Contents

Introduction

Dear Teacher,

We are writing to you to introduce *Focus*, our new course for high school students. This course is the fruit of our many years' teaching, writing, and developing materials. Our aim has been to produce a set of materials that will help you to be the best teacher you can be. In other words, we want to help you to create the optimum conditions for your students to learn English.

Of course, we accept that everybody's teaching context is unique and the perfect English course is an unattainable dream. That said, our own experience in the classroom has taught us to value three things above all when using teaching and learning materials: reliability, flexibility, and credibility.

Reliability

Quite simply, we want the materials to work. We don't want the course to let you down in the classroom. So we've gone for a clean design, clear, easy-to-understand instructions, and a wide variety of engaging topics, texts, and tasks that have been combined in a logical way that will make sense to you and to your students.

Needless to say, the course covers all the necessary language work appropriate for the level and follows the Common European Framework of Reference (CEFR). We hope you will appreciate the stimulating and memorable way in which each carefully selected grammar structure and vocabulary item is presented. But we are well aware that presenting language is not even half the story. We have designed these materials so that they systematically recycle the language that has been presented. 'Use it or lose it' is our motto. You will discover that this course, with all its supporting print-based and digital materials, provides your students with the repeated exposure and practice they require. Reliability = trust. We are confident you will be able to trust *Focus*.

Flexibility

One of the things we learned early in our careers is that you teach the students, not the lesson plan. There is no point in slavishly following a prescribed 'teaching path' through a set of materials if the students are not with you. Your ability to react to emerging classroom situations and adapt your lesson accordingly is a vital teaching skill. We strongly believe that a rigid unit structure does NOT have to be a teaching straitjacket. The lessons themselves are brimming with different ideas, task types, and interesting information. Then the supplementary material we have developed, both print-based and digital, offers you almost limitless flexibility. You can give extra multiple choice grammar exercises, do a communicative A/B information-gap activity, or watch a video clip. Flexibility = choice. We think you will appreciate the range of choice in *Focus*.

Credibility

So, while we are sure that a reliable and flexible course will help you, it's this third characteristic that really counts. We'd like to take this opportunity to summarize our thinking about this and explain what lies at the heart of *Focus*. We can do this by grouping our thoughts under three words beginning with *M*: *Motivation*, *Memory*, and *Meaning*.

Motivation
This is our starting point: students learn best when they are interested in the material. It's as simple as that. We may not have it right every time for your particular teaching context, but our overriding concern has been to select topics, texts, and tasks that engage students both emotionally and intellectually.

Memory
Systematic recycling of new language is a core feature of *Focus*. There is a particular emphasis on vocabulary. In the process of building their own 'Word Store', students using *Focus* will devote valuable time to new vocabulary, as well as learning a variety of ways of recording it.

Meaning
We are strongly opposed to mechanistic practice and drills where form dominates and meaning is irrelevant. Don't practice language for the sake of it. Language exists to make meanings and our learning materials should reflect this.

These are some of the more important ideas that we hold dear. Over the years, they have influenced our teaching and our writing. Credibility = belief. We want you to believe in *Focus*.

So now it's over to you. We'd like to take this opportunity to wish you and your students every success.

Our warmest regards,

Sue and Vaughan

Focus unit walk-through

Vocabulary lesson

Every unit begins by focusing on vocabulary, which is then recycled throughout the unit.

1. Real-life quotations can be used as a conversation starter for introducing the unit or as a tool to find out what students already know.
2. The UNIT LANGUAGE AND SKILLS menu describes the flow of the unit. It highlights the language skills practiced, as well as the extra resources available.
3. The SHOW WHAT YOU KNOW box reviews vocabulary students should already know, to ensure they all begin the unit at the same level.
4. The FOCUS EXTRA section directs students to additional practice materials such as the WORD STORE booklet, the Workbook or MyEnglishLab and the *Focus* website, where they can find the audio recordings for the unit.

Vocabulary and Word store

In the WORD STORE booklet attached to the back of the Students' Book, there are additional vocabulary exercises which accompany the Vocabulary, Listening, and Reading lessons in the unit.

1. When students reach the WORD STORE section of a Vocabulary lesson, they flip open the booklet at the back of the Students' Book and leave it open alongside the main Students' Book page.
2. Students use Exercises A, B, C, and D in the Vocabulary lesson to practice key topical vocabulary and collocations. Students can use the WORD STORE page to complete additional supporting exercises, which provide students with a personal mini dictionary they can refer to as and when necessary.
3. The WORD IN FOCUS section takes specific words or language from the unit and shows students different collocations and uses of it. This can be used to practice dictionary skills.

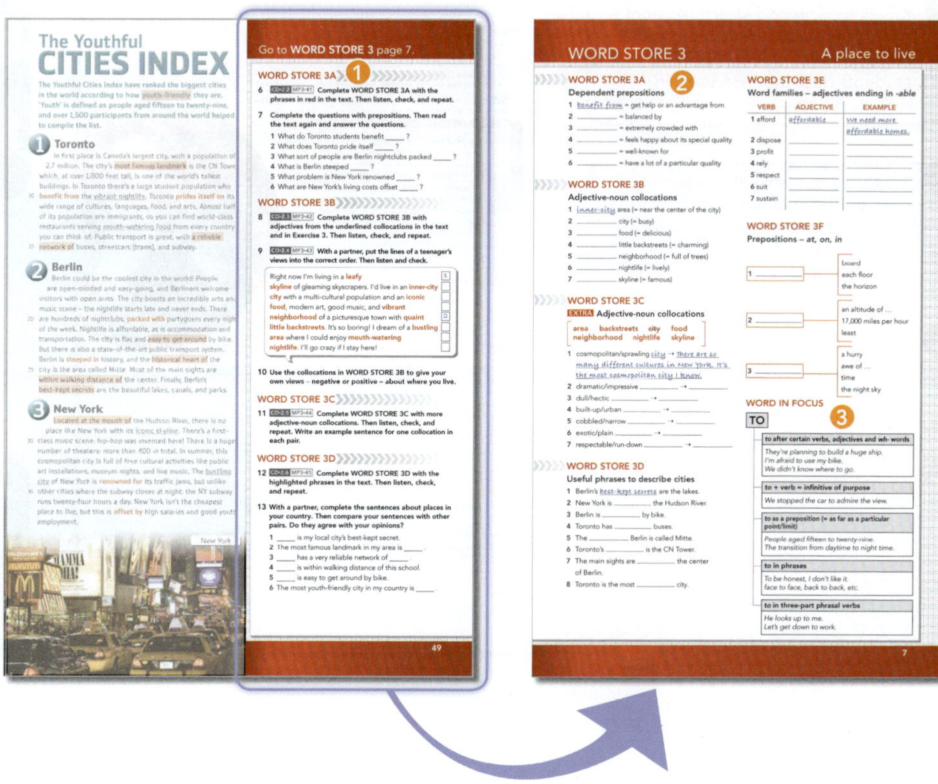

Grammar lessons

The second and fifth lessons of every unit are both Grammar lessons. These lessons are supported by grammar animation videos, which make them more attractive and motivate students to focus on the grammar being covered.

1. The grammar in each lesson is presented in context and highlighted, to make it easily identifiable.
2. The GRAMMAR FOCUS box gives students explanations of how to use the grammar, as well as clear examples. This is followed by a variety of exercises which provide practice with new structures in contexts relevant to students' lives.
3. Each lesson ends with a production exercise, where students actively use the grammar from the lesson.
4. The GRAMMAR FOCUS reference can be used for review at the end of a Grammar lesson or during unit review. It can also be used by fast-finishers or students who require extra practice. Each structure presented in Grammar lessons has its own section in GRAMMAR FOCUS, which includes a detailed explanation of the structure and additional practice exercises.

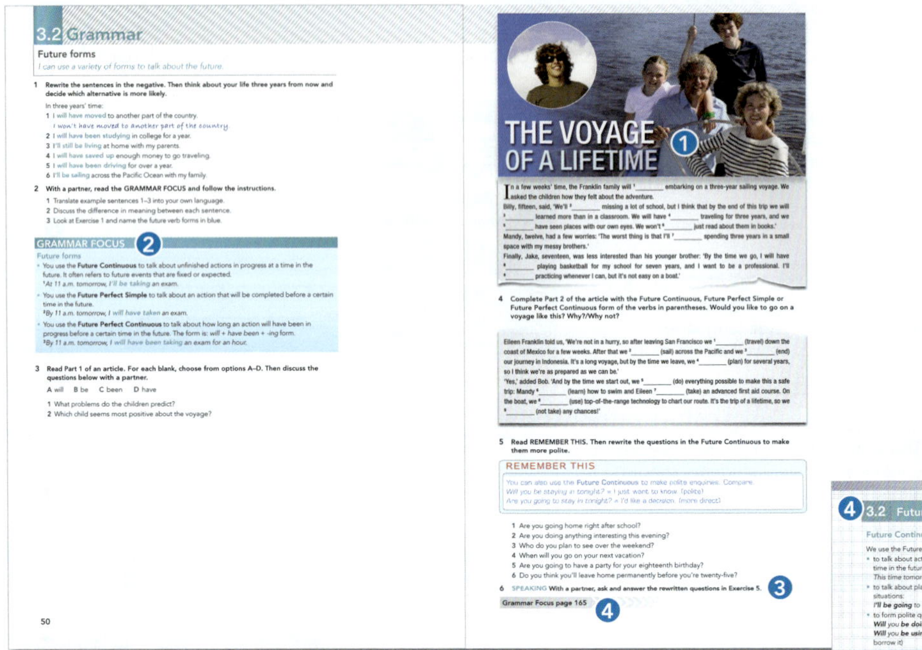

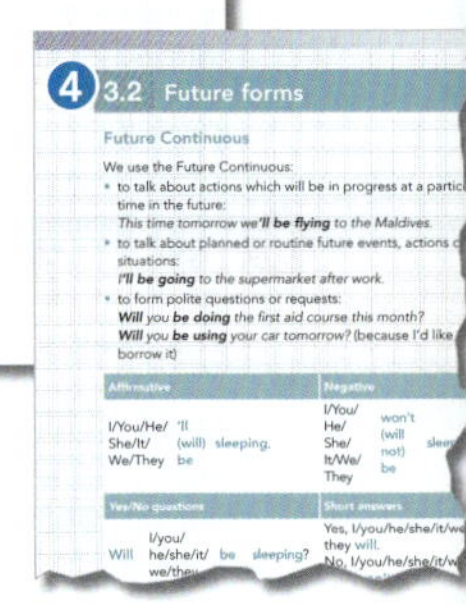

Grammar animation videos

Grammar animation videos are used to support new structures through lively animations. The animated videos can be used for presenting new structures, for reinforcement after the teacher has presented the grammar point, or as a general tool for review.

1. Key language and structures from the Grammar lessons are used in context in the videos, showing students how they are used in real-life situations.
2. There are two animations per unit. Further teacher's notes on how to use the grammar animations are available on pages 11–12 of the Teacher's Book.
3. Each video is accompanied by a teacher's commentary, where the grammar point is clearly explained. Students can use the video and commentary to analyze the grammar point at their own pace.

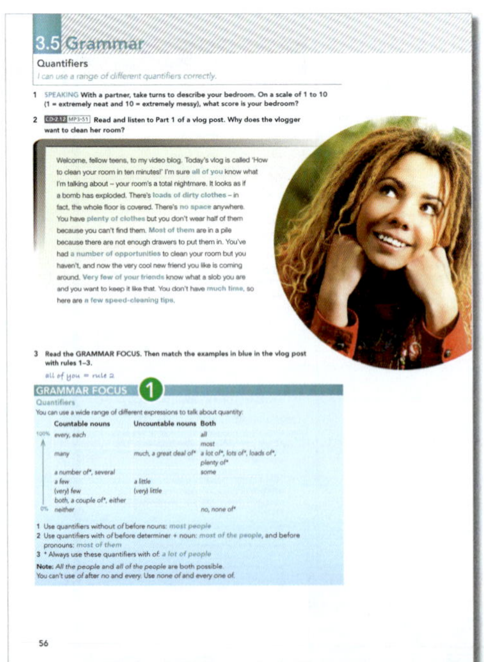

FOCUS

Listening lesson

The Listening lessons offer varied tasks and opportunities for students to practice listening skills with new vocabulary, as well as with exam task types.

1. EXAM FOCUS exercises are exam-specific tasks, which help students prepare for the *Cambridge English: First* exam.
2. The PRONUNCIATION FOCUS boxes in the Listening lessons focus students' attention on different aspects of pronunciation, such as long and short vowel sounds or shifting stress in word families.
3. WORD STORE Exercise E at the end of the Listening lesson consolidates new language. Students can also access the audio from the unit at english.com/focus/american to review and practice.

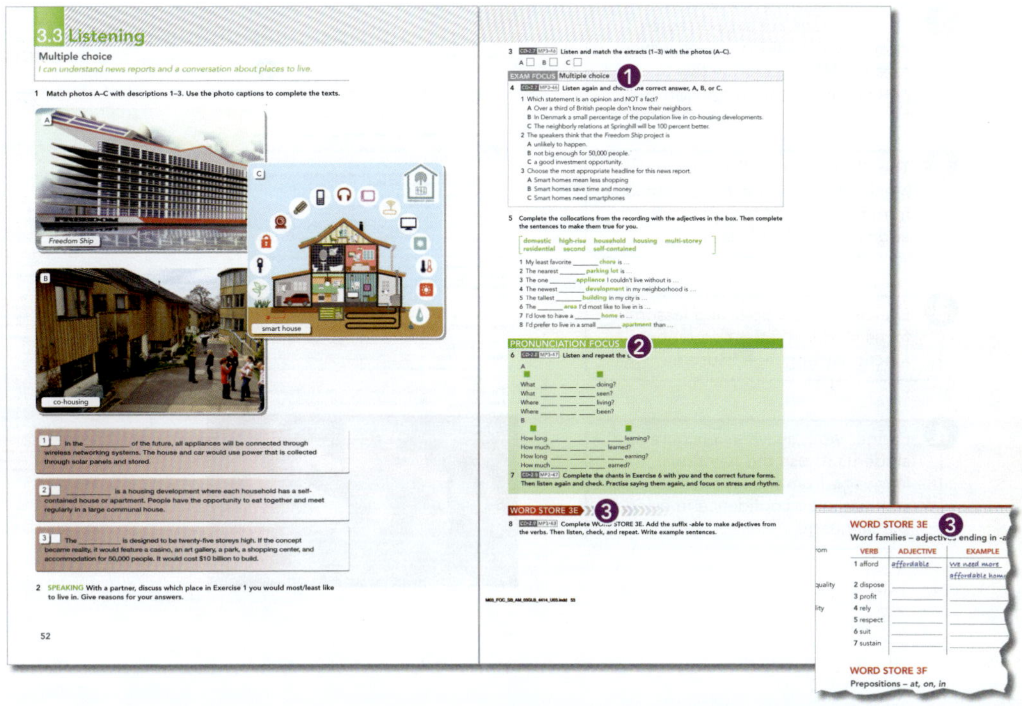

Reading lesson

The Reading lessons feature a variety of reading texts, which also present factual information that is interesting and relevant to teenagers.

1. Audio files accompany each text, allowing additional listening practice to support reading.
2. WORD STORE Exercise F is a language extension activity, linked to the end of the Reading lesson.

Speaking lesson

The Speaking lessons prepare students for everyday interactions such as asking for and giving advice, giving an opinion, or asking for information.

1. These lessons are supported by interactive speaking videos, which give students opportunities to practice functional language.
2. The SPEAKING FOCUS box highlights useful functional language from the unit and also presents additional useful phrases.
3. Exercises in the Speaking lesson focus students' attention on how functional language is used.
4. Partner work activities encourage students to use the functional language from the lesson and increase their confidence in using the language.

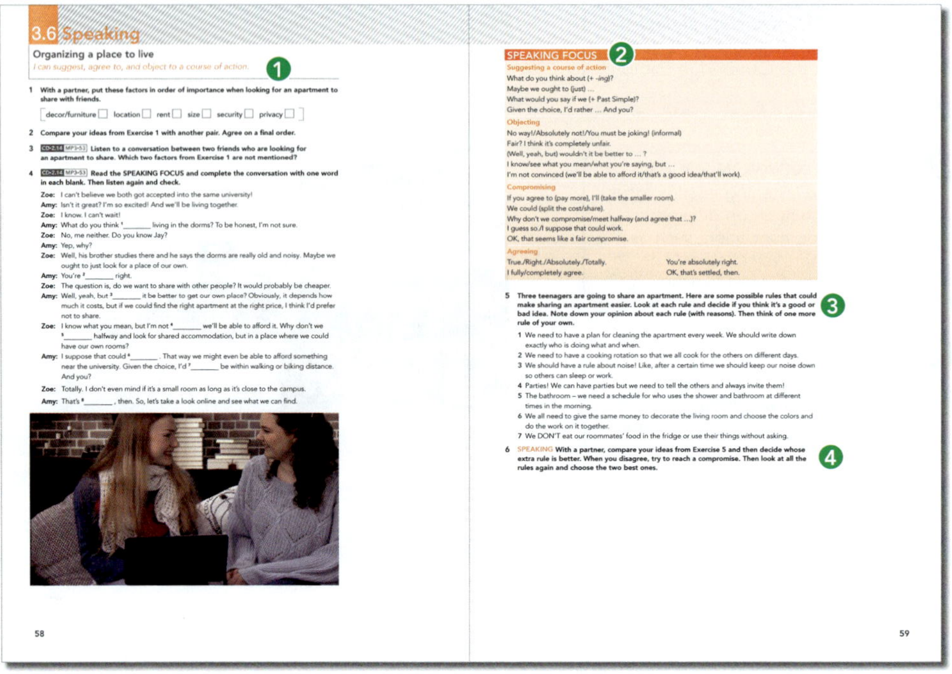

3.6 Speaking

Organizing a place to live

I can suggest, agree to, and object to a course of action. (1)

1 With a partner, put these factors in order of importance when looking for an apartment to share with friends.

decor/furniture ☐ location ☐ rent ☐ size ☐ security ☐ privacy ☐

2 Compare your ideas from Exercise 1 with another pair. Agree on a final order.

3 CD-2.14 MP3-53 Listen to a conversation between two friends who are looking for an apartment to share. Which two factors from Exercise 1 are not mentioned?

4 CD-2.14 MP3-53 Read the SPEAKING FOCUS and complete the conversation with one word in each blank. Then listen again and check.

Zoe: I can't believe we both got accepted into the same university!
Amy: Isn't it great? I'm so excited! And we'll be living together.
Zoe: I know. I can't wait!
Amy: What do you think [1]_______ living in the dorms? To be honest, I'm not sure.
Zoe: No, me neither. Do you know Jay?
Amy: Yep, why?
Zoe: Well, his brother studies there and he says the dorms are really old and noisy. Maybe we ought to just look for a place of our own.
Amy: You're [2]_______ right.
Zoe: The question is, do we want to share with other people? It would probably be cheaper.
Amy: Well, yeah, but [3]_______ it be better to get our own place? Obviously, it depends how much it costs, but if we could find the right apartment at the right price, I think I'd prefer not to share.
Zoe: I know what you mean, but I'm not [4]_______ we'll be able to afford it. Why don't we [5]_______ halfway and look for shared accommodation, but in a place where we could have our own rooms?
Amy: I suppose that could [6]_______. That way we might even be able to afford something near the university. Given the choice, I'd [7]_______ be within walking or biking distance. And you?
Zoe: Totally. I don't even mind if it's a small room as long as it's close to the campus.
Amy: That's [8]_______, then. So, let's take a look online and see what we can find.

SPEAKING FOCUS (2)

Suggesting a course of action
What do you think about (+ -ing)?
Maybe we ought to (just) ...
What would you say if we (+ Past Simple)?
Given the choice, I'd rather ... And you?

Objecting
No way!/Absolutely not!/You must be joking! (informal)
Fair? I think it's completely unfair.
(Well, yeah, but) wouldn't it be better to ... ?
I know/see what you mean/what you're saying, but ...
I'm not convinced (we'll be able to afford it/that's a good idea/that'll work).

Compromising
If you agree to (pay more), I'll (take the smaller room).
We could (split the cost/share).
Why don't we compromise/meet halfway (and agree that ...)?
I guess so./I suppose that could work.
OK, that seems like a fair compromise.

Agreeing
True./Right./Absolutely./Totally. — You're absolutely right.
I fully/completely agree. — OK, that's settled, then.

5 Three teenagers are going to share an apartment. Here are some possible rules that could make sharing an apartment easier. Look at each rule and decide if you think it's a good or bad idea. Note down your opinion about each rule (with reasons). Then think of one more rule of your own. (3)

1 We need to have a plan for cleaning the apartment every week. We should write down exactly who is doing what and when.
2 We need to have a cooking rotation so that we all cook for the others on different days.
3 We should have a rule about noise! Like, after a certain time we should keep our noise down so others can sleep or work.
4 Parties! We can have parties but we need to tell the others and always invite them!
5 The bathroom – we need a schedule for who uses the shower and bathroom at different times in the morning.
6 We all need to give the same money to decorate the living room and choose the colors and do the work on it together.
7 We DON'T eat our roommates' food in the fridge or use their things without asking.

6 SPEAKING With a partner, compare your ideas from Exercise 5 and then decide whose extra rule is better. When you disagree, try to reach a compromise. Then look at all the rules again and choose the two best ones. (4)

58 59

Interactive speaking video

Interactive speaking videos accompany most of the Speaking lessons, making them more attractive and dynamic. The goal of these videos is to help students focus on and practice functional language in everyday situations.

1. The interactive speaking videos have three parts. First, the complete conversation is acted out, setting the context for students to see the language in use.
2. Then, while character A acts out a shorter version of the conversation, the other half remains silent and timed. This gap in the conversation gives students an opportunity to play the role of character B by performing their lines.
3. Students then switch roles and repeat. It is recommendable to use the interactive videos at the end of the Speaking lesson, once the other speaking activities have been completed. Students can practice either with a partner, as a group, or individually and can repeat the exercise as many times as they like.

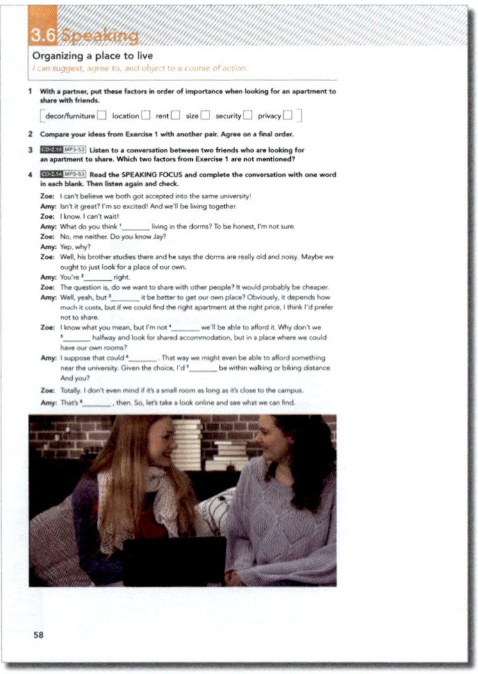

3.6 Speaking

Organizing a place to live

I can suggest, agree to, and object to a course of action.

1 With a partner, put these factors in order of importance when looking for an apartment to share with friends.

decor/furniture ☐ location ☐ rent ☐ size ☐ security ☐ privacy ☐

2 Compare your ideas from Exercise 1 with another pair. Agree on a final order.

3 CD-2.14 MP3-53 Listen to a conversation between two friends who are looking for an apartment to share. Which two factors from Exercise 1 are not mentioned?

4 CD-2.14 MP3-53 Read the SPEAKING FOCUS and complete the conversation with one word in each blank. Then listen again and check.

Zoe: I can't believe we both got accepted into the same university!
Amy: Isn't it great? I'm so excited! And we'll be living together.
Zoe: I know. I can't wait!
Amy: What do you think [1]_______ living in the dorms? To be honest, I'm not sure.
Zoe: No, me neither. Do you know Jay?
Amy: Yep, why?
Zoe: Well, his brother studies there and he says the dorms are really old and noisy. Maybe we ought to just look for a place of our own.
Amy: You're [2]_______ right.
Zoe: The question is, do we want to share with other people? It would probably be cheaper.
Amy: Well, yeah, but [3]_______ it be better to get our own place? Obviously, it depends how much it costs, but if we could find the right apartment at the right price, I think I'd prefer not to share.
Zoe: I know what you mean, but I'm not [4]_______ we'll be able to afford it. Why don't we [5]_______ halfway and look for shared accommodation, but in a place where we could have our own rooms?
Amy: I suppose that could [6]_______. That way we might even be able to afford something near the university. Given the choice, I'd [7]_______ be within walking or biking distance. And you?
Zoe: Totally. I don't even mind if it's a small room as long as it's close to the campus.
Amy: That's [8]_______, then. So, let's take a look online and see what we can find.

58

Writing lesson

Each Writing lesson begins with a motivating text, based on the lesson's writing goal, providing a model for students' own writing.

1. Useful language for the writing task is presented through varied and relevant texts.
2. The WRITING FOCUS box includes exercises which help students to focus, develop, and organize their ideas.
3. The LANGUAGE FOCUS box directs students' attention to language they may find useful in their writing (e.g. expressing contrast, using descriptive language, expressing cause and effect), giving tips on how they can improve their written English.
4. Exam-style writing tasks provide students with realistic opportunities to practice their writing skills.

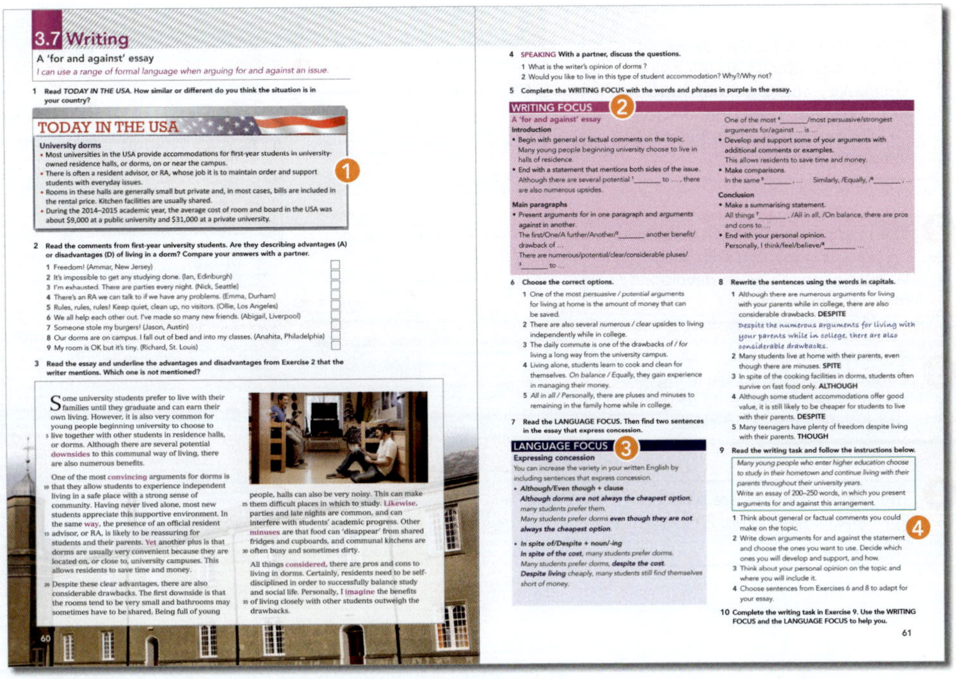

Language in focus and Use of English

The Language in focus lesson and USE OF ENGLISH section in the WORD STORE booklet can be used as part of the unit review.

1. The Language in focus lesson includes a mini presentation and practice of areas that are common in Use of English exam tasks.
2. The USE OF ENGLISH section in the WORD STORE booklet provides opportunities to practice useful language, key phrases, and expressions from the current and the previous unit. These exercises help students to analyze meanings of language and structure, as well as various collocations.
3. Tips help students with more difficult language items, helping them to become more independent as learners.

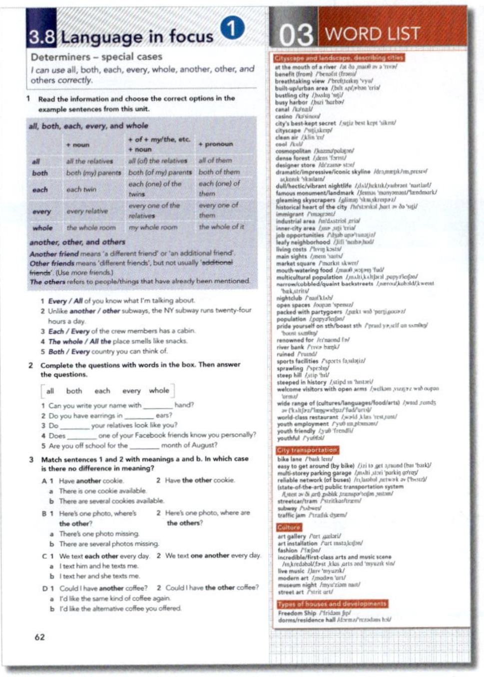

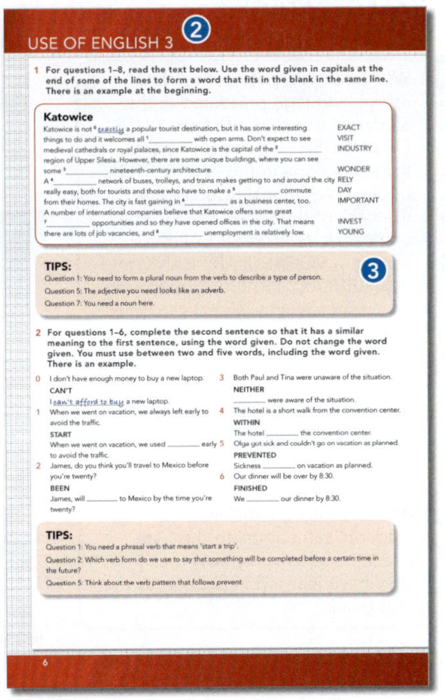

Review lesson

The Review lesson has two parts: a review of grammar and vocabulary, and an integrated skills section.

1. The VOCABULARY AND GRAMMAR and LANGUAGE IN USE sections focus on reviewing vocabulary and grammar structures from the unit. The LANGUAGE IN USE section reviews functional language from the unit.
2. The reading exercises focus students on practicing reading skills and language use. They are developed to mirror the exam tasks.
3. Carefully developed speaking activities guide students to review and practice speaking skills.
4. The writing exercises are based on the *Cambridge English: First* exam tasks.

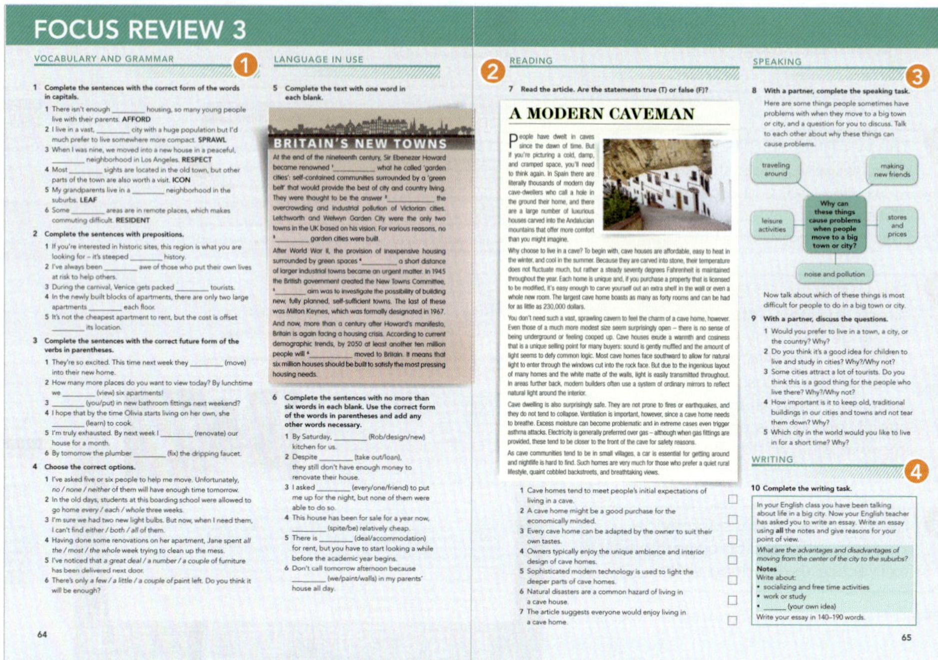

Workbook

The Workbook mirrors the Students' Book lessons and provides extra practice exercises focused on Vocabulary, Reading, Writing, Speaking, and Grammar lessons from each unit. It is also designed to help students prepare for their exam. Tips on exam strategies for Listening, Reading, Writing, Speaking, and Use of English can be found in the EXAM STRATEGIES section at the back of the Workbook.

1. Workbook exercises consolidate use of language presented in the Students' Book. In addition, a USE OF ENGLISH page complements the same page in the WORD STORE booklet. Additional resources at the back of the Workbook include a FUNCTION PHRASE BANK for writing, a VOCABULARY BANK, and VOCABULARY PRACTICE exercises.
2. The Workbook encourages students to actively assess how much they have learned, through the Self-assessment page in every unit.
3. After assessing their own learning, students can complete the Self-check page to verify how much they have learned in relation to the unit goals.

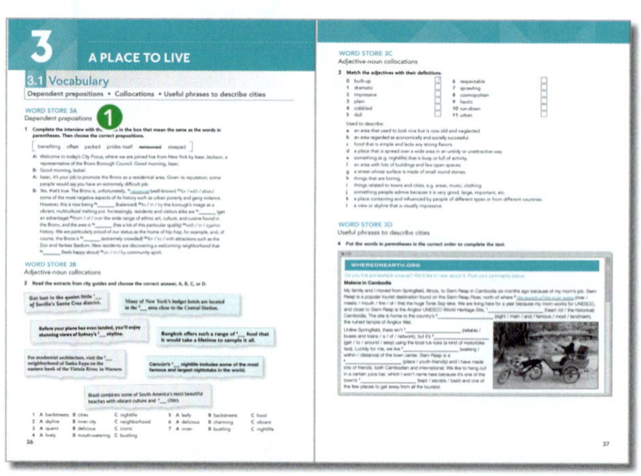

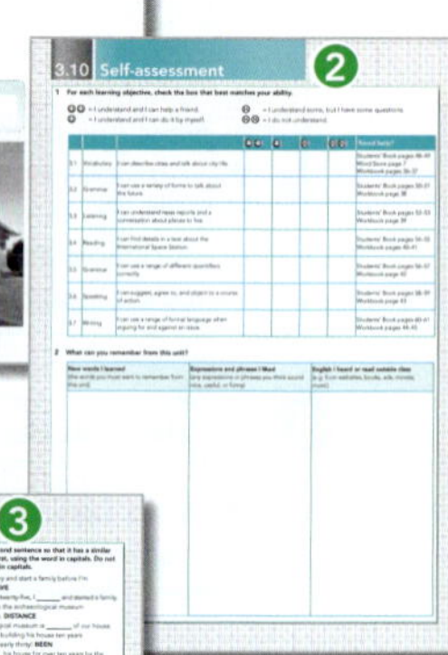

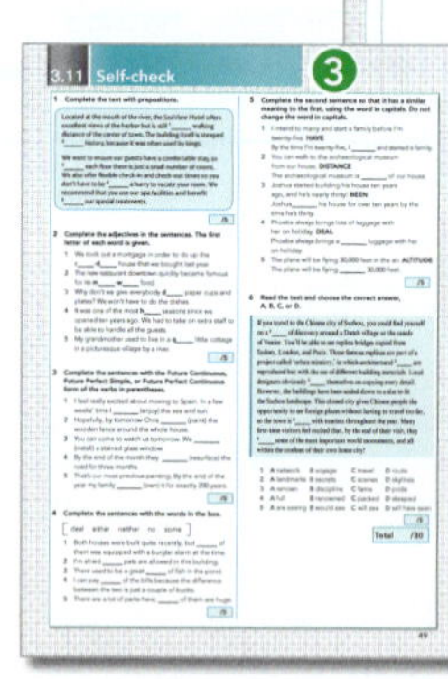

Grammar animations

What are the grammar animations?

The grammar animations are a new and innovative resource for teaching grammar. They appear in each grammar lesson, so there are two grammar animations in each unit. They are available on the Teacher's MultiROM, ActiveTeach, the Teacher's website, and the Students' website, which means they can be used by both teachers and students, in the classroom or outside the classroom. Each animation is composed of two parts: the animated cartoon, which presents the target grammar structure in context, and the teacher's explanation, which reinforces understanding and learning of the structure.

Why are the grammar animations an innovative resource to teach grammar?

In the modern image-driven world, using video in the classroom is one of the most effective ways to engage and motivate students. There is a tradition of teaching speaking via videos with real characters, and methodologists of language teaching agree the method is very effective as students can see the target language in a visual context and identify with the characters. However, such methods are rarely used in teaching grammar, despite it being proven that seeing the target grammar structures in a video context enables students to understand them better and remember them longer.

The grammar animations not only add more context to the grammar lessons but also provide a context that is very different and which really appeals to students. The videos are short and up-to-date, the plots engaging, and the characters funny. In the *Focus 4* grammar animations students will meet not only teenagers like them in different social situations (e.g. on a school trip, in a clothing store, or at a wedding), but also such characters as a cartoonist, a deception specialist working for the police, and geeks who want to live on Mars. Students will also hear amusing stories, for example, about the worst candidates at job interviews or embarrassing technology. The teacher's explanation is concise and ready to use.

How to use the grammar animations in the classroom

- The grammar animations do not compete with the on-page context in the lesson – they add much more for the teacher and the student. The fact that the video context is not connected with the on-page context of the lesson and is not a part of the flow of the lesson makes it a priceless resource, as it can be used when the teacher finds it necessary, independently of the other resources.
- Depending on the lesson plan, the teacher can decide to work with the animation at the beginning of the lesson as an introduction, after explaining the grammar point via the dialogue or text on the page, or at the end of the lesson.
- Some groups might find the grammar animation the most attractive part of the lesson, so it is a great tool to be used when the students' attention begins to fall or as a certain 'prize' for students.
- Teachers very often decide to cover the grammar point on more than one lesson, as the grammar often causes problems. Then the animation can be a good starting point at the beginning of the second lesson. It can also be used for review when needed.
- The teacher's part can, but does not have to, be used during the lesson. Some teachers may prefer to explain the grammar point in the students' L1 or compare it to structures in the students' L1.

  Other teachers find it really helpful, as some students might need to hear the explanation more than once and they have a concise explanation at hand and ready to use: they can make students watch it and then answer their questions. The video can be stopped at any place, which gives the teacher two possibilities: play the whole video or stop it after the animation, before the teacher's part starts.
- The topic of the animation is consistent with the topic of the unit and new vocabulary is avoided, which makes students feel comfortable while watching the animation. The easy lexical context enables students to focus on the grammar structures without being distracted by new lexis.
- Subtitles can be switched on or off, which gives the teacher more options to work with a given animation and adjust the lesson to the level of the group.

How to use the grammar animations outside the classroom

- As the grammar animations are available on the Students' website, they can be used by students outside the classroom. This makes them an invaluable resource for students.
- Students who were absent from school have a ready grammar explanation and the grammar in context to watch at home. This is especially good for auditory learners who like hearing the explanation and watching language in a video context more than reading the dry information on the page.
- Weaker students who find the grammar explanation insufficient can always watch the animation at home at their own pace.
- Students who review before tests or exams can use this resource to go through the grammar points covered. The explanations are concise and the video that has already been watched quickly reminds them of a given grammar topic. Timewise, it's probably one of the most efficient ways of reviewing grammar.

Suggested teaching procedure

Example: grammar animation for Lesson 1.2, Present and past habits

Introduction

- Explain to students that they are going to watch an animated cartoon which will give them more context for the grammar.
- Start the video and stop at the very beginning [00:10] Students will see the main character, Sarah (the journalist), standing next to Max Anthony's door. Ask students a few warm-up questions like: *Who is the girl? Where is she? Who is she going to do the interview with? How do you know?* You can ask students to describe the cartoons they can see on the door.

Comprehension

- Play the video with the subtitles off and ask students to watch and listen carefully. Ask a few general comprehension questions like: *What kind of student was Max? How did he behave in the classroom? What did his sister think of him? What does she think of his work now?*
- Play the whole video once again, with subtitles. Ask students to pay special attention to the sentences with *used to* and *would*.

Video practice

- Explain to students that the animation provides more context for the topic of the lesson and remind them that the lesson is about present and past habits. Ask them if they remember any sentences about past habits from the video. Make a list on the board. Don't worry if students don't remember all the sentences – use the script to read out the sentences with the target language and put them on the board. It's a good idea to elicit some target language from the cartoons and put it on the board; it will serve as prompts for the speaking exercise at the end.
- Ask students additional questions to check if they understand that the simplest way of talking about habits is the Present Simple and the Past Simple, the difference between *used to* and *would*, and using the Present and Past Continuous for irritating habits. Ask them to give you more examples of each category.
- If you realize that students still have problems with present and past habits, use the teacher's part to remind them of the different ways of expressing them. If you feel they are doing well and can list a few examples and provide explanation, then you can omit the teacher's part.
- You can play the animation for a third time in weaker groups or if students really want to watch it. Then pause after each sentence which expresses a present or past habit and ask students to repeat.

Extra practice

- Explain to students that they are going to prepare similar dialogues in groups. One of them will be a journalist, the other one a famous person (a model, an actor, a scientist, etc.). Explain that the topic of the dialogue should be similar (what kind of students they used to be). Tell them to use different structures: *used to*, *would*, Past Simple, Present Simple, Past Continuous, and Present Continuous.
- Let students prepare their dialogues with a partner. Check the language in the meantime. Students should present their dialogues in front of the class, to make it more engaging.

If you are short of time, some elements of the introduction and extra practice can be omitted.

Focus Assessment Package

Test type	Quantity	Total scores	Timing
Placement test	1	100	60 mins
Grammar quiz	16	15	10–20 mins
Vocabulary quiz	8	15	10–20 mins
Unit tests			
Vocabulary and Grammar (A/B)	8	40	25–35 mins
Dictation, Listening, and Reading (A/B)	8	30	20–30 mins
Writing	8	30	30–45 mins
Review tests			
Vocabulary, Grammar, and Use of English (A/B)	4	50	35–40 mins
Writing	4	30	30–45 mins
Speaking (A/B/Teacher's notes)	4	20	8–10 mins per pair
End-of-year test			
Listening, Use of English, and Reading (A/B)	1	60	40–55 mins
Writing	1	20	30–45 mins
Speaking (A/B/Teacher's notes)	1	20	12–15 mins per pair
Progress (optional) Beginning, middle, and end of course	3	GSE score	60 mins

Overview of package

The *Focus* Assessment Package provides a wide range of tests that can be used at different points in the course. Each level has:

- 1 Placement test
- 16 A and B Grammar quizzes
- 8 A and B Vocabulary quizzes
- 8 A and B Unit tests
- 4 A and B Review tests
- 1 A and B End-of-year test

Assessment *of* learning or assessment *for* learning?

Any test can be used as either assessment *of* learning or assessment *for* learning. Assessment *of* learning usually takes place after the learning has happened and provides information about what the student is achieving by assigning a grade. You can also use the tests as assessment *for* learning by providing specific feedback on students' strengths and weaknesses, and suggestions for improvement as part of the continual learning process.

It is a combination of both types of assessment that can provide powerful tools for helping your students' progress.

Grading Writing and Speaking tests

Writing and Speaking tests have detailed grading scales to help you grade consistently and give students meaningful feedback. If you have the grading scale for the exam your students will ultimately take, you may prefer to refer to this.

Whichever grading scale you use, it can be very useful to go through it with your students before they take the test so they know how they are going to be graded. You can then refer back to these grading criteria in your feedback.

Versions of tests

Most tests have two versions: A and B. Versions A and B are designed to be at exactly the same level of difficulty and feature the same task types; however, the test items in each are different. For listening tests, the tasks are different but the audio is the same in both A and B versions, making it easy to administer.

You can use the A/B tests in two ways:

- give half of the class A versions and half of the class B versions – this helps to deter cheating
- give all students the A test and then use the B test either for students who missed the test or as a re-test or remedial work for students whose score shows they need a little more work on the unit objectives.

Exam preparation

As your students are going to be working towards their exam, the tests also provide regular opportunities for them to try exam-style tasks in a low-stakes test environment, which should help them feel more confident going into the final exam.

We would recommend using past papers or practice papers in addition as you get close to the date of the exam.

Expected outcomes

We would expect all students who have completed the instructional material to score at least 50 percent, and the best students to score 90–100 percent on any given test. We have deliberately included more challenging questions in each test so as to help you identify students performing above level.

Tests on paper

The tests are provided in both PDF and Word format. We recommend using the PDF versions, but if you need to edit the tests, this is possible in Word.

When you are marking tests, there is an extended answer key to help you explain why a question is right or wrong, or which part of the text an answer can be found in.

Tests on MyEnglishLab

All of the Unit tests can be taken through the MyEnglishLab platform. On MyEnglishLab, all students take the A test. The B test becomes remediation for those students who need it.

Most parts of the test are automatically scored, and students get instant detailed feedback showing them where they made mistakes or how to improve if you have allowed a 'try again' option. The free writing and speaking parts need to be teacher-graded. You assign each part separately, so you can choose whether to add these or not.

Placement test

The *Focus* Placement tests are designed to help the teacher to place students at the right level of the *Focus* series. Each test contains 100 multiple-choice questions and is designed to last for an hour. If students get less than 60 percent of the answers right, they should use the lower level indicated in the title, e.g. for the *Focus 2/Focus 3* test they should use *Focus 2*. If they get more than 70 percent of the answers right, they should use the higher level indicated in the title. If students can achieve 60-70% of right answers, this puts them in the middle of the two levels and your decision as to where to place these students should depend on the level of the rest of the class.

Grammar quizzes

There are sixteen short A and B Grammar quizzes (two per unit), which test the grammar taught in each Grammar lesson in the Students' Book. The Grammar quizzes can be used at the end of a lesson, for homework, as a review at the beginning of the next lesson, or later in the unit as quick revision.

Vocabulary quizzes

There are eight A and B Vocabulary quizzes, which test the vocabulary taught in each Vocabulary lesson in the Students' Book. Depending on the quiz, they should take between ten and twenty minutes each.

Unit tests

There are eight Unit tests, which test the learning objectives from each unit. These should be administered after each respective unit review.

Each test has three parts: Vocabulary and Grammar; Dictation, Listening, and Reading; Writing. The Vocabulary and Grammar and Dictation, Listening, and Reading parts have A and B versions. There is only one version of the Writing task.

You can assign all or none of these, depending on the time available. If you are including the Listening test, it is best to do the listening first, and then students can do the other sections in their own time.

Review tests

There are four Review tests (one every two units). These are cumulative achievement tests, and so test the learning objectives from all units so far:

Review test 1: Units 1–2
Review test 2: Units 1–4
Review test 3: Units 1–6
Review test 4: Units 1–8

Depending on your school year, you may wish to do all of these or just some of them.

Each test has three parts: Vocabulary, Grammar, and Use of English; Writing; Speaking. The Vocabulary, Grammar, and Use of English parts have A and B versions. There is only one version of the Writing task. Students do the Speaking tasks with a partner and there are separate materials for Students A and B, as well as notes for the teacher with questions, which are incorporated into the Answer key.

As with the Unit tests, you can assign all or none of the parts of the test, depending on the time available.

End-of-year test

The End-of-year test provides a skills-based test covering learning objectives from the whole course.

Each test has three parts: Listening, Use of English, and Reading; Writing; Speaking. The Listening, Use of English, and Reading part has A and B versions. There is only one version of the Writing task. Students do the Speaking tasks with a partner, and there are separate materials for Students A and B, as well as notes for the teacher with questions, which are incorporated into the Answer key.

You can assign all or none of the parts of the test, depending on the time available.

Using *Progress* to track progress

Progress is an optional addition to the *Focus* corpus. It is a standardized package of three tests that allows uniform testing and comparison of results to improve learning outcomes and accurately show learners' progress.

The tests can be conveniently taken either at school or at home, and results are delivered very quickly. *Progress* is scored on Global Scale of English and empirically aligned to the CEFR to accurately measure small amounts of progress within a CEFR band. The test reports overall scores and scores by skill, highlighting strengths and weaknesses to help students and teachers focus learning. For more information, see pearsonelt.com/progress.

The Global Scale of English

The Global Scale of English is a standardized, granular scale from 10 to 90, which measures English language proficiency. Unlike other benchmarks that describe attainment in broad bands, it identifies what a learner can do at each point on the scale across speaking, listening, reading, and writing skills. For instance, a person who has a speaking ability of 47 'can describe their dreams, hopes, and ambitions.'

The scale is designed to motivate learners by demonstrating incremental, step-by-step progress in their language ability. Teachers can use their knowledge of their students' Global Scale of English level to choose materials that are precisely matched to ability and learning goals.

The Global Scale of English serves as a standard against which English language courses and assessments worldwide can be benchmarked, offering a truly global and shared understanding of language proficiency levels.

Visit English.com/gse to learn more about the Global Scale of English.

Assessment for learning

Focus includes elements of Assessment for learning methodology. The aim is to enhance learning by supporting students in understanding what they know and what they need to do next, making them active in their own learning. At the same time, using assessment for learning helps teachers to understand where their students are in their learning and to make decisions about how to help students improve.

When we talk about assessment for learning, we're really talking about assessing students formatively, watching and listening to our students to see how far they understand and using this to help decide what we need to do next. This can be during any activity in class or using a test from the Assessment Package.

In *Focus*, a handful of assessment for learning techniques and activities have been integrated into each unit to give students an awareness of what and how they are learning and give you, the teacher, lots of opportunities to assess how each student is doing.

Each unit starts with the unit objectives, to help students understand the goals. There is a thought-provoking quote linked to the topic of the unit to get students thinking about the theme as a whole, as well as help them remember any topic vocabulary that they already know. The SHOW WHAT YOU KNOW section at the start of the unit reinforces this and helps all students start from a confident beginning.

Throughout the unit, you can use class activities and/or the quizzes in the Assessment Package to check students' learning and deal with any misunderstandings or areas of weakness during the cycle of learning. Consider using the quizzes and other tests in alternative ways: have students work on them together or grade each other's papers. Ask them to highlight areas for review or further work. Rather than grading papers right or wrong, indicate how many are wrong and ask students to work together to find the errors, using their classmates' feedback, the Internet, or reference books to help make the corrections.

The Workbook units finish with a Self-assessment page, followed by a Self-check. The Self-assessment page asks students to reflect on their learning for each of the learning objectives in the unit and points them to where they can go to review any point or get more help. Students also note down new vocabulary items they want to learn, which helps reinforce the intention and focus their attention on an achievable goal, and their out-of-class English experience during that unit, which will help them think about the wider opportunities for learning and using English. The Self-check pages are a traditional review of the grammar and vocabulary from the unit and will help students to confirm their self-assessment.

Components

Students' Book and Word Store

Focus 4 Students' Book contains eight thematic units, each of which is sixteen pages long and divided into the following sections: Vocabulary, Grammar, Listening, Reading, Speaking, Writing, and Language in focus. Additionally, the Students' Book opens with an Intro unit consisting of eight individual lessons that help students review the material from the preceding level. Each main unit is followed by a two-page FOCUS REVIEW section, which reviews the material covered in that unit. The majority of the task types in this section are exam oriented. The GRAMMAR FOCUS section at the back of the book contains grammar explanations for each grammar point, with additional practice exercises. The Students' Book also comes with a twenty-five-page WORD STORE booklet inserted at the back. By completing the exercises in the WORD STORE, students compile their own mini dictionaries of the most important words and phrases from the unit. The WORD STORE also contains a wealth of support material such as a list of phrasal verbs with example sentences, a list of prepositional phrases, and additional Use of English activities focusing on language from the unit.

Class CDs

The audio material is an important element of *Focus*. The class CDs include dialogues and listening activities from the Students' Book, which include use of all the vocabulary from the WORD STORE.

Workbook

The Workbook has been specifically developed to help students pass their exams. It activates all of the language introduced in the Students' Book. It mirrors the organization of the Students' Book and its helpful features include:

- EXAM STRATEGIES: explanation of the different exam task types students will encounter, as well as coaching students in the best techniques to use in the actual exam.
- FUNCTION PHRASE BANK, WRITING: reference for the writing exercises in the Workbook.
- Function phrase bank, speaking: a collection of phrases from the SPEAKING FOCUS boxes in the Students' Book, providing reference for the speaking exercises in the Workbook.
- VOCABULARY BANK: this section at the back of the book contains all the vocabulary from the course, which is organized by topic and lexical set, followed by practice exercises. Students are advised to do the exercises from this section once they have completed the corresponding unit in the Students' Book.
- Vocabulary and Grammar sections: each unit provides further practice exercises to accompany respective sections in the Students' Book.
- Skills sections: each unit provides further exam oriented practice of Reading, Listening, Speaking, Writing, and Use of English.

  The LISTENING LANGUAGE PRACTICE sections include exercises that further exploit the audio scripts from the Students' Book Listening lessons.

  Both the READING and LISTENING LANGUAGE PRACTICE sections also contain exercises which practice the language items from the respective WORD STORE sections in the Students' Book.

  Speaking exercises help students memorize and practice the functions introduced in the Students' Book and in the interactive speaking videos.

  Writing sections include further exercises to support and develop students' writing skills.
- SELF-CHECK sections: these sections in every unit help students prepare for the tests in the Assessment Package. And as the key to these sections is provided in the Workbook, students can assess their progress and decide if they need further practice.

MyEnglishLab

This is an online Workbook which can be accessed by teachers and students at http://myenglishlab.com. It provides additional motivating material for self-study and allows teachers instant access to their students' scores.

MyEnglishLab:

- contains the same material as the paper Workbook in an interactive format
- contains all the video content of the course
- contains SHOW WHAT YOU HAVE LEARNED: mini-test exercises that help students assess whether they have mastered the material adequately
- has self-check and remediation functionality to save teachers some time
- allows students to monitor their own progress
- is intuitive and easy to use
- requires an Internet connection.

You can also add *Progress*, an optional separate test component to help track students' progress in a granular way (see full description on page 14).

Teacher's Book

The Teacher's Book contains a wealth of additional material for teachers. The introductory pages provide information about the unique features of the Students' Book as well as the other course components, including the video elements. They contain a Unit walk-through (see pages 5–10) which gives a visual presentation of how the Students' Book units work, ideas on how to use the WORD STORE at the back of the Students' Book and what additional resources and material are available as part of the Students' Book.

The Teacher's Book contains slightly reduced reproductions of the Students' Book pages, complete with answers, suggestions for extra activities and detailed information about the contents of all the other components that can be used with a given lesson.

It also contains the Students' Book audio script and the Workbook answer key.

The Culture notes provide a wealth of information connected with the people, history, and photos in the Students' Book.

The Teacher's Book is bundled with the MultiROM, which contains the following materials:

- Bank of photocopiable activities (see the list at the back of this TB)
- Grammar animations
- Interactive speaking videos
- Testing package

The bank of photocopiable activities contains the following:

- vocabulary and grammar activities
- Test yourself partner work activities
- activities providing support for the speaking and writing tasks from the Focus Review sections
- Language in use activities, for additional practice and review of functional language
- three mini-tests.

ActiveTeach

ActiveTeach is interactive whiteboard software which includes many innovative features and a wealth of materials. It contains the Students' Book pages in electronic format, where all exercises have the built-in functionality for teachers to check and/or show answers. The majority of activities are interactive exercises in which students can fill in blanks, drag and drop, and match items, as well as check their answers. Open-ended practice tasks also include sample answers that students can follow when preparing their own dialogues, monologues, or written assignments.

Additional games are available to aid extra practice in the classroom and teachers can save their work and notes directly into the software. Included are instant links to all of the audio and video from the course, along with optional subtitles for the teacher to use if he or she wishes to.

Most teacher's resource materials are accessible on ActiveTeach in downloadable formats, such as photocopiable activities, and audio or video scripts. The Assessment Package can also be downloaded in either PDF or editable Word formats, with all documents clearly organized by unit.

Video

Available either via MyEnglishLab, ActiveTeach, or the Teacher's MultiROM, the video element of *Focus* is particularly rich and varied. The three types of video available are:

- Grammar animations: every Grammar lesson is illustrated through these lively animations. Key language is used in context in these videos, providing evidence for students of how the language is used in real-life situations. The animation is followed by teacher commentary on the grammar point, which provides a brief, simple summary of the language and serves as further back-up for the practice activities done in class. However, the animations can be played either at the beginning of the Grammar lesson, to show the grammar in context, after the teacher has explained the grammar point in detail, or at the end of the class, as a tool for review. Students can also access the animation and the teacher's commentary to analyze the grammar point at their own pace and as many times as they need.
- Interactive speaking videos: these videos accompany most Speaking lessons and demonstrate a conversation that appears on the Students' Book page in the Speaking sections. Each interactive speaking video is filmed with native speakers, who model the conversation in order for students to visualize the context. The same conversation is then repeated with optional subtitles, although only one actor speaks their half of the conversation and the other part remains silent and timed. This gap in the conversation allows students to take on a role of either Student A or Student B and act out the missing part of the conversation or work with a partner and perform both parts A and B. Students may like to repeat this exercise several times, either individually or as a group. This provides a simple but effective tool for improving speaking and pronunciation fluency, as well as helping students to focus on using functional language in everyday conversations (such as asking for directions, giving an opinion, or buying food). We recommend using the interactive videos at the end of the Speaking lesson, once the speaking activities in the Students' Book have been completed.

Assessment Package

The Assessment Package is more than just a collection of tests. It offers a coherent system of evaluation and grading which covers a wide range of test types which reflect common external exams. All tests can be used as assessment for learning or assessment of learning. (See pages 13–15 for more detail.)

0.1 Diet

Grammar: Present tenses – review
Vocabulary: Food

SHOW WHAT YOU KNOW

1 **With a partner, list food and drinks that can be described using the adjectives in the box.**

~~bitter~~	dried	fattening	fresh	greasy	raw
ripe	salty	sour	spicy	stale	sweet

bitter = black coffee

2 SPEAKING **Tell your partner which items on your list you like and how often you eat or drink them.**

3 CD•1.2 MP3•2 **Read the comments about three cult diets and choose the correct options. Then listen and check.**

THE HONEY DIET

[1] *I try* / **I'm trying** the Honey Diet right now. Basically, [2] **you use** / *you're using* honey instead of sugar. Also, [3] **you avoid** / *you're avoiding* junk food, [4] *you're always having* / **you always have** breakfast and [5] **you drink** / *you're drinking* lots of water and whole milk. Since I started the diet, [6] *I've been having* / **I've had** so much more energy! [7] **I've lost** / *I've been losing* two pounds this week.

Winnie19 Jan 20, 8:15 a.m.

THE PALEO DIET

[8] *I've done* / **I'm doing** the Paleo Diet. I eat like the cavemen! My diet [9] **consists** / *is consisting* of meat, fish, fresh fruit and vegetables, eggs, nuts, and seeds. [10] *I give up* / **I've given up** wheat and dairy. [11] **I think** / *I'm thinking* it's a very natural way to eat. [12] *I'm following* / **I've been following** the Paleo Diet [13] **for** / *since* two months but [14] *I don't lose* / **I haven't lost** any weight yet.

Flintstone# Jan 21, 9:40 p.m.

THE 5:2 DIET

[15] *I'm doing* / **I've been doing** the 5:2 Diet [16] *for* / **since** January 1. It's simple: [17] **you eat** / *you're eating* normally on five days of the week, but on two days [18] *you're only eating* / **you only eat** 500 calories. I'm on a 500-calorie day today and [19] *I have* / **I'm having** my breakfast – scrambled egg and some grilled salmon. That's the kind of diet [20] **I like** / *I'm liking*!

C@lorieCounter Jan 22, 7:14 a.m.

4 **Read the comments again. Which diet do you think would be the easiest to do?**

4

Exercise 7
1 Have you ever tried spicy Thai food?
2 Are food prices going up right now?
3 Have you ever cut your finger preparing food?
4 How often do you cook a meal for the family?
5 How long have you been having school lunches?
6 How long have you had the same dining table?

REFERENCES
CULTURE NOTES ››› *p. 191*
WORKBOOK
p. 4

5 **Read REMEMBER THIS. Then complete the cartoon caption with the correct form of the verbs in parentheses. Use each tense once only.**

REMEMBER THIS

NOW
- **Present Simple** = facts, habits, routines
- **Present Continuous** = activities in progress

TIME UP TO NOW
- **Present Perfect Simple** = finished actions or unfinished states
- **Present Perfect Continuous** = unfinished or 'just finished' actions

Amy: Wow, you look great! [1] *Have you lost* (you/lose) weight?
Mia: Yes, I have. For the past two weeks I [2] *'ve been following* (follow) the 5:2 Diet.
Amy: Well, I [3] *eat* (eat) all the time! I just tell people that, right now, I [4] *'m doing* (do) the 24:7 Diet.

Grammar Focus page 156

6 **Complete the sentences with the correct present form of the verbs in parentheses. Explain your choice of tense. Then check the sentences that are true for you.**

1 I *think* (think) coffee *tastes* (taste) bitter. I *don't like* (not like) it.
2 My grandma *bakes* (bake) a lot. She *'s probably making* (probably/make) a cake right now.
3 My dad *doesn't see* (not see) why young people *love* (love) fast food so much.
4 I *'ve never been* (never/be) on a diet in my life.
5 I *'m thinking* (think) of giving up chocolate.
6 I *'ve been doing* (do) some cooking. That's why I *smell* (smell) like onions!

7 **Use the prompts to write questions in the correct present tense. Then, with a partner, ask and answer the questions.**

1 you / ever / try / spicy Thai food?
2 food prices / go up / right now?
3 you / ever / cut / your finger / preparing food?
4 how often / you / cook / a meal / for the family?
5 how long / you / have / school lunches?
6 how long / you / have / the same dining table?

0.2 Fun and games

Grammar: Past tenses – review
Vocabulary: Sports

SHOW WHAT YOU KNOW

1 With a partner, match the verbs in box A with the nouns in box B to make collocations.

A	B
~~beat~~ break come go score stay throw win	a ball biking first a goal ~~an opponent~~ a prize a record in shape

beat an opponent

2 Choose three collocations and write three true sentences.

The opponent I like beating most is my brother!

3 CD•1.3 MP3•3 Read the joke and choose the correct options. Then listen and check. Do you like the joke? Why?/Why not?

The other day I [1]*was speeding* / *had sped* down a narrow, twisting mountain road on my bicycle. A man [2]*had driven* / *was driving* very slowly uphill towards me.
As I [3]*passed* / *had passed* him, he [4]*was honking* / *honked* his horn and he [5]*had yelled* / *yelled* at me. 'COW!' he yelled.

I was surprised because I [6]*didn't do* / *hadn't done* anything wrong. But it [7]*wasn't* / *hadn't been* the first time a driver [8]*was yelling* / *had yelled* names at me, so I [9]*ignored* / *was ignoring* him and I [10]*went on* / *was going on*.

I turned the corner and crashed into a cow.

4 Read REMEMBER THIS. Then complete the cartoon caption with the correct form of the verbs in parentheses. Use each tense once only.

REMEMBER THIS

- **Past Simple** = describing the main events of a story: completed past actions
- **Past Continuous** = setting the scene: an activity in progress around a time in the past
- **Past Perfect** = clarifying, if necessary, that one past event happened before another

I [1]was playing (play) chess with my friend. We [2]had played (play) several games when he said, 'Let's find a way of making this game more interesting.' So we [3]stopped (stop) playing chess.

Grammar Focus page 156

5 CD•1.4 MP3•4 Complete two more jokes with the correct past form of the verbs in parentheses. Then listen and check.

A I have a good joke about soccer. The Football Association Cup Final dinner and dance [1]was taking (take) place in London. The party [2]had already started (already/start) when three men [3]arrived (arrive). They [4]had forgotten (forget) their tickets, but they told the bouncer, 'It's all right, we're friends of the referee.'

So the bouncer said, 'I've never heard of a referee with three friends,' and [5]threw (throw) them out.

B A man [1]was riding (ride) a tandem bike when a police officer [2]stopped (stop) him. 'What's the matter, officer?' asked the rider.

'You clearly haven't noticed, sir, but your wife [3]fell off (fall off) your tandem a couple of miles back …'

'Oh, that's a relief,' said the rider. 'I [4]thought (think) I [5]'d gone (go) deaf!'

6 Complete the sentences with the correct past form of the verbs in the box.

break never beat not bring score skate train

1 Tom slipped on the ice and broke his leg when he was skating.
2 It was 2–2. Then Joe scored the winning goal in injury time.
3 Beth couldn't take part in PE because she hadn't brought her PE uniform.
4 Jack was ecstatic. He had never beaten his brother before.
5 Tess couldn't believe she had broken the school record!
6 Lucy was training for a triathlon when she twisted her ankle.

7 With a partner, put the underlined verb into the Past Perfect. Discuss how this changes the meaning. Then check the sentences that are true for you.

1 I started walking when I was eighteen months old.
I had started walking when I was eighteen months old.
2 When I was four, I learned how to ride a bike.
3 I had swimming lessons when I started grade school.
4 When I started playing for the school, they didn't win a game.
5 At 7 o'clock this morning I left my house.
6 This discussion started when I arrived in class.

Exercise 1
break a record
come first
go biking
stay in shape
score a goal
throw a ball
win a prize

Exercise 7
2 had learned
3 had had
4 hadn't won
5 had left
6 had started

REFERENCES
CULTURE NOTES ››› p. 191
WORKBOOK
p. 4

0.3 Teenage types

Grammar: Conditionals • *wish* and *if only*
Vocabulary: Family • People

SHOW WHAT YOU KNOW

1 With a partner, decide whether these adjectives are positive (+) or negative (–) ways of describing personality. Put ? if they can be both.

assertive +	caring +	charming +
fussy ?	immature –	rude –
selfish –	spoiled –	thoughtful +

2 Choose three adjectives and give examples of typical behavior for each one.

If you are selfish, you only think about yourself and you don't care about other people. For example, when …

3 Complete the questionnaire with the correct form of the verbs in parentheses. Then do the questionnaire and compare with a partner.

Exercise 5
Reasons for circled answers:
1 live = it's likely
2 lived = it's unlikely
3 go = you think it's likely / went = you think it's less likely
4 went = an imaginary future situation
5 was = the situation is different
6 had been = talking about an imaginary past event
7 forget = talking about a probable future situation
5 had forgotten = talking about an imaginary past situation

Exercise 6
The boy/son is unhappy with the situation – would prefer the white car to be red.
The father is unhappy with the boy's reaction (= someone's behavior).

GOODY-GOODY? OR SPOILED BRAT

1 What are your parents most likely to say before your birthday?

A If you *want* (want) a new car, we'll get you one.
B If you *continue* (continue) to do well in school, we'll pay for a few driving lessons.

2 If your parents *asked* (ask) you to babysit a younger sibling, would you …

A refuse and tell them you're not their slave?
B accept and do it willingly?

3 If you *were* (be) at a restaurant and your parents *ordered* (order) something you hated, would you …

A make a big fuss?
B eat it and say nothing?

4 What are your parents most likely to say about you?

A If we *hadn't done* (not do) so much for him/her, he/she wouldn't have turned into a spoiled brat.
B If he/she *hadn't been* (not be) such a goody-goody at the summer camp he/she would have had more fun.

Mostly As: You're spoiled! Somebody needs to challenge your selfish behavior before it's too late!
Mostly Bs: You're a thoughtful person and you're kind of a goody-goody. You need to be more assertive.

WORKBOOK p. 5

4 Read REMEMBER THIS I and find examples of the First, Second, and Third Conditional in the questionnaire.

REMEMBER THIS I

- **First Conditional** = the probable future result of an action *1A, 1B*
- **Second Conditional** = the present or future result of an imaginary action *2, 3*
- **Third Conditional** = the imaginary past result of an imaginary past event *4A, 4B*

5 Choose the most appropriate verb form and explain the reasons for your choices. Then complete the conditional sentences.

1 If I (live) / *lived* to be seventy, …
2 If I *live* / (lived) to be 170, …
3 If I (go) / *went* out tonight, …
4 If I *go* / (went) out every night, …
5 If it (was) / *had been* sunny right now, …
6 If it *was* / (had been) sunny yesterday, …
7 If I (forget) / *had forgotten* my mom's next birthday, …
8 If I *forget* / (had forgotten) my mom's last birthday, …

6 Read REMEMBER THIS II and the cartoon. Who is unhappy with the situation? Who is unhappy with someone's behavior?

REMEMBER THIS II

- ***wish/if only* + Past Simple** = you want a present situation to be different
- ***wish/if only* + *would* + verb** = you want someone's present behavior to change

Grammar Focus page 157

7 Write sentences with *wish* or *if only* to show that you would like the situation (S) or behavior (B) to be different. Then check the wishes that are true for you.

1 I don't live overseas. (S)
I wish/If only I lived overseas.
2 I can't read music. (S)
I wish/If only I could read music.
3 My sister doesn't help around the house. (B)
I wish/If only my sister would help around the house.
4 My dad has to work very long hours (S)
I wish/If only my dad didn't have to work long hours.
5 My sister doesn't let me use her laptop. (B)
I wish/If only my sister would let me use her laptop.
6 My brother is very annoying. (S)
I wish/If only my brother weren't/wasn't annoying.
7 My mom always embarrasses me in front of visitors. (B)
I wish/If only my mom wouldn't embarrass me in front of visitors.
8 Our neighbors play loud music at night. (B)
I wish/If only our neighbors wouldn't play loud music at night.

0.4 Visitors from space

Grammar: Modal verbs for speculation
Vocabulary: Science

SHOW WHAT YOU KNOW

1 With a partner, write the noun forms of the verbs in the box. Include nouns for people if appropriate. Then underline the stressed syllables.

analyze conclude destroy evolve explore investigate observe preserve research

analyze = analysis, analyst

2 SPEAKING With a partner, discuss which of these three things governments should spend most money on.

a preservation of planet Earth
b space exploration
c medical research

3 Read REMEMBER THIS and choose the correct options in the cartoon caption. Then tell your partner which opinion is closest to your own.

REMEMBER THIS

- ***must* + infinitive/perfect infinitive*** = you're sure something is/was true
- ***might/may/could* + infinitive/perfect infinitive** = you think it's possible something is/was true
- ***might not/may not* + infinitive/perfect infinitive** = you think it's possible something isn't/wasn't true
- ***can't* + infinitive/perfect infinitive** = you're sure something isn't/wasn't true

*perfect infinitive = *have* + past participle

Grammar Focus page 157

4 Replace the underlined verb structures with alternatives using *can't, could, may, might* and *must* and an infinitive or perfect infinitive. Use each modal verb once only.

IS ANYBODY OUT THERE?

According to a recent UK survey, many people still believe that aliens ¹have possibly visited Earth. When people report sightings of Unidentified Flying Objects (UFOs), they usually describe strange lights and shapes. Other people say aliens ²definitely haven't approached our planet because otherwise there would be some proof. They believe that all 'sightings' of UFOs ³are definitely either natural weather events or man-made, i.e. aircraft, Chinese lanterns, or even hoaxes. But certain government officials think that aliens ⁴have possibly been to Earth for military reconnaissance, scientific research, or tourism and that they ⁵will possibly continue to do so in future.

5 SPEAKING With a partner, discuss your views on space exploration and whether you think there is 'anybody out there'.

6 Choose the correct meaning, A or B, for the underlined phrases.

1 Space exploration might lead to the discovery of other life forms.
A It's possible. B It's certain.
2 So you're a scientist. You must be very intelligent.
A It's compulsory. B It's my opinion.
3 Many explorers may not have understood the significance of their discoveries.
A I don't know if they understood or not.
B They didn't understand.
4 Early computer analysts couldn't have imagined how important the Internet would become.
A I'm sure about this. B I'm not sure about this.
5 It must have been a very interesting documentary.
A I watched it. B I didn't watch it.

7 Rewrite the comments using the modal verb in capitals. Then think about situations when you might make such comments.

1 I'm sure you're very pleased. **MUST**
2 It's possible that she is sleeping. **MIGHT**
3 What? I'm sure she isn't that old! **CAN'T**
4 It's possible that he hasn't received it yet. **MAY NOT**
5 I'm certain you left it at home. **MUST**
6 I'm sure you're not serious. **CAN'T**
7 It's possible that you don't want to hear this. **MIGHT NOT**
8 It's possible that they overheard what we said. **COULD**

Exercise 1
conclusion
destruction
evolution
exploration, explorer
investigation, investigator
observation, observer
preservation
research, researcher

Exercise 4
1 may (might/could) have visited
2 couldn't have approached
3 must be
4 might (could/may) have been to
5 could (may/might) continue

Exercise 7
1 You must be very pleased.
2 She might be sleeping.
3 She can't be that old.
4 He may not have received it yet.
5 You must have left it at home.
6 You can't be serious.
7 You might not want to hear this.
8 They could have overheard what we said.

WORKBOOK
p. 5

Exercise 5
Reporting statements: she'd started using ..., it would require ..., her children loved, she had hidden ..., was impossible
Reporting questions: if they ever bought, whether they believed, when they were going to invent
Reporting imperatives: not to believe
Other changes: you – they, me – her, my – her, a few months ago – a few months before

Exercise 6
1 She asked him if he remembered her. She said she'd bought some sneakers there the previous month.
2 She said they were not working. She asked if she looked any thinner and said that she wasn't. She said she was the same weight then as she had been four weeks before.
3 She said he had made false claims about the sneakers. She told him not to offer her a replacement. She told him she wanted a refund.
4 He told her he couldn't refund her that day because he needed his manager's permission. He asked her if she could come back the next/following day.
The next day:
5 She asked the manager how she could get a refund. She said that the sneakers hadn't made her lose weight.
6 The manager said he was sorry. He told her that she had twenty-eight days to return purchases. From that day, it was twenty-nine days since she had bought them.

0.5 Advertising

Grammar: Reported Speech
Vocabulary: Advertising

SHOW WHAT YOU KNOW

1 **Match the words in box A with the words in box B to make a shopping list.**

A	~~a bag of~~ a pair of a bottle of a box of a bunch of a can of a jar of a tube of

B	anti-aging cream flowers matches mouthwash ~~potato chips~~ sneakers soda toothpaste

a bag of potato chips *a box of matches, a bunch of flowers, a can of soda, a jar of anti-aging cream, a bottle of mouthwash, a pair of sneakers, a tube of toothpaste*

2 SPEAKING **With a partner, choose four products from Exercise 1 and decide why a consumer might complain about them.**

This bag of potato chips is past its sell-by date.

3 **Read the slogans in blue below and, with a partner, discuss whether you think they are believable. Then read the report and find out what other people thought.**

Do products live up to their advertising claims?

I asked three people <u>if they ever bought</u> these products and <u>whether they believed</u> their claims. Here are their reactions.

This cream will make you look ten years younger!

One woman said that <u>she'd started using anti-aging cream a few months before</u>, but she knew that it <u>would require</u> more than a cream to keep <u>her</u> young.

This chocolate spread is a healthy breakfast for children.

A mother said that <u>her children loved</u> chocolate spread. She said that <u>she had hidden the jar away</u> because it <u>was</u> full of sugar and fat. She asked me <u>when they were going to invent</u> healthy chocolate!

You can avoid colds and flu if you use our mouthwash every day.

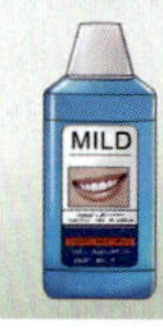

One man I spoke to was a doctor. He told me that it <u>was impossible</u> for a mouthwash to prevent sickness. He told me <u>not to believe</u> everything I read in ads.

4 CD•1.5 MP3•5 **Look at the underlined words in the report. Complete these sentences from the reporter's notes with one word in each blank. Then listen and check.**

1 Questions: *Do* you ever buy these products? *Do* you believe their claims?
2 Woman: I *started* using anti-aging cream a few months *ago* but I know that it *will* require more than a cream to keep *me* young.
3 Mother: *My* children *love* chocolate spread. I *'ve* hidden it away because it *is* full of sugar and fat. When *are* they going to invent healthy chocolate?
4 Doctor: It *'s* impossible for a mouthwash to prevent illness. *Don't* believe everything you read in ads.

5 **Read REMEMBER THIS. Find at least one example for each rule in Exercises 3 and 4.**

REMEMBER THIS

- **Reporting statements** = after *he said/he told me*, move 'one tense back'
- **Reporting questions** = after *she asked me* put the subject before the verb; don't use *do/does/did*; use *if* or *whether* for *yes/no* questions
- **Reporting imperatives** = use *I asked/told him (not) to move/to sing/to go*, etc.
- **Other changes depending on the context** = time and place words, pronouns and possessive adjectives

GRAMMAR FOCUS page 158

6 **Look at the cartoon. Why is the customer dissatisfied? Rewrite the sentences to report the situation.**

These sneakers aren't working. I haven't lost any weight. The store assistant told me that I'd use more calories when I wore them. He said that was why they were so expensive.

1 Customer: Do you remember me? I bought some sneakers here last month.
She asked him if he remembered her. She said ...
2 Customer: They're not working. Do I look any thinner? I'm not! I'm the same weight now as I was four weeks ago.
3 Customer: You made false claims about the sneakers. Don't offer me a replacement. I want a refund.
4 Store assistant: I can't refund you today because I need my manager's permission. Can you come back tomorrow?

The next day:

5 Customer: How can I get a refund? These sneakers haven't made me lose weight.
6 Manager: Oh, I'm sorry. You have twenty-eight days to return purchases. From today, it's twenty-nine days since you bought them.

7 **Think about things you have said to other people today. Write three sentences using *said*, *told*, and *asked*.**

I got up late, so I asked my mom if she could drive me to school.

WORKBOOK p. 6

0.6 Performers

Grammar: Articles
Vocabulary: Culture • The arts

SHOW WHAT YOU KNOW

1 **With a partner, list as many types, genres, or styles as you can for each category in sixty seconds.**

1 Art: *watercolors,*
2 Books/Literature:
3 Dance:
4 Movies:
5 Music:
6 Theater:

2 **SPEAKING** **Choose three subjects from Exercise 1 and tell your partner how you feel about them.**

Art is really important to me. I enjoy painting with watercolors but not so much with …

3 CD•1.6 MP3•6 **Read the article and choose *a/an*, *the* or Ø (no article) to complete it. Then listen and check.**

PRE-SHOW RITUALS

In theaters all over ¹the / **(Ø)** London, artists are getting ready to perform. Most of them are too nervous to have ²**(Ø)** / a dinner before the show, so how do they spend the few hours before the show begins? Here, three performers talk about their pre-show rituals.

Tinie Tempah

TINIE TEMPAH is ³(a) / Ø singer.
He prepares for a gig in the same way ⁴**(an)** / the athlete gets ready for ⁵the / **(a)** big event. About an hour before the gig, he does a lot of stretching. Sometimes he has ⁶**(a)** / Ø massage.

Stephen Mangan

STEPHEN MANGAN is ⁷a / (an) actor.
After six months of doing the same show eight times ⁸the / **(a)** week, ⁹**(the)** / a biggest challenge is getting himself into exactly the same mental state every night. He comes to ¹⁰a / **(the)** theater, and sometimes he doesn't want to be there. But ¹¹a / **(the)** fact that people are waiting to see him is ¹²**(a)** / Ø great motivating factor.

Sara Pascoe

SARA PASCOE is a comedian.
She always gets nervous before a gig. She looks at ¹³a / **(the)** script and tries not to think about ¹⁴Ø / **(the)** things that could go horribly wrong. She tells herself ¹⁵**(Ø)** / the positive things like 'Who cares? Even if you're ¹⁶**(the)** / a worst comedian in ¹⁷a / **(the)** world, you have ¹⁸Ø / **(a)** boyfriend who you love.'

4 **Read the article again and match the performers with their main worry a, b, or c.**

a making mistakes *Sara Pascoe*
b getting into character *Stephen Mangan*
c feeling relaxed *Tinie Tempah*

5 **Read REMEMBER THIS. Complete the cartoon caption with *a/an*, *the* or Ø (no article). Then find examples for the rules in the text in Exercise 3.**

REMEMBER THIS

Indefinite article *a/an*
• new information when it means 'one of many' *a gig*
• jobs – *an artist* *an athlete*
• frequency – *twice a day* *eight times a week*
• actions with *have* – *have a snack* *has a massage*

Definite article *the*
• known information when the listener knows 'which one(s)' *the show, the gig*
• places in a town – *the park* *the theater*
• superlatives – *the best* *the worst, the biggest*
• some countries – *the US, the UK*

No article
• things in general when it means 'all this or all these things' *positive things*
• meals – *have lunch* *have dinner*
• most countries, continents, and cities – *Mexico* *London*

Reporter: What's your pre-show ritual?
Singer: Oh, I'm ¹ *a* singer, not ² *a* diva! I just need ³ *ϕ* cheese, ⁴ *a* bowl of candy, and some water. ⁵ *The* cheese must be from ⁶ *ϕ* France, ⁷ *the* candy should be blue, and ⁸ *the* water has to be ⁹ *ϕ* Swiss spring water served in ¹⁰ *a* Viennese glass. I'm ¹¹ *the* least demanding singer in ¹² *the* world!

Grammar Focus page 159

6 **With a partner, look at the sentence pairs and explain how the use of different articles changes the meaning.**

1 a I love listening to music on my phone.
  b I love listening to the music on my phone.
2 a I'd like to go to an art exhibition.
  b I'd like to go to the art exhibition.
3 a I prefer reading books to watching movies.
  b I prefer reading the book to watching the movie.

7 **SPEAKING** **With a partner, complete the question in eight different ways using the words in the box. Use *a* where necessary. Then ask and answer the questions.**

When was the last time you had … ?

argument	bad day	breakfast in bed
dream	flu	fun
lunch at home	nap	

When was the last time you had a bad day?

9

Exercise 6
1a = a general statement
1b = the music I have downloaded on my phone
2a = any art exhibition
2b = a specific exhibition
3a = books and movies in general
3b = a particular book that was made into a movie

Exercise 7
When was the last time you had:
breakfast in bed?
a dream?
flu?
fun?
lunch at home?
a nap?
an argument?

REFERENCES
CULTURE NOTES ››› *p. 191*
WORKBOOK
p. 6

0.7 The UK vs The US

Grammar: Comparative structures
Vocabulary: Adjectives and adverbs

Exercise 1
closet (US) = wardrobe (UK)
elevator (US) = lift (UK)
garbage (US) = rubbish (UK)
sidewalk (US) = pavement (UK)
subway (US) = underground (UK)
vacation (US) = holiday (UK)

SHOW WHAT YOU KNOW

1 **Find pairs of words that describe the same thing in American and British English. Use a dictionary if necessary.**

~~biscuit~~ closet ~~cookie~~ elevator garbage holiday lift pavement rubbish sidewalk subway underground vacation wardrobe

cookie (US) = *biscuit* (UK)

2 CD•1.7 MP3•7 **With a partner, read the blog entry and discuss which option you think is correct. Then listen to Jess talking to a friend and check your ideas with hers.**

Exercise 4
extreme/more extreme/the most extreme
hot/hotter/the hottest
late/later/the latest
healthy/healthier/the healthiest
soon/sooner/the soonest
well-dressed/better-dressed/the best-dressed

An American in London

I've been chatting to a British friend, comparing life in the US with life here in the UK. Here are some of my conclusions.

In the UK ...
- the cost of living is a lot [1]*higher* / *lower* than
- salaries are [2]*quite a bit* / *a little* lower than
- food portions are a lot [3]*smaller* / *bigger* than
- most people live in [4]*slightly* / *much* smaller houses than
- housework is a lot [5]*harder* / *easier* because there are [6]*more* / *fewer* appliances than
- health care [7]*is more expensive than* / *isn't as expensive as*
- employees get [8]*a lot* / *slightly* more time off than
- people visit museums far [9]*more* / *less* frequently than

... in the US.

(Circled answers: higher, quite a bit, smaller, much, harder, fewer, isn't as expensive as, a lot, more)

where I lived in the US

where I live now in the UK

Exercise 6
1 British soccer players are much better-paid than American soccer players.
2 Big Ben is a little higher than the Statue of Liberty.
3 US life expectancy is a little shorter than UK life expectancy.
4 US military expenditure is much greater than UK military expenditure.

3 **Read REMEMBER THIS. Then complete the cartoon caption with *as, less, much, quite, than,* or *the*.**

REMEMBER THIS

- Adjective forms = add ***-er/the -est*** to short adjectives, ***more/the most*** to long adjectives; irregular adjectives: ***good, bad, far***
- Adverb forms = add ***more/the most*** or ***less/the least*** to adverbs; exceptions include ***early/earlier, fast/faster, well/better***
- Modifying comparisons = ***far/much/a lot/quite a bit/a bit/a little/slightly*** + comparative adjective/adverb
- Other structures = ***as ... as, not as/so ... as, the ... the***

A: Wow, that coffee cup is as big [1] *as* my head! Is everything [2] *much* larger in the US than in the UK?
B: Yes, except one thing: bathtubs are [3] *quite* a bit smaller.
A: Why? There's much more space in American houses [4] *than* British ones.
B: Americans take baths [5] *less* regularly than British people. They prefer showers. But their bathrooms are [6] *the* biggest in the world!

Grammar Focus page 160

4 **Form the comparative and superlative forms of the adjectives and adverbs in the box.**

badly-paid (adj) extreme (adj) hot (adj) late (adv) healthy (adj) soon (adv) well-dressed (adj)

badly-paid/worse-paid/the worst-paid

5 **Complete the second sentence so that it has a similar meaning to the first. Use the words in capitals.**

1 British comedies aren't as funny as American comedies. **THAN**
American comedies are *funnier than* British ones.
2 Andy Roddick's serve is faster than Andy Murray's. **AS**
Andy Murray's serve *isn't as fast as* Andy Roddick's.
3 The One World Trade Center in New York is much taller than the Shard in London. **LESS**
The Shard in London is *less tall than* the One World Trade Center in New York.
4 If you live in Boston, you grow to love it more each day. **MORE**
The longer you live in Boston, *the more* you love it.
5 English rock music is better than any other. **BEST**
English rock music is *the best in the* world.

6 **Use the prompts and the words in parentheses to write comparative sentences. Which facts did you already know?**

1 British soccer players / well-paid / American soccer players (much)
2 Big Ben / high / Statue of Liberty (a little)
3 US life expectancy / short / UK life expectancy (a little)
4 US military expenditure / great / UK military expenditure (much)

10

REFERENCES
CULTURE NOTES ››› pp. 191–192
AUDIO SCRIPT ››› p. 201
WORKBOOK
p. 7

0.8 The US vs The UK

Grammar: The Passive • *have something done*
Vocabulary: Politics • Society

SHOW WHAT YOU KNOW

1 **Complete the table. Put words and phrases with similar meanings side by side under *The US* or *The UK*.**

~~Congress~~ Conservatives 50 States Pound Constitutional Monarchy 98 Counties Dollar Democrats ~~Houses of Parliament~~ Labour President Prime Minister Republic Republicans

The US	The UK	Your country
Congress	Houses of Parliament	

2 **SPEAKING Add equivalent words to describe the institutions in your country. Then, with a partner, discuss similarities and differences between all three countries.**

3 **Read the quiz and choose the correct options.**

1 This country **hasn't been** / *hasn't* invaded since 1066, when King Harold **was** / *has* defeated by William the Conqueror.

2 Until 1913 it was legal to **have** / *be* children sent to other parts of this country by the postal service.

3 One in eight workers in this country *has had* / **has been** employed by McDonald's at one time or another.

4 Eighty percent of everything on sale in this country **is** / *has* bought by women.

5 When Abraham Lincoln became president of this country in 1861, slaves **were still being** / *had still* imported from Africa. During his presidency, Lincoln **had** / *was* slavery abolished.

6 In 1918 women over thirty **were** / *have* allowed to vote in elections in this country. Women over twenty-one **weren't** / *haven't* allowed to vote until 1928.

7 Eight billion chickens **are** / *have* consumed in this country each year.

8 This country's king, Henry VIII, **had been** / *had had* married six times and *had been* / **had** two of his wives executed by the time he died in 1547.

4 CD•1.8 MP3•8 **Replace *this country* with *the US* or *the UK* in Exercise 3. Then listen and check. Which facts did you find surprising?**

1 UK 2 US 3 US 4 UK 5 US 6 UK 7 US 8 UK

5 **Read REMEMBER THIS. Then complete the cartoon caption with the correct auxiliary verbs.**

REMEMBER THIS

- **The Passive** = it isn't important or you don't know who performed an action
- **Passive sentence + *by* + agent** = a way to mention who (or what) performed an action
- ***have something done*** = you don't perform an action yourself (somebody does it for you)

American: I love your royal family, especially William and Kate. Their wedding in 2011 [1] was shown by the biggest American TV stations. I [2] had my hair done like Kate's for the occasion! Do you think George [3] will be crowned King one day?

Brit: Um, maybe, but he's just a child now, so he's only interested in [4] having his meals served and the TV tuned into his favorite cartoons.

Grammar Focus page 161

6 **Read some more trivia facts about the US and the UK. Rewrite the sentences in the passive, using *by* + agent only if it is necessary.**

1 Most people think that Christopher Columbus discovered the US.
Most people think that the US was discovered by Christopher Columbus.
2 Every year in the US, judges sentence around 100 criminals to death.
3 In 1811 in the UK, parents named nearly a quarter of all girls Mary.
4 People in the UK drink more tea than in any other country.
5 French people built the Statue of Liberty in France.

7 **Use the prompts to write questions with *have something done*. Then, with a partner, ask and answer the questions.**

1 have you ever / repair / a bicycle?
Have you ever had a bicycle repaired?
2 when did you last / test / your eyes?
When did you last have your eyes tested?
3 will you ever / color / your hair?
Will you ever have your hair colored?
4 are you going to / paint / your bedroom?
Are you going to have your bedroom painted?
5 have you / pierce / your ears?
Have you had your ears pierced?
6 when did you last / take / a passport photo?
When did you last have a passport photo taken?

11

Exercise 1
The US
Republicans
Republic
50 States
Democrats
Dollar
President
The UK
Conservatives
Constitutional Monarchy
98 counties
Labour
Pound
Prime Minister

Exercise 6
2 Every year in the US around 100 criminals are sentenced to death.
3 In 1811 in the UK, nearly a quarter of all girls were named Mary.
4 More tea is drunk by people in the UK than in any other country.
5 The Statue of Liberty was built in France.

REFERENCES
CULTURE NOTES ››› pp. 192–193
AUDIO SCRIPT ››› p. 201

WORKBOOK
p. 7

NEXT CLASS
Ask students to research and prepare a presentation for the next class. They can choose to work on one of the topics from the unit and must create a question they are going to answer (e.g. *Does advertising really work?*).

Exercise 1
drop a class/
a subject
fail an exam/
a subject/a class
pass an exam
pursue a career
skip an exam/
a class/a subject
study a subject
take a class/
an exam/
a subject

1 DO YOUR BEST

If you think education is expensive, try ignorance.

DEREK BOK (B. 1930), FORMER PRESIDENT OF HARVARD UNIVERSITY

UNIT LANGUAGE AND SKILLS

Vocabulary:
- *Show what you know* – verb-noun collocations
- phrasal verbs – education
- collocations
- synonyms – personality adjectives
- word families – verbs ending in *-ize*
- collocations
- *Word in focus – do*

Grammar:
- present and past habits
- verb patterns

Listening:
- people talking about memory
- multiple matching

Reading:
- an article about experiments in education
- cloze text

Speaking:
- describing and speculating about photos

Writing:
- a report

FOCUS EXTRA

- Grammar Focus page 162
- WORD STORE booklet pages 2–3
- Workbook pages 8–21 or MyEnglishLab
- MP3s – www.english.com/focus

12

1.1 Vocabulary

Education • Phrasal verbs • Collocations • Personality adjectives

I can talk about education and different kinds of student.

SHOW WHAT YOU KNOW

1 With a partner, make as many verb-noun collocations as you can in sixty seconds.

verbs			+	nouns	
attend	drop	fail		a career	a class
pass	pursue	skip		an exam	a subject
study	take			college/a university	

attend a class/attend college

2 SPEAKING Write three questions with different collocations from Exercise 1. Then, with a partner, ask and answer your questions.

Which college would you most like to attend? Why?

3 Look at the photos and read about four kinds of student. Which one describes you best? Compare with a partner.

SELF-MOTIVATED

You're very well-organized and you usually remember to bring the right books to your classes. You want to do well and you try not to fall behind with your homework. You're studious and eager to learn. You get good grades because you pay attention in class. You're an enthusiastic learner.

SOCIABLE

You're gregarious and fun to be with. You sometimes get into trouble in class because you can't stop talking. You particularly like interaction with other people at school. You have a gift for languages and you enjoy taking part in interactive activities. You're a team-player and a communicator.

SPORTY

You're a popular member of the class with a good circle of friends. You particularly enjoy teamwork and learning in an active way. However, you'd rather be outside on the sports field than in the classroom. You're competitive and single-minded, but you're also a cooperative learner who likes motivating other people.

BRAINY

You're lucky – you're naturally bright. You're curious about the world, and you soak up knowledge like a sponge. You have a thirst for knowledge and you excel at subjects that many other students struggle with, such as Math and Sciences. You're a deep thinker and an analytic learner.

EXTRA ACTIVITIES
- Photocopiable resource 1 (education and character – 10 mins)
MultiROM and ActiveTeach
- Photocopiable resource 2 (Test yourself partner work activities)

MultiROM and ActiveTeach
- MyEnglishLab – assignable *Show what you have learned* mini-test

WORKBOOK
pp. 8–9

NEXT CLASS
- Ask students to prepare for a 10–15 minute vocabulary quiz: *Focus* Assessment Package, Unit 1.1, Vocabulary.

4 Take the questionnaire and check your score. Do you get the same answer as in Exercise 3?

WHAT KIND OF STUDENT ARE YOU?

Take our questionnaire and find out.

1 The summer vacation is over and the school year begins on Monday. What are your thoughts?

A I'm looking forward to reaching my goals.
B I can't wait to see old classmates again.
C I'm going to train really hard this semester.
D I can't wait to tackle some advanced Math.

2 Teachers are most likely to say to you:

A 'Thank you for turning in your assignment on time.'
B 'Yes, very funny. Now get on with your work.'
C 'Can you keep still for a moment, please?'
D 'Good for you, you got the best grade again.'

3 You have a free period. What do you do?

A Go to the library and do some research for your school project.
B Hang out with your friends in the cafeteria and chat.
C Get two teams together and play basketball.
D Go to the IT room and catch up on the latest science news.

4 You have an exam tomorrow. What do you do?

A Your study schedule tells you to take the night off.
B You go out - it's Thursday night!
C You go to the gym and put off thinking about the exam.
D You've always done well on exams, so you watch a movie.

5 Your number one reason for liking school is because ...

A you want to go on to further studies and a great career.
B it's where your friends are.
C it has the best football team in the region.
D it has a great science lab.

WHAT DOES IT MEAN?

Mainly **A**s = You're **self-motivated**.
Mainly **B**s = You're **sociable**.
Mainly **C**s = You're **sporty**.
Mainly **D**s = You're **brainy**.

5 SPEAKING With a partner, discuss how you would describe the worst student in the world.

Go to WORD STORE 1 page 3.

WORD STORE 1A

6 CD•1.9 MP3•9 Complete WORD STORE 1A with the base form of the phrasal verbs in red in the texts. Then listen, check, and repeat.

7 Complete the questions with prepositions or particles. Then, with a partner, ask and answer the questions.

1 At the beginning of the semester, what do you look forward _to_ ?
2 Do you get started on you homework as soon as you get home, or do you put it _off_ ?
3 Have you ever finished an assignment and then forgotten to turn it _in_ ?
4 When you go online, what's the first thing you catch up _on_ ?
5 Is there a particular college you want to go _to_ ?
6 Are there any subjects where you are falling _behind_ ?

WORD STORE 1B

8 CD•1.10 MP3•10 Complete WORD STORE 1B with the underlined phrases in the texts. Then listen, check, and repeat. Add a translation.

9 With a partner, match the sentence halves. Which statements do you agree with?

1 To become a deep [d]
2 It's difficult to pay [g]
3 If you don't reach [a]
4 Students who have a gift [e]
5 Children soak up [c]
6 It's important to have a supportive circle [b]
7 Most teenagers aren't very eager [f]

a your educational goals, it doesn't matter.
b of friends at school.
c knowledge like a sponge. It's easy for them.
d thinker, you need a thirst for knowledge.
e for drama should attend special drama schools.
f to learn. They find classes boring.
g attention in class right before lunch.

WORD STORE 1C

10 CD•1.11 MP3•11 Complete WORD STORE 1C with the highlighted adjectives in the texts. Then listen, check, and repeat.

11 Replace the underlined adjective with a synonym from WORD STORE 1C.

1 Hannah is very hard-working (studious). She's always in the library.
2 Dan has a logical (analytic) way of thinking. He likes problem-solving.
3 Jim is a sociable (gregarious) person. He loves a good party!
4 Eva is very determined (single-minded). She never gives up.
5 Tom likes to discover new things. He's always interested (curious).
6 Rosa is really intelligent (bright). She gets everything right.

12 Replace the names in Exercise 11 to describe students in your school. Does your partner agree with you?

WORD STORE 1D

13 CD•1.12 MP3•12 Complete WORD STORE 1D with more synonyms for personality adjectives. Then listen, check, and repeat. Write example sentences.

1.2 Grammar

Present and past habits

I can talk about present and past habits.

1 **Read Gillian Lynne's story. What do you think she did when her mom and the psychologist left the room?** *She got up and started dancing.*

THE RIGHT EDUCATION

Ken Robinson is an educationalist. In his book *The Element*, he interviews people who have made a successful living doing what they love. This is Gillian Lynne's story.

Gillian has had a successful career in the theater, but life **didn't use to be** so good. When she was eight, her schoolwork was a disaster, her handwriting was awful, and she **used to fail** all her exams. Her teachers **would complain** about her disruptive behavior; she **was always fidgeting** and turning in her homework late. They told her mother that she had a learning disorder. So Gillian's mother took her to see a psychologist and listed some of the problems: she never pays attention in class – she**'ll get up** and move around instead of listening to the teacher, she**'s always disturbing** people, and her homework's always late. Finally, the doctor turned to Gillian and said, 'Gillian, I need to speak to your mother privately now. Don't worry. We won't be long.' As they left the room he turned on the radio on his desk ...

2 CD•1.13 MP3•13 **Listen to two friends talking about Gillian's story and check your ideas in Exercise 1. With a partner, discuss what lessons this story teaches us about educating children.**

3 **Complete the GRAMMAR FOCUS with the phrases in blue in the text.**

GRAMMAR FOCUS

Present and past habits

- You can use the **Present Simple** and the **Past Simple** to talk about habits.
- You can use ***used to*** to talk about regular past actions that don't happen any more or past states that are no longer true.
  She ¹*used to fail* *all her exams.*
  Life ²*didn't use to be* *so good.*
- You can use ***will*** (present) or ***would*** (past) to talk about characteristic, repeated, or predictable actions. You don't use them to talk about states.
  She ³*'ll get up* *and move around instead of listening to the teacher.*
  Her teachers ⁴*would complain* *about her disruptive behavior.*

  Note: You don't usually ask questions with this use of *will* and *would*.
- You can use the **Present** or **Past Continuous** with ***always*** to stress the repetitiveness of an action and sometimes to show your annoyance.
  She ⁵*'s always disturbing* *people.*
  She ⁶*was always fidgeting* *and handing in her homework late.*

REFERENCES
CULTURE NOTES ››› *p. 193*
AUDIO SCRIPT ››› *p. 201*

EXTRA ACTIVITIES
• Photocopiable resource 2 (Test yourself partner work activities)

MultiROM and ActiveTeach
• MyEnglishLab – assignable *Show what you have learned* mini-test

WORKBOOK
p. 10

NEXT CLASS
• Ask students to prepare for a 10–15 minute grammar quiz: *Focus* Assessment Package, Unit 1.2, Grammar.

4 **Complete the sentences with the correct form of the verbs in parentheses. Use *would* where possible. If *would* is not possible, use *used to*. If *used to* is not possible, use the Past Simple.**

1 This school used to be (be) smaller than it is now.
2 Mom would take (take) me to school every day.
3 I didn't use to like (not like) going to school.
4 I used to hate (hate) having school lunches.
5 I would go (go) swimming every week.
6 I went (go) on a school trip to California.

5 **Write *yes/no* questions for the sentences in Exercise 4. Use *used to* or the Past Simple. Then, with a partner, ask and answer your questions.**

1 Did this school use to be smaller than it is now?

Exercise 5
2 Did your mom use to take you to school every day?
3 Did you use to like going to school?
4 Did you use to hate having school lunches?
5 Did you use to go swimming every week?
6 Did you go on a school trip to California?

6 **Write sentences comparing your routine in grade school and now. Then compare with a partner. Who has changed the most?**

	Grade school	Now
1 For breakfast	I'd …	I'll …
2 Before setting off for school	I'd …	I'll …
3 At break time	I'd …	I'll …
4 At lunchtime	I'd …	I'll …
5 After school	I'd …	I'll …
6 Before going to bed	I'd …	I'll …

For breakfast I'd have cereal with milk in grade school, but now I'll just have a piece of toast.

7 **Complete the sentences about annoying habits with the correct form of the verbs in the box.**

check ~~chew~~ lose talk tell

1 Before, Tim was always chewing the end of his pen. Now he's always chewing gum.
2 Before, Julie ________ her make-up. Now she ________ her phone.
3 Before, Sam ________ about himself. Now he ________ about his girlfriend.
4 Before, Dave ________ his temper. Now he ________ his keys.
5 Before, Mary ________ lies. Now she ________ people what to do.

Exercise 7
2 was always checking / 's always checking
3 was always talking / 's always talking
4 was always losing / 's always losing
5 was always telling / 's always telling

8 **SPEAKING With a partner, list the habits in Exercise 7 from least to most annoying. Do you know people who had or have any of these habits?**

Grammar Focus page 162

1.3 Listening

Multiple matching

I can understand the main points in short monologues.

1 SPEAKING **With a partner, discuss how good you are at remembering the different things in the box.**

dates and times	English words	faces
items on a shopping list	names	song lyrics

2 CD•1.14 MP3•14 **Read about two methods of memorizing a shopping list. Choose the best heading from the list (A–E) for each method. Then listen and check.**

A Use your imagination
B Make up a dramatic narrative
C Learn how to give a speech
D Imagine what each item tastes like
E Visualize the items in a familiar place

Memory tips

Greek philosopher Socrates famously said, 'Learning is remembering.' So how can we improve our memory? The key is to use your imagination. Here are two ways of remembering a shopping list of eight items:

1 B

First, imagine a huge loaf of bread. Suddenly, coffee squirts out of the top and makes a fountain of dark brown liquid. After a few seconds, the dark brown changes to white yogurt. The yogurt forms a river and it goes under a bridge – the bridge is a steak. Some black and green olives are crossing the bridge and some big brown eggs are chasing them. The olives hide behind a big carton of orange juice. You lift an olive to your mouth to eat and it turns into an onion, which tastes horrible. That's it! You got to the end.

2 E

Think of your home and get a mental image of the rooms in your house. Then put the items on the list, one by one, in specific places in the rooms. For instance, you imagine the bread on the doormat as you come in the door. Then you go into the living room and the coffee is in front of the television, the yogurt is on the sofa, and the steak is stuck to the mirror on the wall, and so on; it's all about making personal associations – you get the idea. This method isn't just useful for memorizing shopping lists. Some famous people have used it to give a speech without using notes.

3 **With a partner, test your memory. Follow the instructions.**

- Make a shopping list of eight items and give it to your partner.
- Study your partner's list for sixty seconds using one of the methods in the text.
- After sixty seconds, take turns to recall your lists. Did the memory tip help?

16

REFERENCES
AUDIO SCRIPT ››› *p. 202*
WORKBOOK
p. 11

EXAM FOCUS Multiple matching

4 CD•1.15 MP3•15 **Listen to four people talking about memory. Choose from the list (A–F) what each speaker says. Use the letters only once. There are two extra letters.**

Speaker 1: B | **Speaker 3:** E
Speaker 2: C | **Speaker 4:** A

The speaker:

A refers to someone who is incapable of forgetting anything.
B wanted a family member to confirm whether his/her memory was correct.
C disagrees with someone about how they keep a good memory.
D wishes they could forget a memory of witnessing a crime.
E has problems remembering the names of things well.
F can describe someone accurately after seeing them for only a few seconds.

5 CD•1.15 MP3•15 **Complete the questions with the words in the box. Then listen again and answer the questions.**

detail earliest good losing slip vividly

1 What is Speaker 1's _earliest_ **memory**? *Christmas before he was three*
2 What is the first birthday party Speaker 1 can **remember** _vividly_ ? *Third*
3 Is Speaker 2's grandfather _losing_ **his memory** or does he manage to **recall things in** _detail_ ? *He manages to recall things in detail.*
4 Does Speaker 3 **have a** _good_ **memory for** names or faces or both? *good for faces but bad for names*
5 Do key facts in TV programs sometimes _slip_ Speaker 4's **mind**? *yes*

6 **SPEAKING With a partner, ask and answer the questions in Exercise 5. Give details wherever possible.**

1 What is your earliest memory?

PRONUNCIATION FOCUS

7 CD•1.16 MP3•16 **Listen and repeat the words in the box. Do any of the words have the same vowel sound?** *No, all six are different.*

bread clear learn mean steak wear

8 CD•1.17 MP3•17 **Add the words from Exercise 7 to the table. Then listen, check, and repeat.**

Sound	Typical spelling	Occasional spelling
/i/	need detail [1] *mean*	piece
/ɪr/	here career [2] *clear*	
/ɚ/	reserved squirt turn	[3] *learn*
/ɛ/	egg	[4] *bread*
/eɪ/	made detail pay	[5] *steak*
/ɛr/	pair rare	[6] *wear*

WORD STORE 1E

9 CD•1.18 MP3•18 **Complete WORD STORE 1E. Add nouns, adjectives, or verbs to the table. Mark the stress. Then listen, check, and repeat.**

1.4 Reading

Cloze text

I can understand the structure of a text.

1 **SPEAKING With a partner, discuss how you use technology to help you learn. Think about in school and out of school.**

2 **Read the article and answer the questions.**

1 What two experiments did Dr. Sugata Mitra set up in India? Why?
2 How did technology help Indian children learn?

Exercise 2
1 Hole-in-the-Wall experiment, and Skype Grannies. To help students in poor and remote areas and to test Dr. Sugata Mitra's theories
2 In the Hole-in-the-Wall experiment, technology provided an environment for students to learn unsupervised, using their natural curiosity.
In the Skype Grannies experiment, technology allowed children from remote and poor places to listen to stories being read in English.

EXAM FOCUS Cloze text

3 **Read the article again. Choose from the sentences (A–E) the one which fits each blank. There is one extra sentence.**

A 'The children are forming relationships with them and the teachers, many of whom were upset at the thought of having finished their careers, have realized they're more important than ever,' he says.
B For many years he has been interested in a form of learning in which children are unsupervised and involved in self-learning and peer-teaching.
C Traditional education models assume that children are empty vessels who need to be filled with content, but Dr. Mitra's experiments prove that wrong.
D 'Computers cannot replace good teachers, but they can get a high standard of education into the schools where they are needed most,' he says.
E He then left them to use it unsupervised and found that after only a month, the children had taught themselves how to use the computer and go online.

4 **Complete the sentences with the correct form of the words in capitals. Then check your answers in the article.**

1 Dr. Sugata Mitra thinks the current education system is _outdated_ and not fit for purpose. **DATE**
2 Using a child's natural _curiosity_ is at the heart of Mitra's ideas. **CURIOUS**
3 He put a computer in a hole in the wall between his work premises and an _adjoining_ slum. **JOIN**
4 The experiment became the _inspiration_ for a very successful movie. **INSPIRE**
5 In 2010 Mitra _initiated_ a new project for Indian children involving Skype. **INITIAL**
6 _Surprisingly_, the children wanted to listen to British grandmothers reading them fairy tales. **SURPRISE**
7 There are now 200 _volunteers_ reading to Indian children via Skype. **VOLUNTARY**
8 Mitra has won a prize for the project he calls '_Minimally_ Invasive Education'. **MINIMUM**

5 **SPEAKING Do you think these things will be more, less, or equally important in the schools of 2025? Discuss with a partner.**

books blackboards computer rooms desks exams and tests
group-work homework hand-held computers language laboratories
paper teachers whiteboards wi-fi

WORD STORE 1F

6 CD•1.20 MP3•20 **Complete WORD STORE 1F. Replace the underlined word with a word in the box to make another collocation with a similar meaning. Then listen, check, and repeat.**

18

REFERENCES
CULTURE NOTES ››› *p. 193*

EXTRA ACTIVITIES
• Photocopiable resource 3 (word formation: adverbs – 8 mins)
MultiROM and ActiveTeach

WORKBOOK
pp. 12–13

NEXT CLASS
• Ask students to write a short blog post about their learning. *How did they learn best in the past? Has it changed? How would they like to learn?* Share in the next class.

CD•1.19 MP3•19

Lighting the spark of learning

Dr. Sugata Mitra, Professor of Educational Technology at Newcastle University, England, thinks it's time for a radical shake-up of education. He believes that the present education system is outdated because it doesn't prepare children for the jobs of the future, which have changed thanks to technology. [1] ____ Dr. Mitra calls this methodology 'Minimally Invasive Education' and explains that it is based on the idea of using children's natural curiosity and then providing an environment where they can learn on their own.

children from India learning from a 'Skype Granny'

Dr. Sugata Mitra

In 1999 he decided to test his ideas and set up an experiment, now known as the Hole-in-the-Wall Experiment, with children living in slums who didn't have access to good teachers. At the time he was working in New Delhi and his place of work shared a wall with a slum. He cut a hole in the wall between his work premises and the adjoining slum, and placed a computer with Internet access in a kiosk where children could use it freely. [2] ____. He then repeated the Hole-in-the-Wall experiment in a village with no Internet access. This time he left the computer in a kiosk with just a few CDs in English and when he went back after two months, the children surprised him by asking in English for a faster processor and a better mouse! When he asked how they knew all this, they said that they taught themselves some English so that they could understand the machine that only talked in English.

children learning from a computer in a wall, India

The project was so successful that it became the inspiration for the hugely successful movie, *Slumdog Millionaire*. The movie was based on a book entitled *Q&A* by Vikas Swarup. Swarup said that his book was inspired by the Hole-in-the-Wall experiment. He said, 'I realized that there's an innate ability in everyone to do something extraordinary, provided they are given an opportunity.'

In 2010 Dr. Mitra initiated another project for children in India – this time using a Skype connection. Mitra explains: 'When I last visited India, I asked the children what they would like to use Skype for most, and surprisingly they said they wanted British grandmothers to read them fairy tales.' Dr. Mitra recruited a British woman to spend a few hours a week reading to the children and set up webcams so that a life-size image of the storyteller is projected on to a wall in India. He now has 200 volunteers reading to the children via Skype. He also has retired teachers and educators regularly teaching slum children in India by Skype. [3] ____ Hundreds of children in India are now learning from 'Skype Grannies', but Dr. Mitra's plan is to create a School in the Cloud using retired teachers as a resource for children all around the world to tap into.

In 2013 Dr. Sugata Mitra was the winner of the $1 million TED* prize for his revolutionary work with Indian children and for showing the power of 'Minimally Invasive Education'. Dr. Mitra believes that technology should be seen not as a threat to teachers, but as an asset. [4] ____ With the prize money he will continue to fulfil his wish of building a School in the Cloud, where children can find information and learn from one another.

*TED (Technology, Entertainment, Design) is a global set of conferences under the slogan 'Ideas Worth Spreading'.

1.5 Grammar

Verb patterns

I can use a wide range of verb patterns.

1 **CD•1.21 MP3•21 Listen to Part 1 of a podcast about being left-handed. What jobs seem to be more suited to 'lefties'?** Jobs that are creative / visual – in music, the arts and media / architects / sports people

2 **CD•1.21 MP3•21 Listen to the podcast again. Are the statements true (T) or false (F)?**

1 No one knows what **makes someone use** their right or left hand. F
2 Left-handers **tend to choose** creative professions. T
3 Dominance of the left hemisphere **enables left-handers to be** better at 3D perception. F
4 Rafael Nadal **keeps winning** because he is naturally left-handed. F

3 **Read and complete GRAMMAR FOCUS I with the verb patterns in blue in Exercise 2.**

GRAMMAR FOCUS I

Verb patterns

1 verb + *to* infinitive: tend to choose
2 verb + object + *to*-infinitive: enables left-handers to be
3 verb + object + infinitive without *to*: makes someone use
4 verb + *-ing*: keeps winning

4 **Match the verbs in the box with verb patterns 1–4 in GRAMMAR FOCUS I. Check the lists in Grammar Focus page 162 if you are not sure.**

advise 2 allow 2 arrange 1 avoid 4 can't afford 1 can't help 4
can't stand 4 cause 2 decide 1 expect 1,2 encourage 2 force 2
imagine 4 intend 1 let 3 manage 1 offer 1 refuse 1
remind 2 seem 1 spend/waste time 4 urge 2 warn (not) 2

5 **CD•1.22 MP3•22 Complete Part 2 of the podcast with the correct form of the verbs in parentheses. Then listen and check. How many left-handed people do you know?**

So that's the good news about being left-handed. The bad news is that manufacturers don't remember to make tools and machinery for left-handers. Society [1] forces us to use (force/us/use) objects that are designed for right-handed people and this [2] makes us look (make/us/look) clumsy.

As a child, I don't remember deciding that I was left-handed. But when my elementary school teacher saw me using my left hand for writing and drawing, she [3] encouraged me to swap (encourage/me/swap) hands. She didn't [4] manage to change (manage/change) my natural inclination and I didn't stop writing with my left hand. Why [5] waste time trying (waste/time/try) to change someone's natural handedness? Just [6] let them use (let/them/use) the hand they feel comfortable with – you can't [7] expect people to do (expect/people/do) what isn't natural to them!

I once heard someone say that left-handed people were strange. But when you stop to think about famous historical figures who were left-handed, you can't [8] avoid concluding (avoid/conclude) that they were brilliant! I'm sure Leonardo Da Vinci, Mahatma Gandhi, Albert Einstein, Winston Churchill and Marie Curie would agree!

President Obama writing with his left hand

REFERENCES

CULTURE NOTES ››› pp. 193–194
AUDIO SCRIPT ››› p. 202

EXTRA ACTIVITIES

- Photocopiable resource 4 (verb patterns – 12 mins) MultiROM and ActiveTeach
- Share students blog posts from the previous class
- MyEnglishLab – assignable *Show what you have learned* mini-test

WORKBOOK

p. 14

6 Read GRAMMAR FOCUS II. Find examples of verb patterns with *remember, stop, hear,* and *see* in the text. Explain the changes in meaning.

GRAMMAR FOCUS II

Verb patterns – change in meaning

- You can use *remember, forget, stop,* and *try* with the *-ing* form or a *to*-infinitive, but with a change in meaning.

  *I **remember doing** my homework. Sadly, I **didn't remember to turn** it **in**.*

  *Jim **will never forget going** on that school trip.*

  *He **forgot to take** any money.*

  *'I've **stopped eating** chocolate.' 'Really? Why **did you stop to buy** some on the way home?'*

  *'I **tried to convince** Jane but she doesn't want my advice.' 'Why don't you **try talking** to her best friend? Jane always listens to her.'*

- You use *feel, hear, see, watch* + object + *-ing* to describe ongoing actions or the same verbs + object + infinitive without *to* to describe finished actions.

  *I **watched Dan playing** soccer and I **saw him score** the winning goal.*

Exercise 6
REMEMBER:
lines 2–3: manufacturers don't remember to make tools …
line 7: I don't remember deciding …
STOP:
line 12: I didn't stop writing …
line 18: when you stop to think …
HEAR:
line 17: I once heard someone say …
SEE
lines 8–9: teacher saw me using …

7 Complete the sentences with the correct form of the verbs in parentheses. Then check the sentences that are true for you.

1 I often forget _to bring_ (bring) my pens to school.
2 I'll never forget _meeting_ (meet) my best friend.
3 I don't remember _learning_ (learn) how to swim.
4 I always remember _to turn_ (turn) my phone off in class.
5 I stopped _taking_ (take) piano lessons a while ago.
6 I usually stop _to buy_ (buy) candy on my way home.
7 If my laptop freezes, I try _restarting_ (restart) it.
8 I've never seen my father _lose_ (lose) his temper.
9 I often see my neighbor _driving_ (drive) to work.

Grammar Focus page 162

NEXT CLASS

- Ask students to prepare for a 10–15 minute grammar quiz: *Focus* Assessment Package, Unit 1.5, Grammar.

1.6 Speaking

Describing a photo

I can speculate about photos and answer a related question.

1 SPEAKING **Look at the adjectives in the box. With a partner, talk about the last time you experienced these feelings while you were learning something.**

confused	determined	enthusiastic	
frustrated	relieved	terrified	thrilled

The last time I felt really confused was when I was trying to understand when to use the Present Perfect tense in English! But, fortunately, I understand it now …

2 SPEAKING **Describe photos A and B.**

- Say what the photos show.
- Speculate about the people and their feelings.

3 CD•1.23 MP3•23 **Listen to someone describing photos A and B. Does the speaker have the same ideas about the situations as you?**

REFERENCES
AUDIO SCRIPT ››› *p. 202*
WORKBOOK
p. 15

4 CD•1.23 MP3•23 **Read the SPEAKING FOCUS and complete the description of photos A and B with one word in each blank. Then listen again and check.**

These are both photos of people learning new things. In the first photo a girl is in a car. It's [1]_hard_ to tell whether she's having a driving lesson or taking her driving test. The man in the passenger seat has a pen, so the [2]_chances_ are he's an examiner. [3]_Based_ on his body language, I'd say they might be [4]_about_ to crash! [5]_Clearly_, something is wrong.
In the second photo a boy is learning to play the guitar. He [6]_might_ be learning from a teacher or a friend. It's not [7]_easy_ to say whether he's a beginner or not, but he [8]_appears_ to be enjoying himself. The girl in the car, however, [9]_judging_ by the expression on her face, isn't enjoying the situation much at all!

SPEAKING FOCUS

Speculating about people

Based on … , I'd say he's/she's/it's …
Judging by … , I (don't) think …
It looks/seems as if/like …
He/She/It appears/doesn't appear to be …
The chances are (that) he's/she's/it's …

Showing certainty

Clearly, (there's a problem/something is wrong).
It's obvious/clear (from the expression on his/her face) that …
He/She/It is definitely/certainly (not) …

Showing uncertainty

It's hard to be sure (whether/if) …
It's not easy to say (whether/if) …
I can't really tell (whether/if) …

Speculating about the situation

He/She could/might have ('ve) *just* + past participle (recent past)
He/She could/might be + *-ing* (present)
He/She could/might be about to + infinitive (near future)

5 SPEAKING **Work with a partner. Go to WORD STORE page 23 and take it in turns to describe and speculate about the photos.**

6 CD•1.24 MP3•24 **Listen to a teenager answering a question. Which of these questions has he been asked?**

1 Which school subject do you feel is the most useful? Why?
(2) Is it important for you to learn to drive? Why?/Why not?
3 What qualities should a good teacher or instructor have?
4 Given the choice, which new subjects or skills would you like to learn and why?

7 CD•1.24 MP3•24 **Listen again and check the phrases you hear.**

- Personally, I think … ✓
- In my opinion, … ☐
- Actually, … ✓
- To be honest, … ☐
- I intend to … ✓
- For this reason, I feel … ✓
- That's why I think … ☐

8 SPEAKING **With a partner, ask and answer the questions in Exercise 6. Use the phrases in Exercise 7 to help you.**

23

1.7 Writing

A report

I can write a report that summarizes information from a meeting.

1 Read Mandy's post on the school website. Then, with a partner, discuss the questions.

1 What is the next school meeting about? *social events for the summer term*
2 What does Mandy want students in her year to do? *send her any points they would like her to talk about*
3 What does a student representative do? *represents his or her class or year group*

2 Read the report and choose the best answer.

When writing a report of a meeting, the writer needs to
A write down exactly what people said.
(B) summarize the main points to inform the readers.

3 Read the report again and answer the questions.

1 What are the three types of event that Mandy writes about? *parties, barbecue, a charity event*
2 Which two of these events also happened last year? *barbecue, charity event*
3 What was Mandy's impression of the meeting? *it gave her lots of information*
4 What action do students need to take? *put some ideas on the website*

4 A report is usually divided into sections with headings. Match these headings with the paragraphs in Mandy's report.

1 Summer charity event [D]
2 Conclusion [E]
3 End-of-year parties [B]
4 Introduction [A]
5 Summer barbecue [C]

5 Complete the WRITING FOCUS with the examples in purple in Mandy's report.

Stoneberry High School

About | Students | School programs | Parents | News | Diary | Contact

Latest news

Student representatives' meeting

Posted on January 9 at 9:03 AM

Hi everyone,

As you know, I'm your Student Representative for this year and I'm going to a big meeting on Thursday, where we'll be discussing school social events for the summer term. One of these will be an important charity event to raise money for the local children's hospital.

If you've got anything you'd like me to say at the meeting, please email me and I'll try to mention it on Thursday.

I'll upload my report of the meeting next week.

Remember: my job is to represent you, so let me know what ideas you have!

Mandy

School meeting about summer social and charity events

Report by Mandy Collins, ninth grade Student Representative

A The aim of this report is to inform students of the summer social events that were discussed at the recent school meeting and to recommend action that needs to be taken.

B The school will fund end-of-year parties for each grade level. These will be organized by students in those classes. The parties should be held at school in the week before the end of the year and could take place at lunchtime, after school, or in the evening.

C We have decided to hold another summer barbecue near the river. Any ideas for a theme for the barbecue from students would be welcome.

D There will be another charity event in June to raise money for Belford Hospital. It is hoped that this year the school can raise even more money than last year. Each grade level is asked to put forward an idea that they can organize for the day.

E The meeting was very informative and several students' ideas were considered. Students should now think about what we can do for the charity event. Any suggestions should be posted on the website.

EXTRA ACTIVITIES
- MyEnglishLab – assignable *Show what you have learned* writing task and *Show that you have checked* checklist

WORKBOOK
p. 16

WRITING FOCUS

A report

Overall structure

- Organize your report clearly. Divide it into different sections, each with a heading.
- Include an introduction, sections giving different information, and a conclusion with suggestions or recommendations.
- Use a semi-formal style.

Introduction

- In your introduction, explain the reason for your report. This doesn't need to be long or detailed.

The purpose of this report is to describe …

1 The aim of this report is to inform

Main sections

- Divide your report into different sections relating to different types of information. Give each section a heading.
- Give factual statements using simple active and passive verb forms.

The school will fund …

2 These will be organized by

It is hoped/advised that …

3 We have decided to

Conclusion

- In your conclusion, summarize your findings in a summary sentence.

4 The meeting was very informative

A lot of points were discussed.

There are still a number of decisions to be made.

Make recommendations/suggestions.

I would recommend/suggest that …
We hope that students will …
One suggestion/idea would be to …
We should consider …
It would benefit everyone if …

5 Students should now think about

Use a semi-formal style.

- Use full forms, not contractions: it is, not ~~it's~~
- Don't leave out words or have one-word sentences: *I will write a new report later*, not ~~*New report later.*~~
- Don't use exclamation marks: *It was very informative*, not ~~*It was very informative!*~~
- Don't use idiomatic expressions: *They appreciated our ideas* not ~~*They loved our ideas.*~~

6 Rewrite these sentences using language from the WRITING FOCUS.

1 In this report I want to describe some changes to the school schedule.
2 I learned a lot from the lecture.
3 Let's think about some alternatives.
4 It would be a good idea to go on the website and look at the plans.
5 Some of the ideas were absolutely fantastic!

7 Read the LANGUAGE FOCUS and choose the correct options.

1 The students suggested *to have* / *having* a big end-of-term party.
2 The people at the meeting recommended *to reconsider* / *that we reconsider* the proposals.
3 We intend *to discuss* / *discuss* the subject again next month.
4 The suggestions caused us *to have* / *that we had* some concerns.
5 It was decided *to have* / *having* a fashion show.
6 Everyone is advised *to wear* / *wearing* warm clothes.

8 Read Jack's email about a meeting he attended. Note down points for his report under these headings.

1 Introduction
2 Where and when
3 Facilities
4 Conclusion and recommendations

LANGUAGE FOCUS

Verb patterns

You can use these verbs in reports to make recommendations and suggestions. Note the verb patterns.

- *advise + person + to-infinitive*
  *You **are advised to check** the website.*
- *intend + to-infinitive*
  *The committee **intends to contact** all members.*
- *cause + noun/pronoun + to-infinitive*
  *Poor weather **caused us to reconsider** our plans for a barbecue.*
- *suggest + that + a person + to-infinitive/-ing*
  *The principal **suggests that we donate** the money to charity.*
  *The principal **suggests donating** the money to charity.*
- *recommend + that + noun + infinitive without to*
  *We **recommend that the barbecue takes** place in August.*
- *decide + to-infinitive*
  *It was **decided to delay** the plans until next term.*

Hi Ella,

Just got back from my student rep meeting – all about the new school sports building. It's going to be at the back of the school where the old parking lot used to be. The builders say that they'll start work during the summer vacation. So, who knows – it might be ready for the new term!

The facilities are going to be great. There's going to be a new indoor swimming pool with locker rooms. Next to that, they hope to have a big room for indoor games like ping-pong and badminton. Fantastic!

The school has the money for the building, but they need us to raise some money for equipment. We talked about having a talent contest and maybe a sponsored walk. We're hoping students will give us some more ideas for fundraising and we can talk about those at the next meeting.

Must write up my report now,

Jack

9 Write Jack's report for the school website in 140–190 words. Use the WRITING FOCUS and the LANGUAGE FOCUS to help you.

Exercise 6
(Example answers)
1 The aim of this report is to describe some changes to the school schedule.
2 The lecture was very informative.
3 We should consider some alternatives.
4 I suggest we go …
5 Some of the ideas were excellent.

1.8 Language in focus

-ing forms

I can use -ing forms in a range of different contexts.

1 Read the information about *-ing* forms and match uses 1–6 with examples a–f from this unit.

All ***-ing* forms** express some sense of 'ongoing activity'. ***-ing* forms** can be used as verbs (*I'm **learning** Spanish*); as adjectives (*The classes are **boring***); or as nouns (***Reading** is easier than **listening***).

1 Use *-ing* forms in continuous tenses.
2 Use *-ing* forms after certain verbs.
3 Use *-ing* forms in certain adjective/noun constructions.
4 Use *-ing* forms after prepositions.
5 Use *-ing* forms to describe people or things.
6 Use *-ing* forms as the subject or object of a sentence.

a **Learning** is **remembering**. [6]
b Nadal keeps **winning**. [2]
c a **shocking** piece of news [5]
d ideas worth **spreading** [3]
e She's always **disturbing** people. [1]
f I'd be good at **recognizing** criminals. [4]

2 Translate examples a–f in Exercise 1. What are the differences between your language and English?

3 Use the prompts to write sentences with the *-ing* form. Which sentences do you agree with?

1 know how to type / useful skill
Knowing how to type is a useful skill.
2 take exams / very stressful
3 watch TV / waste of time
4 copy your friend's homework / cheat
5 always be late / annoy habit
6 not have breakfast / bad for you

Exercise 3
2 Taking exams is very stressful.
3 Watching TV is a waste of time.
4 Copying your friend's homework is cheating.
5 Always being late is an annoying habit.
6 Not having breakfast is bad for you.

4 Read REMEMBER THIS. Then complete the sentences using the words in parentheses. Add *but* and any other words necessary.

REMEMBER THIS

Certain adjective/noun constructions begin with *it* or *there*.
***It**'s **nice being** here. Is **there** any **use trying** to explain?*

1 It's <u>no good talking</u> (no/good/talk) to her – she never listens.
2 Is it <u>worth buying</u> (worth/buy) that textbook? All the information is online.
3 It's <u>no use complaining</u> (no/use/complain) about your exam results. You didn't study!
4 There's <u>no point discussing</u> (no/point/discuss) this any more. I've made up my mind.

5 Complete the questions with the correct form of the words in the box. There are two extra words. Then answer the questions.

do fail forget pass speak write

1 Have you been <u>doing</u> much studying recently?
2 Have you ever listened to yourself <u>speaking</u> English?
3 Do you think speaking is more difficult than <u>writing</u> ?
4 Has the thought of <u>failing</u> your English exams ever entered your head?

26

01 WORD LIST

Education and school work

attend college/a class /ə'tɛnd 'kɑlɪdʒ/ə 'klæs/
do research (into sth) /ˌdu rɪ'sɚtʃ (ˌɪntə ˌsʌmθɪŋ)/
do well (in exams) /ˌdu ˌwɛl (ɪn ɪg'zæmz)/
drama school /'drɑmə skul/
drop a class/a subject /ˌdrɑp ə 'klæs/ə 'sʌbdʒɛkt/
education model /ˌɛdʒə'keɪʃən ˌmɑdl/
educator /'ɛdʒəkeɪṱɚ/
fail an exam/a subject /ˌfeɪl ən ɪg'zæm/ə 'sʌbdʒɛkt/
get good/top grades /ˌgɛt gʊd/tɑp 'greɪdz/
handwriting /'hændˌraɪṱɪŋ/
have/pursue a career /ˌhæv/pɚˌsu ə kə'rɪr/
(high) standard of education /(haɪ) ˌstændɚd əv ˌɛdʒə'keɪʃən/
learn in an active way /ˌlɚn ɪn ən ˌæktɪv 'weɪ/
learner /'lɚnɚ/
learning disability /'lɚnɪŋ dɪsə'bɪləṱi/
mentor (n, v) /'mɛntɔr/
pass an exam /ˌpæs ən ɪg'zæm/
peer-teaching /ˌpɪr 'titʃɪŋ/
period /'pɪriəd/
problem-solving /'prɑbləm ˌsɑlvɪŋ/
study for exams /stʌdi fɚ ɪg'zæmz/
study schedule /stʌdi 'skɛdʒəl/
school management /ˌskul 'mænɪdʒmənt/
skip an exam/a class/a subject /ˌskɪp ən ɪg'zæm/ə 'klæs/ə 'sʌbdʒɛkt/
spokesperson (for a class) /'spoʊksˌpɚsən (fɚ ə 'klæs)/
spread ideas /ˌsprɛd aɪ'diəz/
student representative /ˌstudnt ˌrɛprɪ'zɛntəṱɪv/
take a class/an exam/a subject /ˌteɪk ə 'klæs/ən ɪg'zæm/ə 'sʌbdʒɛkt/
take part in interactive activities /teɪk ˌpɑrt ɪn (ˌɪntərˌæktɪv) æk'tɪvəṱiz/
tap into a resource /ˌtæp ˌɪntə ə rɪ'sɔrs/
teach yourself sth /'titʃ yɚˌsɛlf ˌsʌmθɪŋ/
teamwork /'timwɚk/
train hard /ˌtreɪn 'hɑrd/
volunteer /ˌvɑlən'tɪr/

School discipline

cheat /tʃit/
complain about sth /kəm'pleɪn əˌbaʊt ˌsʌmθɪŋ/
disruptive behavior /dɪsˌrʌptɪv bɪ'heɪvyɚ/
disturb /dɪ'stɚb/
fidget /'fɪdʒət/
get in trouble /ˌgɛt ˌɪn 'trʌbəl/
keep still /ˌkip 'stɪl/
pay attention in class /ˌpeɪ ˌətɛnʃən ɪn 'klæs/
unsupervised /ˌʌn'supɚvaɪzd/

Abilities and learning styles

3D perception /ˌθriˌdi pɚ'sɛpʃən/
analytic /ˌænə'lɪṱɪk/
brainy/bright/sharp/intelligent /'breɪni/braɪt/ʃɑrp/ɪn'tɛlədʒənt/
competitive /kəm'pɛṱəṱɪv/
curiosity /ˌkyʊri'ɑsəṱi/
curious/interested /'kyʊriəs/'ɪntrɪstɪd/
deep thinker /ˌdip 'θɪŋkɚ/
determined/single-minded /dɪ'tɚmɪnd/ˌsɪŋgəl 'maɪndɪd/
diligent /'dɪlədʒənt/
do your best /ˌdu yɚ 'bɛst/
dominance (of the left hemisphere) /'dɑmənəns (əv ðə ˌlɛft 'hɛməsfɪr)/
eager to learn /ˌigɚ tə 'lɚn/
enthusiastic /ɪnˌθuzi'æstɪk/
excel at /ɪk'sɛl ət/
gift for /'gɪft fɚ/
hard-working /ˌhɑrd 'wɚkɪŋ/
incapable of doing sth /ɪnˌkeɪpəbəl əv 'duɪŋ ˌsʌmθɪŋ/
inquisitive /ɪn'kwɪzəṱɪv/
(innate) ability to do sth /(ɪˌneɪt) əˌbɪləṱi tə 'du ˌsʌmθɪŋ/
logical way of thinking /ˌlɑdʒɪkəl ˌweɪ əv 'θɪŋkɪŋ/
motivate /'moʊṱəˌveɪt/
natural inclination /ˌnætʃərəl ˌɪŋklə'neɪʃən/
self-motivated /ˌsɛlf 'moʊṱəˌveɪṱɪd/
struggle with (Math) /ˌstrʌgəl wɪð ('mæθ)/
studious /'studiəs/

EXTRA ACTIVITIES
- Photocopiable resource 5 (*-ing* forms – 15 mins) MultiROM and ActiveTeach

WORKBOOK
p. 17

NEXT CLASS
- Ask students to study the Word list on pp. 26–27.
- Ask students to review for Focus review 1.

Personality

communicator /kə'myunəkeɪṭɚ/
cooperative /koʊ'ɑprəṭɪv/
fair-minded /ˌfɛr 'maɪndɪd/
fun to be with /ˌfʌn tə 'bi wɪð/
fun-loving /'fʌn ˌlʌvɪŋ/
gregarious/sociable /grɪ'gɛriəs/'soʊʃəbəl/
level-headed /ˌlɛvəl 'hɛdɪd/
persistent /pɚ'sɪstənt/
popular /'pɑpyəlɚ/
self-confident /ˌsɛlf 'kɑnfədənt/
sensible/rational /'sɛnsəbəl/'ræʃənəl/
sporty /'spɔrṭi/
tactful /'tæktfəl/
team-player /ˌtim 'pleɪɚ/
well-organized /ˌwɛl 'ɔrgənaɪzd/

Feelings and emotions

be relieved /ˌbi rɪ'livd/
confused /kən'fyuzd/
frustrated /frʌ'streɪṭɪd/
lose one's temper /ˌluz wʌnz 'tɛmpɚ/
scared /skɛrd/
terrified /'tɛrəfaɪd/
thrilled /θrɪld/
trust /trʌst/
upset (at the thought of doing sth) /ˌʌp'sɛt (ət ðə ˌθɔt əv 'duɪŋ ˌsʌmθɪŋ)/

Social life

be supportive /ˌbi sə'pɔrṭɪv/
charity/social/environmental event /'tʃærəṭi/'soʊʃəl/ɪnˌvaɪɚn'mɛntl ɪ'vɛnt/
chat /tʃæt/
circle of friends /ˌsɚkəl əv 'frɛndz/
form relationships /ˌfɔrm rɪ'leɪʃənˌʃɪps/
interaction with other people /ˌɪnṭə'rækʃən wɪð ˌʌðɚ 'pipəl/

Memory

(earliest) memory /(ˌɚliəst) 'mɛmri/
keep a good memory /ˌkip ə gʊd 'mɛmri/
lose your memory /ˌluz yɚ 'mɛmri/
memorable /'mɛmrəbəl/
memorize /'mɛməraɪz/
recall/remember something vividly/in detail /rɪˌkɔl/rɪˌmɛmbɚ ˌsʌmθɪŋ 'vɪvɪdli/ɪn 'diteɪl/
remember/forget doing sth /rɪˌmɛmbɚ/fɚˌgɛt 'duɪŋ ˌsʌmθɪŋ/
remember/forget to do sth /rɪˌmɛmbɚ/fɚˌgɛt tə 'du ˌsʌmθɪŋ/
slip one's mind /ˌslɪp wʌnz 'maɪnd/

Speculating and recommending

admire /əd'maɪɚ/
appear to be /ə'pɪr tə bi/
assume /ə'sum/
based on/judging by /'beɪsd ɑn/'dʒʌdʒɪŋ baɪ/
be regarded as /ˌbi rɪ'gɑrdɪd əz/
clear/obvious /klɪr/'ɑbviəs/
clearly /'klɪrli/
conclude /kən'klud/
conclusion /kən'kluʒən/
confirm /kən'fɚm/
considering /kən'sɪdərɪŋ/
contribute to a discussion /kən'trɪbyut tə ə dɪ'skʌʃən/
(dis)agree /(ˌdɪs)ə'gri/
hesitate /'hɛzəˌteɪt/
it looks/seems as if/like … /ɪt 'lʊks/'simz əz ɪf/laɪk/
nominate /'nɑməˌneɪt/
nominee /ˌnɑmə'ni/
notice /'noʊṭəs/
point of view /ˌpɔɪnt əv 'vyu/
prove /pruv/
realize /'riəlaɪz/
suggest /sə'dʒɛst/
the chances are that … /ðə 'tʃænsɪz ɑr ðæt/

Phrasal verbs

catch up on /ˌkætʃ 'ʌp ɑn/
do away with /ˌdu ə'weɪ wɪð/
do up /ˌdu 'ʌp/
fall behind with (your homework) /ˌfɔl bɪ'haɪnd wɪð (yɚ 'hoʊmwɚk)/
get started on (your homework) /ˌgɛt stɑrtəd ɑn (yɚ 'hoʊmwɚk)/
go on to (further studies) /ˌgoʊ 'ɑn tə (fɚðɚ 'stʌdiz)/
hang out (with) /ˌhæŋ 'aʊt (wɪð)/
look forward to (new challenges) /ˌlʊk 'fɔrwɚd tə (nu tʃæləndʒəz)/
put forward /ˌpʊt 'fɔrwɚd/
put off /ˌpʊt 'ɔf/
set off /ˌsɛt 'ɔf/
set up /ˌsɛt 'ʌp/
soak up (knowledge) /ˌsoʊk 'ʌp (nɑlɪdʒ)/
turn in (an assignment) /ˌtɚn 'ɪn (ən ə'saɪnmənt)/

Other

access to /'æksɛs tə/
accurately /'ækyərɪtli/
adjoining /ə'dʒɔɪnɪŋ/
asset /'æsɛt/
avoid doing sth /əˌvɔɪd 'duɪŋ ˌsʌmθɪŋ/
be involved in /bi ɪn'vɑlvd ɪn/
current /'kʌrənt/
do harm /ˌdu 'hɑrm/
drama /'drɑmə/
dramatic /drə'mæṭɪk/
dramatize /'dræməˌtaɪz/
enable sb to do sth /ɪ'neɪbəl ˌsʌmbɑdi tə ˌdu ˌsʌmθɪŋ/
expect sb to do sth /ɪk'spɛkt ˌsʌmbɑdi tə ˌdu ˌsʌmθɪŋ/
familiar /fə'mɪlyɚ/
familiarity /fəˌmɪl'yærəṭi/
familiarize /fə'mɪlyəˌraɪz/
force sb to do sth/make sb do sth /'fɔrs ˌsʌmbɑdi tə ˌdu ˌsʌmθɪŋ/'meɪk ˌsʌmbɑdi ˌdu ˌsʌmθɪŋ/
fulfil one's wish /fʊlˌfɪl wʌnz 'wɪʃ/
initiate /ɪ'nɪʃieɪt/
inspiration /ˌɪnspə'reɪʃən/
inspired /ɪn'spaɪɚd/
keep doing sth /ˌkip 'duɪŋ ˌsʌmθɪŋ/
left-handed /ˌlɛft 'hændɪd/
left-hander /ˌlɛft 'hændɚ/
let sb do sth /'lɛt ˌsʌmbɑdi ˌdu ˌsʌmθɪŋ/
manage to do sth /'mænɪdʒ tə ˌdu ˌsʌmθɪŋ/
minimally invasive /ˌmɪnɪməli ɪn'veɪsɪv/
outdated /ˌaʊt'deɪṭɪd/
personal /'pɚsənəl/
personalize /'pɚsənəlaɪz/
personally /'pɚsənəli/
piece of news /ˌpis əv 'nuz/
reach one's goal /ˌritʃ wʌnz 'goʊl/
recognition /ˌrɛkəg'nɪʃən/
recognizable /ˌrɛkəg'naɪzəbəl/
recognize /'rɛkəgˌnaɪz/
replace /rɪ'pleɪs/
represent /ˌrɛprɪ'zɛnt/
revolutionary work /ˌrɛvə'luʃəˌnɛri 'wɚk/
shake-up /'ʃeɪk ʌp/
surprisingly /sɚ'praɪzɪŋli/
swap /swɑp/
tackle sth /'tækəl sʌmθɪŋ/
tend to do sth /ˌtɛnd tə 'du ˌsʌmθɪŋ/
threat /θrɛt/
urge sb to do sth /'ɚdʒ ˌsʌmbɑdi tə ˌdu ˌsʌmθɪŋ/
vessel /'vɛsəl/
vision /'vɪʒən/
visual /'vɪʒuəl/
visualize /'vɪʒuəˌlaɪz/
waste time doing sth /ˌweɪst taɪm 'duɪŋ ˌsʌmθɪŋ/

FOCUS REVIEW 1

VOCABULARY AND GRAMMAR

1 Choose the correct options.

1 She's always had a positive (*outlook*) / *approach* / *goal* on life.
2 Would you say that girls have a natural *thirst* / *attention* / (*gift*) for languages because they're more talkative than boys?
3 Do you think that success at school is down to being (*diligent*) / *gregarious* / *persistent* and spending hours studying?
4 Will you *memorize* / (*recognize*) / *familiarize* your school friends when you meet them at a school reunion?
5 Only those who have some kind of *inquisitive* / *sharp* / (*innate*) ability to get on well with people should become teachers.

2 Match verbs from box A with prepositions from box B to make phrasal verbs. Then use them to complete the sentences.

A	set fall put hand soak

\+

B	up in up off behind

1 The principal may ___*hand in*___ his resignation if many students fail.
2 Don't ___*put off*___ doing your assignments until the last minute. You may miss the deadline.
3 Recently, several students wanted to ___*set up*___ a committee to organize a charity event.
4 I was sick for three weeks and I have ___*fallen behind*___ with school work.
5 It's often said that children will ___*soak up*___ information very quickly if they are left to discover things for themselves.

3 Complete the text with one word in each blank.

Last week I went to a school reunion and I was amazed how different the school looks now. To start with, the building where we [1] ___used___ to have PE classes has been demolished and a new sports center has been built instead. I clearly remember how we [2] ___would___ beg our PE teacher to allow us to play games every afternoon.
Then I bumped into Caroline, who I [3] ___was___ always having arguments with. I hardly recognized her. She didn't [4] ___use___ to wear such elegant clothes. But one thing hasn't changed about her. She [5] ___is___ always talking about others behind their back. It's so unpleasant!
The reunion also reminded me of the importance of discipline and punctuality that our principal talked about so often. I got used to certain things so much that even now I [6] ___will___ arrive at meetings at least fifteen minutes earlier than necessary!

4 Complete the sentences with the correct form of the verbs in parentheses.

1 If you can't find a prospectus, try ___*looking*___ (look) online for the information you need.
2 The Music Academy exam board first listened to us all ___*sing*___ (sing) and then they announced who was admitted.
3 I'm sorry, sir. I forgot ___*to check*___ (check) if my essay is within the word limit you required.
4 Do you think our Chemistry teacher will let ___*us use*___ (we/use) the lab to carry out our own experiments?
5 We were warned ___*not to touch*___ (not touch) any of the exhibits.
6 My sister spent the whole night ___*checking*___ (check) her students' homework and then she left it on her desk at home.

LANGUAGE IN USE

5 Complete the text with the correct form of the words in parentheses.

Book review

MAKING SCIENCE POPULAR

By Nicholas Booker

Science is one of the most difficult subjects and even the most [1] ___*studious*___ (study) students sometimes struggle to solve scientific problems. If you want a book that makes science more [2] ___*accessible*___ (access), I can recommend Bill Bryson's *A Short History of Nearly Everything*. Full of amusing anecdotes and stories about quantum mechanics, evolution, astronomy, and chemistry, it's a book that will satisfy your thirst for [3] ___*knowledge*___ (know) and help you to [4] ___*visualize*___ (vision) certain scientific processes. The author brings science to life by, for example, giving a graphic and entertaining description of the universe. This is both a well-written book and a highly enjoyable one. Not [5] ___*surprisingly*___ (surprise), it is considered a must-read by many.

23

6 Complete the second sentence so that it has a similar meaning to the first, using the word in capitals. Do not change the word in capitals.

1 I was in the habit of skipping early morning classes. **USED**
I ___*used to skip*___ early morning classes.
2 Does it make sense to apply to college or should I take a year off? **WORTH**
___*Is it worth applying*___ to college, or should I take a year off?
3 Our English teacher took us to watch foreign movies once a month. **WOULD**
Our English teacher ___*would take us*___ to watch foreign movies once a month.
4 Mark won't help me with my homework so why should I ask him? **USE**
___*It's no use asking*___ Mark to help me with my homework. He won't help me anyway.
5 My best friend has a very irritating habit of chewing gum loudly. **ALWAYS**
My best friend ___*is always chewing gum*___ loudly.
6 I'm not sure if I've told my parents about the school trip. **REMEMBER**
I ___*don't remember telling*___ my parents about the school trip.

28

REFERENCES

AUDIO SCRIPT >>> *pp. 202–203*

EXTRA ACTIVITIES

- Photocopiable resource 58 (word building – 20 mins) MultiROM and ActiveTeach
- Photocopiable resource 60A (transformations – 20 mins) MultiROM and ActiveTeach
- Photocopiable resource 6 (Speaking – 15 mins) MultiROM and ActiveTeach
- Photocopiable resource 7 (Writing – 15 mins) MultiROM and ActiveTeach

READING

7 Read the text and choose from the sentences (A–E) the one that fits each blank. There is one extra sentence.

AT THE BEIJING DANCE ACADEMY 舞蹈學院

from *Mao's Last Dancer*, by Li Cunxin

Those first few weeks at the Beijing Dance Academy were an agony of loneliness. Nights were the worst. I couldn't wait to get to bed so I could clutch onto my niang's* quilt, my only security.

I knew I had no choice but to stay in Beijing. My parents, my brothers, relatives, friends, my old school teachers and classmates, my village and commune, all of their wishes and expectations made it impossible for me to go back. [1] _C_ My success was my parents' only hope of breaking that vicious cycle of poverty. I couldn't let them down, even if I did feel trapped in a cage of rules and routines. Every day I couldn't wait for the year to end so I could return home to see my family and roam the streets and fields once more.

I wasn't alone in missing home. I witnessed many teary eyes among my fellow classmates. The girls sobbed more than the boys. [2] _D_ The boys would be told that crying was a sign of weakness. […]

Our first weeks weren't made any easier when a virus swept through the school. I was among those who had the severe cough, sore throat, and high fever. [3] _A_ I offered to share it with some of my classmates but it was as though I'd offered them poison. I lost a few friends over that, but I did notice that their symptoms lasted much longer than mine. […]

One of the treats at the academy once a month was watching documentaries and occasionally a movie. All the foreign films were from other communist countries. A North Korean movie I remember particularly well was about a young man who had lost his ambitions for the communist cause, and a beautiful girl, a Communist Youth Party member, who helped him and fell in love with him. What I enjoyed most about this movie wasn't the politics but the love story. [4] _E_ I imagined that if I performed badly enough in class, the political head might send this girl to help me, but the longed-for love never materialized.

*niang: grandmother

A Naturally, I did what my niang would have done – I took out a few pieces of my precious dried snakeskin and wrapped a green onion in them.

B We knew what we had to do – and there was a great determination among all the boys and girls to succeed.

C The loss of face would be unbearable. It would damage my family's reputation forever.

D Our political heads and teachers showed more tenderness towards the girls.

E For the next couple of weeks I started to behave differently towards the captain of the girls' class, a pretty Qingdao girl with big, bright eyes.

LISTENING

8 CD•1.25 MP3•25 **Listen to four people talking about classes they attend. Match questions A–F with speakers 1–4. There are two extra questions.**

Speaker 1 _C_
Speaker 2 _B_
Speaker 3 _A_
Speaker 4 _F_

Which speaker:

A wants to develop a professional goal?
B is struggling with the amount of work on the course?
C is motivated by feedback from the instructor?
D is concerned about other students' motivation?
E is thinking of quitting the course?
F is surprised by the attitude of the tutor?

SPEAKING

9 With a partner, complete the speaking task.

Student A, your photos show people of different ages learning new things. Compare the photos and say how difficult it can be to learn new things at these ages.

Student B, do you prefer to learn by studying or by doing?

10 Now go to WORD STORE page 23 and complete another speaking task.

WRITING

11 Complete the writing task.

You are the student representative for your class. You recently attended a meeting about plans for a new cafeteria for the school. Write a report of the meeting for the website. Your report should:

- include some information you learned about the plans.
- ask for suggestions from the students for the new cafeteria.

Write your report in 140–190 words.

WORKBOOK

Use of English 1.9, pp. 18–19;
Self-assessment 1.10, p. 20

NEXT CLASS

- Ask students to do Self-check 1.11, WB p. 21 as homework.
- Ask students to prepare for Unit test 1 (*Focus* Assessment Package).

2 IT TAKES ALL KINDS

Everybody knows how to raise children, except the people who have them.

P.J. O'ROURKE (B. 1947), AN AMERICAN SATIRIST

UNIT LANGUAGE AND SKILLS

Vocabulary:
- *Show what you know* – compound nouns – family
- family, celebrations, and religious ceremonies
- verb-noun collocations
- common phrases
- dependent prepositions
- word families
- *Word in focus* – *take*

Grammar:
- Past Perfect Simple and Continuous
- relative clauses

Listening:
- a talk by a neuroscientist
- sentence completion

Reading:
- a literary extract and a news report about mysterious events
- multiple choice

Speaking:
- telling a personal anecdote

Writing:
- an article

FOCUS EXTRA

- Grammar Focus pages 163–164
- WORD STORE booklet pages 4–5
- Workbook pages 22–35 or MyEnglishLab
- MP3s – www.english.com/focus

30

2.1 Vocabulary

Family • Celebrations • Religious ceremonies • Verb-noun collocations • Common phrases

I can talk about families and describe ceremonies.

SHOW WHAT YOU KNOW

1 Cross out the family word that cannot be used with the underlined part-word.

1 ex- wife / boyfriend / ~~nephew~~
2 great- ~~child~~ / uncle / grandson
3 half brother / ~~niece~~ / sister
4 single mother / ~~daughter~~ / parent
5 step father / children / ~~husband~~
6 god mother / ~~cousin~~ / son

2 With a partner, form other words with the underlined part-words in Exercise 1. Choose words to describe different people in your family.

My great-grandmother lives in Chihuahua. She is ninety, and ...

3 Look at the photos and read the title and introduction of the article. What does *coming of age* mean?

a getting married (b) becoming an adult c having a party

Coming-of-age ceremonies

Most countries have customs that celebrate young people's journey into adulthood. This is how they do it in two very different cultures.

Aki from Japan

Seijin-no-hi

In Japan, we have a festival called Seijin-no-hi and it takes place on every second Monday of January. Anyone who has their twentieth birthday in that year celebrates on that day.

For the young men and women taking part, it's **a once in a lifetime experience**. **The highlight** of everyone's day is seeing the young women in their kimonos. Women wear a special kimono made of brightly colored silk, with long sleeves. Men get dressed up in formal suits.

The day is divided into several stages. First, everyone goes to the town hall to listen to speeches made by government officials. After that, people usually go to a **shrine** with members of their family. On my coming-of-age day, there were three generations of my family there, including **distant relatives** and great-grandparents who were in their nineties. I was showered with gifts and by the end of the day, my wallet was full of money – I'm an **only child**, so I was **really spoiled**.

After the formalities are over, the rest of the day is for fun. I had a meal with my **extended family**, and then I met up with my friends for a big party. I had **the time of my life**.

EXTRA ACTIVITIES
- Photocopiable resource 8 (collocations related to parties – 10 mins) MultiROM and ActiveTeach
- Photocopiable resource 9 (Test yourself partner work activities) MultiROM and ActiveTeach
- MyEnglishLab – assignable *Show what you have learned* mini-test

WORKBOOK
pp. 22–23

NEXT CLASS
- Ask students to prepare for a 10–15 minute vocabulary quiz: *Focus* Assessment Package, Unit 2.1, Vocabulary.

4 Read the article and make notes about the ceremonies.

Country	Age	Guests	Formal part	Informal part
Japan	20	extended family and friends	town hall, speeches, shrine	meal with family then party with friends
Mexico	15	family and friends	church, special mass and blessing	reception, dinner, danced all night

5 **SPEAKING** With a partner, discuss the questions about your country.

1 At what age are you legally allowed to:
- vote?
- drive a car?
- leave school?
- buy alcohol and tobacco?
- join the army?
- have children?

2 What customs are associated with coming of age?
3 When do you think people really come of age?

I'm Mexican and one of our customs is a celebration for young girls on their fifteenth birthday called Quinceañera. In the past, the Quinceañera ceremony signified that girls were ready for marriage. That's definitely not the case today!

My mom had a **small gathering** for her Quinceañera, just the **immediate family** and some close friends. Nowadays there's a lot of pressure to put on a big party with DJs and fireworks. So we did, and it was worth the effort. It was unforgettable.

My family's very modern, but we didn't want to lose sight of the spiritual side of the celebration. So first we went to church for a special **mass** and a **blessing**. The **priest** and my godparents talked to me about my new responsibilities, and I read a letter thanking my parents for everything. It was very moving – I had a lump in my throat and I could see my parents had tears in their eyes.

After the mass, we went on to the **reception**. Towards the end of the meal my father proposed a toast and he got very emotional when he talked about his hopes for my future. After blowing out the candles on my birthday cake, I danced all night. Everyone made a fuss over me and I enjoyed being the center of attention all day.

Go to **WORD STORE 2** page 5.

WORD STORE 2A

6 CD•1.26 MP3•26 Complete WORD STORE 2A with the words in red in the article. Then listen, check, and repeat. Add a translation.

7 Complete the sentences with names of people you know. Then, with a partner, take it in turns to tell each other something interesting about each person.

1 ______ is an only child.
2 In my extended family, ______ is the oldest relative I have and ______ is the youngest.
3 ______ is one of my distant relatives.
4 ______ is the first person I'd invite to a small gathering for my birthday.
5 I sat next to ______ at the last reception I went to.
6 The people in my immediate family are ______ .

WORD STORE 2B

8 CD•1.27 MP3•27 Complete WORD STORE 2B with a noun from the underlined collocations in the article. Then listen, check, and repeat. Add a translation.

9 With a partner, match the sentence halves. Then check the statements that are true for your country.

1 Parents sometimes have a lump in their [d]
2 The bride's father always proposes [e]
3 People have lost [a]
4 Most families don't put on [f]
5 Couples are often showered [b]
6 It's important to make [c]

a sight of what's important in life.
b with gifts on their engagement.
c a fuss over people on their eighteenth birthday.
d throat when their children leave home.
e a toast at his daughter's wedding.
f a big coming-of-age party.

WORD STORE 2C

10 CD•1.28 MP3•28 Complete WORD STORE 2C with more verb-noun collocations. Then listen, check, and repeat. Write example sentences.

WORD STORE 2D

11 CD•1.29 MP3•29 Complete WORD STORE 2D with the highlighted phrases in the article. Then listen, check, and repeat.

12 **SPEAKING** With a partner, complete the questions with one word in each blank. Then ask and answer the questions.

1 What has been the _highlight_ of your day so far today?
2 Have you ever been the center of _attention_?
3 Were you really _spoiled_ on your last birthday?
4 Do you think big parties are _worth_ the effort?
5 Which once in a _lifetime_ experience would you most like to have?
6 When was the last time you had the _time_ of your life?

2.2 Grammar

Past Perfect Simple and Continuous

I can talk about a past action or situation that took place before another past action or situation.

1 Read the story. Why did Amelia and Steve wait seventeen years to get married? *Because a love letter Steve had sent to Amelia had been lost.*

IT WAS MEANT TO BE

Amelia was studying English in the UK when she met Steve. It was love at first sight and they spent a wonderful summer together. Amelia returned to Brazil **after** her course finished. *4* They tried to keep a long-distance relationship going, but they drifted apart.

A few years later, Steve wrote to Amelia but Amelia's mother put the letter on the mantelpiece and forgot to tell Amelia, and it slipped down the back of the fireplace. Many years later, a builder was removing the fireplace when he found the letter. It **had been** there for ten years. *3*

During that time, Amelia had remained single and had never forgotten the love of her life. Meanwhile, Steve **had been working** in a factory *2* in his home town. He had been thinking about Amelia too, but he assumed that she **had gotten married** to somebody else. *1*

When she finally read the letter, Amelia was too nervous to call because so much time had passed. But she finally plucked up courage and they arranged to meet.

They got married seventeen years after they first met.

2 Read the GRAMMAR FOCUS. Match the underlined examples in the story with rules 1–4. *See text in Exercise 1.*

GRAMMAR FOCUS

Past Perfect Simple and Continuous

You use the **Past Perfect** to make it clear that an activity took place before the main events in a story.

1 You use the **Past Perfect Simple** to describe a completed action.

2 You use the **Past Perfect Continuous** to describe an activity in progress.

3 You use the **Past Perfect Simple** (NOT ~~Continuous~~) with state verbs (*be, have, know*, etc.).

4 You don't have to use the **Past Perfect** if a time expression (i.e. *before or after*) makes the order of events clear.

3 Find other examples of the Past Perfect in the story. Then discuss why the Simple or Continuous forms have been used.

4 Choose the correct options.

1 Amelia didn't know that Steve *wrote* / *had written* to her.
2 Steve didn't know that Amelia *had never received* / *had never been receiving* his letter.
3 Steve thought Amelia *had gotten* / *got* married to somebody else.
4 Amelia found the letter and realized it *was lying* / *had been lying* behind the fireplace for ten years.
5 Amelia was nervous about calling Steve because they *hadn't seen* / *didn't see* each other for a long time.

32

EXTRA ACTIVITIES
- Photocopiable resource 9 (Test yourself partner work activities) MultiROM and ActiveTeach
- MyEnglishLab – assignable *Show what you have learned* mini-test

WORKBOOK
p. 24

NEXT CLASS
- Ask students to prepare for a 10–15 minute grammar quiz: *Focus* Assessment Package, Unit 2.2, Grammar.

5 **Complete the sentences with the Past Perfect Simple or Continuous form of the verbs in parentheses.**

1 The roads were wet this morning. It *had been raining* (rain) all night.
2 Yesterday I was tired. I ________ (not sleep) well the night before.
3 I went to the doctor last week because I ________ (not feel) well.
4 I ________ (have) the same phone for years, so I got a new one last month.
5 I didn't understand yesterday's homework because I ________ (not listen) to the teacher in class.
6 By the time I arrived , the class ________ (already/start).

Exercise 5
2 hadn't slept
3 hadn't been feeling
4 had had
5 hadn't been listening
6 had already started

6 **Check the sentences in Exercise 5 that are true for you. Then write three more sentences using the Past Perfect Simple or Continuous.**

7 **Complete the story with the Past Perfect Simple or Continuous form of the verbs in the box. Why did Eric and Vilma wait forty years to get married?**

grow hear know live make meet move search see work

ERIC AND VILMA

FORTY YEARS LATER

Vilma was my wife's best friend. They [1] *had known* each other since childhood. When Vilma moved away, we lost touch but she [2] *had made* a big impression on me. So when my wife and I separated, I decided to ask my friends if anyone [3] *had heard* from her, but no one had. Vilma was a very compassionate person, so I imagined that she [4] *had moved* to Tibet and [5] *had been working* for a charity for a few years.

Finally, my niece called to say she [6] *had seen* Vilma's profile on Facebook. I called her and found out that she [7] *had been living* in Panama, so I [8] *had been searching* in the wrong place! We met up and when we saw one another, it was magical. We [9] *had grown* older, but that didn't matter. She was widowed and didn't have children.

I proposed immediately. Forty years after we [10] *had met* for the first time, we got married.

8 **Use the prompts to write questions about the story. Then answer the questions.**

1 how long / Eric's ex-wife / know / Vilma?
How long had Eric's ex-wife known Vilma?
2 any of Eric's friends / hear / from Vilma / after she / move away?
3 why / Eric / think / Vilma / move / to Tibet?
4 where / Vilma / live / since Eric / lose / touch with her?
5 Vilma / have / any children / with her late husband?

Exercise 8
2 Had any of Eric's friends heard from Vilma after she moved/had moved away?
3 Why did Eric think Vilma had moved to Tibet?
4 Where had Vilma been living since Eric had lost touch with her?
5 Had Vilma had any children with her late husband?

Grammar Focus page 163

2.3 Listening

Sentence completion

I can understand specific details in a talk.

1 **'What is love?' is the most popular search on Google. With a partner, try to match people 1–4 with their definition of love A–D. Which definition do you like best?**

1 a novelist D
2 a nun C
3 a parent B
4 a neuroscientist A

A Love is a chemical reaction.

B Love is unconditional.

C Love is kindness, generosity, and self-sacrifice.

D Love drives all great stories.

2 CD•1.30 MP3•30 **Listen to a talk by a neuroscientist and answer the questions.**

1 What have scientists become interested in recently? *the nature of love*
2 Why do they think humans first developed the instinct to fall in love? *so that the species could survive*
3 What might happen in the future? *Scientists might develop a cure for love.*

EXAM FOCUS **Sentence completion**

3 CD•1.30 MP3•30 **Listen again and complete the sentences with a word or short phrase.**

1 Ruby Niverton first wanted to be a *biologist* .
2 She refers to some new research that has been carried out in *China* .
3 Ruby compares the reasons we want love to the reasons we want a *drug* .
4 According to Ruby, the need for us to love someone becomes an *addiction* .
5 When they put people in *brain scanners* , Chinese scientists got interesting results.
6 The area of the brain responsible for this function first developed about *65 million* years ago.
7 Ruby mentions *chocolate* as an example of something else that produces similar brain activity.
8 There's a possibility that people could take a *pill* to recover from a failed love affair.

4 **Complete the relationship phrases from the talk with prepositions.**

1 be attracted *to* sb
2 go out *with* sb
3 fall *for* sb
4 be madly *in* love *with* sb
5 be obsessed *with* sth
6 split *up* with sb

REFERENCES
AUDIO SCRIPT ››› *p. 203*

WORKBOOK
p. 25

5 **With a partner, match the phrases in Exercise 4 with these phrases with similar meanings. Can you put the stages in a logical order?**

a like sb = be attracted to sb
b adore sb = be madly in love with sb
c end a relationship = split up with sb
d fall in love with sb = fall for sb
e start seeing sb = go out with sb
f worship sb = be obsessed with sb

6 **With a partner, write a short love story. Use at least four phrases from Exercise 5.**

When Harry met Sally ...

7 **Read other students' love stories and vote for the best one.**

PRONUNCIATION FOCUS

8 CD•1.31 MP3•31 **Listen and repeat the words in the box. Make pairs of words with the same consonant sound.**

[church confusion courage feature Japan measure official pressure]

church – feature

Exercise 8
official – pressure
confusion – measure
courage – Japan

9 CD•1.32 MP3•32 **Add the words from Exercise 8 to the table. Then listen, check, and repeat.**

Sound	Typical spelling	Example
/ʃ/	*sh-* *ti- + vowel* *ci- + vowel* *ss-*	shrine, worship attention, emotional 1 official passionate, 2 pressure
/ʒ/	*s- + -ion* *s- + -ure*	3 confusion, decision 4 measure, pleasure
/tʃ/	*-ch* *t- + -ure*	5 church, match 6 feature, picture
/dʒ/	*j-* *g-*	7 Japan, journey 8 courage, marriage

WORD STORE 2E

10 CD•1.33 MP3•33 **Complete WORD STORE 2E. Replace the underlined words/phrases with words/phrases with similar meanings from the box.**

35

2.4 Reading

Multiple choice

I can find specific detail in a text.

1 Look at the list. Put ✓ for things you often read, ? for things you sometimes read, and ✗ for things you never read.

advertisements ☐ cartoons ☐ comics ☐ information on websites ☐
magazine articles ☐ news reports ☐ novels ☐ non-fiction books ☐
short stories ☐

2 SPEAKING With a partner, compare your answers to Exercise 1 and discuss the questions.

1 How much reading for pleasure do you do in your own language?
2 How much do you do in English?

3 Read text A and check the features that you think it contains. Then compare with a partner. (Answers to points marked with ? are subjective and can differ.)

1 likeable characters	✓	5 a situation you can relate to	?
2 mystery	✓	6 a great opening line	✓
3 humor	✓	7 romance	?
4 believable dialogue	✓	8 descriptive language	✓

4 With a partner, discuss which features from Exercise 3 are important in the first chapter of a novel. What makes you want to read further?

A CD•1.34 MP3•34

– ONE –

299 hours, 54 minutes

One minute the teacher was talking about the Civil War. And the next minute he was gone.

There.

Gone.

No 'poof'. No flash of light. No explosion.

Sam Temple was sitting in third-period History class staring blankly at the blackboard, but far away in his head. In his head he was down at the beach, he and Quinn. Down at the beach with their boards, **yelling**, bracing for that first **plunge** into the cold Pacific water.

For a moment he thought he had imagined it, the teacher disappearing. For a moment, he thought he'd slipped into a daydream.

Sam turned to Mary Terafino, who sat just to his left. 'You saw that, right?'

Mary was **staring** hard at the place where the teacher had been.

'Um, where's Mr. Trentlake?' It was Quinn Gaither, Sam's best, maybe only, friend. Quinn sat right behind Sam. The two of them favored window seats because sometimes, if you caught just the right angle, you could actually see a tiny sliver of sparkling water between the school buildings and the homes beyond.

'He must have left,' Mary said, not sounding like she believed it.

Edilio, a new kid Sam found potentially interesting, said, 'No, man. Poof.' He did a thing with his fingers that was a pretty good illustration of the concept.

Kids were staring at one another, craning their necks this way and that, **giggling** nervously. No one was scared. No one was crying. The whole thing seemed kind of funny.

'Mr. Trentlake poofed?' said Quinn, with a suppressed giggle in his voice.

'Hey,' someone said, 'where's Josh?'

Heads turn to look.

'Was he here today?'

'Yes, he was here. He was right here next to me.' Sam recognized the voice. Bette. Bouncing Bette.

'He just, you know, disappeared,' Bette said, 'Just like Mr. Trentlake.

The door to the hallway opened. Every eye locked on it. Mr. Trentlake was going to step in, maybe with Josh, and explain how he had pulled off this magic trick, and then get back to talking in his excited, strained voice about the Civil War nobody cared about.

But it wasn't Mr. Trentlake. It was Astrid Ellison, known as Astrid the Genius, because she was … well, she was a genius. Astrid was in all the AP* classes the school had. In some subjects she was taking online courses from the university.

Astrid had shoulder-length blond hair, and liked to wear starched white short-sleeved blouses that never failed to catch Sam's eye. Astrid was out of his league, Sam knew that. But there was no law against thinking about her.

'Where's your teacher?' Astrid asked.

There was a collective **shrug**. 'He poofed,' Quinn said, like maybe it was funny.

'Isn't he out in the hallway?' Mary asked.

Astrid shook her head. 'Something weird is happening. My math study group … there were just three of us, plus the teacher. They all just disappeared.'

'What?' Sam said.

Astrid looked right at him. He couldn't look away like he normally would because her **gaze** wasn't challenging, sceptical like it usually was: it was scared. Her normally sharp, discerning blue eyes were wide, with way too much white showing. 'They're gone. They all just … disappeared.'

'What about your teacher?' Edilio said.

'She's gone too,' Astrid said.

'Gone?'

'Poof,' Quinn said, not giggling so much now, starting to think maybe it wasn't a joke after all.

36

REFERENCES
CULTURE NOTES ››› *p. 194*

EXTRA ACTIVITIES
- Photocopiable resource 10 (collocations related to body language – 10 mins) MultiROM and ActiveTeach

WORKBOOK
pp. 26–27

NEXT CLASS
- Investigate online and write a short description of a mysterious event.

EXAM FOCUS Multiple choice

5 Read text A again. For questions 1–5, choose the correct answer, A, B, C, or D.

1 When Mr. Trentlake disappeared,
- (A) Sam wasn't paying attention to the lesson.
- B Quinn was daydreaming about the beach.
- C Mary was sure she saw him leaving the room.
- D he was writing on the blackboard.

2 In line 28 *the concept* refers to
- A the fact that Edilio disagrees with Mary.
- (B) the way the teacher has disappeared.
- C the humor in the situation.
- D the students' lack of understanding.

3 How does Sam feel about Astrid?
- A He envies her.
- B He is embarrassed by her.
- (C) He admires her.
- D He thinks she's bossy.

4 So far, the following people have disappeared:
- A two teachers and a student
- (B) two teachers and three students
- C one teacher and one student
- D two teachers

5 In lines 41–45, the author implies that
- A Astrid knows why people are disappearing.
- B Sam is scared by the situation.
- C the situation has become really serious.
- (D) somebody played a joke.

6 Read text B and answer the questions.

1 In what ways are the themes of texts A and B similar?
2 What are the main differences between the texts?
3 Which text do you find more engaging? Why?

7 Read texts A and B again. Are the statements true (T) or false (F)?

Text A

1 Sam was on the beach, shouting and getting ready to dive into the sea. [F]
2 Mary was looking very intently at the spot where Mr. Trentlake had been standing. [T]
3 The kids were trying to see what had happened and laughing nervously. [T]
4 The gesture of raising their shoulders showed that the class knew where Mr. Trentlake was. [F]
5 On this occasion, Astrid's fixed look showed that she was afraid. [T]

Text B

6 Only small boats such as yachts disappear in the Bermuda Triangle. [F]
7 No remains of *USS Cyclops* were ever found and there was no sign of what had happened. [T]
8 Nobody believes that people are kidnapped by aliens in the Bermuda Triangle. [F]

8 Find words in blue in the texts that have similar meanings to the underlined words in Exercise 7.

1 shouting = yelling, dive = plunge

9 SPEAKING With a partner, discuss possible explanations for the mysteries in texts A and B. Compare your ideas with other students in the class.

WORD STORE 2F

10 CD•1.36 MP3•36 Complete WORD STORE 2F with nouns and the base form of verbs from the texts. Mark the stress. Then listen, check, and repeat.

Exercise 8
2 staring
3 giggling
4 shrug
5 gaze
6 vessels
7 wreckage / trace
8 abducted

Exercise 6
1 Both texts have similar themes of mysterious disappearance.
2 Text A is fiction, Text B is a newspaper article. Text A has dialogue and characters. Text B gives factual information about events.

31

B CD•1.35 MP3•35

July 16, 1997

YACHT FOUND ADRIFT IN BERMUDA TRIANGLE

A Royal Navy ship has found an abandoned yacht in the Western Atlantic. Crew from the Navy ship found clothes and personal belongings, including an open book on a bunk. We have learned that the boat belonged to a German couple hoping to sail around the world.

This incident is another in a catalogue of unexplained events in the area of the Atlantic known as the Bermuda Triangle, where planes, people, and all types of **vessels** seem to go missing in mysterious circumstances. In 1918, the American Naval vessel *USS Cyclops* disappeared without a **trace**. No **wreckage** was found, nor any of the 300 crew. Then there is the case of Flight 19. In December 1945, five US Navy bombers took off from Florida. They made several routine calls to base, but shortly afterwards the planes and fourteen men disappeared and were never seen or heard from again.

There are many theories surrounding the mysteries of the Bermuda Triangle, ranging from strange weather conditions to paranormal events. But whether the ships and planes were destroyed by storms or **abducted** by aliens, it is a fact that numerous ships, planes, and people have disappeared without explanation.

37

2.5 Grammar

Relative clauses

I can identify and use different types of relative clause.

1 SPEAKING **With a partner, discuss the advantages and disadvantages of being the firstborn child in a family.**

2 **Read Part 1 of an article about birth order. Are any of the things you discussed in Exercise 1 mentioned?**

WHAT BIRTH ORDER SAYS ABOUT YOU

Birth order is the key [1]that can unlock your personality. Here are some generalizations that have come out of research [2]carried out over the years.

The firstborn

Parents [3]learning to raise their first child tend to be extremely attentive and protective. Firstborn children, [4]who have their parents' undivided attention, are responsible, reliable, and well-behaved. Firstborns tend to be perfectionists bursting with confidence, [5]which makes it hard for them to admit when they're wrong.

Exercise 3
1 defining relative clause
2 reduced relative clause (passive)
3 reduced relative clause (active)
4 non-defining relative clause
5 comment clause

3 **Read the GRAMMAR FOCUS. What type of clause are the examples in blue (1–5) in Part 1 of the text?**

GRAMMAR FOCUS

Relative clauses

- In **defining relative clauses** you can leave out *who*, or *that* when it is the object of the verb.
  *Olga is the girl **who sits next to me**.* (*Who* is the subject of *sit*.)
  *Olga is the **girl (who) I sit next to**.* (*Who* is the object of *sit*.)
- In **non-defining relative clauses**, which always come after a comma, you cannot leave out *who*, *which*, *where*, or *whose*.
  *Eva is friends with Sam, **who I can't stand**.* (= I can't stand Sam.)
- In **reduced relative clauses** you use a present participle for active verbs and a past participle for passive verbs.
  *There's a new teacher **teaching** fourth grade.* (= … who is teaching)
  *The students **taught** by him are delighted.* (= … who are taught)
- In **comment clauses**, which always come after a comma, you refer to the whole of the main clause using *which*.
  *Eva is friends with Sam, **which I can't stand**.* (= I can't stand the situation)

EXTRA ACTIVITIES
- Photocopiable resource 11 (relative clauses – 10 mins) MultiROM and ActiveTeach
- MyEnglishLab – assignable *Show what you have learned* mini-test

WORKBOOK
p. 28

NEXT CLASS
- Ask students to prepare for a 10–15 minute grammar quiz: *Focus* Assessment package, Unit 2.5, Grammar.

4 **Read Part 2 of the article and choose the correct options.**

The middle child

Middle children, [1]**who have been** / [Ø] given less attention by their parents, are more independent. Middle children [2]*which* / **whose** older siblings boss them around feel life is unfair. They often believe their other siblings get all the attention, [3]**which** / *that* can make them feel left out.

The baby of the family

Parents [4]**who are** / [Ø] raising their youngest children are more lenient, [5]**which** / [Ø] means that last-borns are rarely scolded. Youngest children, [6]*that* / **who** have fewer responsibilities, are carefree and easy-going. The baby of the family, [7]*whose* / **who** is used to having things done for them, tends to be bad at making decisions.

The only child

Only children have many of the same qualities as the oldest child, [8]*that* / **which** is not surprising. Only children, [9]*which* / **who** spend more time with adults, will often act older than their age. The typical only child likes being the center of attention, [10]**which** / *whose* sometimes makes them appear self-centered.

5 **What position are you in your family? Which comments in Parts 1 and 2 of the article do you agree with?**

6 **Rewrite the sentences using reduced relative clauses. Then check the statements you agree with.**

1 Siblings who share a bedroom tend to be less selfish.
Siblings sharing a bedroom tend to be less selfish.
2 Children who have been raised as the baby of the family are often fussy eaters.
3 Firstborns, who are accustomed to accepting rules, are better behaved at school.
4 Middle-born children, who grow up with a younger and older sibling, can be argumentative.
5 Only children who spend a lot of time alone tend to be very creative.
6 The youngest child, who is used to being the center of attention, usually has a good sense of humor.

Exercise 6
2 Children raised as the baby of the family are often fussy eaters.
3 First-borns, accustomed to accepting rules, are better behaved at school.
4 Middle-born children, growing up with a younger and older sibling, can be argumentative.
5 Only children spending a lot of time alone tend to be very creative.
6 The youngest child, used to being the center of attention, usually has a good sense of humor.

7 **Complete the sentences with *who, which, that, where, whose*, or – if you can leave out the relative pronoun. Then check the sentences that are true for you.**

1 My sister always leaves her clothes on the floor, *which* is very annoying!
2 In my family, the person *who* cooks the most delicious food is my grandmother.
3 I'm jealous of people *whose* parents let them do whatever they want.
4 The only place *where* I can get some peace at home is in the bathroom!
5 My mother, *who* thinks I'm still a baby, worries when I go out late.
6 I have several cousins *Ø* living in the same town as me.
7 We live in a house *Ø* built over 100 years ago.

Grammar Focus page 164

2.6 Speaking

Telling a personal anecdote

I can tell a personal anecdote about a memorable day trip.

1 Look at the website. Which day trips would you most like to go on? Why?

Are you tired of doing the same old things with your friends? Why not try something different with one of our alternative day trips?

- go mountain biking
- visit a gallery or photo exhibition
- sing karaoke
- rent a row boat or kayak
- attend a workshop (e.g. dancing or DJing)
- go go-kart racing
- visit an aquarium or zoo

2 SPEAKING With a partner, describe the photo in Exercise 1 and answer the questions.

1 What might the people be thinking/feeling?
2 In your opinion, what factors make a memorable day trip?

3 Put the parts of an anecdote about a memorable day trip in a logical order. (Suggested order)

a where and when the trip took place and other background information [2]
b who was involved [3]
c why the day was so memorable [5]
d what the anecdote is going to be about [1]
e what happened, step by step [4]

4 CD•1.37 MP3•37 Listen to someone describing a memorable day trip and check your ideas in Exercise 3. With a partner, try to retell the anecdote.

REFERENCES
AUDIO SCRIPT ››› pp. 203–204
WORKBOOK
p. 29

5 CD•1.37 MP3•37 **Complete the SPEAKING FOCUS with the words in the box. Then listen again and check.**

[all as as soon as blue doubt funnily initially place]

SPEAKING FOCUS

Introducing the anecdote

(OK) I'm going to tell you about (a great day trip).
(OK, so) this is a story about (a day I'll never forget.)
This took [1] _place_ about (a month ago).

Sequencing events in the anecdote

[2] _As soon as_ /When/Just after (we got there, the sun came out).
[3] _Initially_ /To begin with, (we were the only people there).
As/While (we were sitting there) …
Suddenly/[4] _All_ of a sudden, (the weather changed).

Describing events vividly

Predictably/[5] _As_ expected, (other people soon started) …
Unexpectedly/Out of the [6] _blue_ , (it started pouring with rain).
Luckily/Fortunately, (after it stopped raining, the sun came out again).

Finishing the anecdote

Without a [7] _doubt_ , it was (one of the best days I've had in ages).
When I look back (on that day) now, I feel …
It turned out to be (an unforgettable day trip).
Strangely/[8] _Funnily_ enough, (the best days are often the ones you don't really plan).

6 CD•1.38 MP3•38 **Read the anecdote and choose the correct options. Then listen and check.**

OK, so this [1]*took place* / *is a story* about a day I'll never forget. I've always loved music and last month my friend and I went to a DJing workshop. [2]*To begin with* / *Just after*, we learned about the equipment. We can't afford our own stuff yet but [3]*fortunately* / *out of the blue*, we were able to use the decks, mixers, and laptops at the center. [4]*When* / *While* we had understood the basics, it was time to have a go. [5]*Strangely* / *Predictably*, it was really difficult at first, but after a while I started to get the hang of it. It feels and sounds fantastic when you get it right. It turned out to be an [6]*unexpected* / *unforgettable* day. I can't wait for the next workshop.

7 SPEAKING **With a partner, follow the instructions. Take turns to be A and B.**

Student A: Tell a personal anecdote about a memorable day trip. Use the **SPEAKING** FOCUS to help you.

Student B: Listen to your partner's anecdote and think of a question to ask them when they have finished.

2.7 Writing

An article

I can write an article that attracts and holds the reader's attention.

1 Look at the photos. Which aspects of adolescence do they illustrate?

2 With a partner, read the *Last week's contest* section on the website and discuss the questions.

1 Why is adolescence described as 'a roller coaster ride'?
2 What are the best things about being a young adult?
3 What new challenges do you face as a young adult?

3 Read the winning article on the website and answer the questions.

1 Did the author mention any of the pleasures or challenges you discussed in Exercise 2?
2 What is the author's conclusion? Do you agree? Why?/Why not? *The pleasure of being a young adult outweighs the pain.*

Psychology Magazine

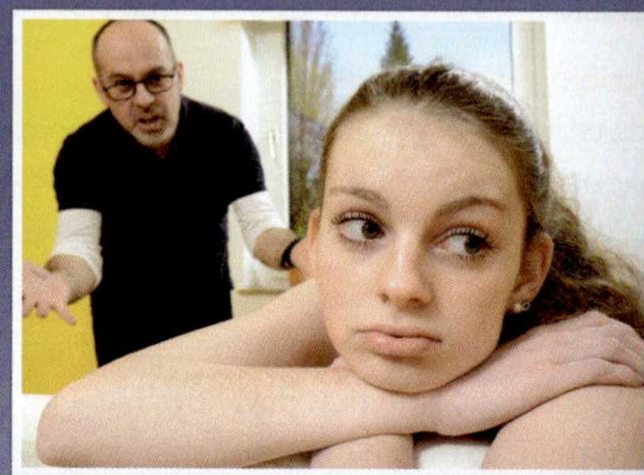

Have your say
Last week's contest

The journey from teenager to adult can bring joy and pain, success and failure, friendship and heartbreak. If you are riding the roller coaster of adolescence right now, then *Psychology Magazine* wants to hear from you.
Send us an article in which you describe some of the very best things about coming of age and discuss the most challenging aspects of life for people living through these 'in-between' years.
As usual, a selection of articles will be published in an upcoming edition of *Psychology Magazine*.

The winning article:

Adolescence: pain and pleasure in equal measure

by Josh Payne

Remember when you were little and school summer vacations seemed to go on forever? Being children, most of us lived carefree and happy lives. Sadly, this does not last and we must all grow up. I can reliably report that the process brings pain and pleasure in equal measure.

First, there is the pain. Adolescence is a time of huge physical and emotional change. For many of us this change is accompanied by feelings of self-doubt, envy, and embarrassment. Apparently, we are neither children nor adults; asked to act like 'grown-ups' in certain situations, but not in others. 'Be responsible and act your age … but be home by 9 p.m.!' These mixed messages can be hard to deal with. Add to this the pressure of schoolwork and it is no wonder we sometimes feel unable to deal with everything.

Thankfully, alongside the pain, there is also pleasure. Though we have to study, few of us need to worry about bills or housework. As a result, whether it is playing sport or online games, we have time to enjoy ourselves. On top of this, we have our friends. Pleasure and pain alike can be shared with those who know exactly how we feel.

Despite the challenges, as far as I am concerned, the pleasure of being a young adult outweighs the pain. Although it may not always seem so now, maybe in the future we will look back on adolescence as 'the best days of our lives'.

This week's contest

There are many unfair gender-based stereotypes concerning the interests and attitudes of adolescents. Write an article of 200–250 words in which you describe some of these common stereotypes and challenge them by explaining why they are untrue or unfair. As usual, a selection of articles will be printed in an upcoming edition of *Psychology Magazine*.

REFERENCES
CULTURE NOTES ››› p. 194

EXTRA ACTIVITIES
• MyEnglishLab – assignable *Show what you have learned* writing task and *Show that you have checked* checklist

WORKBOOK
p. 30

4 **Read the WRITING FOCUS and look at the article again. Check the techniques the author uses for writing a title, an introduction, and a conclusion.**

WRITING FOCUS

An article

Title

Attract the reader's attention from the start:

1 Ask a question. (*Are these the best days of our lives?*) ☐
2 Use vivid adjectives. (*Adolescence: thrilling and terrifying*) ☐
3 Summarize the topic. (*The pains and pleasures of adolescent life*) ☐
4 Use rhyme/wordplay. (*Ten top tips for troubled teens*) ☑

Introduction

Define the topic and hold the reader's attention:

5 Ask a question. ☑
6 Tell a short anecdote. ☐
7 Give an interesting or surprising fact or figure. ☐
8 Give a quotation. ☐

Main paragraphs

Develop the topic and discuss all the issues mentioned in the question.

Conclusion

Give your personal opinion and leave the reader with something to think about:

9 Ask a question. ☐
10 Refer to the future. ☑
11 Make an appeal or suggestion. ☐
12 Return to the idea in your title or introduction. ☑

Note: Articles are usually written in a formal or semi-formal style. In a formal article, avoid informal phrases (~~*I think*~~ … = *As far as I am concerned* …), colloquial language (~~*Most parents figure that*~~ … = *In most parents' opinions* …) and contractions (~~*don't*~~ = *do not*).

5 **Match the article introductions and conclusions with techniques 5–12 in the WRITING FOCUS.**

Introductions

a It's easy to forget that 100 percent of adults alive today were once teenagers like us. As a young man, my 'sensible' father was a real rebel. He rode a motorcycle and got a tattoo at the age of sixteen. [7] and [6]

b In his famous book, American author John Gray said, 'Men are from Mars, women are from Venus.' Does this also apply to adolescents? Are younger men and women really so different from each other? [8] and [5]

Conclusions

c As I began by saying, men and women differ in many ways, but individuals also differ regardless of their gender. We should be wary of stereotyping, respect each other, and cooperate to use our strengths for a common good. [12] and [11]

d So, as a regular teenage girl, am I really that different from the boy sitting opposite me in class? Maybe not. Whether we will become more or less alike in later life remains to be seen. [9] and [10]

6 **Read the LANGUAGE FOCUS and rewrite the underlined parts of the sentences using participle clauses.**

1 <u>Because they want to look stylish</u>, many adolescent boys also enjoy shopping for clothes.
2 <u>Because they attend mixed schools</u>, most adolescent boys and girls receive the same education.
3 <u>Because I grew up with three sisters</u>, I know something about the differences between boys and girls.
4 <u>Because they are stereotypes</u>, such statements do contain an element of truth, of course.
5 <u>Because I have always gotten along well with boys</u>, I think I understand some of their attitudes.

LANGUAGE FOCUS

Participle clauses to express reason

You can use **participle clauses** in formal writing to express the **reason** for a statement made in the main clause.

- Use a present participle (verb + *-ing*) when states or actions occur at the same time.
  Being children, *most of us lived carefree and happy lives.*
  = *Because we were children* (past), *most of us lived carefree and happy lives.* (past)
- Use a perfect participle (*having* + past participle) when one state or action occurs before another.
  Having grown physically, *many adolescents expect to be treated as adults.*
  = *Because they have grown physically* (past), *many adolescents expect to be treated as adults.* (present)

7 **SPEAKING Read the statements and decide if they are stereotypes about adolescent girls or boys. Do they reflect the reality? Discuss with a partner.**

- They find it difficult to talk about their feelings.
- They are always gossiping.
- They love fashion and shopping.
- They love sports and gadgets.
- They are kind and considerate.
- They are rude and aggressive.

8 **You are going to write an article for this week's contest in *Psychology Magazine*. Read the instructions on the website and think about these things.**

1 Where will your article appear and who will read it?
2 Choose two or three gender-based stereotypes you think are untrue or unfair (see Exercise 7 for ideas). Note down reasons to support your views.
3 Select techniques from the WRITING FOCUS to help you attract and hold the reader's attention.
4 Make sure you use a formal or semi-formal style.

9 **Write your article. Include at least one participle clause to express reason. Use the WRITING FOCUS and the LANGUAGE FOCUS to help you.**

Exercise 6
1 Wanting to look stylish
2 Attending mixed schools
3 Having grown up with three sisters
4 Being stereotypes
5 Having always gotten along well with boys

2.8 Language in focus

Collocations

I can recognize and use common collocations.

1 Read the information about collocation and match types of collocation 1–6 with examples a–f from this unit.

Collocation is a central feature of any language. It refers to typical, natural-sounding combinations of words. For example, you can have *strong feelings* but not ~~*tough feelings*~~. You might *break someone's heart* but not ~~*destroy someone's heart*~~. Choosing the right collocation will make your English sound more natural.

1 adjective + noun	c	a	the **center of attention**
2 verb + noun	e	b	It's **absolutely fantastic**.
3 noun + verb	f	c	her **late husband**
4 noun + noun	a	d	Mary **was staring hard**.
5 verb + adverb	d	e	My father **proposed a toast**.
6 adverb + adjective	b	f	The **door** to the hallway **opened**.

Exercise 2
STRONG
center of attention
propose a toast
door opened
WEAK
absolutely (really) fantastic
late (dead / deceased) husband
stare hard (intently / fixedly)

2 Translate the examples in Exercise 1. Discuss how 'strong' each collocation is in your language.

stronger = few or no alternatives e.g. *the center of attention*
weaker = some alternatives e.g. *stare hard/intently/fixedly*

3 Complete the sentences with the correct form of the words in capitals. Could any of the sentences describe people you know?

1 Donna is *painfully* shy in social situations. It's embarrassing for her. **PAIN**
2 Bill has an outgoing *personality* and a great sense of humor. **PERSON**
3 Jane would never swallow her *pride* and admit that she's wrong. **PROUD**
4 Tom is a *faithful* friend. He's always there for me. **FAITH**

4 Choose the correct answer, A, B, C, or D. Then check the sentences that are true for you.

1 Dad says it's important to ________ high standards for yourself.
A aim B put **(C) set** D fix
2 My sister has a ________ imagination and draws incredible pictures.
(A) vivid B detailed C sharp D strong
3 The last movie I saw was terrible. I was ________ disappointed.
A totally B absolutely **(C) bitterly** D completely
4 Most of my Facebook friends are best described as ________ acquaintances.
A occasional **(B) casual** C nearby D relaxed

5 Complete the questions with one word in each blank. Then answer the questions.

1 Is your best friend reliable? Can he/she *keep* a secret?
2 Is anybody in your extended family *expecting/having* a baby? When is it due?
3 Do you tend to *lose* your temper when you are angry?
4 Are you busy right now? Do you have a lot on your *mind* ?
5 Are you emotional? How likely are you to *burst* into tears?
6 Can you remember the last time you roared with *laughter* ?

02 WORD LIST

Family members

cousin /ˈkʌzən/
(distant) relative /(ˌdɪstənt) ˈrɛlət̬ɪv/
ex-wife/ex-boyfriend /ˌɛks ˈwaɪf/ˌɛks ˈbɔɪfrɛnd/
extended family /ɪkˌstɛndɪd ˈfæmli/
firstborn /ˈfɚstbɔrn/
generation /ˌdʒɛnəˈreɪʃən/
godmother/godparents /ˈgɑdˌmʌðɚ/ˈgɑdˌpɛrənts/
godson /ˈgɑdsʌn/
great-grandson/great-grandmother/great-grandparents /ˌgreɪt ˈgrænsʌn/ˌgreɪt ˈgrænˌmʌðɚ/ˌgreɪt ˈgrænˌpɛrənts/
great-uncle /ˌgreɪt ˈʌŋkəl/
half-brother/half-sister /ˈhæf ˌbrʌðɚ/ˈhæf ˌsɪstɚ/
immediate family /ɪˌmidiɪt ˈfæmli/
late husband /ˌleɪt ˈhʌzbənd/
only child /ˌoʊnli ˈtʃaɪld/
siblings /ˈsɪblɪŋz/
single mother/single parent /ˌsɪŋgəl ˈmʌðɚ/ˌsɪŋgəl ˈpɛrənt/
stepchild /ˈstɛpˌtʃaɪld/
stepfather /ˈstɛpˌfɑðɚ/
widowed /ˈwɪdoʊd/

Life stages, life events

adolescence /ˌædlˈɛsəns/
adolescent (n, adj) /ˌædlˈɛsənt/
adulthood /əˈdʌlthʊd/
become an adult /bɪˌkʌm ən əˈdʌlt/
childhood /ˈtʃaɪldhʊd/
come of age /ˌkʌm əv ˈeɪdʒ/
expect a baby /ɪkˌspɛkt ə ˈbeɪbi/
fall in love (with) /ˌfɔl ɪn ˈlʌv (wɪð)/
get married (to) /ˌgɛt ˈmærid (tə)/
grow old /ˌgroʊ ˈoʊld/
grown-up /ˈgroʊn ʌp/
join the army /ˌdʒɔɪn ðə ˈɑrmi/
leave home /ˌliv ˈhoʊm/
leave school /ˌliv ˈskul/
vote /voʊt/

Relationships

adore/worship /əˈdɔr/ˈwɚʃɪp/
be attracted to /bi əˈtrækt̬ɪd tə
be madly in love with /bi ˌmædli ɪn ˈlʌv wɪð/
be obsessed with /bi əbˈsɛst wɪð/
casual acquaintance /ˌkæʒuəl əˈkweɪntˀns/
couple /ˈkʌpəl/
end a relationship /ˌɛnd ə rɪˈleɪʃənʃɪp/
engagement /ɪnˈgeɪdʒmənt/
gender-based stereotypes /ˌdʒendɚ ˌbeɪst ˈstɛriəˌtaɪps/
get/have sb's undivided attention /ˌgɛt/ˌhæv ˌsʌmbɑdiz ˌʌndɪˈvaɪdɪd əˈtɛnʃən/
give sb attention /ˌgɪv ˌsʌmbɑdi əˈtɛnʃən/
heartbreak /ˈhɑrtbreɪk/
lenient /ˈliniənt/
long-distance relationship /ˌlɔŋ ˌdɪstəns rɪˈleɪʃənʃɪp/
lose touch /ˌluz ˈtʌtʃ/
love at first sight /ˌlʌv ət ˌfɚst ˈsaɪt/
love of sb's life /ˌlʌv əv ˌsʌmbɑdiz ˈlaɪf/
make a fool of sb /ˌmeɪk ə ˈful əv sʌmbɑdi/
make an impression on sb /ˌmeɪk ən ɪmˈprɛʃən ɑn sʌmbɑdi/
marriage /ˈmærɪdʒ/
propose /prəˈpoʊz/
respect each other /rɪˈspɛkt itʃ ˌʌðɚ/
romance /roʊˈmæns/
separate /ˈsɛpəreɪt/
shower sb with praise /ˌʃaʊɚ ˌsʌmbɑdi wɪð ˈpreɪz/
single /ˈsɪŋgəl/
start seeing sb /ˌstɑrt ˈsiɪŋ ˌsʌmbɑdi/
stereotyping /ˈstɛriəˌtaɪpɪŋ/
unconditional /ˌʌnkənˈdɪʃənəl/

Celebrations

be the center of attention /bi ðə ˌsɛntɚ əv əˈtɛnʃən/
birthday cake /ˈbɚθdeɪ keɪk/
blessing /ˈblɛsɪŋ/
celebrate /ˈsɛləbreɪt/
coming-of-age party/ceremony /ˌkʌmɪŋ əv ˈeɪdʒ ˌpɑrt̬i/ˌsɛrəmoʊni/
custom /ˈkʌstəm/
DJ /ˈdi ˌdʒeɪ/
festival /ˈfɛstəvəl/

EXTRA ACTIVITIES
- Photocopiable resource 12 (collocations – 10 mins) MultiROM and ActiveTeach

WORKBOOK
p. 31

NEXT CLASS
- Ask students to study the Word list on pp. 44–45.
- Ask students to review for Focus review 2.

fireworks /'faɪɚwɚks/
formalities /fɔr'mælət̬iz/
gathering /'gæðərɪŋ/
get dressed up /ˌget ˌdrest 'ʌp/
have a lump in one's throat /hæv ə ˌlʌmp ɪn wʌnz 'θroʊt/
have the time of one's life /hæv ðə ˌtaɪm əv wʌnz 'laɪf/
highlight /'haɪlaɪt/
make a fuss of sb /ˌmeɪk ə 'fʌs əv sʌmbədi/
make a speech /ˌmeɪk ə 'spitʃ/
mass /mæs/
moving /'muvɪŋ/
once in a lifetime experience /ˌwʌns ɪn ə ˌlaɪftaɪm ɪk'spɪriəns/
priest /prist/
propose a toast /prəˌpoʊz ə 'toʊst/
have a party /ˌhæv ə 'pɑrt̬i/
reception /rɪ'sɛpʃən/
shower sb with gifts /ˌʃaʊɚ ˌsʌmbədi wɪð 'gɪfts/
shrine /ʃraɪn/
spiritual side /'spɪrɪtʃuəl saɪd/
stage /steɪdʒ/
unforgettable /ˌʌnfɚ'gɛt̬əbəl/
worth the effort /ˌwɚθ ði 'ɛfɚt/

Personality, feelings, emotions

act your age /ˌækt yɚ 'eɪdʒ/
aggressive /ə'grɛsɪv/
argumentative /ˌɑrgyə'mɛnt̬ət̬ɪv/
attentive /ə'tɛntɪv/
bitterly disappointed /ˌbɪt̬ɚli ˌdɪsə'pɔɪntɪd/
burst into tears /ˌbɚst ˌɪntə 'tɪrz/
bursting with confidence /ˌbɚstɪŋ wɪð 'kɑnfədəns/
carefree /'kɛrfri/
compassionate /kəm'pæʃənɪt/
considerate /kən'sɪdərɪt/
creative /kri'eɪt̬ɪv/
easy-going /ˌizi 'goʊɪŋ/
embarrassment /ɪm'bærəsmənt/
emotional /ɪ'moʊʃənəl/
enthusiastic /ɪnˌθuzi'æstɪk/
envy /'ɛnvi/
faithful (friend) /ˌfeɪθfəl ('frɛnd)/
fussy /'fʌsi/
generosity /ˌdʒɛnə'rɑsət̬i/
get emotional /ˌget ɪ'moʊʃənəl/
independent /ˌɪndə'pɛndənt/
jealous of /'dʒɛləs əv/
joy /dʒɔɪ/
keep a secret /ˌkip ə 'sikrɪt/
kindness /'kaɪndnɪs/
outgoing personality /aʊtˌgoʊɪŋ ˌpɚsə'nælət̬i/
(painfully) shy /(ˌpeɪnfəli) 'ʃaɪ/
passionate about /'pæʃənɪt əˌbaʊt/
perfectionist /pɚ'fɛkʃənɪst/
protective /prə'tɛkt̬ɪv/
rebel /'rɛbəl/
reliable /rɪ'laɪəbəl/
responsible /rɪ'spɑnsəbəl/
rude /rud/
skeptical /'skɛptɪkəl/
self-centered /ˌsɛlf 'sɛntɚd/
self-doubt /ˌsɛlf 'daʊt/
self-sacrifice /ˌsɛlf 'sækrəfaɪs/
selfish /'sɛlfɪʃ/
sense of humor /ˌsɛns əv 'hyumɚ/
sensible /'sɛnsəbəl/
set high standards for yourself /sɛt ˌhaɪ 'stændɚdz fɚ yɚˌsɛlf/
spoiled /spɔɪld/
strength /strɛŋθ/
strict /strɪkt/
swallow your pride /ˌswɑloʊ yɚ 'praɪd/
vivid imagination /ˌvɪvɪd ɪˌmædʒə'neɪʃən/
well-behaved /ˌwɛl bɪ'heɪvd/

Body language

catch sb's eye /ˌkætʃ ˌsʌmbədiz 'aɪ/
crane your neck /ˌkreɪn yɚ 'nɛk/
discerning eyes /dɪˌsɚnɪŋ 'aɪz/
gaze /geɪz/
gesture /'dʒɛstʃɚ/
giggle /'gɪgəl/
lock your eyes on sth /ˌlɑk yɚ 'aɪz ɑn sʌmθɪŋ/
look hard/intently/fixedly /ˌlʊk 'hɑrd/ɪn'tɛntli/'fɪksɪdli/
lose sight of sb/sth /ˌluz 'saɪt əv sʌmbədi/sʌmθɪŋ/
shake your head /ˌʃeɪk yɚ 'hɛd/
shrug /ʃrʌg/
stare /stɛr/
strained voice /ˌstreɪnd 'vɔɪs/
suppress /sə'prɛs/
suppression /sə'prɛʃən/
yell /yɛl/

Phrasal verbs

blow out (the candles) /ˌbloʊ 'aʊt (ðə 'kændlz)/
boss around /ˌbɔs ə'raʊnd/
bring up (a child) /ˌbrɪŋ 'ʌp (ə tʃaɪld)/
dive/plunge into (the sea) /ˌdaɪv/ˌplʌndʒ 'ɪntə (ðə si)/
drift apart /ˌdrɪft ə'pɑrt/
fall for /'fɔl fɚ/
go out (with) /ˌgoʊ 'aʊt (wɪð)/
grow up /ˌgroʊ 'ʌp/
hear from /'hɪr frəm/
leave out /ˌliv 'aʊt/
look back on /ˌlʊk 'bæk ɑn/
meet up (with) /ˌmit 'ʌp (wɪð)/
pluck up (courage) /ˌplʌk 'ʌp (kɚɪdʒ)/
pull off /ˌpʊl ɔf/
put on /ˌpʊt 'ɑn/
split up (with) /ˌsplɪt 'ʌp (wɪð)/
take off /ˌteɪk ɔf/
tell off /ˌtɛl ɔf/
turn out /ˌtɚn 'aʊt/

Other

abduct /əb'dʌkt/
abduction /əb'dʌkʃən/
accustomed to sth /ə'kʌstəmd tə/
alike /ə'laɪk/
associated with sth /ə'soʊsiˌeɪt̬ɪd wɪð sʌmθɪŋ/
challenge /'tʃæləndʒ/
challenging /'tʃæləndʒɪŋ/
conceive /kən'siv/
concept /'kɑnsɛpt/
daydream /'deɪdrim/
deal with sth /'dil wɪθ sʌmθɪŋ/
disappear without a trace /ˌdɪsə'pɪr wɪðˌaʊt ə 'treɪs/
disappearance /ˌdɪsə'pɪrəns/
explode /ɪk'sploʊd/
explosion /ɪk'sploʊʒən/
focused on sth /'foʊkəst ɑn sʌmθɪŋ/
get the hang of sth /ˌget ðə 'hæŋ əv sʌmθɪŋ/
have a frog in your throat /ˌhæv ə 'frɔg ɪn yɚ θroʊt/
have a lot on your mind /hæv ə ˌlɑt ɑn yɚ 'maɪnd/
illustrate /'ɪləˌstreɪt/
illustration /ˌɪlə'streɪʃən/
involved in sth /ɪn'vɑlvd ɪn sʌmθɪŋ/
it takes all kinds (to make a world) /ɪt teɪks ɔl 'kaɪndz (tə meɪk ə 'wɚld)/
lose count of sth /ˌluz 'kaʊnt əv sʌmθɪŋ/
measure /'mɛʒɚ/
numerous /'numərəs/
nun /nʌn/
outweigh /aʊt'weɪ/
permanent condition /ˌpɚmənənt kən'dɪʃən/
propose a motion /prə'poʊz ə 'moʊʃən/
recognition /ˌrɛkəg'nɪʃən/
recognize /'rɛkəgˌnaɪz/
regardless of sth /rɪ'gɑrdləs əv sʌmθɪŋ/
specialize in sth /'spɛʃəˌlaɪz ɪn sʌmθɪŋ/
take /teɪk/
take a course /ˌteɪk ə 'kɔrs/
take a day off /ˌteɪk ə deɪ 'ɔf/
take part /ˌteɪk 'pɑrt/
take place /ˌteɪk 'pleɪs/
take risks /ˌteɪk 'rɪsks/
unexpectedly/out of the blue /ˌʌnɪk'spɛktɪdli/ˌaʊt əv ðə 'blu/
wary of sth /'wɛri əv sʌmθɪŋ/
weird /wɪrd/

FOCUS REVIEW 2

VOCABULARY AND GRAMMAR

1 Complete the sentences with words from the unit. The first letter of each word is given.

1 The church ceremony was followed by a **r***eception* for over 200 guests.
2 I was **b***itterly* disappointed when I couldn't go to my best friend's birthday party because I had the flu.
3 I have lots of uncles, aunts, and cousins, but my **i***mmediate* family is rather small. I just have one brother.
4 The fireworks display was definitely the **h***ighlight* of my parents' anniversary party.
5 We all **s***howered* my sister's daughter with gifts on her first birthday.

2 Complete the sentences with the correct form of the verbs in the box. There is one extra verb.

do have involve lose make propose put

1 We stood at the shore waving goodbye to the newlyweds until we *lost* sight of their yacht.
2 My older sister has just bought her own apartment and she's planning to *put* on a housewarming party.
3 It's great that Jane wants to get *involved* in organizing a hen party for her younger sister. She always has loads of ideas.
4 I'd like to *propose* a toast to the bride and groom. May they have a long life together.
5 When I got home after traveling for a year, my family *made* a fuss of me. Everyone was super nice to me.
6 The bride's father *had* a lump in his throat when he walked his daughter down the aisle on her wedding day.

3 Complete the sentences with the Past Perfect Simple or Past Perfect Continuous form of the verbs in parentheses.

1 Joshua *had already been* (already/be) married twice before he met Carol.
2 I asked Martha and Sue to organize my wedding because they *had prepared* (prepare) quite a few before.
3 Stewart was really exhausted because he *had been looking* (look) after the twins the whole afternoon.
4 Dad, how long *had you been dating* (you/date) Mom before you got engaged?
5 I split up with my girlfriend because we *had had* (have) a serious fight for the third time that week.
6 When I saw Jane the other day, I could see she *had been crying* (cry), but I didn't know why.

4 Choose the correct options.

1 Maria accepted Niko's invitation to a candlelit dinner, *which* / *that* / *what* made him really happy. (*which*)
2 Last week I bumped into the Smiths, *who* / *that* / *whose* son used to be my boyfriend. (*whose*)
3 Would you like to meet the cousin *which* / *that* / *whose* I told you about yesterday? (*that*)
4 Here are some lovely photos from Greece, *which* / *where* / *that* we went on our honeymoon. (*where*)
5 I can't find my engagement ring, *that* / *which* / *whose* is a complete disaster! (*which*)

46

LANGUAGE IN USE

5 Complete the text with the correct form of the words in the box. There is one extra word.

attend depend grow lazy lose spoil

IT'S NOT ONLY THE ONLY CHILDREN

by Ted Abbott

Don't we often wrongly assume that it's only children who are always the most [1] *spoiled* and selfish ones? Are we right in thinking that because they are raised with no siblings, they often get everything they want from their parents?

[2] *Having grown* up with two older sisters, I think it may not always be the case. As the only son who my mother had always longed for, I was the center of [3] *attention*, leaving my sisters to fight for recognition. It meant that they were always complaining about me, saying what a horrible younger brother I was. That kind of behavior made my blood boil and so I often [4] *lost* my temper with them. At the age of eighteen, I was eager to strike out on my own. I left home to study as far away as I could. That made me more [5] *independent* and mature and also helped my sisters realize that I was actually a pretty decent guy.

6 Choose the correct options.

1 Let me introduce you to Gina, *whose late husband* / *who her late husband* left all his paintings to the Arts Museum in his will. (*whose late husband*)
2 My grandma *had lived* / *was living* in the country for five years before her family moved to the city. (*had lived*)
3 When we got to the reception, we realized that we *had left* / *were leaving* the wedding gift at home! (*had left*)
4 Mark says he didn't have time to make his bed this morning because he *was oversleeping* / *had overslept*. (*had overslept*)
5 My cousin in Argentina called me on my birthday, *that it surprised* / *which surprised* me a great deal. (*which surprised*)

REFERENCES

AUDIO SCRIPT ››› p. 204

EXTRA ACTIVITIES

- Photocopiable resource 59A (word building cloze – 20 mins) MultiROM and ActiveTeach
- Photocopiable resource 60B (transformations – 20 mins) MultiROM and ActiveTeach
- Photocopiable resource 13 (Speaking – 15 mins) MultiROM and ActiveTeach
- Photocopiable resource 14 (Writing – 15 mins) MultiROM and ActiveTeach

WORKBOOK

Use of English 2.9, pp. 32–33; Self-assessment 2.10, p. 34

7 Complete the second sentence so that it has a similar meaning to the first, using the word in capitals. Do not change the word in capitals.

1 First we went out to dinner and then we went to the movies.
BEEN
After we *had been out to dinner*, we went to the movies.

2 Cathy's parents really liked Dan when they met him at the party.
IMPRESSION
Dan *made a good/great impression on* Cathy's parents when they met him at the party.

3 I first met Sally at the restaurant over there.
WHERE
That's the restaurant *where I first met* Sally.

4 After working for years, I decided to take a break.
SO
I'd *been working for years, so* I decided to take a break.

LISTENING

8 CD•1.39 MP3•39 **Listen to a scientist giving a talk and complete the sentences with a word or short phrase.**

1 The speaker has a particular interest in the subject because he is a twin and a *psychologist*.
2 Fraternal twins are babies that are born from *different eggs*.
3 Identical twins make up only *one third* of all the twins in the world.
4 About *twenty* sets of twins in every thousand births are born in some areas of Africa.
5 The record for the greatest number of twins at one school is in *England*.
6 One question the speaker asks is whether twins can tell when their brother or sister is *in danger*.
7 The speaker mentions a story about a twin whose son was born *two hours* after her twin sister's baby.
8 He gives another example of well-known twins whose second wives were both called *Betty*.
9 A problem that twins often experience is that of *competition*.
10 It's difficult for twins to be different because they have similar *DNA*.

SPEAKING

9 With a partner, complete the speaking task.

Student A, your photos show people arguing about different things. Compare the photos and say if you think the people often argue about these things.

Student B, do you often argue with your parents or siblings?

10 Now go to WORD STORE page 23 and complete another speaking task.

WRITING

11 Complete the writing task.

You have seen this announcement on an international students' website.

What do parents and teenagers argue about most in your country?

Write an article about the most common things teenagers and parents argue about in your country. We'll put the best articles on the website next month!

Write your article in 140–190 words.

NEXT CLASS

- Ask students to do Self-check 2.11, WB p. 35 as homework.
- Ask students to prepare for Unit test 2 and Review test 1 (*Focus* Assessment Package).

3 A PLACE TO LIVE

When in Rome, do as the Romans do.

A POPULAR SAYING, ATTRIBUTED TO SAINT AMBROSE

UNIT LANGUAGE AND SKILLS

Vocabulary:
- *Show what you know* – landscapes and cityscapes
- dependent prepositions
- adjective-noun collocations
- useful phrases to describe cities
- word families – adjectives ending in *-able*
- prepositions *at, in, on*
- *Word in focus – to*

Grammar:
- future forms
- quantifiers

Listening:
- news reports and a conversation about places to live
- multiple choice

Reading:
- a text about the International Space Station
- true/false

Speaking:
- suggesting, agreeing to, and objecting to a course of action

Writing:
- a 'for and against' essay

FOCUS EXTRA

- Grammar Focus pages 165–166
- WORD STORE booklet pages 6–7
- Workbook pages 36–49 or MyEnglishLab
- MP3s – www.english.com/focus

48

3.1 Vocabulary

Dependent prepositions • Collocations • Useful phrases to describe cities

I can describe cities and talk about city life.

SHOW WHAT YOU KNOW

1 With a partner, check the cityscape and landscape features you can find near your school.

a breathtaking view ☐ a busy harbor ☐ a dense forest ☐
a famous monument ☐ an industrial area ☐
a market square ☐ a river bank ☐ a ruined castle ☐
a steep hill ☐ a subdivision ☐

2 SPEAKING Discuss how far you need to go to see an example of each feature in Exercise 1. Which is the nearest? Which is the furthest?

3 CD•2.1 MP3•40 Listen to four teenagers talking about what makes a city a good place for young people. Which things are important to them?

1 Lisa
- open spaces and cheap sports facilities ✓
- great nightlife ✓
- affordable things to do ✓

2 Gudrun
- street art and fashion ✓
- expensive designer shops
- cheap public transportation ✓
- safe cycle lanes ✓

3 Liang
- gleaming skyscrapers
- clean air ✓
- job opportunities ✓

4 Josh
- quaint little backstreets
- leafy neighborhoods
- a run-down, inner-city area with a lot going on ✓
- a young, multi-cultural population ✓

4 SPEAKING With a partner, discuss the five most important things for you in a city. Choose from the things in Exercise 3 or add your own ideas.

5 Read *The Youthful Cities Index*. With a partner, decide which city is most suitable for you and explain why.

REFERENCES
CULTURE NOTES ››› *pp. 194–195*
AUDIO SCRIPT ››› *pp. 204–205*

EXTRA ACTIVITIES
- Photocopiable resource 15 (cities – 10 mins) MultiROM and ActiveTeach
- Photocopiable resource 18 (Test yourself partner work activities) MultiROM and ActiveTeach
- MyEnglishLab – assignable *Show what you have learned* mini-test

WORKBOOK
pp. 36–37

The Youthful CITIES INDEX

The Youthful Cities Index have ranked the biggest cities in the world according to how youth-friendly they are. 'Youth' is defined as people aged fifteen to twenty-nine, and over 1,500 participants from around the world helped to compile the list.

1 Toronto

In first place is Canada's largest city, with a population of 2.7 million. The city's most famous landmark is the CN Tower, which, at over 1,800 feet tall, is one of the world's tallest buildings. In Toronto there's a large student population who **benefit from** the vibrant nightlife. Toronto **prides itself on** its wide range of cultures, languages, food, and arts. Almost half of its population are immigrants, so you can find world-class restaurants serving mouth-watering food from every country you can think of. Public transport is great, with a reliable network of buses, streetcars (trams), and subway.

2 Berlin

Berlin could be the coolest city in the world! People are open-minded and easy-going, and Berliners welcome visitors with open arms. The city boasts an incredible arts and music scene – the nightlife starts late and never ends. There are hundreds of nightclubs, **packed with** partygoers every night of the week. Nightlife is affordable, as is accommodation and transportation. The city is flat and easy to get around by bike. But there is also a state-of-the-art public transport system. Berlin is **steeped in** history, and the historical heart of the city is the area called Mitte. Most of the main sights are within walking distance of the center. Finally, Berlin's best-kept secrets are the beautiful lakes, canals, and parks.

3 New York

Located at the mouth of the Hudson River, there is no place like New York with its iconic skyline. There's a first-class music scene: hip-hop was invented here! There is a huge number of theaters: more than 400 in total. In summer, this cosmopolitan city is full of free cultural activities like public art installations, museum nights, and live music. The bustling city of New York is **renowned for** its traffic jams, but unlike other cities where the subway closes at night, the NY subway runs twenty-four hours a day. New York isn't the cheapest place to live, but this is **offset by** high salaries and good youth employment.

New York

NEXT CLASS

- Ask students to prepare for a 10–15 minute vocabulary quiz: *Focus* Assessment Package, Unit 3.1, Vocabulary.

Go to **WORD STORE 3** page 7.

WORD STORE 3A

6 CD•2.2 MP3•41 **Complete WORD STORE 3A with the phrases in red in the text. Then listen, check, and repeat.**

7 **Complete the questions with prepositions. Then read the text again and answer the questions.**

1 What do Toronto students benefit _from_ ?
2 What does Toronto pride itself _on_ ?
3 What sort of people are Berlin nightclubs packed _with_ ?
4 What is Berlin steeped _in_ ?
5 What problem is New York renowned _for_ ?
6 What are New York's living costs offset _by_ ?

Exercise 7
1 vibrant nightlife
2 wide range of cultures, languages, food, and arts
3 partygoers
4 history
5 traffic jams
6 high salaries and youth employment

WORD STORE 3B

8 CD•2.3 MP3•42 **Complete WORD STORE 3B with adjectives from the underlined collocations in the text and in Exercise 3. Then listen, check, and repeat.**

9 CD•2.4 MP3•43 **With a partner, put the lines of a teenager's views into the correct order. Then listen and check.**

Right now I'm living in a **leafy** [1]
skyline of gleaming skyscrapers. I'd live in an **inner-city** [5]
city with a multi-cultural population and an **iconic** [4]
food, modern art, good music, and **vibrant** [7]
neighborhood of a picturesque town with **quaint** [2]
little backstreets. It's so boring! I dream of a **bustling** [3]
area where I could enjoy **mouth-watering** [6]
nightlife. I'll go crazy if I stay here! [8]

10 **Use the collocations in WORD STORE 3B to give your own views – negative or positive – about where you live.**

WORD STORE 3C

11 CD•2.5 MP3•44 **Complete WORD STORE 3C with more adjective-noun collocations. Then listen, check, and repeat. Write an example sentence for one collocation in each pair.**

WORD STORE 3D

12 CD•2.6 MP3•45 **Complete WORD STORE 3D with the highlighted phrases in the text. Then listen, check, and repeat.**

13 **With a partner, complete the sentences about places in your country. Then compare your sentences with other pairs. Do they agree with your opinions?**

1 _____ is my local city's best-kept secret.
2 The most famous landmark in my area is _____ .
3 _____ has a very reliable network of _____ .
4 _____ is within walking distance of this school.
5 _____ is easy to get around by bike.
6 The most youth-friendly city in my country is _____ .

3.2 Grammar

Future forms

I can use a variety of forms to talk about the future.

Exercise 1
2 I won't have been studying
3 I won't still be living
4 I won't have saved up
5 I won't have been driving
6 I won't be sailing

Exercise 2
3
1 future perfect simple
2 future perfect continuous
3 future continuous
4 future perfect simple
5 future perfect continuous
6 future continuous

1 Rewrite the sentences in the negative. Then think about your life three years from now and decide which alternative is more likely.

In three years' time:

1 I **will have moved** to another part of the country.
I won't have moved to another part of the country.
2 I **will have been studying** in college for a year.
3 I'**ll still be living** at home with my parents.
4 I **will have saved up** enough money to go traveling.
5 I **will have been driving** for over a year.
6 I'**ll be sailing** across the Pacific Ocean with my family.

2 With a partner, read the GRAMMAR FOCUS and follow the instructions.

1 Translate example sentences 1–3 into your own language.
2 Discuss the difference in meaning between each sentence.
3 Look at Exercise 1 and name the future verb forms in blue.

GRAMMAR FOCUS

Future forms

- You use the **Future Continuous** to talk about unfinished actions in progress at a time in the future. It often refers to future events that are fixed or expected.
[1]*At 11 a.m. tomorrow, **I'll be taking** an exam.*
- You use the **Future Perfect Simple** to talk about an action that will be completed before a certain time in the future.
[2]*By 11 a.m. tomorrow, I **will have taken** an exam.*
- You use the **Future Perfect Continuous** to talk about how long an action will have been in progress before a certain time in the future. The form is: *will* + *have been* + *-ing* form.
[3]*By 11 a.m. tomorrow, I **will have been taking** an exam for an hour.*

3 Read Part 1 of an article. For each blank, choose from options A–D. Then discuss the questions below with a partner.

A will **B** be **C** been **D** have

1 What problems do the children predict?
2 Which child seems most positive about the voyage?

1 Billy: We'll be missing a lot of school.
Mandy: I'll be spending three years in a small space with my messy brothers.
Jake: I won't be practicing basketball.
2 Billy seems most positive.

EXTRA ACTIVITIES
- Photocopiable resource 16 (future forms – 10 mins) MultiROM and ActiveTeach
- MyEnglishLab – assignable *Show what you have learned* mini-test

WORKBOOK
p. 38

NEXT CLASS
- Ask students to prepare for a 10–15 minute grammar quiz: *Focus* Assessment Package, Unit 3.2, Grammar.

THE VOYAGE OF A LIFETIME

In a few weeks' time, the Franklin family will [1] *be* embarking on a three-year sailing voyage. We asked the children how they felt about the adventure.

Billy, fifteen, said, 'We'll [2] *be* missing a lot of school, but I think that by the end of this trip we will [3] *have* learned more than in a classroom. We will have [4] *been* traveling for three years, and we [5] *will* have seen places with our own eyes. We won't [6] *have* just read about them in books.'

Mandy, twelve, had a few worries: 'The worst thing is that I'll [7] *be* spending three years in a small space with my messy brothers.'

Finally, Jake, seventeen, was less interested than his younger brother: 'By the time we go, I will have [8] *been* playing basketball for my school for seven years, and I want to be a professional. I'll [9] *be* practicing whenever I can, but it's not easy on a boat.'

4 Complete Part 2 of the article with the Future Continuous, Future Perfect Simple or Future Perfect Continuous form of the verbs in parentheses. Would you like to go on a voyage like this? Why?/Why not?

Eileen Franklin told us, 'We're not in a hurry, so after leaving San Francisco we [1] *'ll be traveling* (travel) down the coast of Mexico for a few weeks. After that we [2] *'ll be sailing* (sail) across the Pacific and we [3] *'ll be ending* (end) our journey in Indonesia. It's a long voyage, but by the time we leave, we [4] *'ll have been planning* (plan) for several years, so I think we're as prepared as we can be.'

'Yes,' added Bob, 'And by the time we start out, we [5] *'ll have done* (do) everything possible to make this a safe trip: Mandy [6] *will have learned* (learn) how to swim and Eileen [7] *will have taken* (take) an advanced first aid course. On the boat, we [8] *will be using* (use) top-of-the-range technology to chart our route. It's the trip of a lifetime, so we [9] *won't be taking* (not take) any chances!'

5 Read REMEMBER THIS. Then rewrite the questions in the Future Continuous to make them more polite.

> **REMEMBER THIS**
>
> You can also use the **Future Continuous** to make polite enquiries. Compare:
> *Will you be staying in tonight?* = I just want to know. (polite)
> *Are you going to stay in tonight?* = I'd like a decision. (more direct)

1 Are you going home right after school?
2 Are you doing anything interesting this evening?
3 Who do you plan to see over the weekend?
4 When will you go on your next vacation?
5 Are you going to have a party for your eighteenth birthday?
6 Do you think you'll leave home permanently before you're twenty-five?

6 SPEAKING With a partner, ask and answer the rewritten questions in Exercise 5.

Grammar Focus page 165

Exercise 5
1 Will you be going home right after school?
2 Will you be doing anything interesting this evening?
3 Who will you be seeing over the weekend?
4 When will you be going on your next vacation?
5 Will you be having a party for your eighteenth birthday?
6 Will you be leaving home permanently before you're twenty-five?

3.3 Listening

Multiple choice

I can understand news reports and a conversation about places to live.

1 Match photos A–C with descriptions 1–3. Use the photo captions to complete the texts.

Freedom Ship

smart house

co-housing

1 C In the *smart house* of the future, all appliances will be connected through wireless networking systems. The house and car would use power that is collected through solar panels and stored.

2 B *Co-housing* is a housing development where each household has a self-contained house or apartment. People have the opportunity to eat together and meet regularly in a large communal house.

3 A The *Freedom Ship* is designed to be twenty-five storeys high. If the concept became reality, it would feature a casino, an art gallery, a park, a shopping center, and accommodation for 50,000 people. It would cost $10 billion to build.

2 SPEAKING **With a partner, discuss which place in Exercise 1 you would most/least like to live in. Give reasons for your answers.**

REFERENCES

CULTURE NOTES ››› *p. 195*
AUDIO SCRIPT ››› *p. 205*

WORKBOOK

p. 39

3 CD•2.7 MP3•46 **Listen and match the extracts (1–3) with the photos (A–C).**

A [2] B [1] C [3]

EXAM FOCUS Multiple choice

4 CD•2.7 MP3•46 **Listen again and choose the correct answer, A, B, or C.**

1 Which statement is an opinion and NOT a fact?
  A Over a third of British people don't know their neighbors.
  B In Denmark a small percentage of the population live in co-housing developments.
  (C) The neighborly relations at Springhill will be 100 percent better.
2 The speakers think that the *Freedom Ship* project is
  (A) unlikely to happen.
  B not big enough for 50,000 people.
  C a good investment opportunity.
3 Choose the most appropriate headline for this news report.
  A Smart homes mean less shopping
  (B) Smart homes save time and money
  C Smart homes need smartphones

5 **Complete the collocations from the recording with the adjectives in the box. Then complete the sentences to make them true for you.**

domestic high-rise household housing multi-storey residential second self-contained

1 My least favorite _domestic_ **chore** is …
2 The nearest _multi-story_ **parking lot** is …
3 The one _household_ **appliance** I couldn't live without is …
4 The newest _housing_ **development** in my neighborhood is …
5 The tallest _high-rise_ **building** in my city is …
6 The _residential_ **area** I'd most like to live in is …
7 I'd love to have a _second_ **home** in …
8 I'd prefer to live in a small _self-contained_ **apartment** than …

PRONUNCIATION FOCUS

6 CD•2.8 MP3•47 **Listen and repeat the chants.**

A

What _will_ _you_ _be_ doing?
What _will_ _you_ _have_ seen?
Where _will_ _you_ _be_ living?
Where _will_ _you_ _have_ been?

B

How long _will_ _you_ _have_ _been_ learning?
How much _will_ _you_ _have_ learned?
How long _will_ _you_ _have_ _been_ earning?
How much _will_ _you_ _have_ earned?

7 CD•2.8 MP3•47 **Complete the chants in Exercise 6 with *you* and the correct future forms. Then listen again and check. Practise saying them again, and focus on stress and rhythm.**

WORD STORE 3E

8 CD•2.9 MP3•48 **Complete WORD STORE 3E. Add the suffix *-able* to make adjectives from the verbs. Then listen, check, and repeat. Write example sentences.**

3.4 Reading

True/False

I can find details in a text about the International Space Station.

1 **SPEAKING With a partner, read some facts about living on the International Space Station (ISS) and discuss the questions.**

- Astronauts change their clothes every day – they don't wash them but throw them away.
- Astronauts often lose their sense of smell and taste, so everything tastes like cardboard.
- To use the computer, astronauts have to sit in mid-air, holding onto a wall-strap with their toe.
- In space, astronauts lose muscle power quickly, so they have to exercise at least two hours a day.
- When repairs are necessary on the outside of the ISS, astronauts have to do spacewalks.
- Astronauts' urine is recycled as drinking water.

1 Which facts do you find most surprising?
2 What would you like about living on board the ISS?
3 What would you find most difficult about it?

2 **With a partner, guess which numbers in the box complete the fact sheet about the International Space Station.**

6 16 16 90 217 17,400

ISS Fact sheet

Altitude: [1] 217 miles above the Earth
Speed: [2] 17,400 miles per hour
Power source: [3] 16 solar panels
Permanent crew: [4] 6 astronauts
Time to orbit the Earth: [5] 90 minutes
Number of orbits: [6] 16 per day

3 **Read the article and check your ideas in Exercise 2.**

4 **Read the article again. Are the statements true (T) or false (F)?**

1 Hardly anybody bothers to look out for the International Space Station (ISS). T
2 Astronauts get used to weightless conditions before they go on the ISS. F
3 Lack of gravity prevents astronauts from using fresh water to wash themselves. F
4 The transition from daytime to nighttime lasts a few minutes. F
5 Attaching sleeping bags to the wall solves the problem of falling asleep. F
6 Spacewalkers can't sense the speed at which the space station is flying around the world. T

5 **Put the words and phrases in blue in the article under an appropriate heading.**

Light	Water	Sleep
reflecting		

6 **Complete the questions with the correct form of a word or phrase from Exercise 5.**

1 What does it look like when the sunlight's reflecting off the ISS?
2 What do the astronauts use moist wipes for?
3 How do the astronauts soak up the water and shampoo after washing their hair?
4 What do the astronauts wear when the light is blinding?
5 What color light is the ISS bathed in when day turns into night?
6 Where do the astronauts attach their sleeping bags when they go to bed?
7 What sensation do the astronauts get just when they are starting to snooze?
8 What is used to wake the astronauts up in place of an alarm clock?

7 **Read the article again and answer the questions in Exercise 6.**

8 **SPEAKING Think about the idea of living on a space station for a year. What would you miss most about living on Earth? What would you miss least? Discuss with a partner.**

WORD STORE 3F

9 CD•2.11 MP3•50 **Complete WORD STORE 3F. Add *at*, *in*, and *on* to the diagram. Then listen, check, and repeat.**

Exercise 5
Light: blinding, bathed in light
Water: moist, splashing, wet, soak up
Sleep: sleeping bag, snooze, settle down, alarm clock

Exercise 7
1 a wandering star in the heavens
2 washing
3 with a wet towel
4 sunglasses
5 coppery
6 to the wall of their cabins
7 the sensation of falling off a ten-story building
8 music played by staff on the ground

REFERENCES
CULTURE NOTES ››› p. 195

EXTRA ACTIVITIES
- Photocopiable resource 17 (vocabulary from reading text – 10 mins) MultiROM and ActiveTeach

WORKBOOK
pp. 40–41

NEXT CLASS
- Ask students to think of ideas of how life in space will be in the future.

Students should make a list and discuss in the next class.

CD•2.10 MP3•49

LIFE ON BOARD THE INTERNATIONAL SPACE STATION

At 6:41 p.m. this Thursday, a small bright light will appear low in the night sky before disappearing in the darkness.

Few people will notice and even fewer will care, but for a handful of people, that light on the horizon is a place called home. What looks like a wandering star in the heavens is sunlight **reflecting** off the International Space Station. To get to the space station takes two days. The station flies at an altitude of about 217 miles (that's more than thirty times the cruising height of a jumbo jet) and travels at an incredible 17,400 miles per hour.

In total, the living space on the station is the equivalent of roughly one and a half Boeing 747s. This living space is made up of different 'modules' built by Russians, Americans, and other nations. There are sixteen solar panels attached to the station and they provide electrical power. The space station has a permanent crew of six. Although they have some training in how to live in weightlessness, when they first arrive on board the ISS, they take a while to get used to living without gravity, crashing into things as they try to move from one room to another. In time, people learn to fly down the length of the station without touching anything.

As they live so close together, personal hygiene is essential, but the weightless conditions make washing difficult. Many astronauts use **moist** wipes. Hair-washing is trickier. Sunita Williams, who spent 195 days on the space station, explains how she managed: 'Washing hair took time. I'd put a little water under my hair, pat it down with my hand so it wasn't **splashing** everywhere, then put some shampoo in my hand and move it around. Then I'd **wet** a towel and try to **soak** it **up**.'

It takes the space station one and a half hours to fly around the planet, meaning that it circles the globe sixteen times a day. For those on board, the visual effect is spectacular. If the covers on the windows are opened, the light can be so **blinding** that astronauts reach for their sunglasses. But after forty-five minutes of daylight, a dark line appears on the planet, dividing Earth into night and day. For a couple of seconds, the space station is **bathed in light** that is a coppery color, and then complete darkness. Another forty-five minutes later, the sun rises to fill the station with brilliant light again.

The short days and nights would disrupt the astronauts' body clocks, so a bedtime schedule is imposed by mission controllers: the crew are told when to put the shutters down on the windows and go to bed. Each of the crew has a cabin where they can attach a **sleeping bag** to the wall and **settle down** for the night. Unsurprisingly, falling asleep can be difficult. Just when you are starting to **snooze**, the lack of gravity can make you feel as though you're falling off a ten-storey building. In place of an **alarm clock**, sleeping crews are woken by music played over the communication system controlled by staff on the ground.

When astronauts first arrive at the space station, they're in awe of the views. It is the sight of our planet that takes the breath away. On board, you can get a panoramic view of Earth. But for the really exceptional views, you need to step outside for a spacewalk. One astronaut describes the experience: 'Sometimes you feel that you are on this big flying building and it's going around the world, but most commonly you feel that someone is rolling this huge ball-shaped map beneath you. You have no feeling of motion.'

Those who have visited the space station can look at it shooting across the sky at night. They can imagine the astronauts in their sleeping bags and think, 'My goodness, I was there!'

3.5 Grammar

Quantifiers

I can use a range of different quantifiers correctly.

1 SPEAKING With a partner, take turns to describe your bedroom. On a scale of 1 to 10 (1 = extremely neat and 10 = extremely messy), what score is your bedroom?

2 CD•2.12 MP3•51 Read and listen to Part 1 of a vlog post. Why does the vlogger want to clean her room? *Because a friend she likes is coming over.*

Welcome, fellow teens, to my video blog. Today's vlog is called 'How to clean your room in ten minutes!' I'm sure **all of you** know what I'm talking about – your room's a total nightmare. It looks as if a bomb has exploded. There's **loads of dirty clothes** – in fact, the whole floor is covered. There's **no space** anywhere. You have **plenty of clothes** but you don't wear half of them because you can't find them. **Most of them** are in a pile because there are not enough drawers to put them in. You've had **a number of opportunities** to clean your room but you haven't, and now the very cool new friend you like is coming around. **Very few of your friends** know what a slob you are and you want to keep it like that. You don't have **much time**, so here are **a few speed-cleaning tips**.

Exercise 3
1 – no space / much time / a few speed-cleaning tips
2 – all of you / most of them / very few of your friends
3 – loads of / plenty of / a number of

3 Read the GRAMMAR FOCUS. Then match the examples in blue in the vlog post with rules 1–3.

all of you = rule 2

GRAMMAR FOCUS

Quantifiers

You can use a wide range of different expressions to talk about quantity:

	Countable nouns	Uncountable nouns	Both
100%	*every, each*		*all*
			most
	many	*much, a great deal of**	*a lot of*, lots of*, loads of*, plenty of**
	a number of, several*		*some*
	a few	*a little*	
	(very) few	*(very) little*	
	both, a couple of, either*		
0%	*neither*		*no, none of**

1 Use quantifiers without *of* before nouns: ***most people***
2 Use quantifiers with *of* before determiner + noun: ***most of the people***, and before pronouns: ***most of them***
3 * Always use these quantifiers with *of*: ***a lot of people***

Note: *All the people* and *all of the people* are both possible.
You can't use *of* after *no* and *every*. Use *none of* and *every one of*.

REFERENCES
CULTURE NOTES ››› p. 195

EXTRA ACTIVITIES
• Photocopiable resource 18 (Test yourself partner work activities) MultiROM and ActiveTeach
• MyEnglishLab – assignable *Show what you have learned* mini-test

WORKBOOK
p. 42

NEXT CLASS
• Ask students to prepare for a 10–15 minute grammar quiz: *Focus* Assessment Package, Unit 3.5, Grammar.

4 CD•2.13 MP3•52 **Read Part 2 of the vlog post and choose the correct options. Then listen and check.**

- Find a laundry basket and put [1]*all* / *each* the clothes on the floor into it. Too [2]*much* / *many* clothes? OK, get [3]*a couple* / *a few* of trash bags and put the rest in there. Then hide [4]*both* / *either* of the bags in the closet. If the cool friend sees [5]*plenty* / *either* of the bags, just say it's [6]*a few* / *few* things you're collecting for charity.
- The whole place smells of snacks, so take [7]*every* / *some* half-empty drink and stale half-eaten potato chips bag to the kitchen immediately. There's a big difference between messy and disgusting.
- There are [8]*a number* / *several* of things that would give the wrong impression – things like your huge pink teddy bear. Hide them.
- Make the bed. There's [9]*no* / *any* excuse for an unmade bed.
- Open [10]*plenty* / *all* the windows – now!

You're ready! Just one more thing: check your computer and delete any messages that say something like, 'OMG, I'm so excited! I can't believe X is coming over!'

5 **Complete the sentences with *of* where necessary. Check the sentences that are true for you. Then add other quantifiers to the rest of the sentences to make them true for you.**

1 A couple __of__ my friends are pretty neat.
2 Some __–__ classmates are very messy.
3 Several __–__ people I know share a bedroom.
4 Very few __of__ my neighbors have big yards.
5 Many __of__ the buildings in my street are old.
6 Every __–__ room in my house has wi-fi.
7 None __of__ my friends have a TV in their room.
8 Most __–__ rooms in my house have paintings on the walls.

6 **Write three sentences about yourself – two true and one false. Use a different word from the box in each sentence.**

all	couple	every	little	loads	lots	most	none	plenty

All of my music is on my phone.

7 **With a partner, take turns to read your sentences from Exercise 6 to each other. Can he/she guess which one is false?**

Grammar Focus page 166

57

3.6 Speaking

Organizing a place to live

I can suggest, agree to, and object to a course of action.

1 **With a partner, put these factors in order of importance when looking for an apartment to share with friends.**

decor/furniture ☐ location ☐ rent ☐ size ☐ security ☐ privacy ☐

2 **Compare your ideas from Exercise 1 with another pair. Agree on a final order.**

3 CD•2.14 MP3•53 **Listen to a conversation between two friends who are looking for an apartment to share. Which two factors from Exercise 1 are not mentioned?** decoration/furniture and security not mentioned

4 CD•2.14 MP3•53 **Read the SPEAKING FOCUS and complete the conversation with one word in each blank. Then listen again and check.**

Zoe: I can't believe we both got accepted into the same university!
Amy: Isn't it great? I'm so excited! And we'll be living together.
Zoe: I know. I can't wait!
Amy: What do you think [1] about living in the dorms? To be honest, I'm not sure.
Zoe: No, me neither. Do you know Jay?
Amy: Yep, why?
Zoe: Well, his brother studies there and he says the dorms are really old and noisy. Maybe we ought to just look for a place of our own.
Amy: You're [2] absolutely right.
Zoe: The question is, do we want to share with other people? It would probably be cheaper.
Amy: Well, yeah, but [3] wouldn't it be better to get our own place? Obviously, it depends how much it costs, but if we could find the right apartment at the right price, I think I'd prefer not to share.
Zoe: I know what you mean, but I'm not [4] convinced we'll be able to afford it. Why don't we [5] meet halfway and look for shared accommodation, but in a place where we could have our own rooms?
Amy: I suppose that could [6] work. That way we might even be able to afford something near the university. Given the choice, I'd [7] rather be within walking or biking distance. And you?
Zoe: Totally. I don't even mind if it's a small room as long as it's close to the campus.
Amy: That's [8] settled, then. So, let's take a look online and see what we can find.

WORKBOOK
p. 43

SPEAKING FOCUS

Suggesting a course of action

What do you think about (+ *-ing*)?
Maybe we ought to (just) …
What would you say if we (+ Past Simple)?
Given the choice, I'd rather … And you?

Objecting

No way!/Absolutely not!/You must be joking! (informal)
Fair? I think it's completely unfair.
(Well, yeah, but) wouldn't it be better to … ?
I know/see what you mean/what you're saying, but …
I'm not convinced (we'll be able to afford it/that's a good idea/that'll work).

Compromising

If you agree to (pay more), I'll (take the smaller room).
We could (split the cost/share).
Why don't we compromise/meet halfway (and agree that …)?
I guess so./I suppose that could work.
OK, that seems like a fair compromise.

Agreeing

True./Right./Absolutely./Totally.
I fully/completely agree.
You're absolutely right.
OK, that's settled, then.

5 **Three teenagers are going to share an apartment. Here are some possible rules that could make sharing an apartment easier. Look at each rule and decide if you think it's a good or bad idea. Note down your opinion about each rule (with reasons). Then think of one more rule of your own.**

1 We need to have a plan for cleaning the apartment every week. We should write down exactly who is doing what and when.
2 We need to have a cooking rotation so that we all cook for the others on different days.
3 We should have a rule about noise! Like, after a certain time we should keep our noise down so others can sleep or work.
4 Parties! We can have parties but we need to tell the others and always invite them!
5 The bathroom – we need a schedule for who uses the shower and bathroom at different times in the morning.
6 We all need to give the same money to decorate the living room and choose the colors and do the work on it together.
7 We DON'T eat our roommates' food in the fridge or use their things without asking.

6 SPEAKING **With a partner, compare your ideas from Exercise 5 and then decide whose extra rule is better. When you disagree, try to reach a compromise. Then look at all the rules again and choose the two best ones.**

3.7 Writing

A 'for and against' essay

I can use a range of formal language when arguing for and against an issue.

1 Read *TODAY IN THE USA*. How similar or different do you think the situation is in your country?

TODAY IN THE USA

University dorms

- Most universities in the USA provide accommodations for first-year students in university-owned residence halls, or dorms, on or near the campus.
- There is often a resident advisor, or RA, whose job it is to maintain order and support students with everyday issues.
- Rooms in these halls are generally small but private and, in most cases, bills are included in the rental price. Kitchen facilities are usually shared.
- During the 2014–2015 academic year, the average cost of room and board in the USA was about $9,000 at a public university and $31,000 at a private university.

2 Read the comments from first-year university students. Are they describing advantages (A) or disadvantages (D) of living in a dorm? Compare your answers with a partner.

1 Freedom! (Ammar, New Jersey) A
2 It's impossible to get any studying done. (Ian, Edinburgh) D
3 I'm exhausted. There are parties every night. (Nick, Seattle) D/A
4 There's an RA we can talk to if we have any problems. (Emma, Durham) A
5 Rules, rules, rules! Keep quiet, clean up, no visitors. (Ollie, Los Angeles) D
6 We all help each other out. I've made so many new friends. (Abigail, Liverpool) A
7 Someone stole my burgers! (Jason, Austin) D
8 Our dorms are on campus. I fall out of bed and into my classes. (Anahita, Philadelphia) A
9 My room is OK but it's tiny. (Richard, St. Louis) D

3 Read the essay and underline the advantages and disadvantages from Exercise 2 that the writer mentions. Which one is *not* mentioned? 5

Some university students prefer to live with their families until they graduate and can earn their own living. However, it is also very common for young people beginning university to choose to live together with other students in residence halls, or dorms. Although there are several potential **downsides** to this communal way of living, there are also numerous benefits.

One of the most **convincing** arguments for dorms is that they allow students to experience independent living in a safe place with a strong sense of community. Having never lived alone, most new students appreciate this supportive environment. In the same **way**, the presence of an official resident advisor, or RA, is likely to be reassuring for students and their parents. **Yet** another plus is that dorms are usually very convenient because they are located on, or close to, university campuses. This allows residents to save time and money.

Despite these clear advantages, there are also considerable drawbacks. The first downside is that the rooms tend to be very small and bathrooms may sometimes have to be shared. Being full of young

people, halls can also be very noisy. This can make them difficult places in which to study. **Likewise**, parties and late nights are common, and can interfere with students' academic progress. Other **minuses** are that food can 'disappear' from shared fridges and cupboards, and communal kitchens are often busy and sometimes dirty.

All things **considered**, there are pros and cons to living in dorms. Certainly, residents need to be self-disciplined in order to successfully balance study and social life. Personally, I **imagine** the benefits of living closely with other students outweigh the drawbacks.

EXTRA ACTIVITIES

- MyEnglishLab – assignable *Show what you have learned* writing task and *Show that you have checked* checklist

WORKBOOK

p. 44

4 SPEAKING With a partner, discuss the questions.

1 What is the writer's opinion of dorms ? *The benefits of living in dorms outweigh the drawbacks.*

2 Would you like to live in this type of student accommodation? Why?/Why not?

5 Complete the WRITING FOCUS with the words and phrases in purple in the essay.

WRITING FOCUS

A 'for and against' essay

Introduction

- Begin with general or factual comments on the topic.
  Many young people beginning university choose to live in halls of residence.
- End with a statement that mentions both sides of the issue.
  Although there are several potential [1] *downsides* to ... , there are also numerous upsides.

Main paragraphs

- Present *arguments for* in one paragraph and *arguments against* in another.
  The first/One/A further/Another/[2] *Yet* another benefit/drawback of ...
  There are numerous/potential/clear/considerable pluses/[3] *minuses* to ...
  One of the most [4] *convincing*/most persuasive/strongest arguments for/against ... is ...
- Develop and support some of your arguments with additional comments or examples.
  This allows residents to save time and money.
- Make comparisons.
  In the same [5] *way* , ... Similarly, /Equally, /[6] *Likewise* , ...

Conclusion

- Make a summarising statement.
  All things [7] *considered* , /All in all, /On balance, there are pros and cons to ...
- End with your personal opinion.
  Personally, I think/feel/believe/[8] *imagine* ...

6 Choose the correct options.

1 One of the most *persuasive* / *potential* arguments for living at home is the amount of money that can be saved.

2 There are also several *numerous* / *clear* upsides to living independently while in college.

3 The daily commute is one of the drawbacks *of* / *for* living a long way from the university campus.

4 Living alone, students learn to cook and clean for themselves. *On balance* / *Equally*, they gain experience in managing their money.

5 *All in all* / *Personally*, there are pluses and minuses to remaining in the family home while in college.

7 Read the LANGUAGE FOCUS. Then find two sentences in the essay that express concession.

LANGUAGE FOCUS

Expressing concession

You can increase the variety in your written English by including sentences that express concession.

- ***Although/Even though* + clause**
  Although dorms are not always the cheapest option*, many students prefer them.*
  Many students prefer dorms ***even though they are not always the cheapest option****.*
- ***In spite of/Despite* + noun/-ing**
  In spite of the cost*, many students prefer dorms.*
  Many students prefer dorms, ***despite the cost****.*
  Despite living *cheaply, many students still find themselves short of money.*

8 Rewrite the sentences using the words in capitals.

1 Although there are numerous arguments for living with your parents while in college, there are also considerable drawbacks. **DESPITE**
Despite the numerous arguments for living with your parents while in college, there are also considerable drawbacks.

2 Many students live at home with their parents, even though there are minuses. **SPITE**

3 In spite of the cooking facilities in dorms, students often survive on fast food only. **ALTHOUGH**

4 Although some student accommodations offer good value, it is still likely to be cheaper for students to live with their parents. **DESPITE**

5 Many teenagers have plenty of freedom despite living with their parents. **THOUGH**

9 Read the writing task and follow the instructions below.

> *Many young people who enter higher education choose to study in their hometown and continue living with their parents throughout their university years.*
> Write an essay of 200–250 words, in which you present arguments for and against this arrangement.

1 Think about general or factual comments you could make on the topic.

2 Write down arguments for and against the statement and choose the ones you want to use. Decide which ones you will develop and support, and how.

3 Think about your personal opinion on the topic and where you will include it.

4 Choose sentences from Exercises 6 and 8 to adapt for your essay.

10 Complete the writing task in Exercise 9. Use the WRITING FOCUS and the LANGUAGE FOCUS to help you.

61

Exercise 7
1 Although there are several potential downsides to this communal way of living, there are also numerous benefits.
2 Despite these clear advantages, there are also considerable drawbacks.

Exercise 8
2 Many students live at home with their parents, in spite of the minuses.
3 Although there are cooking facilities in dorms, students often survive on fast food only.
4 Despite some student accommodations offering good value, it is still likely to be cheaper for students to live with their parents.
5 Many teenagers have plenty of freedom even though they live with their parents.

3.8 Language in focus

Determiners – special cases

I can use all, both, each, every, whole, another, other, *and* others *correctly.*

1 Read the information and choose the correct options in the example sentences from this unit.

all, both, each, every, and whole

	+ noun	+ of + my/the, etc. + noun	+ pronoun
all	*all the relatives*	*all (of) the relatives*	*all of them*
both	*both (my) parents*	*both (of my) parents*	*both of them*
each	*each twin*	*each (one) of the twins*	*each (one) of them*
every	*every relative*	*every one of the relatives*	*every one of them*
whole	*the whole room*	*my whole room*	*the whole of it*

another, other, and others

Another friend means 'a different friend' or 'an additional friend'.
Other friends means 'different friends', but not usually 'additional friends'. (Use *more friends*.)
The others refers to people/things that have already been mentioned.

1 ***Every* / *All*** of you know what I'm talking about. (All)
2 Unlike ***another* / *other*** subways, the NY subway runs twenty-four hours a day. (other)
3 ***Each* / *Every*** of the crew members has a cabin. (Each)
4 ***The whole* / *All the*** place smells like snacks. (The whole)
5 ***Both* / *Every*** country you can think of. (Every)

2 Complete the questions with words in the box. Then answer the questions.

all	both	each	every	whole

1 Can you write your name with *each* hand?
2 Do you have earrings in *both* ears?
3 Do *all* your relatives look like you?
4 Does *every/each* one of your Facebook friends know you personally?
5 Are you off school for the *whole* month of August?

3 Match sentences 1 and 2 with meanings a and b. In which case is there no difference in meaning?

A 1 Have **another** cookie. *b* 2 Have **the other** cookie. *a*
a There is one cookie available.
b There are several cookies available.

B 1 Here's one photo, where's **the other**? *a* 2 Here's one photo, where are **the others**? *b*
a There's one photo missing.
b There are several photos missing.

C 1 We text **each other** every day. 2 We text **one another** every day.
a I text him and he texts me. *no difference in meaning*
b I text her and she texts me.

D 1 Could I have **another** coffee? *a* 2 Could I have **the other** coffee? *b*
a I'd like the same kind of coffee again.
b I'd like the alternative coffee you offered.

03 WORD LIST

Cityscape and landscape, describing cities

at the mouth of a river /ət ðə ˌmaʊθ əv ə ˈrɪvɚ/
benefit (from) /ˈbɛnəfɪt (frəm)/
breathtaking view /ˈbrɛθˌteɪkɪŋ ˈvyu/
built-up/urban area /ˌbɪlt ʌp/ˌɚbən ˈɛriə/
bustling city /ˌbʌslɪŋ ˈsɪt̲i/
busy harbor /ˌbɪzi ˈhɑrbɚ/
canal /kəˈnæl/
casino /kəˈsinoʊ/
city's best-kept secret /ˌsɪt̲iz bɛst kɛpt ˈsikrɪt/
cityscape /ˈsɪt̲iˌskeɪp/
clean air /ˌklin ˈɛr/
cool /kul/
cosmopolitan /ˌkɑzməˈpɑlət̲ən/
dense forest /ˌdɛns ˈfɔrɪst/
designer store /dɪˈzaɪnɚ stɔr/
dramatic/impressive/iconic skyline /drəˌmæt̲ɪk/ɪmˌprɛsɪv/aɪˌkɑnɪk ˈskaɪlaɪn/
dull/hectic/vibrant nightlife /ˌdʌl/ˌhɛktɪk/ˌvaɪbrənt ˈnaɪtlaɪf/
famous monument/landmark /ˌfeɪməs ˈmɑnyəmənt/ˈlændmɑrk/
gleaming skyscrapers /ˌglimɪŋ ˈskaɪˌskreɪpɚz/
historical heart of the city /hɪˈstɔrɪkəl ˌhɑrt əv ðə ˈsɪt̲i/
immigrant /ˈɪməgrənt/
industrial area /ɪnˈdʌstriəl ˌɛriə/
inner-city area /ˌɪnɚ ˌsɪt̲i ˈɛriə/
job opportunities /ˈdʒɑb ɑpɚˈtunət̲iz/
leafy neighborhood /ˌlifi ˈneɪbɚˌhʊd/
living costs /ˈlɪvɪŋ kɔsts/
main sights /ˌmeɪn ˈsaɪts/
market square /ˈmɑrkɪt skwɛr/
mouth-watering food /ˌmaʊθ ˌwɔt̲ɚɪŋ ˈfud/
multicultural population /ˌmʌltiˌkʌltʃərəl ˌpɑpyəˈleɪʃən/
narrow/cobbled/quaint backstreets /ˌnæroʊ/ˌkɑbəld/ˌkweɪnt ˈbækˌstrits/
nightclub /ˈnaɪt̚klʌb/
open spaces /oʊpən ˈspeɪsɪz/
packed with partygoers /ˌpækt wɪð ˈpɑrt̲iˌgoʊɚz/
population /ˌpɑpyəˈleɪʃən/
pride yourself on sth/boast sth /ˈpraɪd yɚˌsɛlf ɑn sʌmθɪŋ/ˈboʊst sʌmθɪŋ/
renowned for /rɪˈnaʊnd fɚ/
river bank /ˈrɪvɚ bæŋk/
ruined /ˈruɪnd/
sports facilities /ˈspɔrts fəˌsɪlət̲iz/
sprawling /ˈsprɔlɪŋ/
steep hill /ˌstip ˈhɪl/
steeped in history /ˌstipd ɪn ˈhɪstəri/
welcome visitors with open arms /ˌwɛlkəm ˌvɪzɪt̲ɚz wɪð oʊpən ˈɑrmz/
wide range of (cultures/languages/food/arts) /ˌwaɪd ˌreɪndʒ əv (ˈkʌltʃɚz/ˈlæŋgwɪdʒɪz/ˈfud/ˈɑrts)/
world-class restaurant /ˌwɚld ˌklæs ˈrɛstˌrɑnt/
youth employment /ˈyuθ ɪmˌplɔɪmənt/
youth friendly /ˌyuθ ˈfrɛndli/
youthful /ˈyuθfəl/

City transportation

bike lane /ˈbaɪk leɪn/
easy to get around (by bike) /ˌizi tə ˌgɛt əˌraʊnd (baɪ ˈbaɪk)/
multi-storey parking garage /ˌmʌlti ˌstɔri ˈpɑrkiŋ gəˈrɑʒ/
reliable network (of buses) /rɪˌlaɪəbəl ˌnɛtwɚk əv (ˈbʌsɪz)/
(state-of-the-art) public transportation system /(ˌsteɪt əv ði ˌɑrt) ˌpʌblɪk ˌtrænspɚˈteɪʃən ˌsɪstəm/
streetcar/tram /ˈstritkɑr/træm/
subway /ˈsʌbweɪ/
traffic jam /ˈtræfɪk dʒæm/

Culture

art gallery /ˈɑrt ˌgæləri/
art installation /ˈɑrt ɪnstəˌleɪʃən/
fashion /ˈfæʃən/
incredible/first-class arts and music scene /ɪnˌkrɛdəbəl/ˌfɚst ˌklɑs ˌɑrts ənd ˈmyuzɪk sin/
live music /ˌlaɪv ˈmyuzɪk/
modern art /ˌmɑdɚn ˈɑrt/
museum night /myuˈziəm naɪt/
street art /ˈstrit ɑrt/

Types of houses and developments

Freedom Ship /ˈfridəm ʃɪp/
dorms/residence hall /dɔrmz/ˈrɛzədəns hɔl/

EXTRA ACTIVITIES
- Photocopiable resource 19 (determiners – 15 mins) MultiROM and ActiveTeach

WORKBOOK
p. 45

NEXT CLASS
- Ask students to study the Word list on pp. 62–63.
- Ask students to review for Focus review 3.

housing estate/(co-)housing development /ˈhaʊzɪŋ ɪˌsteɪt/(koʊ)ˌhaʊzɪŋ dɪˈvɛləpmənt/
residential area /ˌrɛzəˈdɛnʃəl ˌɛriə/
second home /ˌsɛkənd ˈhoʊm/
single-family apartment/house /ˌsɪŋgəl fæmli əˈpɑrtˀmənt/ˈhaʊs/
smart house/home /ˈsmɑrt ˌhaʊs/ˌhoʊm/
tall/ten-storey building /ˌtɔl/ˌtɛn ˌstɔri ˈbɪldɪŋ/

Looking for/sharing accommodations

afford sth /əˈfɔrd sʌmθɪŋ/
affordable /əˈfɔrdəbəl/
bill /bɪl/
campus /ˈkæmpəs/
communal house/meal/kitchen /ˌkəˈmyunl ˈhaʊs/ˈmil/ˈkɪtʃən/
communal way of living /ˌkəˈmyunl ˌweɪ əv ˈlɪvɪŋ/
compromise (n, v) /ˈkɑmprəˌmaɪz/
convenient /kənˈvinyənt/
daily commute /ˌdeɪli kəˈmyut/
decoration /ˌdɛkəˈreɪʃən/
domestic chores /dəˌmɛstɪk ˈtʃɔrz/
hometown /ˌhoʊmˈtaʊn/
included in the rental price /ɪnˌkludɪd ɪn ðə ˈrɛntl ˌpraɪs/
kitchen/cooking facilities /ˈkɪtʃən/ˈkʊkɪŋ fəˌsɪləṭiz/
laundry /ˈlɔndri/
living space /ˈlɪvɪŋ speɪs/
located /ˈloʊkeɪtɪd/
location /loʊˈkeɪʃən/
maintain order /meɪnˌteɪn ˈɔrdɚ/
messy /ˈmɛsi/
neighborly relations /ˌneɪbɚli rɪˈleɪʃənz/
noisy /ˈnɔɪzi/
on each floor /ɑn ˌitʃ ˈflɔr/
privacy /ˈpraɪvəsi/
provide accommodations /prəˌvaɪd əˌkɑməˈdeɪʃənz/
rent (v, n) /rɛnt/
resident /ˈrɛzədənt/
resident advisor /rɛzədənt ədˈvaɪzɚ/
run-down/respectable neighborhood /ˌrʌn daʊn/rɪˌspɛktəbəl ˈneɪbɚhʊd/
safe /seɪf/
security /sɪˈkyʊrəṭi/
sense of community /ˌsɛns əv kəˈmyunəṭi/
share a bedroom/apartment /ˌʃɛr ə ˈbɛdrum/əˈpɑrtˀmənt/
shared (fridge/bathroom) /ˌʃɛrd (ˈfrɪdʒ/ˈbæθrum)/
share/split the cost /ʃɛr/ˌsplɪt ðə ˈkɔst/
size /saɪz/
slob /slɑb/
unmade bed /ʌnˌmeɪd ˈbɛd/
within walking/biking distance of sth /wɪðˌɪn ˈwɔkɪŋ/ˈbaɪkɪŋ/ˌdɪstəns əv sʌmθɪŋ/

On board a space station

arrive on board /əˌraɪv ɑn ˈbɔrd/
astronaut /ˈæstrəˌnɔt/
at (100 mi) per hour /ət (ˌwʌn ˌhʌndrəd maɪlz) pər ˈaʊɚ/
at an altitude of ... /ət ən ˈæltəˌtud əv.../
attach /əˈtætʃ/
bathed in light /ˌbeɪðd ɪn ˈlaɪt/
bedtime schedule /ˈbɛdtaɪm ˌskɛdʒəl/
blinding light /ˌblaɪndɪŋ ˈlaɪt/
cabin /ˈkæbɪn/
circle /ˈsɚkəl/
communication system /kəˌmyunəˈkeɪʃən ˌsɪstəm/
cruising height /ˈkruzɪŋ ˌhaɪt/
daylight /ˈdeɪlaɪt/
disrupt the body clock /dɪsˌrʌpt ðə ˈbɑdi klɑk/
electrical power /ɪˌlɛktrɪkəl ˈpaʊɚ/
feeling of motion /ˌfilɪŋ əv ˈmoʊʃən/
globe /gloʊb/
gravity /ˈgrævəṭi/
ground /graʊnd/
heavens /ˈhɛvənz/
in mid-air /ɪn ˌmɪd ˈɛr/
in the night sky /ɪn ðə ˌnaɪt ˈskaɪ/
ISS (International Space Station) /ˌaɪ ɛs ˈɛs (ˌɪntɚˈnæʃənəl ˈspeɪs ˌsteɪʃən)/
lose muscle power/the sense of smell/taste /ˌluz ˈmʌsəl ˌpaʊɚ/ðə ˌsɛns əv ˈsmɛl/ˈteɪst/
mission controller /ˈmɪʃən kənˌtroʊlɚ/
on the horizon /ˌɑn ðə həˈraɪzən/
orbit (v, n) /ˈɔrbɪt/
panoramic view /ˌpænəˌræmɪk ˈvyu/
permanent crew /ˌpɚmənənt ˈkru/
power source /ˈpaʊɚ sɔrs/
put down the shutters /pʊt ˌdaʊn ðə ˈʃʌṭɚz/
reflect off sth /rɪˈflɛkt ɔf sʌmθɪŋ/
rise /raɪz/
shoot /ʃut/
sleeping bag /ˈslipɪŋ bæg/
solar panels /ˌsoʊlɚ ˈpænəlz/
spacewalk /ˈspeɪswɔk/
speed /spid/
transition /trænˈzɪʃən/
wandering star /ˌwɑndərɪŋ ˈstɑr/
weightlessness/weightless conditions /ˈweɪtləsnəs/ˌweɪtləs kənˈdɪʃənz/

Sea travel

chart the route /ˌtʃɑrt ðə ˈrut/
embark on a voyage /ɪmˌbɑrk ɑn ə ˈvɔɪɪdʒ/
sail /seɪl/
top of the line technology /ˌtɑp əv ðə ˌlaɪn tɛkˈnɑlədʒi/
travel down the coast of (Mexico) /ˌtrævəl daʊn ðə ˌkoʊst əv (ˈmɛksɪkoʊ)/
trip/voyage of a lifetime /ˌtrɪp/ˌvɔɪ-ɪdʒ əv ə ˈlaɪftaɪm/

Phrasal verbs

get down to (work) /ˌgɛt ˈdaʊn tə (wɚk)/
hold onto /ˌhoʊld ˈɑntə/
look out for /ˌlʊk ˈaʊt fɚ/
look up to /ˌlʊk ˈʌp tə/
rely on /rɪˈlaɪ ɑn/
settle down /ˌsɛṭl ˈdaʊn/
snooze /snuz/
soak up /ˌsoʊk ˈʌp/
start out /ˌstɑrt ˈaʊt/

Other

alarm clock /əˈlɑrm klɑk/
at least /ˌət ˈlist/
back to back /ˌbæk tə ˈbæk/
balance /ˈbæləns/
be in a hurry /ˌbi ɪn ə ˈhʌri/
be in awe of sth /ˌbi ɪn ˈɔ əv sʌmθɪŋ/
be made up of sth /ˌbi meɪd ˈʌp əv sʌmθɪŋ/
bother /ˈbɑðɚ/
cardboard /ˈkɑrdbɔrd/
coppery /ˈkɑpəri/
disposable /dɪˈspoʊzəbəl/
dispose /dɪˈspoʊz/
downside/drawback/minus /ˈdaʊnsaɪd/ˈdrɔbæk/ˈmaɪnəs/
face to face /ˌfeɪs tə ˈfeɪs/
feature /ˈfitʃɚ/
gain experience /ˌgeɪn ɪkˈspɪriəns/
impose /ɪmˈpoʊz/
in time /ˌɪn ˈtaɪm/
interfere /ˌɪntɚˈfɪr/
investment opportunity /ɪnˈvɛstmənt ɑpɚˈtunəṭi/
moist wipes /ˌmɔɪst ˈwaɪps/
offset/balanced by sth /ˈɔfsɛt/ˈbælənst baɪ/
on the outside /ˌɑn ði aʊtˈsaɪd/
persuasive /pɚˈsweɪsɪv/
plain/exotic food /ˌpleɪn/ɪgˌzɑṭɪk ˈfud/
prevent /prɪˈvɛnt/
profit /ˈprɑfɪt/
profitable /ˈprɑfɪṭəbəl/
reassuring /ˌriəˈʃʊrɪŋ/
respect /rɪˈspɛkt/
self-disciplined /ˌsɛlf ˈdɪsəplɪnd/
sensation /sɛnˈseɪʃən/
sense /sɛns/
splash /splæʃ/
stale /steɪl/
suit /sut/
suitable /ˈsuṭəbəl/
sustain /səˈsteɪn/
sustainable /səˈsteɪnəbəl/
take your breath away /ˌteɪk yɚ ˈbrɛθ əˌweɪ/
to be honest /tə bi ˈɑnɪst/
trash bag /ˈtræʃ bæg/
tricky /ˈtrɪki/
upside/benefit/plus /ˈʌpsaɪd/ˈbɛnəfɪt/ˈplʌs/
wet /wɛt/

FOCUS REVIEW 3

VOCABULARY AND GRAMMAR

1 Complete the sentences with the correct form of the words in capitals.

1 There isn't enough affordable housing, so many young people live with their parents. **AFFORD**
2 I live in a vast, sprawling city with a huge population but I'd much prefer to live somewhere more compact. **SPRAWL**
3 When I was nine, we moved into a new house in a peaceful, respectable neighborhood in Los Angeles. **RESPECT**
4 Most iconic sights are located in the old town, but other parts of the town are also worth a visit. **ICON**
5 My grandparents live in a leafy neighborhood in the suburbs. **LEAF**
6 Some residential areas are in remote places, which makes commuting difficult. **RESIDENT**

2 Complete the sentences with prepositions.

1 If you're interested in historic sites, this region is what you are looking for – it's steeped in history.
2 I've always been in awe of those who put their own lives at risk to help others.
3 During the carnival, Venice gets packed with tourists.
4 In the newly built blocks of apartments, there are only two large apartments on each floor.
5 It's not the cheapest apartment to rent, but the cost is offset by its location.

3 Complete the sentences with the correct future form of the verbs in parentheses.

1 They're so excited. This time next week they will be moving (move) into their new home.
2 How many more places do you want to view today? By lunchtime we will have viewed (view) six apartments!
3 Will you be putting (you/put) in new bathroom fittings next weekend?
4 I hope that by the time Olivia starts living on her own, she will have learned (learn) to cook.
5 I'm truly exhausted. By next week I will have been renovating (renovate) our house for a month.
6 By tomorrow the plumber will have fixed (fix) the dripping faucet.

4 Choose the correct options.

1 I've asked five or six people to help me move. Unfortunately, *no* / *none* / *neither* of them will have enough time tomorrow. [circled: none]
2 In the old days, students at this boarding school were allowed to go home *every* / *each* / *whole* three weeks. [circled: every]
3 I'm sure we had two new light bulbs. But now, when I need them, I can't find *either* / *both* / *all* of them. [circled: either]
4 Having done some renovations on her apartment, Jane spent *all the* / *most* / *the whole* week trying to clean up the mess. [circled: the whole]
5 I've noticed that *a great deal* / *a number* / *a couple* of furniture has been delivered next door. [circled: a great deal]
6 There's only *a few* / *a little* / *a couple of* paint left. Do you think it will be enough? [circled: a little]

Exercise 6
1 Rob will have designed a new
2 taking out / having taken out a loan
3 every one of my friends
4 in spite of being
5 a great deal of accommodation
6 we will be painting the walls

LANGUAGE IN USE

5 Complete the text with one word in each blank.

BRITAIN'S NEW TOWNS

At the end of the nineteenth century, Sir Ebenezer Howard became renowned [1] for what he called 'garden cities': self-contained communities surrounded by a 'green belt' that would provide the best of city and country living. They were thought to be the answer [2] to the overcrowding and industrial pollution of Victorian cities. Letchworth and Welwyn Garden City were the only two towns in the UK based on his vision. For various reasons, no [3] other/more garden cities were built.

After World War II, the provision of inexpensive housing surrounded by green spaces [4] within a short distance of larger industrial towns became an urgent matter. In 1945 the British government created the New Towns Committee, [5] whose aim was to investigate the possibility of building new, fully planned, self-sufficient towns. The last of these was Milton Keynes, which was formally designated in 1967.

And now, more than a century after Howard's manifesto, Britain is again facing a housing crisis. According to current demographic trends, by 2050 at least another ten million people will [6] have moved to Britain. It means that six million houses should be built to satisfy the most pressing housing needs.

6 Complete the sentences with no more than six words in each blank. Use the correct form of the words in parentheses and add any other words necessary.

1 By Saturday, ________ (Rob/design/new) kitchen for us.
2 Despite ________ (take out/loan), they still don't have enough money to renovate their house.
3 I asked ________ (every/one/friend) to put me up for the night, but none of them were able to do so.
4 This house has been for sale for a year now, ________ (spite/be) relatively cheap.
5 There is ________ (deal/accommodation) for rent, but you have to start looking a while before the academic year begins.
6 Don't call tomorrow afternoon because ________ (we/paint/walls) in my parents' house all day.

64

EXTRA ACTIVITIES
• Photocopiable resource 57A (fill in the blanks – 20 mins) MultiROM and ActiveTeach
• Photocopiable resource 61A (sentence formation – 12 mins) MultiROM and ActiveTeach
• Photocopiable resource 20 (Speaking – 15 mins) MultiROM and ActiveTeach
• Photocopiable resource 21 (Writing – 15 mins) MultiROM and ActiveTeach

WORKBOOK
Use of English 3.9, pp. 46–47; Self-assessment 3.10, p. 48

READING

7 Read the article. Are the statements true (T) or false (F)?

A MODERN CAVEMAN

People have dwelt in caves since the dawn of time. But if you're picturing a cold, damp, and cramped space, you'll need to think again. In Spain there are literally thousands of modern day cave-dwellers who call a hole in the ground their home, and there are a large number of luxurious houses carved into the Andalucian mountains that offer more comfort than you might imagine.

Why choose to live in a cave? To begin with, cave houses are affordable, easy to heat in the winter, and cool in the summer. Because they are carved into stone, their temperature does not fluctuate much, but rather a steady seventy degrees Fahrenheit is maintained throughout the year. Each home is unique and, if you purchase a property that is licensed to be modified, it's easy enough to carve yourself out an extra shelf in the wall or even a whole new room. The largest cave home boasts as many as forty rooms and can be had for as little as 230,000 dollars.

You don't need such a vast, sprawling cavern to feel the charm of a cave home, however. Even those of a much more modest size seem surprisingly open – there is no sense of being underground or feeling cooped up. Cave houses exude a warmth and cosiness that is a unique selling point for many buyers: sound is gently muffled and the amount of light seems to defy common logic. Most cave homes face southward to allow for natural light to enter through the windows cut into the rock face. But due to the ingenious layout of many homes and the white matte of the walls, light is easily transmitted throughout. In areas further back, modern builders often use a system of ordinary mirrors to reflect natural light around the interior.

Cave dwelling is also surprisingly safe. They are not prone to fires or earthquakes, and they do not tend to collapse. Ventilation is important, however, since a cave home needs to breathe. Excess moisture can become problematic and in extreme cases even trigger asthma attacks. Electricity is generally preferred over gas – although when gas fittings are provided, these tend to be closer to the front of the cave for safety reasons.

As cave communities tend to be in small villages, a car is essential for getting around and nightlife is hard to find. Such homes are very much for those who prefer a quiet rural lifestyle, quaint cobbled backstreets, and breathtaking views.

1 Cave homes tend to meet people's initial expectations of living in a cave. F
2 A cave home might be a good purchase for the economically minded. T
3 Every cave home can be adapted by the owner to suit their own tastes. F
4 Owners typically enjoy the unique ambience and interior design of cave homes. T
5 Sophisticated modern technology is used to light the deeper parts of cave homes. F
6 Natural disasters are a common hazard of living in a cave house. F
7 The article suggests everyone would enjoy living in a cave home. F

SPEAKING

8 With a partner, complete the speaking task.

Here are some things people sometimes have problems with when they move to a big town or city, and a question for you to discuss. Talk to each other about why these things can cause problems.

Why can these things cause problems when people move to a big town or city?

- traveling around
- making new friends
- leisure activities
- stores and prices
- noise and pollution

Now talk about which of these things is most difficult for people to do in a big town or city.

9 With a partner, discuss the questions.

1 Would you prefer to live in a town, a city, or the country? Why?
2 Do you think it's a good idea for children to live and study in cities? Why?/Why not?
3 Some cities attract a lot of tourists. Do you think this is a good thing for the people who live there? Why?/Why not?
4 How important is it to keep old, traditional buildings in our cities and towns and not tear them down? Why?
5 Which city in the world would you like to live in for a short time? Why?

WRITING

10 Complete the writing task.

In your English class you have been talking about life in a big city. Now your English teacher has asked you to write an essay. Write an essay using **all** the notes and give reasons for your point of view.

What are the advantages and disadvantages of moving from the center of the city to the suburbs?

Notes
Write about:
- socializing and free time activities
- work or study
- ______ (your own idea)

Write your essay in 140–190 words.

NEXT CLASS

- Ask students to do Self-check 3.11, WB p. 49 as homework.
- Ask students to prepare for Unit test 3 (*Focus* Assessment Package).

4 THE COST OF LIVING

Neither a borrower nor a lender be.

SHAKESPEARE – HAMLET

UNIT LANGUAGE AND SKILLS

Vocabulary:
- *Show what you know* – stores
- phrasal verbs – shopping and money
- money idioms
- collocations – buying and selling
- collocations
- word families
- *Word in focus* – *of*

Grammar:
- question tags and reply questions
- present and past modal structures

Listening:
- an interview about market trading
- multiple choice

Reading:
- texts about jeans
- multiple matching

Speaking:
- making and justifying choices

Writing:
- a formal email

FOCUS EXTRA

- Grammar Focus pages 167–168
- WORD STORE booklet pages 8–9
- Workbook pages 50–63 or MyEnglishLab
- MP3s – www.english.com/focus

4.1 Vocabulary

Shopping and money • Phrasal verbs • Collocations • Money idioms

I can talk about shopping and money.

SHOW WHAT YOU KNOW

1 **Put the list of stores in order from 1 (= I go in here a lot) to 12 (= I never go in here). Add any other stores you go to.**

bakery ☐ bookstore ☐ butcher's ☐
department store ☐ florist's ☐ grocery store ☐
hardware store ☐ jeweler's ☐ newsstand ☐
pet store ☐ pharmacy ☐ thrift store ☐

2 **SPEAKING** **With a partner, compare your lists. Then name your top three favorite stores and say why you like them.**

3 **Read the article. Where would you go to:**

a improve your skin? *Dr. Fish Spa*
b take sewing lessons? *Junk Shop UK*
c stroke a pet? *Cat Café*
d buy something that is very healthy? *Molecule Water Café*

COOL PLACES

A recent survey suggests that young people have lost interest in shopping malls, finding the stores overpriced and boring. Instead, they don't mind shopping around for new, fun, and exciting shopping experiences. Here are a few of the trendy and quirky shops and cafés that have opened around the world, hoping to attract young customers.

1 CAT CAFÉ, Tokyo

Japanese people love animals, but pets are often forbidden by landlords. The solution: cafés where customers pay an hourly fee to hang out in a room full of cats. In Cat Café more than a dozen cats of all shapes, sizes, and colors sit on the counter and curl up on customers' laps. Cat Café is a chain of cafés in Japan; there are about forty branches in Tokyo alone.

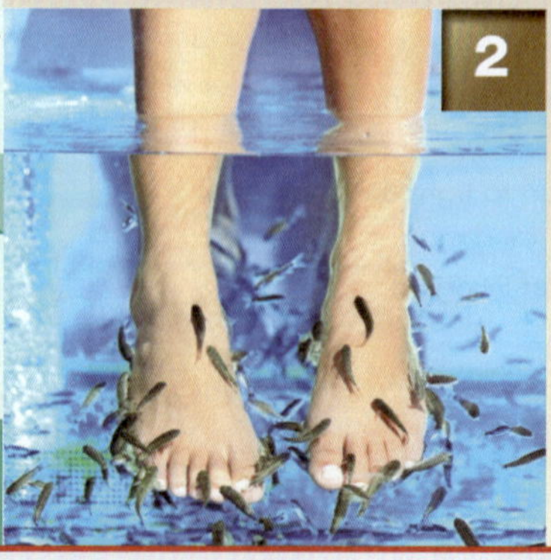

2 DR. FISH SPA, Istanbul

When your feet are tired from all that shopping, how about treating yourself to a fish pedicure? You sit with your feet in a tankful of Garra Rufa fish, often called 'doctor fish'. The tiny fish nibble away the dry skin from your feet, leaving your skin soft and healthy. You'll pay $15 for fifteen minutes but some places will **knock** a few dollars **off** the price if you bring one or two friends. We don't recommend it if you're ticklish!

EXTRA ACTIVITIES
- Photocopiable resource 22 (money and shopping – 12 mins) MultiROM and ActiveTeach
- Photocopiable resource 25 (Test yourself partner work activities) MultiROM and ActiveTeach
- MyEnglishLab – assignable *Show what you have learned* mini-test

WORKBOOK
pp. 50–51

NEXT CLASS
- Ask students to prepare for a 10–15 minute vocabulary quiz: *Focus* Assessment Package, Unit 4.1, Vocabulary.

4 **Read the article again and match comments a–g with places 1–4. Which comments do you agree with?**

a 'I had my first fish pedicure and I didn't have to pay through the nose for it. It only cost $15.' [2]

b 'This place is for people who have money to burn. It's ridiculous to pay for something you can get out of a faucet for free! They're **ripping** people **off**!' [4]

c 'I don't understand this craze for vintage fashion. They're making a fortune out of old junk!' [3]

d 'This sounds disgusting! Anyway, I'm broke, so I'm not **forking out** $15 to have my skin eaten by fish!' [2]

e 'They've uncovered a niche market – clearly it's for affluent, health-conscious New Yorkers who are not struggling to make ends meet.' [4]

f 'These clothes are a bargain – they don't cost an arm and a leg and they're fun.' [3]

g 'I can't imagine anything worse – having to send my coffee back because it has cat hairs in it!' [1]

5 **What's the best, worst, or most unusual shopping experience you've ever had?**

TO HANG OUT IN TOWN

3 JUNK SHOP UK, Manchester

Junk Shop UK is the place to **snap up** a bargain from a range of vintage jewelry and sustainable fashion. This unusual boutique was set up to fill a gap in the market for fun, original, and, most importantly, affordable clothes. They don't only sell unique vintage pieces – they have recently **brought out** their own labels. You can also sign up for dressmaking courses, which don't cost a fortune.

4 MOLECULE WATER CAFÉ, New York

The range of products on sale in this fashionable New York café is somewhat limited: the only drink customers will be sipping here is filtered water costing $2.50 a bottle. Molecule Water Café claims to filter water to its purest form before selling it to customers. To keep costs down, you can fill up your own bottle for a discounted price, and then you can **splash out on** some extras like vitamin A, electrolytes, calcium, and magnesium.

Go to **WORD STORE 4** page 9.

WORD STORE 4A

6 CD•2.15 MP3•54 **Complete WORD STORE 4A with the base form of the phrasal verbs in red in the article and Exercise 4. Then listen, check, and repeat.**

7 **Replace the underlined phrases with phrasal verbs from WORD STORE 4A.**

1 Why are young people looking in different places for new shopping experiences?
2 How can you reduce the price of your fish pedicure?
3 Where can you find and immediately buy a bargain?
4 What new items has Junk Shop UK released recently?
5 What extras can you spend a lot of money on in Molecule Water Café?
6 Which place is cheating their customers?
7 Why is one person unwilling to spend $15 on a fish pedicure?

Exercise 7
1 shopping around
2 knock money off
3 snap up
4 brought out
5 splash out on
6 ripping off
7 fork out

8 **Read the article and comments in Exercise 4 again and answer the questions in Exercise 7.**

Exercise 8
1 Because they are bored with over-priced malls.
2 By bringing in one or two friends.
3 At the Junk Shop.
4 Clothes under their own labels.
5 Vitamin A, electrolytes, calcium, and magnesium.
6 The Water Café.
7 Because they are broke and they think it's disgusting.

WORD STORE 4B

9 CD•2.16 MP3•55 **Complete WORD STORE 4B with the underlined idioms in Exercise 4. Then listen, check, and repeat. Do you have similar idioms in your language?**

10 **Complete the idioms. Then, with a partner, discuss whether you agree or disagree with the statements.**

1 People pay through the _nose_ for popular brands of sneakers.
2 Most college students struggle to make ends _meet_ . Some end up in debt.
3 It costs an _arm_ and a leg to study English in the UK. Few people can afford it.
4 Football players are paid too much. They have money to _burn_ .
5 It's better to be _poor_ and happy than rich and unhappy.

WORD STORE 4C

11 CD•2.17 MP3•56 **Complete WORD STORE 4C with nouns from the highlighted collocations in the article and Exercise 4. Then listen, check, and repeat.**

12 **Complete the questions for a supermarket survey with collocations from WORD STORE 4C. Then, with a partner, ask and answer the questions.**

Supermarket survey
1 What's the biggest _____ in your country?
2 What kind of advertising do supermarkets do to _____ ?
3 Which supermarket has the lowest _____ ?
4 Which supermarket stocks the widest _____ ?
5 Would a new supermarket fill a _____ in your area?

Exercise 12
1 chain of supermarkets
2 attract customers
3 discounted prices
4 range of products
5 gap in the market

WORD STORE 4D

13 CD•2.18 MP3•57 **Complete WORD STORE 4D with more verb-noun collocations. Then listen, check, and repeat. Write example sentences.**

67

4.2 Grammar

Question tags and reply questions

I can use question tags and reply questions.

1 CD•2.19 MP3•58 **Listen to a conversation between Laura and her mom. What is Laura's mom concerned about?** *Buying tickets online. The fact that Laura is wearing her earrings. Jamie driving.*

2 CD•2.19 MP3•58 **Read GRAMMAR FOCUS I and complete the examples from the conversation with auxiliary verbs. Then listen again and check.**

GRAMMAR FOCUS I

Question tags

You form question tags with an auxiliary/modal verb + a pronoun.

Positive statement + negative tag

I'm always careful when I borrow your things, [1] *aren't* *I?*

You know it's risky buying tickets online, [2] *don't* *you?*

Negative statement + positive tag

He hasn't passed his driving test, [3] *has* *he?*

But you never wear them, [4] *do* *you?*

Note: Pay attention to these special cases:

Don't lose them, [5] *will* *you?*

That's Jamie at the door, ***isn't it****?*

Everybody had a good time, ***didn't they****?*

Let's go, ***shall we****?*

Nothing happened, ***did it****?*

3 CD•2.20 MP3•59 **Complete the conversation between Laura and Jamie with appropriate question tags. Then listen and check. What was Laura concerned about?**

Laura: This is the place he told you to meet him, [1] *isn't it*?

Jamie: Yes, it is. He said he'd be waiting at the main entrance.

Laura: Did he? So why are we waiting at the staff entrance?

Jamie: Oh no, you're right! Come on, we'd better hurry.

Laura: Let's call him, [2] *shall we*? I'm sure he'll wait ten minutes. You took his phone number, [3] *didn't you*?

Jamie: No, but he's got mine. If he's wondering where we are, he'll call me, [4] *won't he*?

Laura: Yes – I suppose he wants his cash. Don't lose it, [5] *will you*?

Jamie: What cash?

Laura: For the tickets! You haven't paid him yet, [6] *have you*?

Jamie: Yes, I have – I transferred the money to his account online.

Laura: Did you? Oh – hey, that's him over there, [7] *isn't it*?

Jamie: Is it? How do you know?

Laura: He's holding up a piece of paper with your name on it.

4 CD•2.21 MP3•60 **Complete some things Jamie said at the concert with question tags. Then listen, check, and answer the questions.**

1 We can go in now, *can't we*? ↗
2 There's an opening band on first, *isn't there*? ↘
3 This is a great concert, *isn't it*? ↘
4 Beyoncé toured last year, *didn't she*? ↗
5 Don't forget where we're sitting, *will you*? ↘
6 Excuse me, nobody's seen a silver earring, *have they*? ↗

- Which tags have a rising intonation (↗) and show you expect the listener to answer your question?
- Which tags have a falling intonation (↘) and show you expect the listener to agree with you?

REFERENCES

AUDIO SCRIPT ››› *p. 205*

EXTRA ACTIVITIES

- Photocopiable resource 23 (question tags – 10 mins) MultiROM and ActiveTeach
- MyEnglishLab – assignable *Show what you have learned* mini-test

WORKBOOK

p. 52

NEXT CLASS

- Ask students to prepare for a 10–15 minute grammar quiz: *Focus* Assessment Package, Unit 4.2, Grammar.

5 **Read GRAMMAR FOCUS II. Find three reply questions in the conversation in Exercise 3.**

Did he?
Did you?
Is it?

GRAMMAR FOCUS II

Reply questions

You use reply questions to react to what somebody has said and to show interest. They usually have rising intonation.

Positive statement + positive reply question

'We're going to a concert.' ***'Are you?'*** ↗

Negative statement + negative reply question

'Beyoncé hasn't played here before.' ***'Hasn't she?'*** ↗

6 **Write true sentences about yourself. Then, with a partner, take turns to read your sentences to your partner for him/her to respond with a reply question.**

1 I / need / a new phone
A: *I don't need a new phone.*
B: *Don't you?*
2 my dad / give / me money for my last birthday
3 I / go / shopping recently
4 I / think / I'm a very lucky person
5 my mom / usually / do / the shopping online
6 I / have / a credit card

Exercise 6
Students' own answers/
Suggested answers
2 My dad gave me money for my last birthday. – Did he?
3 I went shopping recently. – Did you?
4 I think I'm a very lucky person. – Do you?
5 My mom usually does the shopping online. – Does she?
6 I have a credit card. – Do you?

7 **Write four more true sentences about yourself. Then, with a partner, take turns to read them to your partner for him/her to respond with a reply question.**

A: *I'm saving up to buy a new laptop.*
B: *Are you?*

8 SPEAKING **You are going to write a conversation between a teenager and a parent. With a partner, follow the instructions.**

- Think of a situation. Choose from the box or use your own ideas.

  The teenager wants to:

form a band   get a tongue piercing
give up a sport or a musical instrument
get more allowance
go to a music festival
go abroad with friends
open a bank account

- Include at least five different question tags and/or reply questions in the conversation.
- Practice your conversation and then act it out.

Grammar Focus page 167

4.3 Listening

Multiple choice

I can understand specific details in an interview.

1 **SPEAKING With a partner, read *TODAY IN THE USA* and discuss the questions.**

1 Do you have similar types of market in your nearest town or city?
2 When did you last go to a market? What did you buy there?
3 What sort of pre-owned goods would or wouldn't you buy?

TODAY IN THE USA

Where do American people go to buy and sell second-hand/pre-owned goods?

- **Flea markets** – The Rose Bowl Flea Market is one of the biggest ones in California. Vendors there sell second-hand clothes as well as furniture, jewelry, and all kinds of merchandise.
- **Garage and yard sales** – Every weekend thousands of people take their unwanted domestic clutter out to their garage, driveway, or front yard. One person's junk is another person's treasure.
- **Online auctions** – More than 17 million people log on to sites like eBay each month to bid for a bargain.
- **Antique markets** – Across the country, antique markets and shows specialize in buying and selling antique and old-fashioned furnishings, ornaments, and bric-a-brac.

2 **SPEAKING Have you ever been to an auction or bid for something online? Discuss with a partner.**

3 CD•2.22 MP3•61 **Listen to an interview. What does Martin do for a living?**

Martin buys lost luggage and sells the contents on his market stall.

REFERENCES
CULTURE NOTES ››› p. 195
AUDIO SCRIPT ››› p. 206
WORKBOOK
p. 53

EXAM FOCUS Multiple choice

4 CD•2.22 MP3•61 **Listen again and choose the correct answer, A, B, or C.**

1 In this episode the interviewer wants to focus on the
   A increased size of the markets that sell second-hand goods.
   B increased earnings of people involved in second-hand selling.
   (C) increased interest in buying second-hand goods.

2 How does Martin get hold of the second-hand goods he sells?
   A He buys them from the owners.
   (B) He gets them at a special sale.
   C He claims them from the airport.

3 What kind of things can Martin find in the suitcases he buys?
   (A) designer clothes
   B electrical goods
   C rotten food

4 The thing that surprises Martin most is that people
   A check in bags in advance.
   (B) forget something important.
   C come to the airport at the last minute.

5 What is Martin most likely to say about the way he earns his living?
   A 'It makes me feel sad.'
   (B) 'It's just a way to earn a living.'
   C 'It's very strange.'

5 Complete the sentences with the words in the box. Then number the sentences in the correct order to explain what can happen to lost luggage at an airport.

auction auctioneers bad belongings
bid checked high lost stall unclaimed

1 Auctioneers throw away things that have gone bad . 3
2 Unclaimed bags go for auction at the auction house. 2
3 Personal belongings from lost luggage end up on a market stall . 5
4 Checked bags get lost at the airport. 1
5 Market stallholders bid for high quality bags. 4

PRONUNCIATION FOCUS

6 CD•2.23 MP3•62 **Listen and repeat the words in the box. Then put them in the correct column depending on the vowel sound.**

~~auction~~ boot bought cotton goods
lose market put rotten stall through

1 /ɔ/	2 /ɑ/	3 /u/	4 /ʊ/
auction	market	boot	could
bought	rotten	lose	goods
stall	cotton	through	put

7 CD•2.24 MP3•63 **Listen, check, and repeat.**

WORD STORE 4E

8 CD•2.25 MP3•64 **Complete WORD STORE 4E. Add the adjectives in the box to complete the collocations. Then listen, check, and repeat. Check the meaning of the other collocations.**

4.4 Reading

Multiple matching

I can find specific details in short texts.

1 CD•2.26 MP3•65 **SPEAKING With a partner, discuss whether you think these 'jean facts' are true (T) or false (F). Then read and listen to *Jeaneology* and check your ideas.**

1 'Denim' and 'jeans' are named after two European cities. T
2 Blue jeans were invented in Germany. F
3 Jeans were mainly worn by cowboys until World War II. T
4 During the 50s and 60s jeans were accepted by mainstream society. F
5 Every American owns about seven pairs of jeans. T

Jeaneology

1800s	Denim was a kind of cotton made in Nîmes ('de Nimes'). The first blue denim jeans were worn by sailors in Genoa – 'Genes' in French. 'Bleu de Genes' became 'blue jeans'.
1850s	Blue jeans as we know them originated during the 1849 Californian Gold Rush. German storekeeper Levi Strauss and Latvian tailor Jacob Davis developed a stronger design using copper rivets.
1930s and 40s	At first jeans were only popular in the western US and worn by cowboys. Their popularity spread after World War II.
1950s and 60s	Young people started wearing jeans to imitate young Hollywood stars like James Dean. But jeans became associated with rebellious behavior and were banned in schools.
2000s	Today jeans are worn by everyone. Every American owns, on average, seven pairs of jeans!

2 **SPEAKING Label the pictures with the words in the box. Then discuss the questions with a partner.**

[baggy ~~bootcut~~ cropped distressed flared skinny straight-leg]

A bootcut B flared C baggy D straight-leg E distressed F cropped G skinny

1 What style of jeans do you like best?
2 When do you wear jeans and when don't you wear jeans?
3 Where can you buy the cheapest/most expensive jeans in your city?

EXAM FOCUS Multiple matching

3 **Read the texts about jeans. For questions 1–8, choose from the texts (A–D). You can choose each text more than once.**

Which text mentions that:

1 jeans can cause health problems for the people making them? B
2 some people think it's worth paying extra for traditionally-made jeans? A
3 a lot of water is wasted in the after-care of jeans? D
4 the fabric of the jeans can make a difference to the health of the wearer? C
5 we need to change our habits to make our jeans last a long time? D
6 most countries today use modern methods of denim production? A
7 new ways of fading jeans require the use of unnatural substances? B
8 people should avoid a particular type of jeans? C

4 **Add the nouns in the box to the lists to make collocations from the texts.**

[cloth colors dyes jeans methods (of production)]

1 dense/mass-produced/stiff cloth
2 deep/intense/rich colors
3 labor-intensive/modern/traditional methods (of production)
4 chemical/toxic/natural dyes
5 affordable/fashionable/hard-wearing jeans

REFERENCES
CULTURE NOTES ››› pp. 195–196

EXTRA ACTIVITIES
• Photocopiable resource 24 (word formation – 8 mins) MultiROM and ActiveTeach

WORKBOOK
pp. 54–55

NEXT CLASS
• Find an interesting article online about how fashion has changed over time.

CD•2.27 MP3•66

A

Japanese denim has a reputation among enthusiasts as being the best in the world. It has a cult following in Europe and America because of its amazing look and feel. The cloth is stiffer, denser, but far more comfortable than the mass-produced denim used in other countries. Japanese denim is different because they use traditional production techniques that have been abandoned elsewhere. Most denim today is produced using chemical dye, but Japanese denim uses natural dye and the material is dipped up to thirty times to produce a deep, intense, and rich color that fades with time. These traditional methods are more labor-intensive, which makes the product more expensive, but Tokyo's trendsetters are willing to splash out on the perfect pair of jeans.

B

We're hooked on jeans! In the UK alone, three pairs are sold every second of every day. But recently, modern methods of production have been causing environmental concerns. Demand for jeans has increased so much that cotton farmers have to rely more and more on pesticides and fertilizers to raise their crops. Traditionally, jeans were dyed with a natural indigo dye. Nowadays, though, the dye is chemical and toxic, and even more chemicals are used to give the denim a vintage appearance. Distressed jeans are increasingly popular, and to achieve this look, the jeans are blasted with sand.

Factory workers complained of breathing problems and as a result, some brands of jeans have banned the process. Another issue is that it takes 1,600 gallons of water to produce one pair of jeans. Jeans are fashionable, affordable, and hard-wearing, but at what cost to the environment?

C

Recent reports have suggested that skinny jeans enthusiasts may be damaging their health. Wearing jeans that are too tight could compress a major nerve on the outside of your thigh. This can lead to pain or loss of feeling in your legs. In most cases, the nerve damage can be reversed simply by taking the tight jeans off. Jeans that are tight around the waist can also make it difficult to digest your food. Health experts are urging young people who are committed to the skinny jeans look to choose a pair that have some stretch in them and are less likely to have a negative effect on the body. If you notice a strange sensation in your legs, it may be time to change your style.

D

So, you've got that top quality pair of jeans you wanted. How can you keep them looking good and stop them from fading? Well, maybe you're washing them too often. The CEO of Levi's caused a stir when he mentioned in public that he hadn't washed his jeans for over a year! He wanted to show how we can help the environment by using less water. Apparently, by washing our jeans in the machine once a week for two years, we use over 900 gallons of water. His view is supported by other professionals who believe that it isn't necessary to wash jeans very often because the material is thick and it's the top of our bodies that sweats and makes clothes smelly, not the bottom! So, to help the environment and also keep our jeans looking good, wash less frequently, soak in cold salt water, turn them inside out and don't dry in sunlight. Oh, yes, and you could wash them in vinegar.

5 Read the texts again and answer the questions. Give reasons for your answers.

1 What effect do Japanese production techniques have on:
   a the color of the denim?
   b the cost of the denim?

2 Why are these products used in modern methods of production?
   a chemicals
   b sand

3 In what ways can skinny jeans have a harmful effect on:
   a your legs?
   b your digestive system?

4 What can we do to
   a help the environment?
   b keep our jeans looking good?

Exercise 5

1 a a deep rich color that fades with time
b more expensive because it's more labor-intensive

2 a used in the dyes to get a vintage look
b used to artificially age the material

3 a loss of feeling by compressing a major nerve on your thigh
b pressure on your stomach making it difficult to digest

4 a use less water by washing our jeans less
b wash less frequently, soak in cold salt water, turn them inside out, and don't dry in the sunlight. You can also wash them in vinegar!

WORD STORE 4F

6 CD•2.28 MP3•67 **Complete WORD STORE 4F with nouns and adjectives from the texts. Mark the stress. Then listen, check, and repeat.**

4.5 Grammar

Present and past modal structures

I can give advice, criticize past actions and talk about past necessity.

1 CD•2.29 MP3•68 **Listen to James talking to his sister Ellie. What is James' problem?**
He hasn't got a present for his girlfriend's birthday yet and doesn't know what to get.

Exercise 2
1 shouldn't – size problems
2 don't need to – doesn't have the same 'meaning' as a ring
3 ought not – in case you split up
4 mustn't – bad idea – teenagers and moms wear different perfumes
5 had better – they know exactly what she likes

2 CD•2.29 MP3•68 **Listen again and choose the advice that Ellie gives. What reasons does she give?**

1 You *shouldn't* / *should* buy her clothes.
2 With a bracelet you *need to* / *don't need to* worry about giving the wrong message.
3 You *ought to* / *ought not to* get her tickets in advance.
4 You *mustn't* / *must* buy her the same perfume as Mom.
5 You *had better* / *had better not* ask her friends for advice.

3 **With a partner, complete the advice with the affirmative or negative form of the verbs in parentheses. Then discuss whether you agree with the advice.**

1 You *shouldn't* (should) leave present buying till the last minute.
2 You *ought not to* (ought to) buy a present unless you are sure about it.
3 You *mustn't* (must) give your credit card details to a stranger.
4 You *need to* (need to) check if you can take the item back.
5 You *had better* (had better) remember your dad's birthday this year!

4 CD•2.30 MP3•69 **Read and listen to a second conversation between James and Ellie. Did James choose a good birthday present for his girlfriend?** *No*

Ellie: How was the birthday?
James: Oh, kind of a disaster, actually. **I should have listened** to your advice, but I didn't. I got a bracelet. I thought it was such a bargain – $25 for a gold bracelet. **I ought to have asked** if it was real gold.
Ellie: You should have realized you couldn't get real gold for $25. But anyway, didn't she like it?
James: She's allergic to metal – she can only wear real gold. She put it on and got a big rash on her arm. And **we had to go** to the doctor's.
Ellie: Oh dear! Did you have to take the bracelet back?
James: Yes, but **I shouldn't have bothered**. They refused to exchange it because I didn't have the receipt. Here you are – you can have it.
Ellie: Oh, thanks!

74

REFERENCES
AUDIO SCRIPT ››› *pp. 206–207*

EXTRA ACTIVITIES
• Photocopiable resource 25 (Test yourself partner work activities) MultiROM and ActiveTeach
• MyEnglishLab – assignable *Show what you have learned* mini-test

WORKBOOK
p. 56

NEXT CLASS
• Ask students to prepare for a 10–15 minute grammar quiz: *Focus* Assessment Package, Unit 4.5, Grammar.

5 **Complete the GRAMMAR FOCUS with the past modal structures in blue in Exercise 4.**

GRAMMAR FOCUS

Past modal structures

- You can use ***should/shouldn't have* + past participle** or ***ought to/ought not to have* + past participle** to criticize a past action or show regret.

  I [1] should have listened *to your advice.*

  I [2] ought to have asked *if it was real gold.*

- You use ***had to/didn't have to* + infinitive** to say a past action was necessary/unnecessary.

  We [3] had to go *to the doctor's.*

- You can also use ***didn't need to* + infinitive** or ***shouldn't have* + past participle** to say a past action was unnecessary. There is a slight difference in meaning:

  I didn't need to bother = I didn't bother because it wasn't necessary.

  I [4] shouldn't have bothered = I bothered, but it wasn't necessary.

6 **Choose the correct meaning for the underlined forms.**

1 I shouldn't have bothered to study last night – my exam was cancelled.
  (A) I studied. B I didn't study.
2 I didn't need to buy a phone – I got one for my birthday.
  A I bought a phone. (B) I didn't buy a phone.
3 I'm tired. I should have gone to bed earlier last night.
  A I went to bed early. (B) I didn't go to bed early.
4 I ought not to have spent so much money last weekend.
  (A) I spent a lot of money. B I didn't spend much money.
5 It's a lovely day. I shouldn't have bothered bringing my umbrella.
  (A) I brought my umbrella. B I didn't bring my umbrella.

7 **Complete the second sentence so that it has a similar meaning to the first, using the word in capitals. Use no more than four words, including the word in capitals. Do not change the word in capitals.**

1 It's a pity we didn't stay at home. **SHOULD**
  We should have stayed at home.
2 It's a shame he didn't tell her. **TO**
  He ought to have told her.
3 It was unnecessary to do what he said. **HAVE**
  You didn't have to do what he said.
4 That was a silly thing for me to say. **SHOULD**
  I shouldn't have said that.
5 It wasn't necessary for her to come. **BOTHERED**
  She shouldn't have bothered coming.

8 CD•2.31 MP3•70 **Listen to three conversations. Choose a sentence from the ones you wrote in Exercise 7 to complete each conversation.**

A [1] B [4] C [5]

9 SPEAKING **With a partner, choose a sentence from Exercise 7 and write your own conversation. Then practise and act out your conversation.**

Grammar Focus page 168

4.6 Speaking

Making and justifying choices

I can evaluate options and justify choices.

1 SPEAKING **With a partner, look at two ways of shopping for food and answer the questions.**

1 What are the pluses and minuses of each option?
2 If you were college students doing your own food shopping, which option would you prefer? Why?

2 CD•2.32 MP3•71 **Listen to Emma and Oscar discussing the options above. Do they mention any of the pluses and minuses you discussed in Exercise 1?**

3 CD•2.32 MP3•71 **Complete the SPEAKING FOCUS with the words in the box. Then listen again and check.**

but choice choose compare likely opt reason simply

SPEAKING FOCUS

Comparing and contrasting options

(Going to the market) is … [1] *but* (shopping online) is …
X is the only one/option that …
When you [2] *compare* the two/X and Y, …
It is (much) more [3] *likely* that …
X is definitely the cheaper/better/more suitable option.

Choosing an option and justifying the choice

That's why I'd [4] *opt* for X.
… and therefore, it's probably/clearly the best [5] *choice* .
The main/Another [6] *reason* (that X would be my choice) is that …
I prefer X mainly/[7] *simply* because …
This option is (clearly) the most/least + *adjective* … because …

Explaining reasons for rejecting other options

X might (require less effort), but I wouldn't [8] *choose* it because …
X isn't the best choice if you consider …
The reason I wouldn't go for/pick/choose X is because …

REFERENCES
AUDIO SCRIPT ››› *p. 207*
WORKBOOK
p. 57

4 In your opinion, which of these is the best place to shop?

- shopping mall
- online auction
- chain store
- thrift store
- street market
- garage/yard sale

5 Complete the sentences about places to shop using the words in parentheses.

1 It is _more likely_ (likely) that you can find what you want in a shopping mall.
2 I _'d opt for_ (opt) the charity store because you can help other people.
3 The _reason I wouldn't pick_ (reason/not pick) the online auction is because you can end up paying more than you had planned!
4 If you want something unusual and cheap, a street market _is definitely the better_ (definitely/better) option.
5 A designer store _is clearly the best_ (clearly/best) place to go shopping if you're looking for good quality.
6 A thrift store _would not be the best choice considering_ (not/best/choice/consider) the quality of the things there.

6 SPEAKING With a partner, complete the speaking task. Use the SPEAKING FOCUS to help you.

Here are some things that can influence people when they are choosing where to buy clothes. Talk to each other about how important these things are when you're deciding which store to buy clothes from.

Now decide which of these things is most important when you are deciding where to buy clothes.

4.7 Writing

A formal email

I can describe an incident and make a complaint about it in writing.

1 SPEAKING Would you hang out with your friends in the places mentioned in the box? Why?/Why not? Discuss with a partner.

coffee shop empty building park
fast-food restaurant shopping center
skate park street corner

2 Read the posts on the website. Do you think Jude and his friends were treated unfairly? What is the advice given by YCN?

3 Read Jude's email below and answer the questions.

1 Are the main events described in the email the same as those in Jude's message to YCN? *Yes*
2 How does the style of the email differ from the style of the message? *More formal*
3 How do you think the manager will react?

Dear Sir or Madam,

I am writing on [1] *behalf* of myself and my friends to [2] *draw* your attention to an incident that **took place** at the Bellevue Plaza Shopping Center last Saturday. I would like to [3] *make* a formal complaint about the way we were treated by staff at the center.

Last Saturday, some friends and I met in the center at Plaza Coffee Shop. We had bought some drinks and were enjoying ourselves when the manager of the coffee shop **approached** our table and **accused** us of being too noisy. When we tried to **reason with** him, he immediately called security. A moment later, two guards arrived and forced us to leave the coffee shop and the shopping center. To make [4] *matters* worse, they **threatened** to call the police and told us not to return in the future.

We are particularly upset because the [5] *truth/fact* is, we were no noisier than some of the other people in the coffee shop. To be honest, we are amazed that the center security guards are allowed to treat customers in this way. Without a doubt, the worst [6] *part* of this whole incident was being thrown out of the busy shopping center like criminals. We were so **humiliated** that we decided to contact you and complain.

As you are the manager of the center, we [7] *urge* you to reconsider your policies towards teenage customers. It is simply unfair to discriminate against young people in this way. We have contacted the local media about the incident and look forward to your response.

Yours faithfully,
Jude Seaborne

YCN

Youth City News

YCN message board

Got comments? Need advice?
This is the place …

Author	Post
Jude	Last Saturday, my friends and I were kicked out of Bellevue Plaza Shopping Center for … no good reason! We were having a coffee at Plaza Coffee Shop when the manager came over and told us to be quiet. We honestly weren't being that loud and my friend explained this to the manager. Next thing, two security guards arrived and told us to leave or they'd call the police! They walked us to the exit and told us not to come back. It was so embarrassing and a total overreaction. What can we do?
YCN	If you really weren't disturbing anyone, then it does seem unfair, Jude. Why don't you write to the shopping center management and explain the situation? Be sure to let us know their reaction.

4 Read the WRITING FOCUS and complete Jude's email. Sometimes more than one answer is possible.

WRITING FOCUS

A formal email – describing an incident and making a complaint

Introduction

- Say why you are writing and summarize your complaint.
  I am writing on behalf of myself and my friends …
  I am writing to draw your attention to …
  I would like to make a formal complaint about …

Main paragraphs

- Use narrative tenses to describe the incident you are complaining about (see REMEMBER THIS p. 5).
- Give your reaction to the incident.
  We are particularly upset because …
  To make matters worse, …
  The truth/fact is (that) …
  Without doubt, the worst part of this whole incident was …
  … I/we decided to contact you and complain.

Conclusion

- Say what you would like to happen.
  I/We urge you to (reconsider your policies).
  I/We ask/demand that you (investigate the matter).
- Make a final statement.
  It is simply unfair to discriminate against young people in this way.
- Mention that you expect a reply.
  I/We look forward to your response.

EXTRA ACTIVITIES

- MyEnglishLab – assignable *Show what you have learned* writing task and *Show that you have checked* checklist

WORKBOOK

p. 58

5 Complete the sentences with the words and phrases in purple in Jude's email. Use the definitions in parentheses to help you.

I am writing to complain about an incident that [1] ~~took place~~ (happened) last night at Skybowl bowling alley.

a We told her we had paid, and we tried to [2] reason with her (persuade her to be more sensible). [3]

b She [3] accused us (said that we had done something bad) of trying to leave without paying for our drinks. [2]

c My friends and I had finished our game and were about to leave when a waitress [4] approached (came towards) us. [1]

d All the other customers heard her shouting and we felt really [5] humiliated (ashamed or embarrassed). [5]

e However, she started shouting at us and [6] threatened (promised to do something bad) to call the police. [4]

In the end, the manager checked the computer and found that it was the waitress's mistake. The worst part of this whole event was that nobody apologized.

6 Put sentences a–e in Exercise 5 in the correct order to form an extract from an email.

7 Read the LANGUAGE FOCUS and complete the questions with *so* or *such* (*a/an*). Then, with a partner, ask and answer the questions.

When was the last time:

1 you were __so__ angry that you shouted at someone?
2 you had __such a__ good time hanging out with your friends that you didn't want the day to end?
3 you felt __so__ humiliated that you turned red in the face?
4 you received __such__ terrible service that you complained or told someone else about it?
5 you had to deal with __such__ rude people that you felt offended?

LANGUAGE FOCUS

Expressing cause and result

You can make your writing more varied by using **so** and ***such* + *that* clause** to give information about a cause and link it to a result:

- ***so* + adjective + *that* clause**
  We were ***so*** *humiliated* ***that we decided to contact you and complain****.*
- ***such* (+ *a*/*an*) (+ adjective) + noun + *that* clause**
  It was ***such a*** *humiliating situation* ***that we decided to contact you and complain****.*

8 You are going to write an email of complaint to a manager. Imagine you experienced one of the situations below. With a partner, make notes about:

- the details of the incident (what happened and how you felt/reacted).
- what you want the manager to do.

1 A bus driver refused to let you and four friends onto a bus late at night. He said he recognized you and that you had caused trouble on the bus the week before. None of you had been on the bus the week before.

2 You and your friends were asked to leave the movie theater after a member of staff accused you of throwing popcorn around. It was actually some young children sitting a few rows in front of you.

3 You were leaving a supermarket when the security alarm went off. The security guards were very aggressive and searched all your bags and pockets. After keeping you there for half an hour, they found there was a fault with the alarm.

9 Choose one of the situations in Exercise 8 and complete the writing task below. Use your notes from Exercise 8, the WRITING FOCUS and the LANGUAGE FOCUS to help you.

Write a formal email complaining about the way you were treated. Describe the incident and say what actions you expect the recipient to take. Write 140–190 words.

4.8 Language in focus

Modality – alternative structures

I can use a range of alternative structures to express modality.

Exercise 1
1 be bound to do …
2 succeeded in doing …
3 be allowed to do …
4 be banned from doing …
5 be supposed to do …

1 Read the information about modality and complete the table with the base form of the structures in blue in sentences a–e.

As well as using modal verbs, you can express modality with adverbs (*perhaps*, etc.), adjectives and participles (*be sure to*, *be obliged to*, etc.), or other verbs (*manage to*, etc.). Here are some of the more common structures:

MODAL CONCEPT	ALTERNATIVE STRUCTURES
probability	be (un)likely to do sth, it is (un)likely that sth, [1] ______ , be sure to do sth, be certain to do sth
ability	be (un)able to do sth, manage to do sth, [2] ______
permission	[3] ______ , be permitted to do sth
prohibition	[4] ______ , be forbidden to do sth/from doing sth
obligation	be obliged to do sth, be required to do sth, [5] ______

a My brothers and sisters **are banned from** entering my bedroom.
b **I'm supposed to** keep my bedroom clean but I just don't care.
c I can't find my house keys but **they're bound to** turn up sooner or later.
d **I succeeded in** transferring all my photos to my new laptop recently.
e My mom says **I'm allowed to** get a tattoo but I don't want one.

2 Translate the sentences in Exercise 1. Then check the sentences that are true for you.

Exercise 3
1 was supposed to be
2 is banned/forbidden from competing
3 didn't succeed in persuading
4 was supposed to call
5 is required to show

3 Rewrite the sentences. Replace the underlined phrases with phrases that include the words in capitals.

1 Tim is late. He should be here by now. **SUPPOSED**
2 Rogers can't compete for three years because he failed a drugs test. **FROM**
3 Janet couldn't persuade her parents to lend her any money. **IN**
4 Terry should have called me last night, but he forgot. **SUPPOSED**
5 Everybody has to show their ID card when they enter the UK. **REQUIRED**

4 Complete the conversation with one word in each blank. Use each word once only. Sometimes more than one answer is possible.

A: I've got a part-time job in the local supermarket. I'm [1] supposed to be there at 7 a.m. but I'm not sure if I'll [2] manage to get up in time!
B: What are you going to wear?
A: You have to wear dress shoes. Sneakers are [3] forbidden , and you're not [4] allowed to wear jewelry or piercings. You are [5] required to put on a uniform and I think I'm [6] supposed to wear a hat if I'm working on the fresh food counter.
B: What about phones?
A: You're [7] permitted to bring a cell phone onto the premises, but it has to be turned off at all times.
B: Knowing you, you're [8] bound to forget. What happens if it rings?
A: I'm not sure, but it's [9] likely that the manager would be very angry, so I'll be [10] sure to turn mine off tomorrow!

80

04 WORD LIST

Types of stores

bakery /ˈbeɪkəri/
bookstore /ˈbukstɔr/
boutique /buˈtik/
branch /bræntʃ/
butcher /ˈbʊtʃɚ/
chain of (restaurants/supermarkets) /ˌtʃeɪn əv (ˈrɛsˌtrɑnts/ˈsupɚˌmɑrkɪts)/
department store /dɪˈpɑrtˈmənt stɔr/
florist's /ˈflɔrɪsts/
hardware store /ˈhɑrdwɛr stɔr/
jeweler's /ˈdʒuələ˞z/
junk store /ˈdʒʌŋk stɔr/
newsstand /ˈnuzˌstænd/
pharmacy /ˈfɑrməsi/
pet store /ˈpɛt stɔr/
produce vendor /ˈproʊdus vɛndɚ/
shopping mall/center /ˈʃɑpɪŋ mɔl/ˌsɛntɚ/
thrift store /ˈθrɪft stɔr/

Buying and selling

advertising /ˈædvɚˌtaɪzɪŋ/
attract customers /əˌtrækt ˈkʌstəmɚz/
counter /ˈkaʊntɚ/
demand for /dɪˈmænd fɚ/
fill a gap in the market /fɪl ə ˌgæp ɪn ðə ˈmɑrkɪt/
launch/release /lɔntʃ/rɪˈlis/
new shopping experience /ˌnu ˈʃɑpɪŋ ɪkˌspɪriəns/
niche market /ˈnɪtʃ mɑrkɪt/
on sale /ˌɑn ˈseɪl/
promote a product /prəˌmoʊt ə ˈprɑdʌkt/
range of products /ˌreɪndʒ əv ˈprɑdʌkts/
reputation /ˌrɛpyəˈteɪʃən/
serve customers /ˌsɚv ˈkʌstəmɚz/
specialize in sth /ˈspɛʃəˌlaɪz ɪn sʌmθɪŋ/
stock /stɑk/
storekeeper /ˈstɔrkipɚ/
supply/monopolize the market /səˌplaɪ/məˈnɑpəˌlaɪz ðə ˈmɑrkɪt/
trade /treɪd/
treat yourself to sth /ˈtrit yɚˌsɛlf tə ˌsʌmθɪŋ/

Auctions and market places

antiques market /ænˈtiks ˌmɑrkɪt/
auction house /ˈɔkʃən haʊs/
auctioneer /ˌɔkʃəˈnɪr/
bid for sth /ˈbɪd fɚ ˌsʌmθɪŋ/
flea market /ˈfli ˌmɑrkɪt/
garage sale /gəˈrɑʒ seɪl/
market stall /ˈmɑrkɪt stɔl/
market stallholder /ˌmɑrkɪt ˈstɔlˌhoʊldɚ/
online auction /ˌɑnlaɪn ˈɔkʃən/

Money and prices

affluent /ˈæfluənt/
allowance /əˈlaʊəns/
borrow /ˈbɑroʊ/
broke /broʊk/
cash /kæʃ/
charge /tʃɑrdʒ/
cheat /tʃit/
cost an arm and a leg /ˌkɔst ən ˌɑrm ənd ə ˈlɛg/
cost of living /ˌkɔst əv ˈlɪvɪŋ/
cost/be worth a fortune /ˌkɔst/bi ˌwɚθ ə ˈfɔrtʃən/
credit card details /ˈkrɛdɪt kɑrd ˌditeɪlz/
cut/raise prices /ˌkʌt/ˌreɪz ˈpraɪsɪz/
discounted price /dɪsˌkaʊntɪd ˈpraɪs/
earn a living /ˌɚn ə ˈlɪvɪŋ/
have money to burn /ˌhæv ˈmʌni tə bɚn/
hourly fee /ˌaʊɚli ˈfi/
in debt /ˌɪn ˈdɛt/
make a fortune /ˌmeɪk ə ˈfɔrtʃən/
make ends meet /ˌmeɪk ɛndz ˈmit/
open a bank account /ˌoʊpən ə ˈbæŋk əˌkaʊnt/
overpriced /ˌoʊvɚˈpraɪst/
owe sb money /ˌoʊ ˌsʌmbɑdi ˈmʌni/
pay through the nose /ˌpeɪ θru ðə ˈnoʊz/
reasonably-priced /ˌrizənəbli ˈpraɪst/
reduce the price /rɪˌdus ðə ˈpraɪs/

EXTRA ACTIVITIES
- Photocopiable resource 26 (modality – 15 mins) MultiROM and ActiveTeach

WORKBOOK
p. 59

NEXT CLASS
- Ask students to study the Word list on pp. 80–81.
- Ask students to review for Focus review 4.

spend a lot of money on sth /ˌspend ə lɑt əv ˈmʌni ɑn ˌsʌmθɪŋ/
thirty percent off /ˌθɚti pɚˌsent ɔf/
transfer /ˈtrænsfɚ/
withdraw money /wɪðˌdrɔ ˈmʌni/

Goods

antique /ænˈtik/
bracelet /ˈbreɪslət/
brand/label /ˈbrænd/ˈleɪbəl/
consumer goods /kənsumɚ ˈgʊdz/
designer clothes /dɪˈzaɪnɚ ˈkloʊðz/
domestic clutter /dəˌmestɪk ˈklʌt̬ɚ/
electrical goods /ɪˈlektrɪkəl gʊdz/
evening/party/wedding dress /ˈivnɪŋ/ˈpɑrt̬i/ ˈwedɪŋ dres/
fashion /ˈfæʃən/
item /ˈaɪt̬əm/
jewelry /ˈdʒuəlri/
ornament /ˈɔrnəmənt/
perfume /pɚˈfyum/
pre-owned/second-hand/used goods /ˌpri oʊnd/ˌsekənd ˌhænd/ˌyuzd ˈgʊdz/
vintage piece /ˈvɪntɪdʒ pis/

Adjectives describing goods

affordable /əˈfɔrdəbəl/
fashionable/trendy /ˈfæʃənəbəl/ˈtrendi/
fun /fʌn/
hard-wearing /ˌhɑrd ˈwerɪŋ/
high quality /ˌhaɪ ˈkwɑlət̬i/
one-off /ˈwʌn ɔf/
quirky /ˈkwɚki/
unwanted /ʌnˈwɑntɪd/
vintage /ˈvɪntɪdʒ/

Complaints

apologize /əˈpɑlədʒaɪz/
complain /kəmˈpleɪn/
demand /dɪˈmænd/
draw sb's attention to sth /ˌdrɔ ˌsʌmbɑdiz əˈtenʃən tə ˌsʌmθɪŋ/
exchange /ɪksˈtʃeɪndʒ/
fault /fɔlt/
incident /ˈɪnsədənt/
investigate the matter /ɪnˈvestəˌgeɪt ðə ˈmæt̬ɚ/
make a formal complaint about sth /ˌmeɪk ə ˌfɔrməl kəmˈpleɪnt əˌbaʊt ˌsʌmθɪŋ/
receipt /rɪˈsit/
reconsider your policies /ˌrikənˌsɪdɚ yɚ ˈpɑləsiz/
refuse /rɪˈfyuz/
response /rɪˈspɑns/

Jeans

Production process

blast with sand /ˌblæst wɪð ˈsænd/
chemical/toxic/natural dye /ˌkemɪkəl/ˌtɑksɪk/ˌnætʃərəl ˈdaɪ/
dense/stiff/mass-produced cloth /ˌdens/ˌstɪf/ mæs prəˌdusd ˈklɔθ/
dye /daɪ/
indigo dye /ˈɪndɪgoʊ daɪ/
labor-intensive/modern/traditional methods of production /ˌleɪbɚ ɪnˈtensɪv/ˌmɑdɚn/trəˈdɪʃənəl ˌmeθədz əv prəˈdʌkʃən/
produce /prəˈdus/
producer /prəˈdusɚ/
production cycle/technique /prəˈdʌkʃən ˌsaɪkəl/ tekˌnik/

Look and style

baggy /ˈbægi/
bootcut /ˈbutkʌt/
copper rivet /ˌkɑpɚ ˈrɪvət/
cotton /ˈkɑt̚n/
cropped jeans /ˌkrɑpt ˈdʒinz/
deep/rich/intense color /ˌdip/ˌrɪtʃ/ɪnˌtens ˈkʌlɚ/
design /dɪˈzaɪn/
distressed /dɪˈstrest/
fade /feɪd/
feel /fil/
flared jeans /ˌflerd ˈdʒinz/
skinny /ˈskɪni/
stiff/stretch denim /ˌstɪf/ˌstretʃ ˈdenəm/
straight-leg /ˈstreɪt ˌleg/
tight /taɪt/

Phrasal verbs

bring out /ˌbrɪŋ ˈaʊt/
deal with (customers) /ˈdil wɪð (ˈkʌstəmɚz)/
fork out /ˌfɔrk ˈaʊt/
hang out /ˌhæŋ ˈaʊt/
keep (costs) down /ˌkip (kɔsts) ˈdaʊn/
knock (a few dollars) off (the price) /ˌnɑk (ə fyu dɑlɚz) ɔf (ðe ˈpraɪs)/
rely on /rɪˈlaɪ ɑn/
rip off /ˌrɪp ˈɔf/
run out (of) /ˌrʌn ˈaʊt (əv)/
save up /ˌseɪv ˈʌp/
shop around /ˌʃɑp əˈraʊnd/
sign up /ˌsaɪn ˈʌp/
snap up (a bargain) /ˌsnæp ˈʌp (ə ˈbɑrgɪn)/
splash out on /ˌsplæʃ ˈaʊt ɑn/
take/send (an item) back /ˌteɪk/ˌsend (ən aɪt̬əm) ˈbæk/

Other

abandon /əˈbændən/
accuse (of) /əˈkyuz (əv)/
be banned from doing sth /bi ˈbænd frəm ˌduɪŋ ˌsʌmθɪŋ/
be bound to do sth /bi ˌbaʊnd tə ˈdu ˌsʌmθɪŋ/
be committed to sth /bi kəˈmɪt̬ɪd tə ˌsʌmθɪŋ/
be hooked on sth /bi ˈhʊkt ɑn ˌsʌmθɪŋ/
be permitted to do sth /bi pɚˌmɪt̬ɪd tə ˈdu ˌsʌmθɪŋ/
checked/unclaimed luggage /ˌtʃɛkt/ʌnˌkleɪmd ˈlʌgɪdʒ/
chemical /ˈkemɪkəl/
compress /kəmˈpres/
concern /kənˈsɚn/
craze for /ˈkreɪz fɚ/
digest /daɪˈdʒest/
digestive system /daɪˈdʒestɪv ˌsɪstəm/
discriminate against /dɪˈskrɪməneɪt əˌgenst/
domestic/long-haul/international flight /dəˌmestɪk/ˌlɔŋ hɔl/ˌɪnt̬ɚˌnæʃənəl ˈflaɪt/
enthusiasm /ɪnˈθuziˌæzəm/
enthusiast /ɪnˈθuziəst/
enthusiastic /ɪnˌθuziˈæstɪk/
environment /ɪnˈvaɪɚnment/
environmental /ɪnˌvaɪɚnˈmentl/
environmentalist /ɪnˌvaɪɚnˈmentl-ɪst/
expert (n, adj) /ˈekspɚt/
expertise /ekspɚˈtiz/
fertilizer /ˈfɚt̬əˌlaɪzɚ/
fish pedicure /ˈfɪʃ ˌpedɪˌkyʊr/
go missing /ˌgoʊ ˈmɪsɪŋ/
go bad /ˌgoʊ ˈbæd/
hips /hɪps/
humiliated /hyuˈmɪliˌeɪt̬ɪd/
increase /ɪnˈkris/
intellectual/private property /ˌɪntəlˌektʃuəl/ ˌpraɪvɪt ˈprɑpɚt̬i/
likely /ˈlaɪkli/
loss of feeling /ˌlɔs əv ˈfilɪŋ/
lost property /ˌlɔst ˈprɑpɚt̬i/
major/root/common cause /ˌmeɪdʒɚ/ˌrut/ˌkɑmən ˈkɔz/
member of staff /ˌmembɚ əv ˈstæf/
offended /əˈfendɪd/
on behalf of sb /ɑn bɪˈhæf əv sʌmbɑdi/
opt for sth /ˈɑpt fɚ sʌmθɪŋ/
perfect /ˈpɚfɪkt/
perfection /pɚˈfekʃən/
perfectionist /pɚˈfekʃənəst/
personal belongings /ˌpɚsənəl bɪˈlɔŋɪŋz/
pesticide /ˈpest̬əˌsaɪd/
productive /prəˈdʌkt̬ɪv/
rebellious /rɪˈbelyəs/
recent /ˈrisənt/
risky /ˈrɪski/
security alarm /sɪˈkyʊrət̬i əˌlɑrm/
security guard /sɪˈkyʊrət̬i gɑrd/
stolen goods /ˌstoʊlən ˈgʊdz/
stroke /stroʊk/
succeed in doing sth /səkˌsid ɪn ˈduɪŋ ˌsʌmθɪŋ/
threaten /ˈθret̚n/
to make matters worse /tə ˌmeɪk ˌmæt̬ɚz ˈwɚs/
tongue piercing /ˈtʌŋ ˌpɪrsɪŋ/
tradition /trəˈdɪʃən/
traditional /trəˈdɪʃənl/
traditionalist /trəˈdɪʃənl-ɪst/
trendsetter /ˈtrendˌset̬ɚ/
turn red in the face /tɚn ˌred ɪn ðə ˈfeɪs/
waist /weɪst/
wardrobe /ˈwɔrdroʊb/

FOCUS REVIEW 4

VOCABULARY AND GRAMMAR

1 Match the sentence halves.

1 Have you ever been ripped c
2 When did you last pay e
3 What do you like to splash a
4 Why is it a good idea to shop d
5 Do you think you'll manage to get a few dollars knocked b

a out on when you're feeling rich?
b off the original price of the headphones you want to buy?
c off while shopping abroad?
d around before choosing what you want to get?
e through the nose for a piece of electronic equipment?

2 Complete the sentences with the words in the box. There is one extra word.

consumer fork make market snap bargain withdraw

1 You'll have to move fast if you want to _snap_ up a bargain during the sale. The best items disappear in no time.
2 I think that our brand new car is a _bargain_. It's very economical.
3 It's difficult to _make_ ends meet when you only work part-time.
4 You must be joking! Why should I _fork_ out $20 on something that I don't really like?
5 The prices of most _consumer_ goods have risen recently.
6 A bank clerk explained to me how to _withdraw_ money from a cash machine using PayPal.

3 Complete the sentences with question tags or reply questions.

1 Nobody has gotten a refund yet, _have they_?
2 That's a nice dress she's wearing tonight, _isn't it_?
3 Let's talk about insuring the house, _shall we_?
4 A: Tim had to take out a loan to buy a car.
B: _Did he_?
5 A: I'm not going to lend him money ever again!
B: _Aren't you_?
6 A: Eve wants to pay a deposit on the house next week.
B: _Does she_?

4 Choose the correct options.

1 We *had better* / (*had to*) find the receipt before we even attempted to take the camera back to the store.
2 I told you not to order a wedding dress online. You *should listen* / (*ought to have listened*) to me then, and we wouldn't have to look for one now!
3 Amy is a shopaholic. She really (*mustn't*) / *hadn't* spend any more on unnecessary purchases.
4 I *didn't need to spend* / (*shouldn't have spent*) a fortune on all this fancy food. They didn't come after all.
5 Hurry up, Kate. There are (*bound*) / *supposed* to be crowds trying to get into the shop when it opens.

LANGUAGE IN USE

5 Read the text and choose the correct answer, A, B, C, or D.

BAR CODE

You may have never heard of Joe Woodland or Bernard Silver, but you [1]________ to come across their groundbreaking invention on a daily basis – the bar code.

While studying engineering, Woodland and Silver were approached by a retail food company and asked to find ways to automate checkout operations. They designed and then [2]________ a bar code in the shape of a bull's eye. It meant that employees no longer [3]________ manually input prices for every single product at the checkout or replace price tags whenever an item's cost changed. [4]________ the idea didn't catch on at first, the food industry didn't give up looking for an easy way to scan products. Finally, an IBM employee, George Laurer, designed the bar code as a rectangular box with vertical lines and numbers. The first ever item was scanned on 26 June 1974. It was a pack of chewing gum, [5]________ is now a museum exhibit, together with the scanner used.

Nowadays, not only food but a wide [6]________ of products are branded with a bar code. It has even become a feature in some modern paintings.

	A	B	C	D
1	are supposed	manage	(C) are certain	are required
2	(A) brought out	kicked off	put in	set up
3	ought to	must	should	(D) had to
4	Despite	Only if	(C) Even though	However
5	what	(B) which	that	whose
6	matter	chain	niche	(D) range

6 Complete the second sentence so that it has a similar meaning to the first, using the word in capitals. Do not change the word in capitals.

1 It would have been better if we hadn't given Tony so much money for his birthday. **SHOULD**
We _shouldn't have given_ Tony so much money for his birthday.
2 Sam's advice was so good that I knew immediately which bank account to open. **ADVICE**
Sam gave me _such good advice_ that I knew immediately which bank account to open.
3 It wasn't necessary for Sarah to pay her university fees because they were covered by her employer. **NEED**
Sarah _didn't need to pay_ her university fees because they were covered by her employer.
4 If I were you, I wouldn't exceed the credit card limit just because it's Christmas. **HAD**
You _had better not exceed_ the credit card limit just because it's Christmas.
5 We didn't manage to launch a new campaign due to lack of funding. **SUCCEED**
We _didn't succeed in launching_ a new campaign due to lack of funding.

REFERENCES

AUDIO SCRIPT ››› pp. 207–208

EXTRA ACTIVITIES

- Photocopiable resource 56A (multiple choice – 12 mins) MultiROM and ActiveTeach
- Photocopiable resource 60C (transformations – 20 mins) MultiROM and ActiveTeach
- Photocopiable resource 27 (Writing – 10 mins) MultiROM and ActiveTeach
- Photocopiable resource 28 (Speaking – 10 mins) MultiROM and ActiveTeach

LISTENING

7 CD•2.33 MP3•72 **Listen to an interview with Anne, a mystery shopper. Choose the correct answer, A, B, or C.**

1 Anne is asked by her clients to
- (A) buy specific products.
- B dress in a particular way.
- C go to any store she wants.

2 The services of mystery shoppers are in demand mainly because
- A stores want to attract more customers.
- B they provide information on the competition.
- (C) online shopping is becoming a danger to regular stores.

3 Anne believes she is doing a good job because the stores she has visited
- A are hiring more staff.
- B are cleaner than they were before.
- (C) are winning awards for customer service.

4 What does Anne say about being a mystery shopper in expensive restaurants?
- (A) It's a task requiring a good memory.
- B She has to take notes during the meal.
- C She finds it a rather disappointing experience overall.

5 What is Anne's attitude to her job?
- (A) It isn't always easy.
- B It's quite monotonous.
- C It pays well.

WRITING

8 Complete the writing task.

Read part of an email you sent to an English friend. Write an email of complaint to the manager of the museum.

> I really enjoyed our visit to the museum yesterday, but I can't believe that they wouldn't let you go into the Egyptian room. They said that your wheelchair might damage the delicate exhibits in there! I think their attitude was really wrong and totally unfair. I'm going to write an email to the director of the museum and complain about their behavior.

Write your email in 140–190 words.

SPEAKING

9 With a partner, complete the speaking task.

Here are different ways in which companies advertise their products or services. Talk to each other about how effective these forms of advertising are.

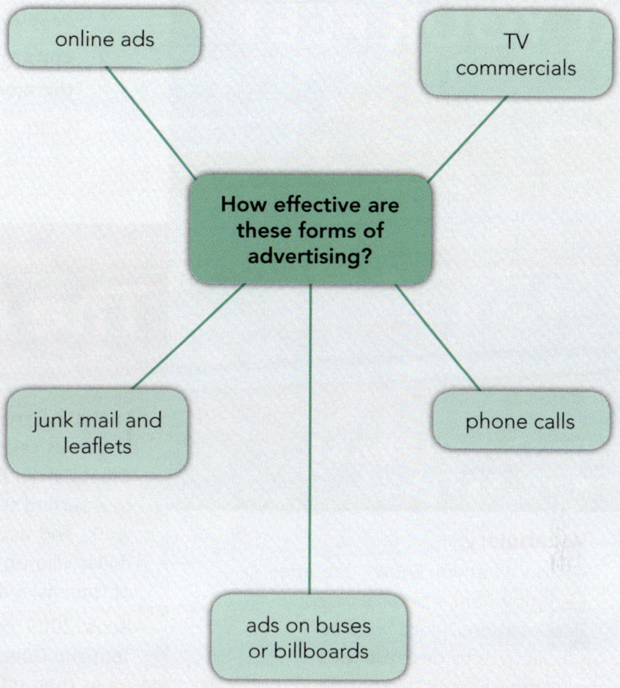

Which form of advertising do you think irritates people the most?

10 With a partner, discuss the questions.

1 Do you often buy things because of ads? Why?/Why not?
2 What's your favorite TV commercial right now?
3 Do you think a personal recommendation is better than an ad? Why?/Why not?
4 Some people say that ads persuade us to buy things we don't need. What do you think?
5 Which forms of advertising do you think will become less common in the future? Why?

WORKBOOK

Use of English 4.9, pp. 60–61; Self-assessment 4.10, p. 62

NEXT CLASS

- Ask students to do Self-check 4.11, WB p. 63 as homework.
- Ask students to prepare for Unit test 4 and Review test 2 (*Focus* Assessment Package).

5 THE WORLD AT YOUR FEET

If a job is worth doing, it's worth doing well.

A PROVERB

UNIT LANGUAGE AND SKILLS

Vocabulary:
- *Show what you know* – job titles
- employment – phrasal verbs, collocations, word families
- adjectives to describe jobs
- linking phrases
- *Word in focus – at*

Grammar:
- Reported Speech
- reporting verbs

Listening:
- an interview on the future of work
- people talking about their jobs
- multiple matching

Reading:
- a literary text about men's and women's roles
- multiple choice

Speaking:
- discussing problems and solutions, expressing annoyance

Writing:
- an article

FOCUS EXTRA

- Grammar Focus pages 168–169
- WORD STORE booklet pages 10–11
- Workbook pages 64–77 or MyEnglishLab
- MP3s – www.english.com/focus

5.1 Vocabulary

Employment • Phrasal verbs • Collocations • Word families

I can talk about work and employment.

SHOW WHAT YOU KNOW

1 **With a partner, try to note down a job title for each letter of the alphabet. How many can you think of in two minutes?**

accountant beautician civil servant detective

2 SPEAKING **With a partner, choose three jobs from your list and discuss the advantages and disadvantages of each one. Compare the following:**

- requirements (qualifications/training/experience)
- terms and conditions (salary/working hours/place of work)

The return of the Best Job

In 2009, Ben Southall applied for 'The Best Job in the World' and after a rigorous selection process, he **was taken on** as Island Caretaker on the Great Barrier Reef. The dream post was not just an opportunity to **pick up** new surfing skills: it came with a pay package of $150,000 for six months' work, and accommodation in a five-million-dollar villa on Hamilton Island, off the coast of Queensland, Australia.

Ben's 2009 contract expired long ago, but Tourism Queensland decided to **keep him on** as their official Ambassador. The new role that he **took up** still involves traveling and blogging about his adventures.

In 2013, as he **stepped down from** his Island Caretaker job and became an official Ambassador for Tourism Queensland, he said this: 'Unfortunately for me, my time is up. But luckily for the world, "The Best Job in the World" is back. It was one of the most successful tourism campaigns in recent times, so they decided to do it again, but this time they're recruiting for several vacancies around Australia!'

The successful applicant for each job was paid a six-month package of up to $100,000, including living expenses. More than 330,000 people from 196 countries expressed interest in the dream jobs, and Tourism Australia had to deal with more than 40,000 video applications. A final shortlist of eighteen candidates **was drawn up** and they were flown in to Australia for interview.

The aim of the promo was to push Australia's lucrative vacation industry and target the international youth market from around the world – they wanted to attract people on vacation but also employ people who wanted to work, helping to fill many vacant posts in the tourism industry. Here are four of the jobs and the lucky people who were hired to do them:

Allan, Ireland

OUTBACK ADVENTURER
DUTIES
This role requires a sense of adventu
his job is to uncov
the best vacation experiences in the Outback of Northern Australia
PERKS
Being immersed in indigenous Aborigi
culture.

Rober
Braz

LIFESTYLE PHOTOGRAPHER
DUTIES
He's responsible for documenting Melbourne's unique culture and lifestyle.
PERKS
Trying out the coolest dining places in Melbourne.

REFERENCES
CULTURE NOTES ››› p. 196

EXTRA ACTIVITIES
- Photocopiable resource 29 (employment – 8 mins) MultiROM and ActiveTeach
- Photocopiable resource 32 (Test yourself partner work activities) MultiROM and ActiveTeach
- MyEnglishLab – assignable *Show what you have learned* mini-test

WORKBOOK
pp. 64–65

3 **How would you define the best job in the world? Complete the table and compare with a partner.**

Location	Working hours	Duties	Salary	Perks

4 **Read the article and answer the questions.**

1 What was the original Best Job in the World?
2 What does the role of official Ambassador for Tourism Queensland involve?
3 How did people apply for the new vacancies?
4 Why did Tourism Australia run the competition again?
5 What are the key responsibilities of each job described?

5 **Which of the four jobs described in the article is the closest to your ideas in Exercise 3?**

in the World!

Elisa, France

PARK RANGER
DUTIES
Her primary responsibilities are protecting Australian native plants and animals and informing people about them.
PERKS
Experiencing the Great Barrier Reef.

CHIEF FUNSTER
DUTIES
He's in charge of promoting and reviewing gigs, parties, VIP events, and festivals in Sydney.
PERKS
Having fun!

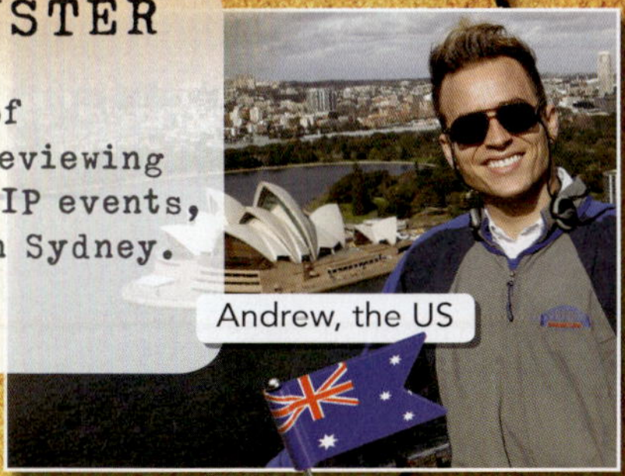
Andrew, the US

Go to WORD STORE 5 page 11.

WORD STORE 5A

6 CD•2.34 MP3•73 **Complete WORD STORE 5A with the base form of the phrasal verbs in red in the article. Then listen, check, and repeat.**

7 **Replace the underlined verbs in the questions with the correct form of a phrasal verb. Then read the article again and answer the questions.**

1 When was Ben Southall employed *(taken on)* as an Island Caretaker?
2 What new skill could Ben learn *(pick up)* as an Island Caretaker?
3 When Ben's contract expired, did Tourism Queensland retain *(keep him on)* him?
4 What is the title of the new post Ben accepted *(took up)* in 2013?
5 How do you think Ben felt about leaving *(stepping down from)* his island job?
6 What happened to the candidates after the shortlist had been prepared *(drawn up)*?

WORD STORE 5B

8 CD•2.35 MP3•74 **Complete WORD STORE 5B with the underlined collocations in the article. Then listen, check, and repeat. Add a translation.**

9 **Complete the text with collocations from WORD STORE 5B. Did the person find their dream job? Why?/ Why not?**

When I left school, I [1] *filled* a vacant post in a restaurant but I didn't enjoy the job. So when my contract [2] *expired*, I left. At school I had always [3] *expressed* an interest in working overseas. I have a good [4] *sense* of adventure, and so when I found out that the tourist industry were targeting the youth [5] *market*, I took a restaurant job on a cruise ship. The perks were good – my living [6] *expenses* were covered. But the job was the same as my previous one, just on a ship.

WORD STORE 5C

10 CD•2.36 MP3•75 **Complete WORD STORE 5C with the words in the box to make more collocations. Then listen, check, and repeat. Write example sentences.**

WORD STORE 5D

11 CD•2.37 MP3•76 **Complete WORD STORE 5D with words from the article. Then listen, check, and repeat. Which verbs and nouns have the same forms?**

12 **Complete the sentences with words from WORD STORE 5D.**

1 You should always _____ your homework before you turn it in.
2 Most people would prefer to be an _____ than an interviewee.
3 Few local companies _____ teenagers for part-time jobs.
4 Very few men _____ for elementary school teaching posts.
5 Full _____ is an impossible dream for this country.

13 **SPEAKING With a partner, discuss whether you agree or disagree with the statements in Exercise 12.**

Exercise 4
1 Island Caretaker
2 traveling and blogging about his adventures
3 They sent video applications.
4 to get more young tourists visiting
5 **Chief Funster:** in charge of promoting and reviewing gigs, parties, VIP events, and festivals in Sydney
Park Ranger: protecting Australian native plants and animals and informing people about them
Lifestyle Photographer: documenting Melbourne's unique culture and lifestyle
Outback Adventurer: uncovering the best vacation experiences in the Outback of Northern Australia

Exercise 7
1 taken on / in 2009
2 pick up / surfing
3 keep him on / yes
4 took up / Ambassador
5 stepping down from / sad
6 drawn up / they were flown to Australia for interview

Exercise 12
1 review
2 interviewer
3 recruit
4 apply
5 employment

NEXT CLASS
- Ask students to prepare for a 10–15 minute vocabulary quiz: *Focus* Assessment Package, Unit 5.1, Vocabulary.

5.2 Grammar

Reported Speech

I can report speech naturally and fluently, making appropriate grammatical changes.

1 CD•2.38 MP3•77 **Listen to three people in job interview situations. Would you employ them? Why?/Why not?**

2 CD•2.38 MP3•77 **Read the reports of the interviews in Exercise 1. Rewrite the underlined parts in Direct Speech. Then listen again and check.**

1 We were interviewing someone to be a part-time postman. We asked him to tell us about his[4] weaknesses. He told us that he[1] wasn't a morning person. In fact, he said he had[1] struggled to get up that[4] morning. He said he[3] would like to start work after lunch.

A: Tell us *about your weaknesses* .

B: I *'m not a morning person. In fact, I struggled to get up this morning. I'd like to start work after lunch* .

2 We interviewed two young men for jobs as waiters. We said it was[1] a pity that they hadn't had any experience of restaurant work. They told us not[6] to worry. They were very good at eating and that was why they thought they should[3] get the job.

A: It's a *pity you haven't had any experience of restaurant work* .

B: Don't *worry. We're very good at eating and that's why we think we should get the job.*

3 We're currently interviewing somebody for a receptionist position. We just asked her whether[5] she likes the job she has now. She says she[2] doesn't because she has to answer the phone a lot, and she hates that.

A: Do *you like the job you have now?* ?

B: No, *I don't because I have to answer the phone a lot, and I hate that* .

3 **Read the GRAMMAR FOCUS. Then look at the way Direct Speech is reported in Exercise 2 and find examples for each rule.** *See numbers in Exercise 2.*

GRAMMAR FOCUS

Reported Speech

When you report someone's words, remember these rules:

- You usually move the verbs 'one tense back' when your reporting verb is in a past tense (*She said* ...).
- You **don't** change the verb form if your reporting verb is in a present tense (*She says* ... or *He has told me* ...).
- You **don't** change verbs in the Past Perfect or modal verbs such as *would, should, could, might*.
- You change pronouns, possessive adjectives and words for time and place as necessary.
- You change the word order in questions and don't use *do, does* or *did*.
- You use *told* + sb + *to*-infinitive to report orders and *ask* + sb + *to*-infinitive to report requests.

REFERENCES

AUDIO SCRIPT ››› *p. 208*

EXTRA ACTIVITIES

- Photocopiable resource 30 (Reported Speech – 12 mins) MultiROM and ActiveTeach
- MyEnglishLab – assignable *Show what you have learned* mini-test

WORKBOOK

p. 66

NEXT CLASS

- Ask students to prepare for a 10–15 minute grammar quiz: *Focus* Assessment Package, Unit 5.2, Grammar.

4 Harry is preparing for a job interview. Report his parents' comments. Don't change the tense if it isn't necessary.

1 'You didn't prepare well enough for your last interview.' They said *that he hadn't prepared well enough for his previous interview.*
2 'You'll never get a job if you don't have your hair cut.' They said …
3 'You forgot to clean your shoes last time and they always look at shoes.' They said …
4 'You should buy a new suit.' They said …
5 'You mustn't drink too much coffee beforehand because you'll be nervous.' They said …
6 'Don't worry if you don't get it. Something better might come up.' They told him …

Exercise 4
2 They said that he'd never get a job if he didn't have his hair cut.
3 They said that he'd forgotten to clean his shoes the previous time and that they always looked at shoes.
4 They said he should buy a new suit.
5 They said he mustn't drink too much coffee beforehand because he would be nervous.
6 They told him not to worry if he didn't get it. They told him something better might come up.

5 Report the interview questions. Don't change the tense if it isn't necessary. Which questions would you be happy with/worried about? Why?

1 'Did you write this résumé?'
They asked me *whether I had written that résumé.*
2 'Don't call us, we'll call you.' They told me …
3 'I'll be contacting your references tomorrow.' He says …
4 'Will you be available to start here next month?' They asked me …
5 'You're exactly the person we're looking for.' She says …
6 'Could we give you some advice?' They asked me …

Exercise 5
2 They told me not to call them. They would call me.
3 He says he'll be contacting my references tomorrow.
4 They asked me whether I'd be available to start there next month.
5 She says I'm exactly the person they're looking for.
6 They asked me whether they could give me some advice.

6 Complete the reported statements to make them true for you.

1 The last time my friends gave me good advice, they told me …
2 My brother/sister annoys me when he/she tells me …
3 I think I'm pretty good/bad at English. My teacher says …
4 I heard something interesting recently. Somebody told me …
5 I don't know what I want to do when I leave school. My parents say …
6 The last person who spoke to me was ________ . He/She said …

Grammar Focus page 168

5.3 Listening

Multiple matching

I can understand an interview about the future of work and people talking about their jobs

1 SPEAKING With a partner, look at the photos and discuss which of these categories each job belongs to. Think of three more jobs for each category.

- jobs that will always be needed
- jobs that are at risk
- jobs of the future

A lawyer

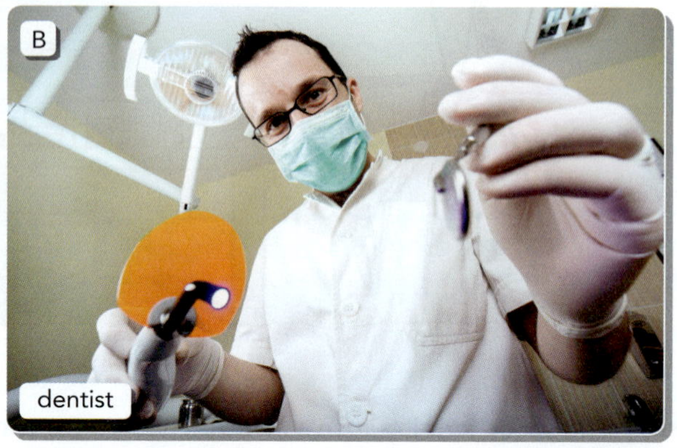
B dentist

C store assistant

D wind turbine technician

2 CD•2.39 MP3•78 **Listen to an interview with a data analyst. Compare his findings with your ideas in Exercise 1.**

3 CD•2.39 MP3•78 **Complete the sentences with the words in the box. Then listen again and check.**

decline marked rise sharp unchanged

1 There's been **a steady** rise **in** people working from home.
2 There's been **a** sharp **drop in** the number of people commuting to work.
3 Jobs in the medical and teaching professions will **be** unchanged.
4 There will be **a** marked **increase in** jobs connected with alternative energy.
5 There will be **a gradual** decline **in** jobs in retail.

4 Match the phrases in green in Exercise 3 with these phrases with similar meanings.

a a sharp rise in 4
b a growing number of 1
c remain constant 3
d a drop in the number of 5
e a rapid decline in 2

5 SPEAKING With a partner, describe trends in your country using the phrases in Exercise 4. Think about the things in the box.

cost of going out biking to work/school getting married in your twenties shopping online studying English

Exercise 2
Jobs that will always be needed: actors, artists, carers, doctors, fire fighters, lawyers, managers, politicians, solar panel engineers, wind turbine technicians, writers
Jobs that are at risk: factory workers, office workers, shop assistants
Jobs of the future: body-part makers, robot mechanics, space tourist guides

REFERENCES
AUDIO SCRIPT ››› pp. 208–209
WORKBOOK
p. 67

EXAM FOCUS Multiple matching

6 CD•2.40 MP3•79 **Listen to four people talking about their jobs. Choose from the list (A–F) what each speaker says. Use the letters only once. There are two extra letters.**

Speaker 1: B **Speaker 2:** F **Speaker 3:** A **Speaker 4:** E

The speaker:

A is concerned about his/her elderly customers.
B believes that technology has replaced parts of the jobs in his/her industry.
C has seen a decrease in his/her salary.
D thinks that it's better to do an internship than go to college.
E has a hobby that has taught him/her skills that are relevant for his job.
F thinks technology has led to a better experience for his/her clients.

7 CD•2.40 MP3•79 **Listen again and answer the questions.**

1 What makes law such a stable profession?
2 Why are law firms now offering internships?
3 How have dental patients benefited from medical advances?
4 Why is it useful to have good interpersonal skills as a store assistant?
5 What qualifications and skills do you need to be a wind turbine technician?

Exercise 7
1 Laws don't change fast.
2 so trainees can earn a salary
3 There's less pain.
4 to handle difficult customers
5 two-year course in applied science, to be good with your hands, to have some experience of mechanics

8 SPEAKING **With a partner, discuss the questions.**

1 Would you prefer to work from home or commute? Why?
2 What are the pros and cons of working freelance?
3 What kind of qualifications and skills do you hope to gain in the future?

PRONUNCIATION FOCUS

9 CD•2.41 MP3•80 **Listen and repeat the words said as nouns and as verbs. Mark the stress. Which pairs have different stress patterns?**

[~~contract~~ export import increase market recruit review target]

a <u>con</u>tract/to con<u>tract</u>

10 **With a partner, take turns to say a word from Exercise 9. Your partner must decide whether the word is a noun or a verb.**

Exercise 9
an <u>ex</u>port/to ex<u>port</u>
an <u>im</u>port/to im<u>port</u>
an <u>in</u>crease/to in<u>crease</u>
a <u>mar</u>ket/to <u>mar</u>ket
a re<u>cruit</u>/to re<u>cruit</u>
a re<u>view</u>/to re<u>view</u>
a <u>tar</u>get/to <u>tar</u>get

WORD STORE 5E

11 CD•2.42 MP3•81 **Complete WORD STORE 5E. Match the adjectives in the box with the synonym that has the closest meaning. Then listen, check, and repeat.**

5.4 Reading

Multiple choice

I can understand a literary and a factual text about men and women's roles.

1 With a partner, read *TODAY IN THE USA* and answer the questions.

1. What percentage of women earn the biggest salary in the family? *40%*
2. How much time do men spend doing the housework and child care? *161 minutes per day*
3. What is the trend for couples where both people work compared to previous eras? *numbers are rising*

TODAY IN THE USA

Work/Home life for the average American family

- Seventy percent of American children live in households where both parents are employed.
- Women **are primary breadwinners** in forty percent of homes with children. Two thirds of these women are single parents.
- With the rise of **dual-income marriages**, women do less housework than in previous **generations**, and men do more. However, women still tend to do more housework than men; in the USA, women spend 248 minutes per day on domestic work, while American men spend 161 minutes per day cooking, cleaning, or on **child-rearing duties**.

2 Replace the underlined words and phrases in Exercise 1 with the words and phrases in blue in *TODAY IN THE USA*.

3 SPEAKING With a partner, discuss what similarities/ differences there are between working life in the US and in your country.

4 Read the text and answer the questions.

1. What was the author's mother's job and what did his father think about it?
2. How many siblings did the author have and what kind of house did they live in?
3. Which of these descriptions do you think best describes the book that this extract was taken from?
   - a historical novel
   - a memoir
   - a travel guide

CD•2.43 MP3•82

CHAPTER 1

Harper's magazine in December 1951 published an article by Nancy B. Mavity on an unsettling new phenomenon, the two-income family, in which husband and wife both went out to work to pay for a more ambitious lifestyle. Mavity's worry was not how women would cope with the demands of employment on top of child-rearing and housework, but rather what this would do to the man's traditional status as breadwinner. 'I'd be ashamed to let my wife work,' one man told Mavity tartly, and it was clear from her tone that Mavity expected most readers to agree. Remarkably, until the war many women in America had been unable to work whether they wanted to or not. Up until Pearl Harbor, half of the forty-eight states had laws making it illegal to employ a married woman.

In this respect, my father was commendably – I would even say enthusiastically – liberal, and was completely in favor of my mother working. She worked for the *Des Moines Register*, as the Home Furnishings Editor, in which capacity she provided calm reassurance to two generations of homemakers who were anxious to know whether the time had come for paisley in the bedroom and whether they should have square sofa cushions or round. […]

Because they both worked, we were better off than most people of our socio-economic background (which in Des Moines in the 1950s was most people). We – which is to say, my parents, my brother, Michael, my sister, Mary Elizabeth (or Betty), and I – had a bigger house on a larger lot than most of my parents' colleagues. It was a white clapboard house with black shutters and a big screened porch on top of a shady hill on the best side of town. […]

The only downside of my mother's working was that it

Exercise 2
1 primary breadwinners
2 child-rearing duties
3 dual-income marriages, generations

Exercise 4
1 Mrs. Bryson was home furnishings editor for *The Des Moines Register*. Mr. Bryson was completely in favor of Mrs. Bryson working.
2 Bryson had two siblings – a brother and a sister. They lived in a large house which was made of white clapboard, with black shutters and a big screened porch.
3 A memoir.

90

REFERENCES
CULTURE NOTES ››› p. 196

EXTRA ACTIVITIES
- Photocopiable resource 31 (vocabulary from reading text – 10 mins) MultiROM and ActiveTeach

WORKBOOK
pp. 68–69

NEXT CLASS
- Write a paragraph describing the similarities or differences between working lives in your country and the US.

The Life and Times of the Thunderbolt Kid, by Bill Bryson

put a little pressure on her with regard to running the home and particularly with regard to dinner, which, frankly, she wasn't very good at anyway. My mother always ran late and was dangerously forgetful. You soon learned to stand aside about ten to six every evening, for it was then that she would fly in the back door, throw something in the oven and disappear into some other quarter of the house to embark on the thousand other household tasks that greeted her each evening. In consequence, she nearly always forgot about dinner until a point slightly beyond way too late. As a rule, you knew it was time to eat when you could hear potatoes exploding in the oven. We didn't call it the kitchen in our house. We called it the Burns Unit.

'It's a bit burned,' my mother would say apologetically at every meal, presenting you with a piece of meat that looked like something – a much-loved pet perhaps – salvaged from a tragic house fire. 'But I think I scraped off most of the burned part,' she would add, overlooking that this included every bit of it that had once been flesh.

Happily, all this suited my father. His palate only responded to two tastes – burned and ice cream – so everything was fine by him so long as it was sufficiently dark and not too startlingly flavorful. Theirs truly was a marriage made in heaven, for no one could burn food like my mother or eat it like my dad.

As part of her job, my mother bought stacks of housekeeping magazines – *House Beautiful*, *House and Garden*, *Better Homes and Gardens*, *Good Housekeeping* – and I read these with a certain avidity, partly because they were always lying around and in our house all idle moments were spent reading something, and partly because they depicted lives so absorbingly at variance with our own. The housewives in my mother's magazines were so collected, so organized, so calmly on top of things, and their food was perfect – their lives were perfect. They dressed up to take their food out of the oven!

EXAM FOCUS Multiple choice

5 Read the text again. For questions 1–6, choose the correct answer, A, B, C, or D.

1 Nancy B. Mavity
- **A** believed both husbands and wives should work.
- **B** worried about women who were ambitious in their work.
- **C** wondered how couples would share housework.
- **D** thought that gender roles should not be changed.

2 The writer's family
- **A** were sure that their home furnishings were up-to-date.
- **B** came from a better socio-economic background than most people.
- **C** had a more comfortable lifestyle thanks to their dual income.
- **D** knew a lot of people with large houses in a good part of town.

3 In paragraph 4, the writer
- **A** sympathizes with his mother's situation.
- **B** complains that his mother was always late.
- **C** suggests that his mother was overworked.
- **D** recommends that women shouldn't work.

4 How does the writer's mother feel about the food she cooks?
- **A** upset that her food is burned
- **B** uncaring about the family's reaction
- **C** aware that it is not perfect
- **D** confident that the family will enjoy it

5 What does *this* refer to in line 62?
- **A** the lack of meat on the plate
- **B** his wife's way of cooking
- **C** his wife's apology
- **D** the appearance of his meal

6 The writer liked reading the magazines because
- **A** they showed a different way of living.
- **B** he didn't have anything else to read.
- **C** he wanted to learn about his mother's job.
- **D** he envied the lifestyle they portrayed.

6 SPEAKING Think about your grandparents', your parents', and your own generation. Discuss how family/working life has changed.

WORD STORE 5F

7 CD•2.44 MP3•83 **Complete WORD STORE 5F with the phrases in the box. Then listen, check, and repeat. Find and underline examples in the text on pages 90–91.**

5.5 Grammar

Reporting verbs

I can use a range of reporting verbs correctly.

1 With a partner, look at the title of the article below. What do you think it means? Then read Part 1 of the article. What's the answer?

SPOILED BRAT OR NEGLECTED CHILD?

US teenager Rachel Canning took her parents to court and tried to sue them for financial support. She accused them of abandoning her when she had turned eighteen and refusing to fund her college education. She **claimed** that they had thrown her out of her home and **explained** that she had been living at a friend's house.

Mr. Canning refused to accept his daughter's version of events. He denied kicking Rachel out and **assured** the court that she had left voluntarily after an argument about household rules and her choice of boyfriends. He **suggested** that Rachel's friends had encouraged her to take the matter to court. He **insisted** that he and his wife loved and missed their child and **added** that the situation was having a terrible effect on them. He begged his daughter to come home soon.

Exercise 2
claimed, explained, suggested, insisted, added can be replaced with *said* because they don't take an object
assured can be replaced with *told* because it takes an object

2 Translate the verbs in blue in Exercise 1. Which five can be replaced with *said*? Which one can be replaced with *told*?

3 Read the GRAMMAR FOCUS. Then find five more reporting verbs in Exercise 1. Which verb patterns do they illustrate?

GRAMMAR FOCUS

Reporting verbs

1 Verbs without a direct object

- **verb + *that* clause:** *add, admit, agree, claim, deny, explain, insist, promise, propose, recommend, suggest*
  *She **promised that** she would come home.*
- **verb + *to*-infinitive:** *agree, claim, offer, promise, refuse* refuse
  *He **offered to help**.*
- **verb + *-ing* form:** *admit, deny, propose, recommend, suggest* deny
  *They **suggested talking** to the lawyer.*
- **verb + preposition + *-ing* form:** *apologize for, object to, insist on*
  *I **insisted on paying** for everything.*

2 Verbs with a direct object

- **verb + object + *that* clause:** *assure, convince, inform, promise, remind, warn*
  *She **assured me that** she was OK.*
- **verb + object + *to*-infinitive:** *advise, beg, convince, encourage, invite, order, persuade, remind, urge, warn (not)* beg, encourage
  *He **begged them to leave**.*
- **verb + object + preposition + *-ing* form:** *accuse sb of, blame sb for, congratulate sb on, thank sb for* accuse sb of
  *I **accused her of telling** lies.*

92

EXTRA ACTIVITIES
- Photocopiable resource 32 (Test yourself partner work activities) MultiROM and ActiveTeach
- MyEnglishLab – assignable *Show what you have learned* mini-test

WORKBOOK
p. 70

NEXT CLASS
- Ask students to prepare for a 10–15 minute grammar quiz: *Focus Assessment Package*, Unit 5.5, Grammar.

4 Read Part 2 of the article and choose the correct answer, A, B, C, or D. Do you agree with the judge's decision?

The judge rejected the teenager's demands and [1] _______ everyone in the court that in future, children may consider suing their parents for a smartphone. The judge [2] _______ Rachel and her family to have family counseling. The teenager has [3] _______ to return home and the Cannings have [4] _______ the media to give the family some privacy while they work things out. The parents have [5] _______ to relax the house rules and in return, Rachel has [6] _______ them that she won't leave home again.

Rachel Canning and her father in court

1	A warned	B explained	C promised	D suggested
2	A denied	B insisted	C advised	D reminded
3	A agreed	B proposed	C reminded	D ordered
4	A refused	B warned	C insisted	D urged
5	A convinced	B offered	C suggested	D told
6	A agreed	B denied	C warned	D promised

5 Some reporting verbs can follow two or more patterns. Report each of these sentences in two different ways.

1 'I did not kick my daughter out!' Rachel's father denied …
2 'We figure you should take your parents to court.' Rachel's friends suggested …
3 'We have been terribly upset.' Her parents admitted …
4 'You should have some family counseling.' The judge recommended …
5 'OK. We'll relax some of the house rules.' Rachel's parents promised …
6 'All right. I'll move back in.' Rachel agreed …

6 Complete the sentences with the correct form of the verbs in the box. Use the correct verb pattern. Add *me* if necessary.

buy	have	lose	not copy	owe	repaint

Recently:
1 my friends have persuaded _me to have_ a haircut.
2 my brother/sister has accused _me of losing_ his/her camera.
3 a teacher has warned _me not to copy_ homework from the Internet.
4 a friend has reminded _me that I owe_ him/her some money.
5 my grandparents have offered _to buy_ me a laptop.
6 Dad has suggested _repainting_ my bedroom.

7 SPEAKING With a partner, discuss whether the sentences in Exercise 6 are true for you. Use the sentence beginnings to report other things that people have said to you.

Grammar Focus page 169

Exercise 5
1 kicking his daughter out/(that) he had kicked his daughter out.
2 taking her parents to court/(that) she (should) take her parents to court.
3 being terribly upset/(that) they had been terribly upset.
4 having some family counseling/(that) they should have some family counseling.
5 to relax some of the house rules/(that) they would relax some of the house rules.
6 to move back in/(that) she would move back in.

5.6 Speaking

Problem solving

I can discuss problems and solutions, and express annoyance.

1 SPEAKING **With a partner, describe what happened last time you experienced one of these problems.**

- Something was lost or stolen (bag, keys, bike, etc.).
- Something was broken (computer, car, phone, etc.).
- Something was forgotten (test, alarm, appointment, etc.).

Exercise 2
1 The door to the store wouldn't open. The key broke off in the lock. Then Hannah tried to get into the store through an open window at the back, but she got stuck and the alarm went off.

2 CD•2.45 MP3•84 **Listen to two friends, Hannah and Daniel, discussing a problem and answer the questions.**

1 What was the problem and how did Hannah and Daniel try to solve it?
2 What would be a better solution in your opinion?
3 What do you think might happen next?

3 CD•2.45 MP3•84 **Choose the correct options to complete the SPEAKING FOCUS. Then listen again and check.**

SPEAKING FOCUS

Talking about a problem

What's wrong/the matter?
What's [1]*up/on* (with it)?
I seem/appear to have lost/forgotten/broken …
I haven't (got) a clue./I have no [2]*thought/idea.*/I wish I knew.
Every time I try to …, it …
Maybe there's something wrong/a problem with the …

Talking about a solution

Have you tried … + *-ing*?
It's worth a try, I suppose.
I [3]*doubt/know* that'll work/help, but let's see.
Problem solved!
No, that doesn't/didn't make any [4]*solution/difference.*

Expressing annoyance

What are we [5]*about/supposed* to do now?
Why in the world did/didn't you … ?
How should I [6]*know/think*?
You should've checked/asked first.
You should've thought about that earlier.

REFERENCES
AUDIO SCRIPT ››› *p. 209*

WORKBOOK
p. 71

4 CD•2.46 MP3•85 **Complete the conversations with one word in each blank. Sometimes more than one answer is possible. Then listen and check.**

1

Abi and Beth are working in a supermarket during the school vacation.

Abi: What's [1] ___up___ ?

Beth: Well, unfortunately, I [2] ___seem/ appear___ to have broken the bar code scanner.

Abi: Oh no. What happened?

Beth: I put it on the table during the break and spilled my coffee on it – like an idiot!

Abi: Whoops. The manager isn't going to be happy.

Beth: Yeah, tell me about it. [3] ___Every___ time I try to turn it on, it beeps and turns off again.

Abi: Have you [4] ___tried___ drying it under the hand dryer in the restroom?

Beth: Actually, no, but it's worth a try, I [5] ___suppose___ .

2

Leo is working on his uncle's farm in the summer.

Pete: Hello, Woodtop Farm.

Leo: Uncle Pete, it's me. I'm in the bottom field. The tractor has broken down.

Pete: What? What's the [6] ___matter___ with it?

Leo: Um … I [7] ___wish___ I knew.

Pete: OK, listen, are the lights working?

Leo: Hang on a second … Yep.

Pete: OK, then it's not the battery. You did remember to put some gas in it, right?

Leo: Um … oh.

Pete: Leo! I told you it was nearly empty.

Leo: I, um … I forgot. Sorry.

Pete: Well, you'll have to walk back up here and get some, won't you?

Leo: What? It's a long way!

Pete: Well, you should have thought about that [8] ___before___ . Next time, maybe you'll remember.

Leo: Can't you bring some down in the … Hello? Hello?

5 **With a partner, follow the instructions to prepare a conversation. Use the SPEAKING FOCUS to help you.**

As part of a school project, you are giving a joint presentation about summer job opportunities in your local area. Together, you prepared notes and visuals on a laptop at home.

Student A: You were responsible for bringing a thumb drive with all the notes and visuals. The presentation is in twenty minutes and you just realized you left the thumb drive at home.

Student B: You worked hard on the presentation and you are very annoyed that your partner forgot to bring the thumb drive.

There isn't enough time to go home. Together, you need to come up with a solution.

6 **SPEAKING Practice your conversation and act it out.**

5.7 Writing

An article

I can introduce the topic of main paragraphs, generalize and discuss consequences in an article.

1 You are going to suggest a suitable job for your partner based on his/her interests. With a partner, follow the instructions.

1 Thinking about yourself, make a list of the following items:
- two personal interests
- the two school subjects you enjoy most
- two college majors that interest you

2 Exchange lists with your partner and suggest at least one job that would suit him/her, based on their interests.

3 Do you like your partner's suggestion(s)? Why?/Why not?

2 Read the writing task and Ben's article. Do you agree with the author's point of view? Why?/Why not?

An increasing number of young people choose a college major based on what is likely to lead to a good job rather than what interests them. Write an article for a website in which you explain the reasons for such a decision and discuss the possible consequences.

3 Read Ben's plan. Then mark the paragraphs in his article. *See ⌐ in the text.*

Introduction
Introduce the topic. Refer to school. Ask the reader what they would do.

Main paragraph 1
Though interesting, some majors are unlikely to lead to a career. Graduates have to be lucky, or the best, to get a job.

Main paragraph 2
Even if some majors are likely to lead to a job, how will you motivate yourself to study a subject you find boring? Likely to lead to low grades and unhappiness.

Conclusion
Difficult decision. I'll take my chances on a major I enjoy. Four years is a long time, so think carefully!

4 Underline two sentences in Ben's article that tell you what the topic of each main paragraph will be. *See ⬭ in the text.*

Ben, Atlanta posted on March 7, 8:17 p.m.

We are not robots

In school, we all have to study the subjects we do not like alongside the ones we find interesting. However, would you consider spending four years studying a single subject that does not interest you in order to have a bigger chance of getting a good job? Although some university subjects sound very interesting, young people often avoid them because in many cases they don't lead to an obvious career. Examples include media studies, popular music, and philosophy. To get a job in one of these areas, graduates have to be very lucky or be the very best. It is fair to say that there are not many millionaire philosophers in this world! Understandably, many students decide that a more practical degree, in accounting or engineering, for example, is a safer option, even if the particular subject doesn't really interest them. However, we are humans, not robots, and opting for a subject we find boring creates significant problems when it comes to motivation. The outcome of such a choice could be low grades and a very unhappy time at university.

Deciding which way to go is difficult, but personally, I think I will take my chances and choose a subject I am interested in. Four years is a long time to dedicate yourself to anything, especially if you do not enjoy it. It is a good idea to think very carefully before you make your choice. It could affect the rest of your life.

96

Comments (18)

EXTRA ACTIVITIES
- MyEnglishLab – assignable *Show what you have learned* writing task and *Show that you have checked* checklist

WORKBOOK
p. 72

5 Read three main paragraphs from other articles on this subject. Then choose the best topic sentence for each paragraph.

> [1]______ According to recent figures, nearly half of new UK graduates work in jobs that don't normally require a degree. **Some** would say they are the fortunate ones, compared to around ten percent of new graduates who can't find employment at all.

A More and more young people are completing college degrees these days.
(B) It is increasingly difficult for college graduates to find jobs that suit their qualifications.
C Unemployment among young people has reached worrying levels in recent years.

> [2]______ Compared to decades spent in a poorly-paid and unsatisfying job, a few years of working on a major that you may not always find stimulating seems like a small sacrifice. This should be a strong enough motivation for most young people.

A People **tend** to retire much later in life nowadays.
B Most people **agree** there is no such thing as a job for life these days.
(C) When deciding what to major in, it is important to consider the long-term future.

> [3]______ It is therefore often the case that, once you have chosen to major in one of these subjects, your other career options are limited. As a **consequence**, before you decide on one of these subjects, you need to be certain that this is the career for you.

(A) Majors such as nursing, architecture, and grade school teaching lead to very specific jobs.
B Examples of traditional degrees include medicine, law, and economics.
C Such majors as management or business studies prepare graduates for a wide range of jobs.

6 Complete the WRITING FOCUS with the words in purple in Ben's article and Exercise 5.

WRITING FOCUS

An article

Generalizing

Broadly speaking,/In general,/On the whole, …
In some/certain/[1] __many__ /most cases …
It is rarely/sometimes/often/usually the case that …
Many/Most people/of us feel/believe/[2] __agree__ …
People [3] __tend__ (not) to …
[4] __Some__ would say (that) …

Describing possible consequences

The result/consequence/[5] __outcome__ of (such a decision/choice) could be (that) …
This could lead to/result in/cause/trigger …
As a [6] __consequence__/result/Consequently, …

7 Make the following statements more general using the prompts in parentheses and phrases from the WRITING FOCUS.

1 High school students in my country don't have weekend jobs. (tend)
High school students in my country tend not to have weekend jobs.
2 In my country, lots of people think students should focus only on their studies. (most/agree)
3 High school students don't need to work to help pay for their education. (rarely/case)
4 Work experience is as valuable as a college education. (some/say)
5 The skills young people learn through a part-time job are valued by future employers. (most/cases)

8 Match the underlined adjectives in Ben's article with the adjectives with similar meanings in the LANGUAGE FOCUS.

LANGUAGE FOCUS

Range of adjectives

Hold the reader's attention by using a wide range of adjectives in your writing.

1 __interesting__ = stimulating
2 __very interesting__ = fascinating
3 __boring__ = dull
4 __difficult__ = tough
5 __bigger__ = greater
6 __very unhappy__ = miserable
7 __lucky__ = fortunate

9 Read the writing task. Then follow the instructions below.

> You have seen this announcement on an international students' website.
>
> **Get a part-time job!**
> Have you had or would you like to have a part-time job? Why? Can a part-time job be useful for your education or future career?
> Write an article for our website answering these questions.
>
> Write your article in 140–190 words.

1 Note down your ideas for each of the questions in the task.
2 Organize your notes into a plan similar to the one in Exercise 3.
3 Think about how you will attract and hold the reader's attention (see page 43 if necessary).
4 Write sentences that tell the reader what each main paragraph is going to be about.
5 Develop these sentences into full paragraphs, and then add a title, an introduction, and a conclusion.

10 Complete the writing task in Exercise 9. Use the WRITING FOCUS and the LANGUAGE FOCUS to help you.

97

Exercise 7
2 In my country, most people agree (that) students should focus only on their studies.
3 It is rarely the case that high school students need to work to help pay for their education.
4 Some would say (that) work experience is as valuable as a college education.
5 In most cases, the skills young people learn through a part-time job are valued by future employers./ The skills young people learn though a part-time job are valued by future employers in most cases.

5.8 Language in focus

Phrasal verbs

I can recognize and use common phrasal verbs.

1 Read the information about phrasal verbs and complete the table with examples a–d.

With phrasal verbs you need to think about:

- the **meaning**: is it literal – *she picked the baby up* (= lifted), or idiomatic – *she picked a skill up* (= learned)?
- the **grammar** and syntax: you can say *she picked French up, she picked up French, she picked it up* but NOT ~~she picked up it~~.

Phrasal verbs are usually divided into four types:

GRAMMAR (SYNTAX)	EXAMPLES
verb + particle + object	1 deal with them
verb + particle	2 Hang on
verb + object + particle verb + particle + object (NOT pronouns)	3 taken her on We took on Jo.
verb + particle + particle + object	4 made up for it

a The service was bad but the food **made up for** it.
b I'm busy. Can you **deal with** them?
c Sarah's good, so we've **taken** her **on**./We've **taken on** Jo.
d **Hang on**, I'm not ready yet!

2 Complete the phrasal verbs with *in*, *off*, or *out*. Then answer the questions.

1 separate sth by cutting
2 stop working (a machine, an engine) — CUT *out*

3 admit that you can't guess the answer
4 accept that you can't win — GIVE *up*

5 remove sth (clothing)
6 become successful very fast (a business) — TAKE *off*

- Which phrasal verbs have a literal meaning? *1, 5*
- Which phrasal verbs have an idiomatic meaning? *2, 3, 4, 6*

3 For each blank, choose from options A–D to complete the sentences. Which statements do you agree with?

A come B take C get D put

1 People always try to *get* out of paying their taxes.
2 Do tasks you hate right away and don't *put* them off.
3 On your first day in a new job, there's always a lot to *take* in.
4 It's important to *come* across as confident in an interview.

4 Rewrite the sentences. Replace the underlined phrases with phrasal verbs that include the words in capitals. Which sentences are true for you?

1 My friend once cheated on a test, but he didn't get caught (*got away with it*). **GOT**
2 Police officers are people who I really respect (*look up to*). **TO**
3 My sister is always inventing (*making up*) stories that aren't true. **UP**
4 I'd never reject (*turn down*) part-time work. I need the money! **DOWN**
5 I just ended a relationship (*broke up*) with my girlfriend. **UP**
6 Half the workforce has been dismissed (*laid off*) at a local factory. **LAID**

98

05 WORD LIST

Jobs

accountant /ə'kaʊntənt/
beautician /byu'tɪʃən/
caretaker /'kerˌteɪkɚ/
civil servant /ˌsɪvəl 'sɚvənt/
detective /dɪ'tektɪv/
lifestyle photographer /'laɪfstaɪl fəˌtɑgrəfɚ/
official ambassador /əˌfɪʃəl æm'bæsədɚ/
park ranger /'pɑrk ˌreɪndʒɚ/
wind turbine technician /'wɪnd ˌtɚbaɪn tekˌnɪʃən/

Career

accept a post /əkˌsept ə 'poʊst/
application /ˌæplɪ'keɪʃən/
apply for /ə'plaɪ fɚ/
available /ə'veɪləbəl/
be in charge of /bi ɪn 'tʃɑrdʒ əv/
be responsible for /bi rɪ'spɑnsəbəl fɚ/
candidate /'kændədeɪt/
career prospects/options /kə'rɪr ˌprɑspekts/ˌɑpʃənz/
colleague /'kɑlig/
commute to work /kəˌmyut tə 'wɚk/
contract /'kɑntrækt/
create a vacancy/vacant post /kriˌeɪt ə 'veɪkənsi/ˌveɪkənt 'poʊst/
dedicate yourself to /'dedəkeɪt yɚˌself tə/
degree /dɪ'gri/
dismiss /dɪs'mɪs/
do an internship /ˌdu ən 'ɪnˌtɚnʃɪp/
duties /'dut̬iz/
employ/hire /ɪm'plɔɪ/'haɪɚ/
employee /ɪm'plɔɪ-i/
employer /ɪm'plɔɪɚ/
experience of restaurant work /ɪkˌspɪriəns əv 'resˌtrɑnt wɚk/
expire /ɪk'spaɪɚ/
express interest in/concern about /ɪkˌspres 'ɪntrɪst ɪn/kən'sɚn əˌbaʊt/
fill a vacancy/vacant post /ˌfɪl ə 'veɪkənsi/ˌveɪkənt 'poʊst/
find employment /ˌfaɪnd ɪm'plɔɪmənt/
gain skills/qualifications /ˌgeɪn 'skɪlz/ˌkwɑləfə'keɪʃənz/
graduate /'grædʒuɪt/
interpersonal skills /ˌɪntɚˌpɚsənl 'skɪlz/
interview (n, v) /'ɪntɚvyu/
interviewee /ˌɪntɚvyu'i/
interviewer /'ɪntɚvyuɚ/
involve /ɪn'vɑlv/
job opportunities /ˌdʒɑb ˌɑpɚ'tunət̬iz/
(key/primary) responsibilities /(ˌki/ˌpraɪmeri) rɪˌspɑnsə'bɪlət̬iz/
leave a job /ˌliv ə 'dʒɑb/
living expenses /'lɪvɪŋ ɪkˌspensɪz/
living standards /'lɪvɪŋ ˌstændɚdz/
long-term future /ˌlɔŋ tɚm 'fyutʃɚ/
medical/teaching profession/post /'medɪkəl/'titʃɪŋ prəˌfeʃən/poʊst/
morning person /'mɔrnɪŋ ˌpɚsən/
motivate yourself to do sth /'moʊt̬əˌveɪt yɚˌself tə du ˌsʌmθɪŋ/
motivation /ˌmoʊt̬ə'veɪʃən/
pay package of ... /'peɪ pækɪdʒ ˌəv .../
perk /pɚk/
place of work /ˌpleɪs əv 'wɚk/
position/post /pə'zɪʃən/poʊst/
prepare a shortlist of candidates /prɪˌper ə ˌʃɔrtlɪst əv 'kændədeɪts/
promote /prə'moʊt/
recruit (v, n) /rɪ'krut/
recruitment /rɪ'krutmənt/
reference /'refrəns/
relevant /'reləvənt/
replace /rɪ'pleɪs/
require /rɪ'kwaɪɚ/
requirements /rɪ'kwaɪɚmənts/
retail /'riteɪl/
retain sb as ... /rɪ'teɪn ˌsʌmbɑdi əz .../
retire /rɪ'taɪɚ/
review (n, v) /rɪ'vyu/
reviewer /rɪ'vyuɚ/
(rigorous) application/selection process /(ˌrɪgərəs) ˌæplɪ'keɪʃən/sə'lekʃən ˌprɑses/
run a competition /ˌrʌn ə ˌkɑmpə'tɪʃən/
salary /'sæləri/
sense of achievement /ˌsens əv ə'tʃivmənt/

EXTRA ACTIVITIES

- Photocopiable resource 33 (phrasal verbs – 10 mins) MultiROM and ActiveTeach

WORKBOOK

p. 73

NEXT CLASS

- Ask students to study the Word list on pp. 98–99.
- Ask students to review for Focus review 5.

sense of adventure /ˌsens əv ədˈventʃɚ/
stable profession /ˌsteɪbəl prəˈfeʃən/
(successful) applicant /(səkˌsesfəl) ˈæplɪkənt/
suit your qualifications /ˌsut yɚ ˌkwɑləfəˈkeɪʃənz/
target the youth market/the college sector /ˌtɑrgɪt ðə ˈyuθ ˌmɑrkɪt/ ðə ˈkɑlɪdʒ ˌsektɚ/
terms and conditions /ˌtɚmz ənd kənˈdɪʃənz/
tourism industry /ˈtʊrɪzəm ˌɪndəstri/
training /ˈtreɪnɪŋ/
unemployment /ˌʌnɪmˈplɔɪmənt/
VIP event /ˌvi aɪ ˈpi ɪˌvent/
weaknesses /ˈwiknəsɪz/
work freelance /ˌwɚk ˈfrilæns/
work from home /ˌwɚk frəm ˈhoʊm/
workforce /ˈwɚkfɔrs/
working hours /ˈwɚkɪŋ ˌaʊɚz/

Adjectives to describe jobs

challenging/demanding /ˈtʃæləndʒɪŋ/dɪˈmændɪŋ/
fulfilling/rewarding /fʊlˈfɪlɪŋ/rɪˈwɔrdɪŋ/
high-powered /ˌhaɪ ˈpaʊɚd/
lucrative/well-paid /ˈlukrət̬ɪv/ˌwel ˈpeɪd/
monotonous/tedious /məˈnɑtˀənəs/ˈtidiəs/
part-time /ˌpɑrt ˈtaɪm/
poorly-paid /ˌpʊrli ˈpeɪd/
secure/stable /sɪˈkyʊr/ˈsteɪbəl/
unsatisfying /ʌnˈsæt̬ɪsˌfaɪɪŋ/

University subjects

Accounting /əˈkaʊntɪŋ/
Architecture /ˈɑrkətektʃɚ/
Business studies/Management /ˈbɪznəs ˌstʌdiz/ˈmænɪdʒmənt/
Economics /ˌekəˈnɑmɪks/
Engineering /ˌendʒəˈnɪrɪŋ/
Grade School Teaching /ˈgreɪd skul ˌtitʃɪŋ/
Law /lɔ/
Medicine /ˈmedəsən/
Nursing /ˈnɚsɪŋ/
Philosophy /fɪˈlɑsəfi/

Gender roles, family issues

abandon /əˈbændən/
be engaged in /bi ɪnˈgeɪdʒd ɪn/
childcare/child-rearing duties /ˈtʃaɪldker/ˈtʃaɪld ˌrɪrɪŋ ˌdut̬iz/
disagreement /ˌdɪsəˈgrimənt/
do the housework/domestic work/domestic duties/household tasks /ˌdu ðə ˈhaʊswɚk/dəˈmestɪk wɚk/dəˌmestɪk ˈdut̬iz/ˈhaʊshoʊld tæsks/
dual-income/two-income family /ˌduəl ˌɪŋkʌm/ˌtu ˌɪŋkʌm ˈfæmli/
family counseling /ˌfæmli ˈkaʊnsəlɪŋ/
fund /fʌnd/
homemaker /ˈhoʊmˌmeɪkɚ/
neglect /nɪˈglekt/
overworked /oʊvɚˈwɚkt/
primary breadwinner /ˌpraɪˌmeri ˈbredˌwɪnɚ/
privacy /ˈpraɪvəsi/
put pressure on /ˌpʊt ˈpreʃər ɑn/
quarrel /ˈkwɑrəl/
reject sb's demands /rɪˌdʒekt ˌsʌmbɑdiz dɪˈmændz/
relax the house rules/household rules /rɪˌlæks ðə ˌhaʊs ˈrulz/ ˌhaʊshoʊld ˈrulz/
run late /ˌrʌn ˈleɪt/
run the home /ˌrʌn ðə ˈhoʊm/
sacrifice /ˈsækrəfaɪs/
siblings /ˈsɪblɪŋz/
socioeconomic background /ˌsoʊsioʊekəˈnɑmɪk ˈbækgraʊnd/
spoiled brat /ˌspɔɪld ˈbræt/
take sb/sth to court/sue sb (for sth) /ˌteɪk ˌsʌmbɑdi/ˌsʌmθɪŋ tə ˈkɔrt/ ˈsu ˌsʌmbɑdi (fɚ ˌsʌmθɪŋ)/
turn (eighteen) /ˌtɚn (ˌeɪˈtin)/

Statistics

average /ˈævrɪdʒ/
be unchanged/remain constant /ˌbi ʌnˈtʃeɪndʒd/rɪˌmeɪn ˈkɑnstənt/
gradual decline/drop in the number of /ˌgrædʒuəl dɪˌklaɪn/ˌdrɑp ɪn ðə ˈnʌmbər əv/
marked increase/sharp rise in sth /ˌmɑrkt ˈɪnkris/ˌʃɑrp ˈraɪz ɪn sʌmθɪŋ/
recent figures /ˌrisənt ˈfɪgyɚz/
sharp drop/rapid decline in /ˌʃɑrp ˈdrɑp/ˌræpɪd dɪˈklaɪn ɪn/
steady rise in/growing number of /ˌstedi ˈraɪz ɪn/ˌgroʊɪŋ ˈnʌmbɚ əv/

Phrasal verbs

carry out (a study) /ˌkæri ˈaʊt (ə stʌdi)/
come across as (polite) /ˌkʌm əˈkrɔs əz (pəˈlaɪt)/
cut out /ˌkʌt ˈaʊt/
deal with /ˈdil wɪð/
draw up (a list) /ˌdrɔ ˈʌp (ə lɪst)/
embark on (household tasks) /ɪmˈbɑrk ɑn (haʊshoʊld tæsks)/
get away with /ˌget əˈweɪ wɪð/
get along /ˌget ˈəˈlɔŋ/
get out of /ˌget ˈaʊt əv/
give up /gɪv ˈʊp/
hang on /ˌhæŋ ˈɑn/
keep on (as ...) /ˌkip ˈɑn (æs ...)/
kick/throw out /ˌkɪk/θroʊ ˈaʊt/
lay off /ˌleɪ ɔf/
lead to /ˈlid tə/
look down on /ˌlʊk ˈdaʊn ɑn/
look up to /ˌlʊk ˈʌp tə/
make up /ˌmeɪk ˈʌp/
make up for /ˌmeɪk ˈʌp fɚ/
pick up (new skills) /ˌpɪk ˈʌp (nu skɪlz)/
put off /ˌpʊt ɔf/
step down (from a job) /ˌstep ˈdaʊn (frəm ə dʒɑb)/
take in /ˌteɪk ˈɪn/
take off /ˌteɪk ɔf/
take on /ˌteɪk ˈɑn/
take up (a post) /ˌteɪk ˈʌp (ə poʊst)/
try out /ˌtraɪ ˈaʊt/
turn down /ˌtɚn ˈdaʊn/
work (things) out /ˌwɚk (θɪŋz) ˈaʊt/

Other

at dawn /ˌət ˈdɔn/
at last /ˌət ˈlæst/
at once /ˌət ˈwʌns/
at present /ˌət ˈprezənt/
at risk /ˌət ˈrɪsk/
attract /əˈtrækt/
be immersed in /bi ɪˈmɚst ɪn/
be short of money /bi ˌʃɔrt əv ˈmʌni/
benefit (n, v) /ˈbenəfɪt/
blame /bleɪm/
campaign (n, v) /kæmˈpeɪn/
campaigner /kæmˈpeɪnɚ/
collective responsibility /kəˌlektɪv rɪˌspɑnsəˈbɪlət̬i/
congratulate /kənˈgrætʃəleɪt/
consequently/in consequence/as a consequence /ˈkɑnsəkwentli/ ɪn ˈkɑnsəkwens/əz ə ˈkɑnsəkwens/
dull /dʌl/
fortunate /ˈfɔrtʃənɪt/
indigenous culture /ɪnˌdɪdʒənəs ˈkʌltʃɚ/
memoir /ˈmemwɑr/
miserable /ˈmɪzərəbəl/
object /ɑbˈdʒekt/
outcome /ˈaʊtˀkʌm/
persuade /pɚˈsweɪd/
phenomenon /fɪˈnɑmənɑn/
provide reassurance /prəˌvaɪd ˌriəˈʃʊrəns/
stimulating /ˈstɪmyəleɪt̬ɪŋ/
tough /tʌf/
warn /wɔrn/
well-off /ˌwel ɔf/

FOCUS REVIEW 5

VOCABULARY AND GRAMMAR

1 Complete the sentences with the correct form of the words in capitals.

1 It is important that interviewees try to be relaxed when they talk to their prospective employers. **INTERVIEW**
2 Having done the same monotonous job for five years, Alan decided to leave and set up his own business. **MONOTONY**
3 My brother's salary covers his __living__ expenses, but he doesn't save anything at all. **LIFE**
4 There aren't many __vacancies__ in the car factory right now. **VACANT**
5 Rob felt a certain sense of achievement when an extensive leisure center was built to his avant-garde design. **ACHIEVE**

2 Choose the correct options.

1 Now that we've won the contract, we need to *keep on / pick up / take on* some new architects.
2 Are you going to apply for a job in a different company once your contract has *expired / secured / declined*?
3 How long are you going to *put off / draw up / hold up* asking the boss for a raise?
4 Since you have so many family issues, have you thought of *looking down on / stepping down from / coming up with* the position of Finance Director?
5 Josh found his first job so *high-powered / tedious / fulfilling* that he quit after a month.

3 Rewrite the sentences in Reported Speech.

1 'You should take a few days off,' the manager said.
The manager said that you ________ a few days off.
2 'I've been working in this company for ten years,' Ann told them.
Ann said ________ for ten years.
3 'I must notify the police because some important documents have disappeared,' Mr. Jones explained.
Mr Jones explained ________ disappeared.
4 'When are you going to look for a permanent post?' my parents keep asking me.
My parents keep asking me ________ a permanent post.

4 Complete the sentences using the words in parentheses.

1 The other day mom's boss ________ (refuse/give/she) a raise.
2 Our new interpreter ________ (suggest/make) a few changes in the speech so that it would sound more natural.
3 The manager ________ (thank/team/work) so hard.
4 My team leader ________ (convince/I/sign) for a training course.
5 Last month my dad ________ (offer/show/I/class) around different departments in his company.
6 Yesterday the chief accountant ________ (deny/boss/spend) any of the company's money on personal expenses.

LANGUAGE IN USE

5 Complete the article with the correct form of the verbs in the box. There are two extra verbs.

apply	come	get	look	prize	reward

My first summer job

I was just twenty-one and studying Tourism when I took my first summer job. A friend of mine told me that the hotel where she was a receptionist 1 was looking for more staff to work in reception during the summer vacation.

I applied and, to my surprise, I got the job. I realized that it wasn't going to be the most 2 rewarding job, but it would probably be good enough to gain some experience. My duties included answering the phone and dealing with the guests' questions and complaints. Apparently, I 3 __came__ across as communicative and efficient, which was nice to know.

After three months, it was time for me to go back to college. I was happy to return home but, at the same time, I knew I had been extremely lucky to have been chosen from all the 4 applicants for the job. The hotel manager offered me a permanent post, which I obviously declined. But I promised to be back the following summer.

6 Rewrite the sentences using the verbs in parentheses.

1 'Congratulations on winning the scholarship, Amanda!' said her mom.
Amanda's mom ________ . (congratulate)
2 'I'll help you prepare for the job interview, Karen,' said Dave.
Dave ________ . (offer)
3 'Do you want to become a fitness instructor, Dan?' asked Ronny.
Ronny ________ . (ask)
4 'I'm sorry I made a mistake with your flight reservation,' the travel agent told me.
The travel agent ________ . (apologize)
5 'Don't forget to fill in the questionnaire,' the teacher said to the class.
The teacher ________ . (remind)

Exercise 3
1 should take
2 that she had been working in that company
3 explained that he had to notify the police because some important documents had
4 when I am going to look for

Exercise 4
1 refused to give her
2 suggested making / suggested that we make
3 thanked the team for working
4 convinced me to sign up
5 offered to show my class
6 denied that the boss had spent

Exercise 6
1 congratulated her on winning the scholarship
2 offered to help Karen prepare for the job interview
3 asked Dan if he wanted to become a fitness instructor
4 apologized for making a mistake with my flight reservation
5 reminded the class to fill in the questionnaire

100

EXTRA ACTIVITIES

- Photocopiable Resource 59B (word building cloze – 20 mins) MultiROM and ActiveTeach
- Photocopiable resource 60D (transformations – 20 mins) MultiROM and ActiveTeach
- Photocopiable resource 34 (Writing – 10 mins) MultiROM and ActiveTeach

WORKBOOK

Use of English 5.9, pp. 74–75; Self-assessment 5.10, p. 76

READING

7 Read the article and choose the correct answer, A, B, C, or D.

The human scarecrow

Being told to bring a deckchair and a good book for the first day in a new job might not be the kind of advice you'd expect to receive from your new boss, but that's exactly the advice Jamie Fox was given when he took up a post to help out a local farmer.

Fox, twenty-two, a music graduate from New York University, uses a range of musical instruments to scare off partridges that have been destroying crops because ordinary scarecrows don't quite seem up to the job. Despite working from 7:30 a.m. to 4:00 p.m. for minimum wage, Fox, who is saving up to finance a trip to Chile, is quite content with his unique position. Indeed, he'd much rather be out in the open air reading and playing instruments, he says, and time passes much quicker than sitting at home doing nothing and claiming unemployment benefit.

Fox can do anything he likes to pass the time. As well as playing musical instruments and reading to relieve the monotony, other perks of the job include doing Sudoku puzzles, observing the wildlife, and daydreaming. He does, however, need to get out of the comfort of his chair occasionally to scare the partridges off the fields. And although the work is far from lucrative, some of Jamie's friends, including those with more generously paid jobs, are reportedly envious of his position and the fact that he spends a large part of the day doing mostly as he pleases.

His employer, farmer William Youngs, claims that he was forced to take someone on as a human scarecrow after the partridges didn't respond to more traditional methods of frightening them away. Since losing thirty acres' worth of crops to the birds at a cost of thousands of dollars, Youngs has tried a variety of approaches to protect his livelihood. Now, however, he is happy with the solution, and he claims that Jamie's presence in the fields is proving very effective and making a real difference.

1 Jamie Fox's plans include
- A joining a band.
- B becoming a farmer.
- **(C)** traveling overseas.
- D earning more money.

2 Jamie Fox is happy with his job because
- A he never gets bored.
- B he uses his educational background.
- C he has plenty of free time during the day.
- **(D)** he thinks it is better than being out of work.

3 What is true about Jamie's job?
- A He doesn't need to move.
- B He has replaced another person.
- C He gets uncomfortable.
- **(D)** He makes a lot of noise.

4 Jamie's friends are envious because of
- A the hours he works.
- **(B)** the nature of his work.
- C the money he earns.
- D the fact he enjoys what he is doing.

5 Mr Youngs decided to employ Jamie because
- A he can pay him a low wage.
- B he considered Jamie a good worker.
- **(C)** he lost lots of crops previously.
- D he wants to help with the problem of unemployment.

SPEAKING

8 With a partner, discuss the questions.

1 What types of part-time jobs are offered to teens in your area?
2 What are the advantages and disadvantages of setting up your own business?
3 Is it better to choose a job that you like doing or one that has a good salary?
4 How can young people find out about the best job for them?
5 Some famous people, like professional athletes, earn very high salaries. Is this a good thing? Why?/Why not?

WRITING

9 Complete the writing task.

You have seen this advertisement in an international students' website.

Taking a year off? We want articles!

Are you considering taking a year off before college, or have you already done this?

Write an article for our magazine about your plans for a year off or your experiences. How can a year off help or hinder your education?

The best articles will be published in the next edition.

Write your article in 140–190 words.

101

NEXT CLASS
- Ask students to do Self-check 5.11, WB p. 77 as homework.
- Ask students to prepare for Unit test 5 (*Focus* Assessment Package).

6 TRUE OR FALSE?

Exercise 1
Some possibilities:
ginger / gray / etc. HAIRED
blue / hazel / wide / etc. EYED
pale / olive / dark / etc. SKINNED
thin / round / etc. FACED
good / messy / etc. LOOKING
well / elegantly / etc. DRESSED

Never let the truth get in the way of a good story.

MARK TWAIN (1835–1910), AN AMERICAN WRITER

UNIT LANGUAGE AND SKILLS

Vocabulary:
- *Show what you know* – adjectives to describe people
- describing truth and falsehood
- phrases with *take*
- compound adjectives
- word families
- phrasal verbs
- *Word in focus* – *or*

Grammar:
- conditional clauses – alternatives to *if*
- mixed conditionals

Listening:
- a conversation about a street artist
- sentence completion

Reading:
- an article about an imposter
- cloze text

Speaking:
- answering questions, expressing tentative opinions

Writing:
- an opinion essay

FOCUS EXTRA

- Grammar Focus pages 169–170
- WORD STORE booklet pages 12–13
- Workbook pages 78–91 or MyEnglishLab
- MP3s – www.english.com/focus

102

6.1 Vocabulary

Truth and falsehood • Phrases with *take* • Compound adjectives

I can describe people and talk about the media.

SHOW WHAT YOU KNOW

1 **With a partner, make two compound adjectives with each word in the box.**

-haired -eyed -skinned -faced -looking -dressed

wavy-haired, dark-haired

2 **SPEAKING With a partner, take turns to describe people you know using your compound adjectives from Exercise 1.**

3 **SPEAKING With a partner, describe the photos of people in the article using the words in the box.**

acne bags under the eyes crow's feet wrinkles furrowed brow fine lines greying hair

Why can't you believe everythi[ng] you see in the media?

Models and celebrities are airbrushed

When celebrities and models appear on posters with smooth skin, the aim is to **create the illusion** that they are perfect. Most celebrities take it for granted that their photos will be digitally improved. But it's far-fetched to suggest that anybody over the age of thirty would have wrinkle-free skin, and this is why Brad Pitt has refused airbrushing because he felt it was inauthentic – he prefers his photos to show his crow's feet and furrowed brow.

Eighteen-year-old singer Lorde tweeted two photos of herself: one had been airbrushed to remove her acne and the other one was left as she is. She commented that imperfections are fine. Other celebrities such as Keira Knightley take pride in the fact that they reject any digital alteration.

Most people recognize digitally improved images and take them with a grain of salt, but these images can affect young people's self-image. Photographers, designers and editors should take some responsibility for showing true images that don't **distort the truth**. But it's unlikely to happen, so young people must become more world-wise and learn to see the difference between **fake** images and **genuine** ones.

REFERENCES
CULTURE NOTES ››› *pp. 196–197*

EXTRA ACTIVITIES
- Photocopiable resource 35 (appearance and the media – 10 mins) MultiROM and ActiveTeach
- Photocopiable resource 36 (Test yourself partner work activities) MultiROM and ActiveTeach
- MyEnglishLab – assignable *Show what you have learned* mini-test

WORKBOOK
pp. 78–79

4 **Read the article and answer the questions.**

1 What do Brad Pitt and Keira Knightley have in common?
2 How does Lorde feel about her skin?
3 What is an important message for young people in Part 1 (lines 1–33) of the article?
4 Why was the photographer of the Obama selfie angry with the press?
5 Does the writer think the photo of the shark in New York was real? How do we know?

5 **SPEAKING With a partner, talk about some of the weird or hilarious photos and video clips you have seen online. How do you know whether they are true or false?**

Photos can be taken out of context

When President Obama posed for a selfie with the Danish and British Prime Ministers at Nelson Mandela's funeral, the press went crazy. The photo showed three Heads of State sharing a light-hearted moment. Meanwhile, Michelle Obama remained stony-faced and appeared unamused. Newspapers around the world thought it was ill-advised to pose for a selfie on such a somber occasion and published it on their front pages.

However, you can't take everything you read in the press at face value. The photographer responsible for the shot claimed that the press had taken his photo out of context and called it 'a **misleading** image'. He wrote on his blog: 'Photos can lie. In reality, just a few seconds earlier Mrs. Obama was joking with those around her.' This is an example of how photos can **manipulate** public opinion. The photograph is **authentic** and the photographer's intention was not to **deceive** the public, but the press saw an opportunity to **sensationalize the story**.

Some photos are doctored

This is the most extreme form of digital alteration, and often just for fun. Photos like this went viral during floods in New York. Real or **doctored**? You decide!

Go to **WORD STORE 6** page 13.

WORD STORE 6A

6 CD•3.1 MP3•86 **Complete WORD STORE 6A with the base form of the words in red in the text. Then listen, check, and repeat. Are the words verbs (v) or adjectives (adj)?**

7 **Complete the sentences about the text with words or phrases from WORD STORE 6A.**

1 Journalists and photographers often try to distort the truth.
2 Not all celebrities want to create the illusion that they are perfect.
3 Fake images can be harmful for young people.
4 The Obama selfie was authentic.
5 The photographer described the Obama selfie as misleading.
6 The press used the selfie to deceive the public.

WORD STORE 6B

8 CD•3.2 MP3•87 **Complete WORD STORE 6B with the underlined phrases with *take* in the text. Then listen, check, and repeat. Add a translation.**

9 **Complete the sentences with phrases from WORD STORE 6B. Then check the sentences that are true for you.**

1 I admire people who admit their mistakes and take responsibility for their actions.
2 I don't realize how much my parents do for me. I just take them for granted.
3 I tend to believe what people tell me. I generally take things at face value.
4 I think the media manipulate the truth by taking things out of context.
5 I don't believe most of the silly stories I read online. I usually take them with a pinch of salt.
6 I'm a perfectionist and like to do my homework well. I take pride in my work.

WORD STORE 6C

10 CD•3.3 MP3•88 **Complete WORD STORE 6C with the highlighted compound adjectives in the text. Then listen, check, and repeat.**

11 **Complete each question with a contrasting compound adjective. Then, with a partner, ask and answer the questions.**

1 Are people in your family usually serious or light-hearted?
2 Is it wise or ill-advised to believe everything you read in the media?
3 Would you describe your best friend as naive or world-wise?
4 Is it more natural for older people to have wrinkles or be wrinkle-free?
5 Is the chance of your national soccer team winning the World Cup likely or far-fetched?
6 Does your English teacher look cheerful or stony-faced when you don't do your homework?

WORD STORE 6D

12 CD•3.4 MP3•89 **Complete WORD STORE 6D with more compound adjectives. Then listen, check, and repeat. Write example sentences.**

Exercise 4
1 They both rejected airbrushing.
2 She thinks it's OK not to be perfect/accepts her acne.
3 Young people need to become more world-wise.
4 Because he thought the press used the image in a different context from that in which it was taken and added a story to it.
5 No, the text suggests it's been doctored.

NEXT CLASS

- Ask students to prepare for a 10–15 minute vocabulary quiz: *Focus* Assessment Package, Unit 6.1, Vocabulary.

6.2 Grammar

Conditional clauses – alternatives to *if*

I can form conditional sentences using if, unless, imagine, provided, suppose, *and inversion.*

1 **'The dog ate my homework' is a typical excuse used by students. With a partner, think of other excuses.**

2 **Read the story. What excuse did the students use for missing their exam? What happened next?** *They said they had a flat tire. They took the exam and Q2 was 'Which tire?'*

The exam question

Imagine you were taking an important exam on Monday, what would you do the weekend before? You almost certainly wouldn't do what two Chemistry students did in Kansas, Missouri. They went to a different city and partied all weekend. They had a great time, but they knew that **unless they got back in time for the exam**, they wouldn't be able to take it. So they drove through the night and got back to college in the early hours of Monday morning. Sadly for them, they overslept and missed the exam.

When they found their professor afterwards, they decided to invent a story. They told him that they would have gotten back for the exam **had they not had a flat tire**. The professor thought about this for a moment and then agreed that, **provided they arrived before 9 a.m.**, they could take the exam the next day. He placed them in separate rooms and gave them the exam paper. The first question was simple and worth five points. But they were unprepared for the question on the next page:

Question 2 (95 points): Which tire?

Exercise 3
If you were taking an important exam on Monday, ...
... if they didn't get back in time for the exam ...
... if they hadn't had a flat tire.
... if they arrived before 9 a.m.

3 **Read the GRAMMAR FOCUS. Then rewrite the conditional clauses in blue in the story using *if*.**

GRAMMAR FOCUS

Conditional clauses – alternatives to *if*

- You use ***unless*** to mean 'except if'.
  I wouldn't lie to you unless it was necessary (= … if it wasn't necessary.)
- You use ***imagine*** or ***suppose/supposing*** to ask questions.
  Imagine you were getting married, how would you feel? (= If you were getting married, …)
- You use ***provided/providing*** to create a condition.
  I'll lend you $10 provided you pay me back tomorrow … (= if you pay me back …)
- You can use **inversion** in formal contexts – mostly with the auxiliary verbs *were, had,* or *should.*
  Had they followed my instructions, they wouldn't have got lost. (= If they had followed …)

Note: In inversion, you do not contract negative forms.
… had they not called, we wouldn't have known. (NOT ~~*… hadn't they called …*~~)

EXTRA ACTIVITIES
- Photocopiable resource 36 (Test yourself partner work activities) MultiROM and ActiveTeach
- MyEnglishLab – assignable *Show what you have learned* mini-test

WORKBOOK
p. 80

NEXT CLASS
- Ask students to prepare for a 10–15 minute grammar quiz: *Focus* Assessment Package, Unit 6.2, Grammar.

4 Rewrite the conditional sentences using *unless*. Then check the sentences that are true for you.

1 I'll fail all my exams if I don't study hard.
I'll fail all my exams unless I study hard.
2 I wouldn't be able to do my homework if I didn't have a laptop.
3 I wouldn't study English if I didn't need it to get a job.
4 My parents wouldn't have let me go out last night if I hadn't finished my homework.
5 I'd never get to school on time if my mom didn't wake me up.
6 I can't understand American movies if I don't watch them with subtitles.

Exercise 4
2 I wouldn't be able to do my homework unless I had a laptop.
3 I wouldn't study English unless I needed it to get a job.
4 My parents wouldn't have let me go out last night unless I had finished my homework.
5 I'd never get to school on time unless my mom woke me up.
6 I can't understand American movies unless I watch them with subtitles.

5 Complete the second sentence so that it has a similar meaning to the first, using the word in capitals. Use no more than six words, including the word in capitals. Do not change the word in capitals. Then check the sentences that are true for you.

1 I'll probably go out this evening if I don't get too much homework. **PROVIDED**
I'll probably go out this evening *provided I don't get* too much homework.
2 If my mom hadn't reminded me, I would've forgotten her birthday. **NOT**
Had *my mom not reminded* me, I would've forgotten her birthday.
3 I'd never eat fast food unless I was absolutely starving. **WASN'T**
If *I wasn't absolutely starving*, I'd never eat fast food.
4 I would've watched Mr. Bean if I'd known it was on TV last night. **WAS**
Had *I known Mr. Bean was* on TV last night, I would've watched it.
5 I don't watch football unless my team is playing. **IF**
I don't watch football *if my team isn't playing*.
6 If I wasn't so tired, I'd go out this evening. **NOT**
Were *I not so tired*, I'd go out this evening.
7 If I should ever get married, I'd want a huge party. **EVER**
Should *I ever get married*, I'd want a huge party.

6 Use the prompts to write conditional questions. Begin each question with *Imagine …* or *Suppose …* and complete it with your own ideas.

1 You can't live anywhere in the world.
Imagine/Suppose you could live anywhere in the world, where would you live?
2 You didn't find $100 in the street yesterday. *Imagine/Suppose you had found …*
3 You're not able to travel back in time. *Imagine/Suppose you were able to travel …*
4 You don't have to live without technology. *Imagine/Suppose you had to live …*
5 You didn't see an old man steal something from a store last week. *Imagine/Suppose you had seen an old man …*
6 You can't have three wishes. *Imagine/Suppose you could have …*

7 SPEAKING With a partner, ask and answer your questions from Exercise 6.

Grammar Focus page 169

6.3 Listening

Sentence completion

I can identify specific details in a conversation.

1 **SPEAKING** With a partner, describe these two murals by controversial British artist Banksy. What do you think they mean?

2 CD•3.5 MP3•90 Listen to a news report. Check the information if it has been confirmed. If not, put a question mark.

1	real name is Robin Gunningham	?
2	was born in Bristol in 1973	?
3	trained to be a butcher	?
4	became famous in the 1990s	✓
5	has never been arrested	✓
6	authenticates his work on his website	✓
7	is a multi-millionaire	?

REFERENCES

CULTURE NOTES ››› p. 197
AUDIO SCRIPT ››› pp. 209–210

WORKBOOK

p. 81

3 With a partner, add *pro-* or *anti-* to the words to describe whether you think Banksy is for or against these things.

1 pro-anonymity
2 anti-authority
3 anti-war
4 pro-peaceful protest
5 pro-fairness
6 pro-equality

4 CD•3.6 MP3•91 Listen to Robert and Alice talking about Banksy and check your ideas in Exercise 3.

EXAM FOCUS Sentence completion

5 CD•3.6 MP3•91 Listen again and complete the sentences with a word or short phrase.

1 Robert needs information to write a(n) essay .
2 Alice did something like Robert when she was working on her degree .
3 Alice first thought Banksy was American .
4 Banksy started painting graffiti twenty-five years ago.
5 He used spray cans and stencils instead of paintbrushes so that he could speed up his work.
6 Banksy doesn't want to be identified because his activities are illegal .
7 Some murals show soldiers with flowers in their hands.
8 Robert admires a mural showing a little girl with a red/floating balloon .

6 Complete the sentences with the words in the box.

aware law peaceful stand strong underlying

1 **Breaking** the law is always wrong.
2 It's a bad idea to **make** people aware **of** your political views.
3 Teenagers have no idea what they stand **for**.
4 Street art can be an effective form of peaceful **protest**.
5 Only experts understand the underlying **messages** in modern art.
6 Nobody has strong **beliefs** about anything any more.

7 **SPEAKING** With a partner, discuss whether you agree or disagree with the statements in Exercise 6.

PRONUNCIATION FOCUS

8 CD•3.7 MP3•92 Listen and put these four-syllable words into the correct group A, B, or C.

~~alteration~~ authority ceremony commentator inauthentic photographer uncomfortable underlying vandalism

A ■▪▪▪	B ▪■▪▪	C ▪▪■▪
ceremony	authority	alteration
commentator	photographer	inauthentic
vandalism	uncomfortable	underlying

9 CD•3.8 MP3•93 Listen, check, and repeat.

WORD STORE 6E

10 CD•3.9 MP3•94 Complete WORD STORE 6E. Add nouns or adjectives to the table. Mark the stress. Then listen, check, and repeat.

6.4 Reading

Cloze text

I can understand the structure of a text.

1 Look at the ways of changing one's appearance. Put ✓ if they are reversible and ✗ if they are irreversible. Which changes would/wouldn't you consider?

bleach or dye your hair ✓ change your hairstyle ✓
draw a mole/beauty spot/scar ✓ go on an extreme diet ✓
have a fake/real tattoo ✓,✗ have plastic surgery ✗
wear color-change contact lenses ✓ wear a wig ✓

2 Read the introduction and first paragraph (lines 1–12) of the article. Explain the link between Nicholas Barclay and Frederic Bourdin. *The link is that Bourdin tried to 'be' Barclay.*

3 Read the rest of the article and answer the questions.

1 Why did Bourdin try to make people believe he was Nicholas?
2 How certain was Bourdin that Carey would realize it was a trick?
3 What solemn promise did Carey make in Spain?
4 What made Parker suspect that Bourdin wasn't Nicholas?
5 When did Bourdin stop pretending that he was Nicholas?
6 What suggestions does the writer make about the family's motivations?

Exercise 3
1 To get a new identity and run away from a home for young people in Spain.
2 Very certain.
3 That Bourdin was her brother.
4 Because he analyzed the ears and found they were different.
5 After Parker had discovered the truth.
6 Something more sinister.

EXAM FOCUS Cloze text

4 Read the article again. Choose from the sentences (A–E) the one that fits each blank. There is one extra sentence.

A In spite of Bourdin's brown eyes and French accent, she was in no doubt that this was her long-lost family member.
B In fact, he managed to live as Nicholas for three and a half months, moving into the teenager's bedroom and even attending a local school.
C Conversely, the boy claiming to be him had dark features and spoke with a French accent.
D His mother's health prevented her from making the trip, so Nick's older married sister Carey flew to Spain in order to be reunited with her brother.
E Initially he was puzzled by the boy's accent, but it was when he came across a photo of the missing teenager that he realized something was very wrong.
F Having seen a photo of Nicholas on a missing person's flyer, Bourdin bleached his dark hair.

5 Complete the table with the underlined introductory words and phrases in Exercise 4.

Function	Introductory word/phrase
Showing contrast	despite = [1] *in spite of* in contrast = [1] *conversely*
Giving a reason	because he had = [3] *having* so that = [4] *in order to*
Adding more information	what is more = [5] *in fact*
Sequencing events	at first = [6] *initially*

Exercise 8
1 covered up
2 passed himself off as
3 were taken in
4 see through
5 keeping up the lie
6 swore under oath

6 Complete the sentences about the article with one word in each blank.

1 Bourdin wanted a new identity in order *to* run away from a home in Spain.
2 Bourdin had the wrong colored eyes. *What* is more, he had a French accent.
3 *Initially* Bourdin thought Carey would reject him but she swore he was her brother.
4 Bourdin was twenty-three when he adopted his new identity. *Conversely*, Nicholas would have been much younger.
5 *Despite* Bourdin's deception, the Barclay family happily accepted him as their son.
6 Parker analyzed Bourdin's ears *so* that he could prove that Bourdin was an imposter.

7 Match the phrases in blue in the article with these definitions.

1 continue to pretend – *keep up the lie*
2 hiding the truth about sth – *covering sth up*
3 making people believe he is sb – *pass himself off as s*
4 realize the truth about sth – *see through sth*
5 solemnly promised – *swore under oath*
6 wasn't deceived – *wasn't taken in (by sb/sth)*

8 Complete the text with the correct form of the phrases in Exercise 7.

Frederic Bourdin

Born in June 1974 near Paris, Bourdin was abandoned by his parents. Raised by his poor grandparents, he [1] ________ the truth about his family and claimed his dad was a British secret agent. From the age of sixteen, Frederic Bourdin [2] ________ an orphan. Orphanages, hospitals, and schools [3] ________ by his stories. Authorities in more than sixteen countries failed to [4] ________ more than forty false identities. In particular, he used to lie about his age and he was so good at [5] ________ that when one doctor examined him, she confirmed that he was in his teens, although he was thirty years old at the time. Bourdin finally got married and [6] ________ that he would never pretend to be anyone again.

9 SPEAKING With a partner, discuss who you would choose to be if you could be anybody for one day.

WORD STORE 6F

10 CD•3.11 MP3•96 **Complete WORD STORE 6F. Add particles to complete the phrasal verbs from the article. Then listen, check, and repeat.**

EXTRA ACTIVITIES
- Photocopiable resource 37 (vocabulary from reading text – 10 mins) MultiROM and ActiveTeach

WORKBOOK
pp. 82–83

NEXT CLASS
- Ask students to imagine what would happen if someone stole their identity. Ask them to write sentences describing what might happen in this situation.

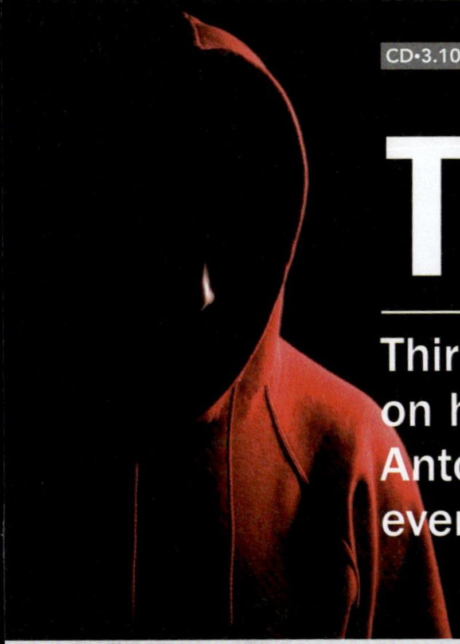

CD•3.10 MP3•95

THE IMPOSTER

Thirteen-year-old Nicholas Barclay disappeared on his way home from a basketball game in San Antonio, Texas. He was never found and was eventually assumed to be dead.

Three and a half years later, Nicholas's family were contacted with the news that the missing boy had been found in Spain. Carey, Nicholas's sister, travelled from Texas to Spain to take her long-lost brother home. It was an emotional reunion, and when she took the boy home to Texas, the family embraced him and told him how much they'd missed him. Nobody in the family questioned how Nicholas, who disappeared in Texas, ended up in Spain. And more surprisingly, nobody questioned the fact that this boy looked nothing like the missing boy. Nicholas was blond-haired and blue-eyed. [1] ____ This is the amazing story of twenty-three-year-old Frederic Bourdin, a mixed-race Parisian who, in the late 90s, adopted the identity of Nicholas Barclay, a sixteen-year-old American.

In 1997 Bourdin was living in a home for young people in Spain and was planning to run away. He needed a new identity, so he tried to **pass himself off as** the missing boy from Texas. [2] ____ He read on the flyer that Nicholas had a cross tattooed between his right index finger and thumb, so he got a friend to give him a tattoo using a needle and ink. There was nothing he could do about his brown eyes, but he decided that he would say his eyes had changed color as a result of the traumas he had been through. When his disguise was ready, he presented himself at a local government office and said that he was Nicholas Barclay.

When Nicholas's sister Carey came to pick him up, Bourdin was sure that she would instantly **see through** his disguise and realize he wasn't her brother. But instead, Carey rushed towards him and hugged him. [3] ____ She even **swore under oath** that he was her brother and an American citizen, and he was granted an American passport.

On the flight back to America, Carey showed Bourdin photos of the family and he listened carefully, learning everyone's name so that he could recognize them later. He was worried that the family would reject him, but they took him in and he quickly blended into family life. [4] ____

Not long after Bourdin had settled into his new home, a TV station heard about the extraordinary return of the sixteen-year-old Nicholas and hired Charlie Parker, a private investigator, to look into the disappearance of Nicholas Barclay for a TV show. Parker and the TV crew showed up at Carey's house to interview Bourdin. From the beginning, Parker **wasn't taken in** by Bourdin. [5] ____ Having once read that ears are distinct, like fingerprints, he told the cameraman to zoom in on his ears. Once he was back in his office, he studied the ears of both boys and found that they didn't match. He passed on his suspicions to the police. He then called Nicholas's family to tell them what he had discovered, yet they still believed that Bourdin was their son.

In the end, Bourdin found it impossible to **keep up the lie** and he finally admitted to Charlie Parker that he was Frederic Bourdin. He was later sentenced to six years in jail.

Many questions remain unanswered: how could the family not recognize that he wasn't their flesh and blood? Were they really taken in by Bourdin or were they **covering up** a more sinister truth?

6.5 Grammar

Mixed conditionals

I can use mixed conditionals to talk about hypothetical situations in the past or present.

1 **Read the article and find out what these two British actors think about their screen characters.** *Radcliffe liked Harry Potter. Pattinson hated Edward Cullen.*

ACTORS LIKE THEIR SCREEN CHARACTERS. OR DO THEY?

Daniel Radcliffe

Daniel Radcliffe doesn't mind being called Harry Potter. **If he hadn't played the part of Harry Potter, he wouldn't be one of the richest young stars in movies today.** *1c* But there have been times when his fame has been difficult for him to deal with. **If he was less famous, he would have gone out dancing with his friends more**, *2a* but sadly, he's never had that freedom.

Robert Pattinson didn't like the character he played in the *Twilight* series. He says that **if Edward Cullen wasn't a fictional character, he would have been an axe murderer.** *3d* Pattinson understands that **he wouldn't be so mega-famous if he hadn't played the role of Edward Cullen**, *4b* but he says it's really weird being famous for a character he doesn't like.

Robert Pattinson

2 **Read the article again and match the situations with the results.**

Situations		Results
1 Radcliffe played Harry Potter.	c	a He didn't go out dancing much.
2 Radcliffe is very famous.	a	b He is very famous.
3 Edward Cullen is fictional.	d	c He is very rich.
4 Pattinson played Edward Cullen.	b	d He wasn't an axe murderer.

3 **Match the conditional sentences in blue in the article with the situations and results in Exercise 2.** *See text in Exercise 1.*

4 **Read the GRAMMAR FOCUS and complete the blanks with *past* or *present*.**

GRAMMAR FOCUS

Mixed conditionals

You use a **mixed conditional** to describe certain imaginary situations and their imaginary results. There are two main types:

1 imaginary [1] *past* condition → imaginary [2] *past* result
if + Past Simple, ***would/wouldn't have*** **+ past participle**
*If he **was** less famous, he **would have gone out** dancing with his friends more.*

2 imaginary [3] *past* condition → imaginary [4] *present* result
if + Past Perfect, ***would/wouldn't*** **+ infinitive**
*If he **hadn't played** the part of Harry Potter, he **wouldn't be** one of the richest young stars in movies today.*

Note: As well as *would*, you can also use *could*, *might*, and *should* in mixed conditional sentences.

REFERENCES
CULTURE NOTES ››› *p. 197*

EXTRA ACTIVITIES
• Photocopiable resource 38 (mixed conditionals – 10 mins) MultiROM and ActiveTeach
• MyEnglishLab – assignable *Show what you have learned* mini-test

WORKBOOK
p. 84

NEXT CLASS
• Ask students to prepare for a 10–15 minute grammar quiz: *Focus* Assessment Package, Unit 6.5, Grammar.

5 **For each sentence, check the explanations (a and b) that are correct.**

1 If I'd watched the *Twilight* movies, I'd know who Edward Cullen was.
   a I didn't watch the *Twilight* movies. ✓
   b I know who Edward Cullen is. ☐
2 If I was interested in Harry Potter, I would've read the books.
   a I'm not interested in Harry Potter. ✓
   b I haven't read any of the books. ✓
3 If Robert Pattinson was ugly, I might not have watched *Twilight*.
   a Robert Pattinson is handsome. ✓
   b I watched *Twilight*. ✓
4 Pattinson and Radcliffe wouldn't be enjoying so much success if they hadn't worked hard on these roles.
   a They aren't enjoying success. ☐
   b They worked hard on these roles. ✓

6 **With a partner, compare your answers to Exercise 5 and correct the explanations that are wrong.**

7 **Use the prompts to write mixed conditional sentences. Begin with the words in parentheses. Then check the sentences that are true for you.**

1 It's cold today, so you came to school by bus. (if)
   If it wasn't cold today, I wouldn't have come to school by bus.
2 You're reading this book because your friend recommended it. (I)
3 You don't like football, so you didn't watch the game last night. (if)
4 You passed all your exams because you're a good student. (I)
5 You didn't have a big breakfast, so you're hungry now. (if)
6 You're learning how to drive because your parents paid for some lessons. (I)

8 **Complete the sentences to make them true for you. Then compare with a partner.**

1 If I didn't have a smartphone, (*imaginary past result*) …
2 If antibiotics hadn't been invented, (*imaginary present result*) …
3 If I had been born in the US, (*imaginary present result*) …
4 If I could fly, (*imaginary past result*) …
5 If I was a better student, (*imaginary past result*) …
6 If my dad hadn't woken me up this morning, (*imaginary present result*) …
7 If my parents were famous actors, (*imaginary past result*) …

Grammar Focus page 170

Exercise 6
1b I don't know who Edward Cullen is.
4a Pattinson and Radcliffe are enjoying success.

Exercise 7
2 I wouldn't be reading this book if my friend hadn't recommended it.
3 If I liked football, I would have watched the game last night.
4 I wouldn't have passed all my exams if I wasn't/weren't a good student.
5 If I had had a big breakfast, I wouldn't be hungry now.
6 I wouldn't be learning how to drive if my parents hadn't paid for some lessons.

6.6 Speaking

Ethical issues

I can express tentative opinions and add comments using adverbials.

1 SPEAKING **Which of these ways of highlighting ethical issues is the most effective and why? Discuss with a partner.**

handing out leaflets   posts on social media   the involvement of public figures
protest marches   petitions

2 **Look at the posters. Which one do you think would be most effective in an anti-fur campaign? Why?**

A

B

3 CD•3.12 MP3•97 **Listen to three extracts from an interview with an anti-fur campaigner. For each extract, choose the question the campaigner is answering.**

1 (a) Do awareness-raising campaigns and protests really make a difference, and if so, how?
  b How important is it to stop the fur trade?
2 c Why do you think fur is still popular with fashion designers and wealthy consumers?
  (d) What are the advantages of getting public figures involved in anti-fur protests?
3 e Apart from avoiding fur products, what else can members of the public do to help?
  (f) If you could send any message to people who wear fur, what would it be?

REFERENCES
AUDIO SCRIPT ››› p. 210
WORKBOOK
p. 85

4 CD•3.12 MP3•97 **Complete the SPEAKING FOCUS with the words in the box. Then listen again and check.**

[argued emphasize firmly obvious particularly]

SPEAKING FOCUS

Beginning your answer

I [1] firmly believe / I'm not convinced they do because …	a
One [2] obvious /clear advantage/disadvantage is that …	d
I think I'd [3] emphasize/explain that/how …	f
It's absolutely vital/quite important, I think, because …	b
As well as (avoiding fur products), other (things that can help) include …	e
I think the main/one/a significant reason is that …	c

Expressing tentative opinions

It could be [4] argued that …
I don't feel [5] particularly strongly about …
I don't have a strong opinion about …
I suppose you could say that …

5 **Match the questions in Exercise 3 with appropriate ways to begin answers to them in the SPEAKING FOCUS.**

6 **Read the extracts from the interview and complete REMEMBER THIS with the words in orange.**

1 Sadly, fur seems to be fashionable again these days …
2 Obviously, protesting is a good way to promote awareness …
3 Frankly, I find some of the pictures extremely difficult to look at.

REMEMBER THIS

You can use comment adverbials to add your opinion to statements you make.

- You use ***clearly***/[1] obviously to introduce something that can easily be noticed or understood.
- You use ***to be honest***/[2] frankly to show that you are saying what you really think about something.
- You use ***regrettably***/[3] sadly to show you wish something was not true.

7 SPEAKING **With a partner, follow the instructions.**

- Decide who is A and who is B.
- Read the questions below and make notes on how you will answer them.
- Use the **SPEAKING** FOCUS and REMEMBER THIS to help you.
- Ask and answer the questions.

Student A: Ask Student B the questions below.

1 How important is it to stop the practice of testing cosmetics on animals?
2 If you could send any message to the governments of countries that still test cosmetics on animals, what would it be?

Student B: Ask Student A the questions below.

1 Why do you think hunting animals for sport is still popular with certain groups and individuals?
2 How important is it to stop the practice of hunting animals for sport?

6.7 Writing

An opinion essay

I can explore an issue in writing from different aspects or viewpoints.

1 **SPEAKING** **With a partner, discuss whether you enjoy celebrity gossip magazines and websites.**

2 **Read the extract from a website. With a partner, discuss which of the opposing opinions you agree with. Give reasons.**

IMHO
IN MY HUMBLE OPINION

YES ? NO

Today's question: should the media have greater respect for the private lives of public figures?

77% say *YES*	23% say *NO*
Latest comment: YES! Politicians, sports personalities, and entertainers do their jobs in the public eye, but they have the same rights to privacy and fair treatment by the media as you or me. Working life and private life are separate, and the media should respect this.	**Latest comment:** NO! Public figures use the media to increase their popularity and sometimes to earn large amounts of money. Dealing with media attention is part of being famous. You can't have it both ways.

3 **Read the writing task and the essay below. Which of the opinions in Exercise 2 do you think the author would agree with?** *probably 'Yes'*

> Magazines, newspapers, and websites often report on the personal lives of politicians, sports stars, and entertainers. In your opinion, should the media be allowed to print stories about the private lives of public figures? Write an opinion essay on this topic, analyzing the two aspects below:
> - public figures' responsibilities as role-models
> - public figures' rights to privacy.

The private lives of public figures are often reported in the media.[1] Personally, I think this should only be allowed when there is a clear benefit to society.[2] To justify this point of view, it is necessary to consider public figures' responsibility as role models as well as their rights to privacy.

In terms of public figures as role models, I believe that those with influence should take responsibility for the example they set.[3] Politicians, for example, are chosen as representatives and lawmakers, and so they have a duty to behave as model citizens. Likewise, entertainers and sports stars should be aware that their behavior influences their fans. With this in mind, I feel the media should be allowed to report unacceptable behavior such as racism or drug abuse among public figures, even if this means looking into their private lives.

It is also important to consider this issue with regard to public figures' rights to privacy. Whereas certain stories may expose unacceptable behavior, others are really only printed to satisfy people's curiosity and make money. [3] Articles concerning celebrities who have gained or lost weight or left their house without make-up, for instance, serve no useful purpose. Unless permission is given, I personally don't think such articles should be allowed.

[4] All in all, I am of the opinion that public figures' private lives should only be reported if this benefits society by exposing irresponsible behavior. Otherwise, I think it is unfair unless the person has specifically given permission. [5] I certainly would not like my own private life to be reported on in this way.

EXTRA ACTIVITIES
- MyEnglishLab – assignable *Show what you have learned* writing task and *Show that you have checked* checklist

WORKBOOK
p. 86

4 Read the WRITING FOCUS. Then find these things in the essay.

1 a sentence that states the writer's main opinion
2 a sentence that says which two aspects will be discussed
3 two sentences that expand the discussion by giving examples
4 a sentence that restates the writer's main opinion
5 a final comment

WRITING FOCUS

An opinion essay

Introduction

- Introduce the topic and state your main opinion.
- Say which two points of view or aspects will be discussed.

To explain the reasons for my opinion, I will explore this issue from the viewpoint of (an old person) and (a teenager).
It is my intention to examine this issue in terms of (freedom of speech) and (public safety).
This essay will look at this question from the perspective of (both) (customers) and (shop owners).

Main paragraphs

- Discuss different aspects of the issue and support the main opinion you stated in the introduction.

In terms of (public figures as role models), I believe …
It is also important to consider this issue with regard to (public figures' rights to privacy).
Another important angle on this issue is (public safety).
From the perspective/viewpoint of (a teenager), …

- Expand the discussion by giving examples.

Conclusion

- Use an introductory word or phrase to introduce a conclusion.

In conclusion, … All things considered, …
To sum up, … All in all, …

- Restate your main opinion.
- Include a final comment.

5 Read the LANGUAGE FOCUS. Then join each pair of sentences in two different ways. Begin with the words in parentheses.

1 Some people claim we should always tell the truth. Others feel there are times when it is acceptable to lie. (some people claim, while others feel)
Some people claim we should always tell the truth, while others feel there are times when it is acceptable to lie.
While some people feel …
2 Some lies are told for the benefit of the liar. Others are told to avoid hurting someone else's feelings. (whereas, some lies)
3 Pretending to like a gift may be acceptable. Lying about your qualifications is clearly wrong. (while, pretending)
4 A white lie can sometimes protect someone's self-esteem. The truth may hurt them. (a white lie, whereas)

LANGUAGE FOCUS

Expressing contrast

You can use the conjunctions ***while*** and ***whereas*** as more advanced alternatives to *but* when expressing contrast. Note the position of the commas and the different word order patterns.

While/Whereas *certain stories may expose unacceptable behavior, others are really only printed to satisfy people's curiosity and make money.*
Certain stories may expose unacceptable behavior, ***while/ whereas*** *others are really only printed to satisfy people's curiosity and make money.*

6 SPEAKING You are going to write an essay about honesty. With a partner, discuss what you would say to a friend in these situations and why. What might the consequences be for you and your friend?

1 A friend has cooked a meal for you. The food is tasteless and looks awful. However, they seem to be enjoying it and ask for your opinion.
2 You saw your friend's new girlfriend/boyfriend on a date with someone else. Your friend is clearly falling in love and asks what you think of their new partner.
3 A friend has spent a lot of money on a new outfit that, in your opinion, doesn't fit well and doesn't suit them. They ask if you think they should wear it for the first date they are going on tonight.

7 Complete the writing task. Use the WRITING FOCUS and the LANGUAGE FOCUS to help you.

In your English class you have been talking about telling the truth. Now your English teacher has asked you to write an essay. Write an essay using all the notes and give reasons for your point of view.

Some people say that it's not always a good idea to be completely honest. Do you agree?

Notes

Write about:

- friends and family
- people in positions of authority
- ______ (your own idea)

Write your essay in 140–190 words.

Exercise 5

2 Whereas some lies are told for the benefit of the liar, others are told to avoid hurting someone else's feelings. Some lies are told for the benefit of the liar, whereas/ while others are told to avoid hurting someone else's feelings.
3 While pretending to like a gift may be acceptable, lying about your qualifications is clearly wrong. Pretending to like a gift may be acceptable, whereas/while lying about your qualifications is clearly wrong.
4 A white lie can sometimes protect someone's self-esteem, while/ whereas the truth may hurt them./ Whereas a white lie can sometimes protect someone's self-esteem, the truth may hurt them.

6.8 Language in focus

Word families – suffixes

I can recognize and form a wide range of words using suffixes.

1 Read the information and complete the table. Mark the stress.

Words are formed and word families are created by adding different suffixes to the same 'root word'. Root words can be nouns, verbs or adjectives. The table lists the most common suffixes for each part of speech.

NOUN (concept)	NOUN (person)	VERB	ADJECTIVE
-al -ance/-ence -cy -dom -ful -hood -ing -ion -ism -ity -ment -ness -ship -y	-ant -ee -ess -er -ian -ist -or	-ate -en -ify -ize	-able/-ible -al -ary -ed -ent -ful -ic -ing -ish -ive -less -like -ly -ous -y
1 employment	3 employer/employee	employ	8 employable
2 perfection	4 perfectionist	6 perfect	perfect
sympathy	5 sympathizer	7 sympathize	9 sympathetic

2 Translate the word families in Exercise 1. How are new words formed from a root word in your language?

3 Complete the statements using the root words in the box. Make any necessary spelling changes. Which statements do you agree with?

employ lead perfect point qualify strong sympathy terror

1 The more ____ions you get, the more ____able you become.
2 You should never ____ize with ____ists. Violence is always wrong.
3 It's ____less looking for ____ion; it's unattainable.
4 There is a need to ____en the political ____ship in our country.

4 Form words from the 'person' nouns in the box and write them in the table. Mark the stress.

~~applicant~~ believer creator dependant pacifist purist

NOUN (concept)	NOUN (person)	VERB	ADJECTIVE
application	applicant	apply	applicable

5 Complete the sentences with the correct form of the words in parentheses. Then check the sentences that are true for you.

1 We should never justify (just) biased or dishonest journalism (journal).
2 I think most fast food is disgusting (disgust) and very fattening (fat).
3 I'd like to deepen (deep) my knowledge (know) of American rock music.
4 I have no idea what the secret to a successful (success) artistic (art) career is.

6 Complete the quote with the noun form of the words in parentheses. Do you agree with the quote?

Six keys to a good relationship: 1______ (friend), 2______ (free), 3______ (honest), 4______ (trust), 5______ (understand), and 6______ (communicate).

Exercise 3
1 qualifications, employable
2 sympathize, terrorists
3 pointless, perfection
4 strengthen, leadership

Exercise 4
NOUN (concept): belief, creation, dependence, peace, purity
NOUN (person): believer, creator, dependant, pacifist, purist
VERB: believe, create, depend, pacify, purify
ADJECTIVE: believable, creative, dependent, peaceful, pure

Exercise 6
1 friendship
2 freedom
3 honesty
4 trust
5 understanding
6 communication

116

06 WORD LIST

Appearance

acne /ˈækni/
bags under the eyes /ˈbægz ˌʌndɚ ði aɪz/
bleach/dye your hair /ˌblitʃ/ˌdaɪ yɚ ˈhɛr/
(blue-/hazel-/wide-)eyed /(ˈblu/ˈheɪzəl/ˈwaɪd) ˌaɪd/
change your hairstyle /ˌtʃeɪndʒ yɚ ˈhɛrstaɪl/
color-change contact lenses /ˌkʌlɚ tʃeɪndʒ ˈkɑntækt ˌlɛnzɪz/
features /ˈfitʃɚz/
fine lines /faɪn ˈlaɪnz/
furrowed brow /ˌfʌroʊd ˈbraʊ/
greying hair /ˌgreɪɪŋ ˈhɛr/
imperfection /ˌɪmpɚˈfɛkʃən/
(messy-)looking /(mɛsi) ˈlʊkɪŋ/
mole/beauty spot /moʊl/ˈbyuṯi spɑt/
outfit /ˈaʊtfɪt/
scar /skɑr/
(pale-/olive-/dark-)skinned /(ˈpeɪl/ˈɑlɪv/ˈdɑrk) ˌskɪnd/
plastic surgery /ˌplæstɪk ˈsɚdʒəri/
(thin-/round-)faced /(ˈθɪn/ˈraʊnd) ˌfeɪst/
(wavy-/red-/grey-/blond-)haired /(ˈweɪvi/ˈrɛd/ˈgreɪ/ˈblɑnd) ˌhɛrd/
wear a wig /ˌwɛr ə ˈwɪg/
(well-/elegantly-)dressed /(ˌwɛl/ˌɛlɪgəntli) ˈdrɛst/
wrinkle-free skin /ˌrɪŋkəl fri ˈskɪn/
wrinkle /ˈrɪŋkəl/

Truth, falsehood and manipulation

adopt a new identity /əˌdɑpt ə nu aɪˈdɛntəṯi/
airbrushed /ˈɛrbrʌʃt/
authentic/inauthentic /ɔˈθɛntɪk/ˌɪnɔˈθɛntɪk/
authenticate /ɔˈθɛntɪkeɪt/
be in no doubt that … /ˌbi ɪn ˌnoʊ ˈdaʊt ðæt …/
be taken in/be deceived /bi ˌteɪkən ˈɪn/ˌbi dɪˈsivd/
believable /bəˈlivəbəl/
claim/pretend to be sb /ˌkleɪm/prɪˌtɛnd tə ˈbi ˌsʌmbɑdi/
create an illusion /kriˌeɪt ən ɪˈluʒən/
deceive (the public) /dɪˌsiv (ðə ˈpʌblɪk)/
deception /dɪˈsɛpʃən/
digital alteration /ˌdɪdʒəṯl ˌɔltəˈreɪʃən/
digitally improved /ˌdɪdʒɪṯəli ɪmˈpruvd/
discover /dɪsˈkʌvɚ/
disguise /dɪsˈgaɪz/
distort/hide the truth about sth /dɪˌstɔrt/ˌhaɪd ðə ˈtruθ əˈbaʊt sʌmθɪŋ/
doctored /ˈdɑktɚd/
fake /feɪk/
false identity /ˌfɔls aɪˈdɛntəṯi/
far-fetched /ˌfɑr ˈfɛtʃt/
genuine /ˈdʒɛnyuɪən/
honest /ˈɑnəst/
honesty /ˈɑnəsti/
imposter /ɪmˈpɑstɚ/
in reality /ˌɪn riˈæləṯi/
invent a story /ɪnˌvɛnt ə ˈstɔri/
liar /ˈlaɪɚ/
lie (to) /ˈlaɪ (tə)/
make sb aware of sth /ˌmeɪk ˌsʌmbɑdi əˈwɛr əv sʌmθɪŋ/
manipulate the truth/public opinion /məˌnɪpyəleɪt ðə ˈtruθ/ˌpʌblɪk əˈpɪnyən/
misleading image /mɪsˌlidɪŋ ˈɪmɪdʒ/
mysterious /mɪˈstɪriəs/
mystery /ˈmɪstəri/
objective /əbˈdʒɛktɪv/
sensationalize /sɛnˈseɪʃənəlaɪz/
solemn promise /ˌsɑləm ˈprɑmɪs/
solemnly promise /ˌsɑləmli ˈprɑmɪs/
suspicion /səˈspɪʃən/
swear under oath /ˌswɛr ˌʌndɚ ˈoʊθ/
take sth at face value /ˌteɪk ˌsʌmθɪŋ ət ˌfeɪs ˈvælyu/
take sth out of context /ˌteɪk ˌsʌmθɪŋ ˈaʊt əv ˈkɑntɛkst/
tell lies/the truth /ˌtɛl ˈlaɪz/ðə ˈtruθ/
trick /trɪk/
white lie /ˌwaɪt ˈlaɪ/

Personality, emotions, attitude

admit one's mistake /ədˌmɪt wʌnz mɪˈsteɪk/
appear unamused /əˌpɪr ʌnəˈmyuzd /
approve /əˈpruv/
become worldly-wise /bɪˌkʌm ˌwɚldli ˈwaɪz/
convinced /kənˈvɪnst/
embrace/hug /ɪmˈbreɪs/hʌg/

EXTRA ACTIVITIES
- Photocopiable resource 39 (word formation – 15 mins) MultiROM and ActiveTeach

WORKBOOK
p. 87

NEXT CLASS
- Ask students to study the Word list on pp. 116–117.
- Ask students to review for Focus review 6.

express your views /ɪkˌsprɛs yɚ ˈvyuz/
kind-hearted /ˌkaɪnd ˈhɑrtɪd/
loyal /ˈlɔɪəl/
loyalty /ˈlɔɪəlti/
naive /naɪˈiv/
perfect (adj) /ˈpɚfɪkt/
perfect (v) /pɚˈfɛkt/
perfection /pɚˈfɛkʃən/
perfectionist /pɚˈfɛkʃənɪst/
puzzled by sth /ˈpʌzəld baɪ sʌmθɪŋ/
reject /rɪˈdʒɛkt/
role model /ˈroʊl ˌmɑdl/
self-esteem /ˌsɛlf ɪˈstim/
self-image /ˌsɛlf ˈɪmɪdʒ/
somber /ˈsɑmbɚ/
stony-faced /ˈstoʊni ˌfeɪst/
strong belief /ˌstrɔŋ bəˈlif/
stupid /ˈstupɪd/
stupidity /stuˈpɪdət̬i/
sympathetic /ˌsɪmpəˈθɛt̬ɪk/
sympathize /ˈsɪmpəθaɪz/
sympathizer /ˈsɪmpəθaɪzɚ/
sympathy /ˈsɪmpəθi/
take pride in sth /ˌteɪk ˈpraɪd ɪn sʌmθɪŋ/
take responsibility (for) /ˌteɪk rɪˌspɑnsəˈbɪlət̬i (fɚ)/
take sth for granted /ˌteɪk ˌsʌmθɪŋ fɚ ˈgræntɪd/
take sth with a grain of salt /ˌteɪk ˌsʌmθɪŋ wɪð ə ˌgreɪn əv ˈsɔlt/
trust /trʌst/
trustworthy /ˈtrʌstˌwɚði/
two-faced /ˈtu ˌfeɪst/
wise /waɪz/
world-wise /ˌwɚld ˈwaɪz/

Ethical issues

anonymity /ˌænəˈnɪmət̬i/
anti-fur protest /ˌænti ˈfɚ ˌproʊtɛst/
anti-war /ˌænti ˈwɔr/
authorities /əˈθɔrət̬iz/
avoid fur products /əˌvɔɪd ˈfɚ ˌprɑdʌkts/
awareness-raising campaign /əˈwɛrnəs ˌreɪzɪŋ kæmˌpeɪn/
benefit society /ˌbɛnəfɪt səˈsaɪət̬i/
benefit to society /ˌbɛnəfɪt tə səˈsaɪət̬i/
break the law /ˌbreɪk ðə ˈlɔ/
drug abuse /ˈdrʌg əˌbyus/
equal /ˈikwəl/
equality /ɪˈkwɑlət̬i/
expose unacceptable behavior /ɪkˌspoʊz ˌʌnəkˌsɛptəbəl bɪˈheɪvyɚ/
fair treatment /ˌfɛr ˈtritˀmənt/
fairness /ˈfɛrnəs/
freedom of speech /ˌfridəm əv ˈspitʃ/
get public figures involved /gɛt ˌpʌblɪk ˈfɪgyɚz ɪnˌvɑlvd/
hunt animals for sport /ˌhʌnt ˌænɪməlz fɚ ˈspɔrt/
involvement of public figures /ɪnˌvɑlvmənt əv ˌpʌblɪk ˈfɪgyɚz/
member of the public /ˌmɛmbər əv ðə ˈpʌblɪk/
peaceful protest /ˌpisfəl ˈproʊtɛst/
petition /pəˈtɪʃən/
pro-(anonymity/fairness) /ˌproʊ (ˌænəˈnɪmət̬i/ˈfɛrnəs)/
promote awareness /prəˌmoʊt əˈwɛrnəs/
protest (v) /prəˈtɛst/
protest march /ˈproʊtɛst mɑrtʃ/
public safety /ˌpʌblɪk ˈseɪfti/
racism /ˈreɪsɪzəm/
respect (v; n) /rɪˈspɛkt/
right to (privacy) /ˌraɪt tə (ˈpraɪvəsi)/
stop the practice of sth /ˌstɑp ðə ˈpræktɪs əv sʌmθɪŋ/
test cosmetics on animals /ˌtɛst kɑzˌmɛt̬ɪks ɑn ˈænɪməlz/
violence /ˈvaɪələns/
wrong /rɔŋ/

Phrasal verbs

blend into /ˌblɛnd ˈɪntə/
come across /ˌkʌm əˈkrɔs/
cover up /ˌkʌvɚ ˈʌp/
end up /ˌɛnd ˈʌp/
go through /ˌgoʊ ˈθru/
hand out /ˌhænd ˈaʊt/
keep up (a lie) /ˌkip ˈʌp (ə laɪ)/
look into /ˌlʊk ˈɪntə/
pass yourself off as sb /ˌpæs yɚˌsɛlf ɔf əz sʌmbɑdi/
pick up /ˌpɪk ˈʌp/
run away /ˌrʌn əˈweɪ/
see through /ˌsi ˈθru/
settle in /ˌsɛt̬l ˈɪn/
show up /ʃoʊ ˈʌp/
stand for /ˈstænd fɚ/
take in /ˌteɪk ˈɪn/
zoom in (on) /ˌzum ˈɪn (ɑn)/

Other

assumed to be dead /əˌsumd tə bi ˈdɛd/
be reunited with sb /bi ˌriyuˈnaɪt̬ɪd wɪð sʌmbɑdi/
clearly /ˈklɪrli/
conversely/in contrast /kənˈvɚsli/ɪn ˈkɑntræst/
crew /kru/
deepen your knowledge /ˌdipən yɚ ˈnɑlɪdʒ/
distinct /dɪˈstɪŋkt/
employable /ɪmˈplɔɪəbəl/
enigma /ɪˈnɪgmə/
enigmatic /ˌɛnɪgˈmæt̬ɪk/
explore/examine/consider an issue /ɪkˌsplɔr/ɪgˌzæmɪn/kənˌsɪdɚ ən ˈɪʃu/
fame /feɪm/
far-reaching consequences /ˌfɑr ˌritʃɪŋ ˈkɑnsɪkwənsɪz/
get in the way /ˌgɛt ɪn ðə ˈweɪ/
grant /grænt/
have a flat tire /ˌhæv ə ˌflæt ˈtaɪɚ/
ill-advised /ˌɪl ədˈvaɪzd/
ill-timed /ˌɪl ˈtaɪmd/
in terms of /ɪn ˈtɚmz əv/
in the public eye /ɪn ðə ˌpʌblɪk ˈaɪ/
lawmaker /ˈlɔmeɪkɚ/
leadership /ˈlidɚʃɪp/
light-hearted /ˌlaɪt ˈhɑrt̬ɪd/
long-lost /ˌlɔŋ ˈlɔst/
missing person's flyer /ˌmɪsɪŋ ˈpɚsənz ˌflaɪɚ/
(model) citizen /(ˌmɑdl) ˈsɪt̬əzən/
obviously /ˈɑbviəsli/
orphan /ˈɔrfən/
orphanage /ˈɔrfənɪdʒ/
oversleep /ˌoʊvɚˈslip/
pointless /ˈpɔɪntləs/
pose (for) /ˈpoʊz (fɚ)/
private investigator /ˌpraɪvət ɪnˈvɛstɪgeɪt̬ɚ/
question a fact /kwɛstʃən ə ˈfækt/
regrettably/sadly /rɪˈgrɛt̬əbli/ˈsædli/
representative /ˌrɛprɪˈzɛntət̬ɪv/
reunion /riˈyunyən/
satisfy people's curiosity /ˌsætɪsfaɪ ˌpipəlz ˌkyʊriˈɑsət̬i/
sb's flesh and blood /ˌsʌmbɑdiz ˌflɛʃ ənd ˈblʌd/
serve a useful purpose /ˌsɚv ə ˌyusfəl ˈpɚpəs/
shot /ʃɑt/
significant /sɪgˈnɪfɪkənt/
sinister /ˈsɪnəstɚ/
streetwise /ˈstritwaɪz/
strengthen /ˈstrɛŋθən/
tax-free /ˌtæks ˈfri/
to start with /tə ˈstɑrt wɪð/
trauma /ˈtrɔmə/
unanswered question /ʌnˌænsɚd ˈkwɛstʃən/
unattainable /ˌʌnəˈteɪnəbəl/
underlying message /ˌʌndəˌlaɪɪŋ ˈmɛsɪdʒ/
unlikely to happen /ʌnˌlaɪkli tə ˈhæpən/
unprepared /ˌʌnprɪˈpɛrd/
viewpoint/point of view /ˈvyupɔɪnt/ˌpɔɪnt əv ˈvyu/
vital /ˈvaɪt̬l/
with regard to /wɪð rɪˈgɑrd tə/
working life /ˌwɚkɪŋ ˈlaɪf/

FOCUS REVIEW 6

VOCABULARY AND GRAMMAR

1 Match words from box A with words from box B to make compound adjectives. Then use them to complete the sentences.

A	B
far- ill- light- tax- two- world-	advised faced fetched free hearted wise

1 The mayor's plan to raise taxes is rather _ill-advised_. It'll make him unpopular.
2 Tessa's articles are never serious, mainly because she chooses such _light-hearted_ topics.
3 Peter is extremely _world-wise_ – he's been a peace negotiator in war zones and created several international companies.
4 How can you be so _two-faced_, praising your brother when you see him and criticizing him behind his back?
5 Suggesting that John committed the crime is pretty _far-fetched_. He's just not capable of breaking the law.
6 Whenever I fly overseas, I buy gifts at the airport because they're _tax-free_, which means they're cheaper.

2 Complete the sentences with words from the unit. The first letter of each word is given.

1 Journalists should never **d**_istort_ the truth when reporting a story.
2 Teenagers often take it for **g**_ranted_ that they'll have Internet access wherever they go.
3 You really shouldn't take all her explanations at face **v**_alue_. She is rarely truthful.
4 I'm sure the photos of the model have been **d**_octored_ – her waist doesn't look natural.
5 My neighbor claims he's climbed Mt. Everest, but I took his story with a **g**_rain_ of salt.

3 Choose the correct options.

1 *Would* / *(Should)* you need any further information, please don't hesitate to ask.
2 *(Had the government not)* / *Hadn't the government* acted, there would soon have been more riots.
3 I would ask people for their IDs before letting them in, *providing* / *(unless)* I knew them personally.
4 We wouldn't get involved in your project *weren't we* / *(were we not)* enthusiastic about it.
5 *(Imagine)* / *Provided* you were offered a job as a foreign affairs correspondent, would you accept it?

4 Complete the sentences with the correct form of the verbs in parentheses.

1 If Karen _had checked_ (check) her sources before submitting her article last week, she _would not be_ (not be) in trouble with the editor today.
2 John _would have told_ (tell) us the truth about the school incident if he _was/were_ (be) an honest person.
3 If Jerry generally _took_ (take) his job seriously, his manager _would have promoted_ (promote) him a long time ago.
4 If my grandparents _were not_ (not be) such generous people, they _would not have helped_ (not help) me financially with college.
5 Of course, we _would not have to_ (not have to) take them to court now if they _had paid_ (pay) the loan back on time.

LANGUAGE IN USE

5 Complete the text with the correct form of the words in parentheses.

THE SECRET KEEPER

Do you know stories that could harm someone if the media tried to [1] _sensationalize_ (sensation) them? Have you ever been told a secret and asked to keep it quiet? Are there any secrets that we shouldn't even try to [2] _deepen_ (deep) our knowledge about?

Dilemmas like this are part of Laurel Nicholson's life, a character in Kate Morton's *The Secret Keeper*. At the age of sixteen, Laurel witnesses an act of shocking [3] _violence_ (violent) committed by her mother, Dorothy. Even as a teenager, Laurel realizes that there is more to the story. She wants to know what is really behind her mother's actions, but at the same time she feels it's [4] _pointless_ (point) trying to discover the truth. Her mother would never share a secret with her teenage daughter.

As a mature woman, Laurel has to take care of her terminally ill mother. One day, prompted by the discovery of a long-forgotten photo, she decides to unearth the [5] _hidden_ (hide) family secret. She knows it's the last chance to find out the truth before her mother dies.

6 Complete the sentences using the words in parentheses.

1 I ______ (not tell) Christie my secret if she were not a trustworthy person.
2 I'm pretty sure that if you ______ (listen/advice) that I gave you last time, you wouldn't be in such a terrible situation now.
3 Suppose ______ (you/miss) your flight last night, what would you have done?
4 If you hadn't forgotten the keys, we ______ (not stand) outside our house in the cold now.
5 I'm sure there will be an investigation ______ (unless/company/release) its financial report.
6 Tim wouldn't be giving you any free lessons ______ (be/he/not) your good friend.

Exercise 6
1 wouldn't have told
2 had listened to the advice
3 you had missed
4 would not be standing
5 unless the company releases
6 were he not

EXTRA ACTIVITIES
- Photocopiable resource 61B (sentence formation – 12 mins) MultiROM and ActiveTeach
- Photocopiable resource 62 (mini-test 1 – 15 mins) MultiROM and ActiveTeach
- Photocopiable resource 40 (Speaking – 12 mins) MultiROM and ActiveTeach
- Photocopiable resource 41 (Writing – 15 mins) MultiROM and ActiveTeach

WORKBOOK
Use of English 6.9, pp. 88–89; Self-assessment 6.10, p. 90

READING

7 Read the article. Choose from the sentences (A–E) the one that fits each blank. There is one extra sentence.

THE CONMAN WHO FIGHTS FRAUD

Frank Abagnale, the former identity thief who inspired the Leonardo DiCaprio movie *Catch Me If You Can*, is now working for the FBI.

There was a time when Frank Abagnale would have come to London having deceived his way onto a plane, engineered a free room for himself at a five-star hotel, and then spent the rest of his time coming up with scams to cheat people out of their money. But those days are well and truly over. 1 _B_ He has now been associated with the US crime-fighting agency for more than three decades.

No longer the slick young man portrayed on screen in the movie *Catch Me If You Can* by Leonardo DiCaprio, Abagnale is now in his mid-sixties, with receding white hair and heavy bags under his eyes. 2 _E_ Despite a lifestyle of crime and running from the law, time it would appear has been rather kind to him.

Recently, Abagnale was in London once again involved in fraud – only this time he was there as a good guy. As the chief executive of Abagnale & Associates, he was helping to launch a verification system that promises to authenticate financial transactions with greater security than ever before. 3 _C_ 'The crooks are now targeting where the real big money is,' he says. His job is to combat the latest craze in cyber crime: the theft of corporate identities in order to steal millions of dollars from well-stocked bank accounts.

So far, the attacks have mostly been in the States, particularly in government-backed enterprises. But large companies, especially banks, have also recently been targeted. Last year, nearly 90 million dollars was drained from a corporate account held in one of America's best-known Wall Street banks. 4 _D_ 'Identity theft has become a big problem in the US and elsewhere, and so it will happen in the UK. It's just a matter of time.' Only now the challenges are bigger than ever.

A Fifteen years ago he set up a company to facilitate electronic payments over the Internet – an 'early version of PayPal', as he describes it.

B After being locked up in a US prison on multiple accounts of forgery, America's legendary imposter was eventually freed by the FBI on the basis that he taught them everything he knew.

C For years, he explains, identity theft has been the problem of individuals and small businesses. But now, modern-day criminals are developing the taste and the technology for far bigger sums.

D Abagnale believes that the UK is likely to start being hit too, and that UK bosses are being far too complacent about the risks.

E There is, however, still very much an air of mischievousness in the warm smile and light-hearted laugh of this smartly-dressed and charismatic elderly man.

SPEAKING

8 With a partner, complete the speaking task.

Student A, your photos show people doing different things to protest against something. Compare the photos and say how useful these ways of protesting are.

A

B

Student B, have you ever taken part in a protest march?

9 Now go to WORD STORE page 24 and complete another speaking task.

10 With a partner, discuss the questions.

1. Should young people get involved in campaigns that concern their local areas? Why?/Why not?
2. Is it better to express one's opinion on a controversial issue or to keep quiet? Why?
3. What's the most effective way to persuade somebody to change their opinion? Why?
4. What are the advantages of using social media to organize an event?

WRITING

11 Complete the writing task.

In your English class you have been talking about journalists and the press. Now your English teacher has asked you to write an essay. Write an essay using **all** the notes and give reasons for your point of view.

Should journalists use information they got illegally when writing about politicians?

Notes

Write about:

- informing the public
- politicians' privacy
- ______ (your own idea)

Write your essay in 140–190 words.

NEXT CLASS

- Ask students to do Self-check 6.11, WB p. 91 as homework.
- Ask students to prepare for Unit test 6 and Review test 3 (*Focus* Assessment Package).

7 LOG ON

One machine can do the work of fifty ordinary men. No machine can do the work of one extraordinary man.

ELBERT HUBBARD (1856–1915), AN AMERICAN WRITER AND PHILOSOPHER

UNIT LANGUAGE AND SKILLS

Vocabulary:
- *Show what you know* – using computers
- collocations to do with Internet use
- health issues
- collocations in set phrases
- electronic communication
- what the body does
- *Word in focus – on*

Grammar:
- advanced passive forms
- passive reporting verbs

Listening:
- a news report and conversations about problems with technology
- multiple choice

Reading:
- an article about wearable technology
- multiple choice

Speaking:
- clarification

Writing:
- a 'for and against' essay

FOCUS EXTRA

- Grammar Focus pages 170–171
- WORD STORE booklet pages 14–15
- Workbook pages 92–105 or MyEnglishLab
- MP3s – www.english.com/focus

120

7.1 Vocabulary

Collocations to do with Internet use • Health issues • Collocations in set phrases

I can talk about technology and the effects it has on people.

SHOW WHAT YOU KNOW

1 **Write four sentences – three true and one false – about things you have/haven't done. Use verbs and nouns from the boxes.**

verbs
attach click download
follow open save
send text visit

\+

nouns
attachment e-book email
file icon music photo
somebody (on Twitter) website

I have never visited this school's website.

2 **With a partner, take turns to read your sentences to each other. Guess which of your partner's sentences is false.**

3 **SPEAKING Look at the title and the headings in the article. Do you agree with the statements? Discuss with a partner. Then read the article and compare your ideas.**

TECHNOLOGY: DANGER OR USEFUL TOOL?

1 Technology makes you lonely.

AGREE

Constant access to social media means teens are always aware of what everyone is doing. When they compare themselves to their online friends, they think that everyone else is having more fun, and this can lead to anxiety.

2 Technology makes you dependent.

AGREE

Parents who have trouble tearing their teens away from their device may think they're addicted to technology. **Withdrawal symptoms** experienced by young people deprived of gadgets and technology are similar to those felt by drug addicts who need their drugs.

3 Technology makes you ill.

AGREE

The number of obese and overweight children is rising due to their **sedentary lifestyle**. This can lead to health problems such as diabetes, high blood pressure, and insomnia, as well as physical problems such as eye strain, joint pain, or new ailments like *WhatsAppitis*, a repetitive strain injury caused by using thumbs for texting.

4 Technology makes you stupid.

AGREE

Technology is making us lazy: why would we think for ourselves when we can google it? Why would we try to work out how to get from A to B when the GPS will plan a route? Our **attention span** is getting shorter.

REFERENCES

CULTURE NOTES >>> p. 197
AUDIO SCRIPT >>> pp. 210–211

EXTRA ACTIVITIES

- Photocopiable resource 42 (technology and its effects – 10 mins) MultiROM and ActiveTeach
- Photocopiable resource 45 (Test yourself partner work activities) MultiROM and ActiveTeach
- MyEnglishLab – assignable *Show what you have learned* mini-test

4 **Complete the questions with prepositions. Then read the article again and answer the questions.**

1 What do teenagers have constant access _to_ ?
2 What are teenagers always aware _of_ ?
3 What can comparisons with online friends lead _to_ ?
4 What do parents think their children are addicted _to_ ?
5 What is the rise in childhood obesity due _to_ ?
6 What is 'WhatsAppitis' caused _by_ ?
7 What kind of ailments can apps help _with_ ?
8 What does technology allow people to focus _on_ ?

5 **SPEAKING With a partner, discuss the questions.**

1 Which of the opinions in the text do you agree with? Why?
2 How would you answer the question in the title?

DISAGREE

Social media **plays a crucial role** in teenagers' lives. Whether they are **updating their status**, **posting comments**, or **uploading photos**, teenagers use social media to supplement face-to-face socializing.

DISAGREE

Some teens enjoy video games so much that they **lose track of time**. But addiction is a serious condition! Checking social media a little too often is one thing, but that doesn't mean you're obsessed with your device **at the expense** of other aspects of your life.

DISAGREE

There are apps to help with those minor ailments. Stressed? Worried about inactivity? Get an app that measures your movements. Weight gain? A fitness app counts calories. A sedentary lifestyle is not the only reason why children suffer from obesity. Until our society **addresses all the issues** connected with childhood obesity, the trend is likely to continue.

DISAGREE

Technology is making us more efficient. With a search engine **at our fingertips**, we can **browse the net**, **bookmark useful sites**, and **share the links** with our friends. We have more head space to focus on other, more interesting things.

Go to WORD STORE 7 page 15.

WORD STORE 7A

6 CD•3.13 MP3•98 **Complete WORD STORE 7A with the base form of the collocations in red in the article. Then listen, check, and repeat. Add a translation.**

7 **For each question, cross out the noun that does not collocate with the verb. Then, with a partner, ask and answer the questions.**

When was the last time you:
1 uploaded ~~a laptop~~ / *a video clip / a photo*?
2 updated your *status* / ~~bookmark~~ / *profile*?
3 posted *a comment / a link* / ~~social media~~?
4 browsed ~~an icon~~ / *a website / the web*?
5 bookmarked *a webpage / a homepage* / ~~a password~~?
6 shared *a link* / ~~an icon~~ / *a Facebook post*?

WORD STORE 7B

8 CD•3.14 MP3•99 **Complete WORD STORE 7B. Match the underlined phrases in the article with typical symptoms. Then listen, check, and repeat.**

9 CD•3.15 MP3•100 **Listen and match conversations 1–6 with ailments a–f.**

a addiction	6	d high blood pressure	1
b diabetes	5	e insomnia	3
c eye strain	2	f joint pain	4

WORD STORE 7C

10 CD•3.16 MP3•101 **Complete WORD STORE 7C with the highlighted phrases in the article. Then listen, check, and repeat.**

11 **With a partner, complete the statements with phrases from WORD STORE C. Then choose four statements to discuss.**

1 Young people spend too much time in front of screens _____ their health.
2 With the Internet _____ , you don't need to 'know' anything anymore.
3 Social media _____ in maintaining friendships.
4 The only way to improve a _____ is to get more exercise.
5 Doctors do not know how to _____ of obesity.
6 It's so easy to _____ when you are online.
7 Drug addicts suffering from _____ deserve our sympathy.
8 Teenagers these days have a very limited _____ .

WORD STORE 7D

12 CD•3.17 MP3•102 **Complete WORD STORE 7D with more collocations. Then listen, check, and repeat. Write example sentences.**

Exercise 4
1 social media
2 what everybody else is doing
3 anxiety
4 technology
5 a sedentary lifestyle
6 using thumbs for texting
7 stress, weight
8 more interesting things

Exercise 11
1 at the expense of
2 at your fingertips
3 plays a crucial role
4 sedentary lifestyle
5 address the issue
6 lose track of time
7 withdrawal symptoms
8 attention span

WORKBOOK
pp. 92–93

Focus Assessment Package, Unit 7.1, Vocabulary.

NEXT CLASS
• Ask students to prepare for a 10–15 minute vocabulary quiz:

Advanced passive forms

I can use a range of advanced passive forms.

1 **SPEAKING** **With a partner, discuss what would happen in your home if all screens were banned for six months. Then read what happened to the Maushart family and compare.**

WHAT HAPPENED WHEN MOM PULLED THE PLUG ON TECHNOLOGY

Susan Maushart with children

Susan Maushart unplugged her teenagers and for six months the family lived without their devices. Family rooms were no longer lit up by the light of screens and no electronic noises **could be heard** through the night.

Maushart decided to unplug the family because nothing was ever really turned off. She'd constantly told her children to turn their devices off when doing their homework but even when they **should have been turned** off, they were bleeping away in the background.

So what happened? Once the children **had been made to turn** off their technology, the family rediscovered small pleasures like board games, books, and listening to music together. Susan Maushart's son **was given** a saxophone and took up music seriously. If the Internet was needed for homework, her older daughter just went to the library. The youngest daughter **hated being** unplugged but Susan Maushart believes her children became more focused thanks to being less dependent on technology. She now believes all families **need to be encouraged** to unplug periodically.

REFERENCES

CULTURE NOTES ››› *p. 197*

EXTRA ACTIVITIES

- Photocopiable resource 43 (advanced passive forms – 15 mins) MultiROM and ActiveTeach
- MyEnglishLab – assignable *Show what you have learned* mini-test

WORKBOOK

p. 94

NEXT CLASS

- Ask students to prepare for a 10–15 minute grammar quiz: *Focus* Assessment Package, Unit 7.2, Grammar.

2 **Read the GRAMMAR FOCUS. Complete the examples with the correct form of *be*. Then check your answers in the text.**

GRAMMAR FOCUS

Advanced passive forms

- Passive forms with present or past modal verb structures
  ... no electronic noises ***could*** [1] be ***heard*** *through the night.*
  ... even when they ***should*** [2] have been ***turned*** *off, they ...*
- Passive forms with verbs that take two objects, i.e. a person and a thing (*give sb sth, send sb sth, show sb sth*, etc.)
  Her son [3] was ***given*** *a saxophone.* (the 'person' is the topic – more common)
  A saxophone was given to her son. (the 'thing' is the topic – less common)
- Verbs followed by passive infinitives or passive *-ing* forms
  The youngest daughter ***hated*** [4] being *unplugged.*
  ... all families need [5] to be *encouraged ...*

Note: *make sb do sth → be made to do sth*
Once the children ***had been made to*** *turn off their technology ...*

3 **Rewrite the sentences in the passive starting with the underlined object.**

1 You can buy absolutely anything on the Internet these days.
Absolutely anything can be bought on the Internet these days.
2 Nobody could have predicted the importance of the Internet back in the 1970s.
3 You must protect your computer by using anti-virus software.
4 Architects may have designed Bill Gates's house on an Apple computer.
5 You can control the volume of a YouTube video with the up/down arrows on your keyboard.
6 They should have given Albert Einstein a Nobel Prize for his theory of relativity.

Exercise 3
2 The importance of the Internet could not have been predicted back in the 1970s.
3 Your computer must be protected by using anti-virus software.
4 Bill Gates's house may have been designed on an Apple computer.
5 The volume of a YouTube video can be controlled with the up/down arrows on your keyboard.
6 Albert Einstein should have been given a Nobel Prize for his theory of relativity.

4 **Underline the indirect object in each sentence. Then rewrite the sentences in the passive, using *by* if necessary. Which sentences are true for you?**

1 Yesterday, people sent me fifty messages.
Yesterday, I was sent fifty messages.
2 My parents might give me a new laptop for my next birthday. I might be given a new laptop for my birthday.
3 They have promised us some new computers for the school. We have been promised some new computers for the school.
4 People owe me lots of money. I am owed lots of money.
5 They should offer my father a new job. My father should be offered a new job.
6 Today a substitute teacher is teaching us IT. Today we are being taught IT by a substitute teacher.

5 **Use the prompts to write sentences using the passive infinitive or *-ing* form. Then, with a partner, discuss the statements.**

Most teenagers:
1 don't enjoy / yell at
Most teenagers don't enjoy being yelled at.
2 can't stand / ignore Most teenagers can't stand being ignored.
3 would prefer / not criticize Most teenagers would prefer not to be criticized.
4 would like / take / seriously Most teenagers would like to be taken seriously.
5 get tired of / judge Most teenagers get tired of being judged.
6 just want / love Most teenagers just want to be loved.
8 dislike / tell / what to do Most teenagers dislike being told what to do.
7 aren't interested in / compare / to other teenagers Most teenagers aren't interested in being compared to other teenagers.

Grammar Focus page 170

7.3 Listening

Multiple choice

I can understand the main points in news reports and conversations.

1 **Look at the cartoons. What problems do they illustrate? Have you had any similar problems?**

Exercise 1
A phone theft
B following your sat-nav to the wrong place
C computer freezing/unreliable support service
D not having enough money/not being tech savvy

2 CD•3.18 MP3•103 **Listen and match three of the cartoons (A–D) with the situations (1–3).**

1 D 2 B 3 A

EXAM FOCUS Multiple choice

3 CD•3.18 MP3•103 **Listen again and choose the correct answer, A, B, or C.**

1 The store assistant wants to
  (A) warn the girl against buying cheap laptops.
  B persuade the girl to increase her planned budget.
  C encourage the girl to store movies and music on a laptop.
2 Which sentence best describes the situation?
  A The sat-nav has taken them the wrong way.
  B The man wants to avoid the interstate.
  (C) The woman thinks that the man should trust the sat-nav.
3 What does the report say about cell phones?
  (A) Cell phone theft is on the rise.
  B Cell phones are a risk to children's safety.
  C Cell phone thieves target male teenagers.

REFERENCES
AUDIO SCRIPT ››› p. 211
WORKBOOK
p. 95

4 CD•3.18 MP3•103 **Listen again and choose the correct options.**

1 a The store assistant *thinks* / *doesn't think* the girl will be able to **do without** a big hard drive in future.

b The girl decides that she *needs* / *doesn't need* to **think it over**.

2 a The couple *can* / *can't* **figure out** which way to go.

b The man is *happy* / *unhappy* that he was **talked into** buying a sat-nav.

c Sat-navs **get on** *the man's* / *the woman's* **nerves**.

3 a Figures have **come out** that show a sharp *fall* / *rise* in cell phone thefts.

b The government wants *companies* / *the police* to **bring in** new security measures.

5 **Match the phrasal verbs in green in Exercise 4 with these definitions.**

1 persuaded = talked sb into sth
2 consider it = think sth over
3 introduce = bring sth in
4 annoy, irritate = get on sb's nerves
5 been released or published = come out
6 understand = figure sth out
7 manage without = do without sth

6 **Complete the sentences to make them true for you. Then compare with a partner.**

1 I couldn't do without my phone because ...
2 The last time I wanted to buy something expensive and I had to think it over was ...
3 I always find it difficult to figure out ...
4 I can't talk my parents into buying me ...
5 The person who really gets on my nerves is ...
6 The government should bring in new laws to ...
7 The next new book/movie/album/game I want to buy is coming out ...

PRONUNCIATION FOCUS

7 CD•3.19 MP3•104 **Listen and complete the table. Then listen again and repeat.**

NOUN	ADJECTIVE	ADVERB
1 science	scientific	scientifically
2 technology	technological	technologically
3 electronics	electronic	electronically
4 electricity	electric	electrically

8 CD•3.20 MP3•105 **Mark the stress in the words in Exercise 7. Then listen, check, and repeat.**

WORD STORE 7E

9 CD•3.21 MP3•106 **Complete WORD STORE 7E. Match the words in the box with the photos. Then listen, check, and repeat.**

7.4 Reading

Multiple choice

I can understand the main points in an article.

1 **SPEAKING With a partner, discuss the questions.**

1 Which five apps on your phone or tablet do you use most?
2 What does each one do and how does it work?
3 Which is your favourite app? Why?

2 **Decide if the statements below are true (T) or false (F). Then read *TODAY IN THE USA* and check your ideas.**

1 The number of Americans interested in wearable technology is growing fast. T
2 More than half of wearable devices in use are used in sport activities. T
3 The majority of people are not worried about privacy issues. F

TODAY IN THE USA

- The wearable technology market grew from $6.3 million in 2010 to $5.1 billion in 2014, and continues to grow rapidly.
- Sixty-one percent of all devices in the wearable technology market are activity or fitness trackers.
- Sixty percent of Americans who own wearable technology devices say that it helps them feel more in control of their lives.
- Fifty-one percent of people reported that privacy is the main thing preventing them from using wearable technology.

3 **SPEAKING With a partner, discuss the infographic. What do you think the function of each wearable gadget is?**

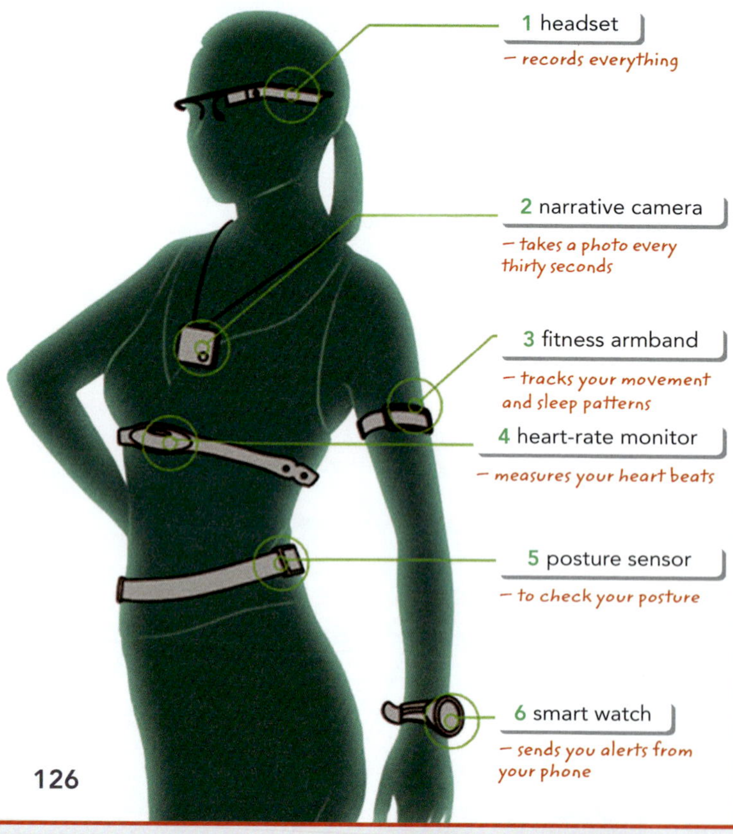

CD•3.22 MP3•107

Rise of the 'inner-net' meet the most connected man on the planet

For most people, keeping track of emails and **staying on top** of their calendar might be hard enough, but for American software developer Chris Dancy life doesn't feel complete without being connected to several hundred devices and applications that collect data about his life at all times. 'I've been called the most connected human on Earth,' he says.

"I've spent the last four years connecting all the devices that I wear to all the smart technology in my home and transmitting all that data through to a single online platform, so I can search my entire life. I call it my "inner-net.""

On a normal day, Dancy 'travels light,' only wearing six devices. Over his eyes sits a headset, which records everything he sees. Around his neck hangs a narrative camera, which requires no photography skills because it takes a picture automatically every thirty seconds. On his wrist is a smart watch, which sends him alerts from his two smartphones, while around the upper arm is a fitness armband, **tracking his movement** and sleep patterns twenty-four hours a day. And then there's the stuff you can't see: a heart-rate monitor strapped to his chest to measure his heart beats and beneath his waistband, a posture sensor, 'which vibrates when I get tired and I forget my posture and slouch,' he beams.

Back in Denver, Colorado, all the data from these devices feeds directly into his home environment, which automatically adjusts according to his mood and needs. 'The house knows my moods,' he says. 'If I've been dashing around all day and get really stressed out so that I don't sleep well, when I wake up, the light is a certain color, the room a particular temperature and certain music plays.'

REFERENCES
CULTURE NOTES ››› *pp. 197–198*

EXTRA ACTIVITIES
- Photocopiable resource 44 (word formation – 12 mins) MultiROM and ActiveTeach

WORKBOOK
pp. 96–97

NEXT CLASS
- Ask students to investigate and read about another advance in technology.

Chris Dancy

Dancy claims this connected environment, which he calls 'data-assisted living,' has revolutionized his life, helping him to lose 100 pounds in eighteen months and letting him live in a state of Zen-like calm, safe in the knowledge that his every moment is being archived. He can cast an eye over this personal data any time he needs to remember something that happened in the past: 'I was at a restaurant in Denver, and I was like, "What did I eat here last time?" So I browsed all the photos from that day and could see exactly what meal it was,' he says. He goes on to give another example: 'When I have a meeting with someone on my calendar, instead of scanning a LinkedIn* profile, I can access information about how they made me feel the first time I met them.'

So, when you're as connected as Dancy, what's the next frontier? 'All this stuff has to go away,' he says. 'It all needs to be in my clothing. Why can't your shoes have sensors in them, so when you're wandering around trying to find a location, you don't need a GPS – your shoe just vibrates left or right. I think this kind of personalized data is really the future, but for now we have to fix all this stuff onto our clothes, and people stare at you because it looks silly.'

But what about the issue of ownership of data and privacy? A lot of data is fed back on the web and a lot of companies now hold huge amounts of data on their customers. Dancy frowns: he is concerned, but is optimistic about the beneficial power of mastering our data, as long as we stop giving it away. 'It's urgent that people look at the data they are creating and giving away – so much of it can be used to make our lives better, rather than lining the pockets of mega corporations.'

*LinkedIn is a networking service for professional people.

4 Read the article and check your ideas from Exercise 3. Which gadget would you most like to own? Why?

EXAM FOCUS Multiple choice

5 Read the article again. For questions 1–6, choose the correct answer, A, B, C, or D.

1 Dancy is called the most connected man because he
A checks his emails and calendar regularly.
(B) uses technology to track every detail of his life.
C wears smart clothes all the time.
D has a personal online platform at home.

2 One of the devices that Dancy wears
A helps him to travel without too much luggage.
B improves his photography skills.
C wakes him up when he's falling asleep.
(D) alerts him when he isn't standing or sitting up straight.

3 Dancy maintains that technology has enabled him to
A improve the quality of his sleep.
B live in a more secure environment.
C find out what other people think of him.
(D) de-stress and lose weight.

4 Dancy thinks that in the future wearable technology will
A disappear. C be worn in the shoes.
(B) be less visible. D look stupid.

5 Dancy thinks people should
A share their data with others online.
B create more data to give away.
(C) protect personal data from big companies.
D improve the economy by sharing data.

6 Which is the best summary of Dancy's attitude to wearable technology?
(A) You can use personal data to improve the quality of your life.
B It's difficult to use personal data to your own advantage.
C Wearable technology can be used to control your environment and people around you.
D It's only large companies that benefit from data analysis.

6 With a partner, complete the questions using the phrases in blue in the article. Then, with a partner, ask and answer the questions.

1 Has any technology ever revolutionized your _life_ ?
2 Do you shop online safe in the _knowledge_ that your personal data is protected?
3 Do you manage to stay on _top_ of your homework?
4 Can your smartphone track your _movements_ ?
5 Does buying things online line the _pockets_ of big corporations?
6 Do you think that shoes and clothing with built-in technology is the next _frontier_ ?

7 SPEAKING With a partner, discuss your thoughts on wearable technology and say whether you agree or disagree with the statements.

1 Chris Dancy is a weirdo! It's not for me.
2 I really want my life to be recorded like this. It's cool!
3 It's dangerous to have too much personal data online.
4 It will help people become healthier and happier.

WORD STORE 7F

8 CD•3.23 MP3•108 Complete WORD STORE 7F. Match the verbs in the box with their definitions. Then listen, check, and repeat.

7.5 Grammar

Passive reporting structures

I can use passive reporting structures to talk about general feelings or beliefs.

1 CD•3.24 MP3•109 **SPEAKING With a partner, discuss the Math facts and choose the option you think is correct. Then listen and check your answers.**

Math facts

1 **It is thought that** numbers and counting began with the number *zero* / *one.* (one)
2 Arithmetic **is considered to have originated** around *20,000* / *6,000* years ago in Sumeria. (6,000)
3 The *Egyptians* / *Romans* **are known to have invented** the numbers one thousand and one million. (Egyptians)
4 Before 1500, the term 'Mathematics' was understood to mean *'Astrology'* / *'Physics'*. ('Astrology')
5 **There are said to be** *limited* / *unlimited* opportunities for mathematicians. (unlimited)
6 *An increasing* / *A decreasing* number of students **are expected to be doing** Math in college in the future. (An increasing)

2 Read the GRAMMAR FOCUS and find examples of each pattern in the text.

GRAMMAR FOCUS

Passive reporting structures

You can use the passive to talk about general feelings or beliefs with reporting verbs like *believe, know, think*, etc. These structures are usually used in more formal contexts.

- *it* + passive verb (present or past) + *that* clause 1
- subject + passive verb (present or past) + *to*-infinitive (*to do/to have done/to be doing*, etc.) 2, 3, 4, 6
- *there* + passive verb (present or past) + *to be/to have been* 5

3 CD•3.25 MP3•110 **Read the text and find one missing word in each of the underlined phrases. Then listen and check.**

Where do our numbers come from?

Around 500BC, the Greek philosopher [1]Pythagoras is understood to *have* come up with the idea of odd and even numbers. [2]It *is* said that Pythagoras prepared the way for many famous Greek mathematicians, including Archimedes. [3]Archimedes is considered *to* be one of the greatest mathematicians of all time and discovered how to measure the volume of an object with an irregular shape. [4]He is believed to *have* been taking a bath when he made the discovery, and leapt out yelling, 'Eureka!' ('I have found it!'). Unfortunately, Archimedes was killed by a Roman soldier in 212BC and Mathematics entered a dark age. [5]It *is* thought that the Romans just weren't interested in Mathematics. [6]There are known to *have* been several other civilizations, including the Maya people in Mexico and scholars in ancient China, who contributed to the advancement of Mathematics. However, the next big breakthrough was probably in 500AD, when the Indians invented 'zero'. They had already created symbols for the numbers 1–9. In fact, [7]it could *be* argued that our 'Arabic numerals' should rather be known as 'Indian numerals'. After all, it was actually the Indians who invented them.

1	2	3	4	5	6	7	8	9
–	=	≡	+	h	ɸ	ʔ	ς	ʔ

Brahmi numerals around 300AD

128

REFERENCES
CULTURE NOTES ››› *p. 198*
AUDIO SCRIPT ››› *pp. 211–212*

EXTRA ACTIVITIES
- Photocopiable resource 45 (Test yourself partner work activities) MultiROM and ActiveTeach
- MyEnglishLab – assignable *Show what you have learned* mini-test

WORKBOOK
p. 98

NEXT CLASS
- Ask students to prepare for a 10–15 minute grammar quiz: *Focus* Assessment Package, Unit 7.5, Grammar.

4 **Complete the sentences using the words in parentheses. Don't change the order of the words provided but add any other necessary words.**

1 It *is understood that Pythagoras came up with* (understand/Pythagoras/come up) the idea of odd and even numbers.
2 Pythagoras ________ (say/prepare) the way for many famous Greek mathematicians.
3 It ________ (be/think/Archimedes) is one of the greatest mathematicians of all time.
4 Archimedes ________ (believe/make) his most famous discovery in the bath.
5 The Romans ________ (not/think/be interested) in Math.
6 Several other civilizations ________ (be/know/contribute) to the advancement of Mathematics.

5 **Rewrite each sentence in two ways. Begin with the words in parentheses.**

1 We know that most mathematical symbols were invented in the 1500s. (It … / Most …)
It is known that most mathematical symbols were invented in the 1500s.
Most mathematical symbols are known to have been invented in the 1500s.
2 Historians consider the seventeenth century to be a high point in the history of Mathematics. (The seventeenth … / It …)
3 Many teachers thought that calculators could harm students' Math skills. (It … / Calculators …)
4 They estimate that there are over 10,000 new Math graduates every year in the UK. (There … / It …)

6 **SPEAKING List the school subjects you study in order from most important to least important. Discuss your list with a partner. How important is Math?**

Grammar Focus page 171

Exercise 4
2 is said to have prepared
3 is thought that Archimedes
4 is believed to have made
5 are not thought to have been interested
6 are known to have contributed

Exercise 5
2 The seventeenth century is considered to have been a high point in the history of Mathematics. It is considered that the seventeenth century was a high point in the history of Mathematics.
3 It was thought that calculators could harm students' Math skills. Calculators were thought to be able to harm students' Math skills.
4 There are estimated to be over 10,000 new Math graduates every year in the UK. It is estimated that there are over 10,000 new Math graduates every year in the UK.

7.6 Speaking

Clarification

I can ask for and give clarification.

1 **SPEAKING Put ✓ next to the machines you would trust in place of a human and ✗ next to the ones you would not. Then, with a partner, discuss your choices.**

1 a self-driving car ☐
2 a robotic surgeon ☐
3 a computer-generated online friend ☐
4 a virtual teacher ☐
5 a robot police officer ☐

2 **SPEAKING Imagine you are going to a technology fair. With a partner, read the ads and discuss which exhibition you would rather visit.**

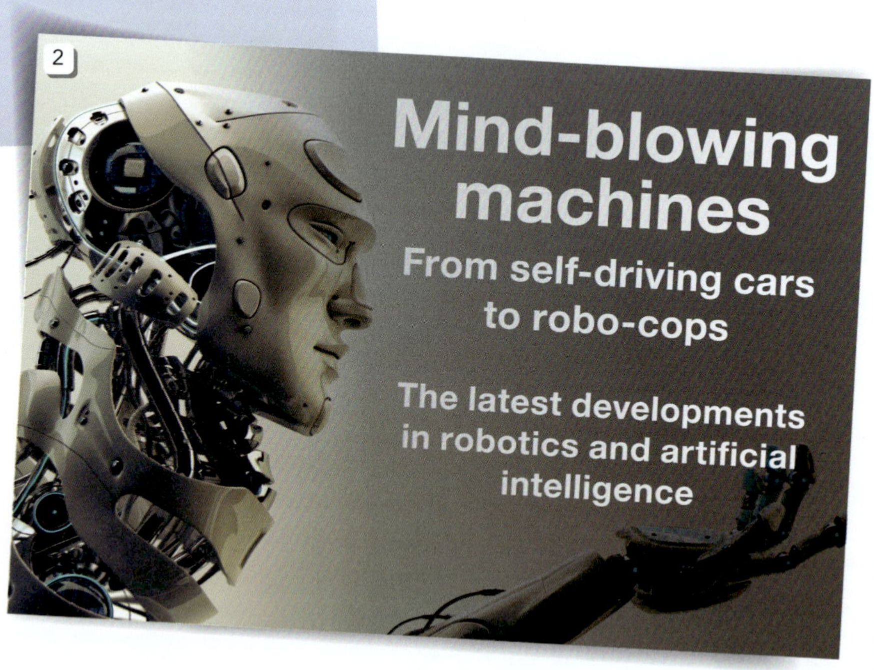

3 CD•3.26 MP3•111 **Listen to a conversation at the Mind-blowing machines exhibition. What type of machine is the 'explainer' describing?** *It's a fully-automated remote surgical unit (robotic surgeon).*

REFERENCES
CULTURE NOTES ››› p. 198
AUDIO SCRIPT ››› p. 212
WORKBOOK
p. 99

4 CD•3.26 MP3•111 **Listen again and check the phrases in the SPEAKING FOCUS that you hear.**

SPEAKING FOCUS

Signaling confusion	
Sorry, I'm not with you.	☐
I'm not sure I follow (you).	☐
I'm afraid you've lost me there.	☑
I don't know what you mean by …	☐
Checking your understanding	
So, in other words, …	☐
Are you saying … ?	☑
If I understand correctly, you mean … , right?	☐
Giving clarification	
Yes, precisely/exactly.	☑
Yes, (that's) pretty much (it).	☐
No, that's not (quite) what I meant.	☐
What I meant was …	☐

5 CD•3.27 MP3•112 **Complete the conversations with words from the SPEAKING FOCUS. Then listen and check.**

1

A: Not many people agree with me, but I think video games are kind of a waste of time. I'd rather kick back with my friends than stare at a screen for hours on end.

B: Um … sorry, but I don't know what you mean [1] *by* 'kick back'.

A: What I [2] *meant* was 'spend time together' – you know, hang out, chat, relax.

2

A: I think I'd die without my phone.

B: 'And this year's Oscar for best actress goes to …'

A: Ha, ha, very funny. Are you [3] *saying* I'm being dramatic?

B: Yes, [4] *exactly* . I think you'd survive without it.

3

A: Dan, I have to answer this question for homework. Can you help, please?

B: Sure, what's the question?

A: 'In what ways might socially intelligent robots benefit human society?'

B: Hmm. Well, I suppose the ability to have conversations with our machines will make a big difference.

A: I'm not sure I [5] *follow* you.

B: Well, we interact with today's machines mostly by typing or pushing buttons, but some phones and tablets already understand voice commands, right? Imagine they and other machines could react to what you say and really talk back to you.

A: Hmm, OK. If I understand [6] *correctly* , you mean we'll be able to have a conversation with our television or our fridge, right?

B: Yes, that's [7] *pretty* much it.

A: I'm not sure I'd want to have a conversation with a fridge.

B: Why not?

A: Well, they have a reputation for being pretty cold.

B: Oh, very funny!

6 SPEAKING **With a partner, discuss the questions. Use the SPEAKING FOCUS to help you.**

1 In what ways are video games good or bad for the people who play them?
2 What do you think has been the most important technological development during your lifetime?
3 Has social media made us more or less sociable? Explain your opinion.
4 In what ways might socially intelligent machines benefit human society?

7.7 Writing

A 'for and against' essay

I can express certainty, contrast, and condition using formal language.

1 Complete the survey by choosing the information that is true for you.

Thanks for taking the time to complete our survey. We appreciate your help!

1. On average, I spend *0–2 / 2–4 / 4 or more* hours a day online.
2. When I search for something online, I *rarely / sometimes / often* look beyond the first few results.
3. I generally believe what I read or watch online. *Yes. / No.*
4. I *never / occasionally / often* contribute to wikis, forums, and readers' comments sections.
5. I *never / occasionally / often* pay for access to online content.
6. I *never / occasionally / often* do research using (paper) reference books.

2 SPEAKING With a partner, discuss any similarities and differences in your answers.

3 Read the writing task and Mark's essay. What arguments for and against does he give?

> The Internet makes it possible to access vast amounts of knowledge, wherever and whenever we like. Write an essay discussing the advantages and disadvantages of having so much information at our disposal.

4 Read Mark's essay again and complete the paragraph plan. Check your answers with the WRITING FOCUS in Unit 3 if necessary.

1. introduction: *general/ factual* comments on the topic and a statement mentioning both sides of the issue
2. arguments *for* the issue
3. arguments *against* the issue
4. conclusion: a summarizing statement and *a personal opinion*

5 Underline three passive structures in Mark's essay. Do they make the essay more or less formal?

1 The Internet and the vast amount of information it contains can now be accessed in an instant, from almost anywhere, at any time. In fact, because of smartphones and tablets, millions of us carry this resource with us constantly and use it on a daily or even hourly basis. **Undeniably**, this is a positive development in many ways, and **yet** there are also certain drawbacks.

2 There is no **doubt** that having online access to most of human knowledge has many advantages. **Provided** that a connection is available, anyone with basic computer skills can search, share, and contribute to this huge digital library. In other words, when it comes to accessibility, information is no longer only for the privileged. Another key benefit is the easy availability of different forms of information such as text, images, videos, and sound on almost every topic imaginable. This leads to a much richer experience than was possible for most people before the Internet existed.

3 **Having** said that, there are also minuses. Since much of the information online is generated by users, there are few checks on accuracy. This means a significant amount of online data is likely to be incorrect or biased. Another potential drawback is the enormous amount of information available. It may **actually** be very hard to find exactly what you are looking for, and good analytical reading skills are often required.

4 All things considered, there are disadvantages and challenges associated with the accuracy and amount of information available online. However, to my mind, the benefits offered by this resource clearly outweigh the drawbacks.

Mark Forest, Grade 11

132

Exercise 3

For:
- Anyone with basic computer skills can search, share, and contribute to this huge digital library.
- Information is no longer only for the privileged.
- Easy availability of different forms of information such as text, images, videos, and sound on virtually every topic imaginable.

Against:
- There are few checks on accuracy.
- A significant amount of online data is likely to be incorrect or biased.
- The enormous amount of information available; it may actually be very hard to find exactly what you are looking for.

EXTRA ACTIVITIES

- MyEnglishLab – assignable *Show what you have learned* writing task and *Show that you have checked* checklist

WORKBOOK

p. 100

6 **Complete the WRITING FOCUS with the words in purple in Mark's essay.**

WRITING FOCUS

- Expressing certainty
  [1] Undeniably, this is a positive development.
  There are undoubtedly certain drawbacks …
  It is undeniable/There is no [2] doubt that having online access (to …) has many advantages.
  Without (a) doubt, there are people who believe the opposite.
- Expressing contrast
  That said/[3] Having said that, there are also drawbacks/minuses.
  Search results may be instant, but nevertheless/even so, careful reading takes time.
- Introducing unexpected or surprising contrasts
  This is a positive development in many ways, and [4] yet there are also certain drawbacks.
  It may [5] actually be very hard to find what you are looking for.
- Expressing condition
  As long as/Providing/[6] Provided that a connection is available, anyone can search the Internet.

7 **Complete the sentences with words from the WRITING FOCUS. Use each word once only.**

1 There are undoubtedly some strong arguments against banning cell phones in schools.
2 It is undeniable that having access to the Internet can be very helpful during some classes.
3 As long as phones are turned off during class, I see no reason to ban them completely.
4 Phones at school may be distracting, but even so, some parents want their children to have one for safety reasons.
5 In some countries, it may actually be illegal for schools to ban cell phones altogether.
6 Without a doubt, some parents want their children to always be contactable.

8 **Read the LANGUAGE FOCUS. Which alternative to *because* does Mark use in his essay?** since

LANGUAGE FOCUS

Introducing reasons in formal writing

You can make your writing more formal by using these alternatives to *because*:

- ***As*** or ***since*** to introduce a reason that you already know.
  As/Since we are overseas, *cell phone charges are more expensive. (We know we are overseas.)*
  *Cell phone charges are more expensive **as/since we are overseas**.*
- ***Due to*** (instead of *because of*) when the reason is a noun.
  Due to customer demand, *Internet connection speeds are constantly increasing.*
  *Internet connection speeds are constantly increasing **due to customer demand**.*

9 **Rewrite each sentence in two ways. For each sentence b, use the same alternative to *because* as in sentence a.**

1 Phones should be banned at school because they are distracting.
   a As phones are distracting, they should be banned at school.
   b Phones should be banned at school as they are distracting.
2 Because of the high price of some phones, theft is not uncommon.
   a Due to … b Theft …
3 Phones should certainly not be allowed in classrooms because they can be used to cheat during tests.
   a Since … b Phones …
4 Discipline has improved because of the ban that was introduced at our school.
   a Due to … b Discipline …

10 **Read the writing task and follow the instructions below.**

> In your English class you have been talking about using cell phones at school. Now your English teacher has asked you to write an essay. Write an essay using all the notes and give reasons for your point of view.
>
> *Should students be banned from using cell phones during the school day?*
>
> **Notes**
> Write about:
> 1 finding important information
> 2 disturbing the class/other students
> 3 ______ (your own idea)
>
> Write your essay in 140–190 words.

1 What general comment could you make on the use of cell phones at school?
2 Write a sentence that mentions both sides of the argument.
3 Use your answers to questions 1 and 2 to help you write the introduction.
4 Note down arguments for and against a ban on cell phones at school and supporting points.
5 Expand these notes into main paragraphs.
6 Add a conclusion that includes your personal opinion.

11 **Complete the writing task in Exercise 10. Use the WRITING FOCUS and the LANGUAGE FOCUS to help you.**

133

Exercise 9
2 a Due to the high price of some phones, theft is not uncommon.
b Theft is not uncommon due to the high price of some phones.
3 a Since they can be used to cheat during tests, phones should certainly not be allowed in classrooms.
b Phones should certainly not be allowed in classrooms since they can be used to cheat during tests.
4 a Due to the ban that was introduced at our school, discipline has improved.
b Discipline has improved due to the ban that was introduced at our school.

7.8 Language in focus

Easily confused words

I can understand and use words that are easily confused.

1 Read the information and choose the correct options in the sentences below.

Certain words are easily confused. Words may look and/or sound similar but have different meanings (e.g. *lose/loose*) or closely related meanings (e.g. *lone/lonely/alone*). Other words look completely different but are confused, either because they have similar meanings (e.g. *include/consist of/comprise*) or because they are 'false friends' (e.g. *actual/current*).

1 It's so easy to (***lose***) / ***loose*** track of time.
2 Technology makes you ***lone*** / (***lonely***) / ***alone***.
3 Did you go to bed (***late***) / ***lately***?
4 What is the ***arise*** / ***raise*** / (***rise***) in childhood obesity due to?
5 The conclusion must (***include***) / ***comprise*** / ***consist of*** your opinion.
6 If (***present***) / ***actual*** trends continue, thefts could reach 1 million.

2 Change one letter in the word in bold to form a different part of speech and complete the sentences.

1 You can advise someone or give someone **advice**.
2 You can **breathe** in deeply or take a deep breath.
3 You can be dependent on someone or be someone's **dependent**.
4 A situation can **affect** you badly or have a bad effect on you.

3 Choose the correct options. Then answer the questions.

1 Is your car very *economic* / (*economical*)?
2 Do you *lay* / (*lie*) on your front when you're sleeping?
3 Are there any (*historic*) / *historical* buildings nearby?
4 Will you ever get an *occasion* / (*opportunity*) to go to Australia?
5 Do you prefer exams or (*continuous*) / *continual* assessment?
6 Are you a *conscious* / (*conscientious*) student?

4 Write example sentences for the words you didn't use in Exercise 3. Use a dictionary if necessary.

There's an economic crisis in my country right now.

5 Replace the underlined words/phrases in the sentences with the words in the box.

actually complement compliment currently
eventually fantastic genial possibly

1 I always say I have lots of Facebook friends but
a in fact (actually), I only have 100. b right now (currently), I only have 100.
2 'Are you going to buy a new laptop?'
a 'In the end (Eventually), yes.' b 'Maybe (Possibly), yes.'
3 My grandma and grandpa always
a work well with (complement) each other. b say nice things to (compliment) each other.
4 We love our family doctor. He's a
a great (fantastic) guy. b friendly (genial) guy.

6 Translate the sentences in Exercise 5. Are there any 'false friends' with these words in your language? Are any sentences true?

134

07 WORD LIST

Electronic communication

access information/knowledge /ˌæksɛs ˌɪnfɚˈmeɪʃən/ˈnɑlɪdʒ/
access to (the Internet/online content) /ˌæksɛs tə (ðə ˈɪntɚnɛt/ˌɑnlaɪn ˈkɑntɛnt)/
accessibility/availability /əkˌsɛsəˈbɪləṯi/əˌveɪləˈbɪləṯi/
adjust /əˈdʒʌst/
alert (n, v) /əˈlɚt/
anti-virus software /ˌæntivaɪrəs ˈsɔftwɛr/
application/app /ˌæplɪˈkeɪʃən/æp/
attach a file /əˌtætʃ ə ˈfaɪl/
attachment /əˈtætʃmənt/
bleep /blip/
bookmark a site/a homepage /bʊkmɑrk ə ˈsaɪt/ə ˈhoʊmpeɪdʒ/
browse the net/a website /ˌbraʊz ðə ˈnɛt/ə ˈwɛbsaɪt/
built-in technology /ˌbɪlt ɪn tɛkˈnɑlədʒi/
collect data /kəˌlɛkt ˈdeɪṯə/
contribute to wikis/forums/readers' comments sections /kənˌtrɪbyut tə ˈwɪkiz/ˈfɔrəmz/ˌridɚz ˈkɑmɛnts ˌsɛkʃənz/
control the volume /kənˌtroʊl ðə ˈvɑlyum/
data analysis /ˈdeɪṯə əˌnæləsɪs/
device /dɪˈvaɪs/
download music/e-books /daʊnˌloʊd ˈmyuzɪk/ˈi bʊks/
external drive /ɪkˌstɚnl ˈdraɪv/
fitness/activity app/tracker /ˈfɪtnəs/ækˈtɪvəṯi æp/ˌtrækɚ/
follow sb (on Twitter) /ˌfɑloʊ ˌsʌmbɑdi (ɑn ˈtwɪṯɚ)/
generate /ˈdʒɛnəreɪt/
google sth /ˈgugəl ˌsʌmθɪŋ/
handset /ˈhændsɛt/
hard drive /ˈhɑrd draɪv/
headset /ˈhɛdsɛt/
Internet connection speed /ˌɪntɚnɛt kəˈnɛkʃən spid/
landline /ˈlændˌlaɪn/
narrative camera /ˌnærəṯɪv ˈkæmrə/
on the web/on Twitter /ˌɑn ðə ˈwɛb/ɑn ˈtwɪṯɚ/
online platform /ˌonlaɪn ˈplætfɔrm/
password /ˈpæswɚd/
personalized /ˈpɚsənəlaɪzd/
post a comment/a link /ˌpoʊst ə ˈkɑmɛnt/ə ˈlɪŋk/
privacy issues /ˈpraɪvəsi ˌɪʃuz/
push a button /ˌpʊʃ ə ˈbʌt̚n/
record / rɪˈkɔrd /
remote control /rɪˌmoʊt kənˈtroʊl/
sat-nav (satellite navigation system)/GPS /ˈsæt næv (ˌsæṯəlaɪt ˌnævɪˈgeɪʃən ˌsɪstəm)/ˌdʒi pi ɛs/
save a file/an attachment /seɪv ə ˈfaɪl/ən əˈtætʃmənt/
scan sb's profile /ˌskæn ˌsʌmbɑdiz ˈproʊfaɪl/
search results /ˈsɚtʃ rɪˌzʌlts/
sensor /ˈsɛnsɚ/
share a link/a Facebook post /ˌʃɛr ə ˈlɪŋk/ə ˈfeɪsbʊk poʊst/
smart technology /ˌsmɑrt tɛkˈnɑlədʒi/
smartphone /ˈsmɑrtfoʊn/
social media /ˌsoʊʃəl ˈmidiə/
software developer /ˈsɔftwɛr dɪˌvɛləpɚ/
store /stɔr/
text sb /ˈtɛkst sʌmbɑdi/
track /træk/
transmit /trænzˈmɪt/
type /taɪp/
unplug /ʌnˈplʌg/
update your status/profile /ʌpˌdeɪt yɚ ˈsteɪṯəs/ˈproʊfaɪl/
upload a photo/a video clip /ʌpˌloʊd ə ˈfoʊṯoʊ/ə ˈvɪdioʊ klɪp/
vibrate /ˈvaɪbreɪt/
virtual /ˈvɚtʃuəl/
voice command /ˈvɔɪs kəˌmænd/
wearable technology /ˌwɛrəbəl tɛkˈnɑlədʒi/
www/World Wide Web /ˌdʌblyu dʌblyu ˈdʌblyu/ˌwɚld waɪd ˈwɛb/

Health and addictions

addicted to /əˈdɪktəd tə/
anxiety /æŋˈzaɪəṯi/
breathe (deeply) /ˌbrið (ˈdipli)/
circulation /ˌsɚkyəˈleɪʃən/
condition /kənˈdɪʃən/
count calories /ˌkaʊnt ˈkæləriz/
deprive of /dɪˈpraɪv əv/
diabetes /ˌdaɪəˈbiṯiz/
drug addict /ˈdrʌg ˌædɪkt/
excess weight /ɛksɛs ˈweɪt/
eye strain/sore eyes /ˈaɪ streɪn/ˌsɔr ˈaɪz/

EXTRA ACTIVITIES
- Photocopiable resource 46 (easily confused words – 20 mins) MultiROM and ActiveTeach

WORKBOOK
p. 101

NEXT CLASS
- Ask students to study the Word list on pp. 134–135.
- Ask students to review for Focus review 7.

heart rate monitor /ˈhɑrt reɪt ˌmɑnət̬ɚ/
high blood pressure /ˌhaɪ ˈblʌd ˌprɛʃɚ/
insomnia /ɪnˈsɑmniə/
joint pain /ˈdʒɔɪnt peɪn/
(minor) ailments /(ˌmaɪnɚ) ˈeɪlmənts/
obese /oʊˈbis/
obesity /oʊˈbisət̬i/
obsessed with /əbˈsɛst wɪð/
obsessive behavior /əbˌsɛsɪv bɪˈheɪvyɚ/
overweight /ˌoʊvɚˈweɪt/
repetitive strain injury /rɪˌpɛt̬ət̬ɪv ˈstreɪn ˌɪndʒəri/
sedentary lifestyle /ˌsɛdnˌtɛri ˈlaɪfstaɪl/
sleep disorder /ˈslip dɪsˌɔrdɚ/
sore elbow/wrist/thumb/hip /ˌsɔr ˈɛlboʊ/ˈrɪst/ˈθʌm/ˈhɪp/
suffer from /ˈsʌfɚ frəm/
surgeon /ˈsɚdʒən/
take a (deep) breath /ˌteɪk ə (ˌdip) ˈbrɛθ/
weight gain /ˈweɪt geɪn/
withdrawal symptoms /wɪðˈdrɔəl ˌsɪmptəmz/

Science and statistics

AD (Anno Domini) /ˌeɪ ˈdi (ænoʊ ˈdɑmɪnaɪ)/
advancement /ədˈvænsmənt/
Arabic numerals /ˌærəbɪk ˈnumərəlz/
arithmetic /əˈrɪθmətɪk/
artificial intelligence /ˌɑrt̬ɪˌfɪʃəl ɪnˈtɛlɪdʒəns/
astrology /əˈstrɑlədʒi/
BC (Before Christ) /ˌbi ˈsi (bɪfɔr ˈkraɪst)/
breakthrough /ˈbreɪkθru/
contribute to /kənˈtrɪbyut tə/
grow rapidly /ˌgroʊ ˈræpɪdli/
high point /ˈhaɪ ˌpɔɪnt/
increase/be on the rise /ɪnˈkris/ˌbi ɑn ðə ˈraɪz/
increasing/decreasing number /ɪnˌkrisɪŋ/dɪˌkrisɪŋ ˈnʌmbɚ/
irregular shape /ɪˌrɛgyulɚ ˈʃeɪp/
limited/unlimited /ˈlɪmɪt̬ɪd/ʌnˈlɪmɪt̬ɪd/
make a discovery /ˌmeɪk ə dɪsˈkʌvəri/
mathematical symbol /mæθˌmæt̬ɪkəl ˈsɪmbəl/
mathematician /ˌmæθməˈtɪʃən/
measure /ˈmɛʒɚ/
odd/even numbers /ˌɑd/ˌivən ˈnʌmbɚz/
robotics /roʊˈbɑt̬ɪks/
scholar /ˈskɑlɚ/
sharp fall/rise (in) /ˌʃɑrp ˈfɔl/ˈraɪz (ɪn)/
technological development /ˌtɛknəˌlɑdʒɪkəl dɪˈvɛləpmənt/
theory of relativity /ˌθiri əv ˌrɛləˈtɪvət̬i/
vast/enormous amount /ˌvæst/ɪˌnɔrməs əˈmaʊnt/
volume /ˈvɑlyum/

What the body does

beam /bim/
browse /braʊz/
cast an eye over /ˌkæst ən ˈaɪ ˌoʊvɚ/
frown /fraʊn/
slouch /slaʊtʃ/
stare at /ˈstɛr ət/
wander around /ˌwɑndɚ əˈraʊnd/

Phrasal verbs

bring in /ˌbrɪŋ ˈɪn/
come out /ˌkʌm ˈaʊt/
consist of /kənˈsɪst əv/
dash around /ˌdæʃ əˈraʊnd/
do without /ˌdu wɪðˈaʊt/
feed into /fid ˈɪntə/
figure out /ˌfɪgyɚ ˈaʊt/
go on and on about sth /ˌgoʊ ˌɑn ənd ˈɑn əˌbaʊt sʌmθɪŋ/
get on sb's nerves /gɛt ɑn sʌmbɑdiz ˈnɚvz/
have nothing on /ˌhæv ˌnʌθɪŋ ˈɑn/
kick back /ˌkɪk ˈbæk/
log on /ˌlɔg ˈɑn/
talk (sb) into (doing sth) /ˌtɔk (sʌmbɑdi) ˈɪntə (duɪŋ sʌmθɪŋ)/
tear sb away from sth /ˌtɛr sʌmbɑdi əˈweɪ frəm sʌmθɪŋ/
think over /ˌθɪŋk ˈoʊvɚ/

Other

accuracy /ˈækyərəsi/
actual /ˈæktʃuəl/
actually /ˈæktʃuəli/
address an issue/problem /əˌdrɛs ən ˈɪʃu/ˈprɑbləm/
alone /əˈloʊn/
and so on /ənd ˈsoʊ ɑn/
arise /əˈraɪz/
at sb's disposal /ət ˌsʌmbɑdiz dɪˈspoʊzəl/
at the expense of sth /ət ðə ɪkˈspɛns əv sʌmθɪŋ/
at your fingertips /ət yɚ ˈfɪŋgɚtɪps/
ban /bæn/
beneficial /ˌbɛnəˈfɪʃəl/
benefit (n) /ˈbɛnəfɪt/
benefit from /ˈbɛnəfɪt frəm/
biased /ˈbaɪəst/
complement /ˈkɑmpləmənt/
compliment /ˈkɑmpləmənt/
comprise /kəmˈpraɪz/
conscientious /ˌkɑnʃiˈɛnʃəs/
conscious /ˈkɑnʃəs/
constant /ˈkɑnstənt/
constantly/at all times /ˈkɑnstəntli/ət ɔl ˈtaɪmz/
continual /kənˈtɪnyuəl/
continuous assessment /kənˌtɪnyuəs əˈsɛsmənt/
current /ˈkʌrənt/
currently /ˈkʌrəntli/
dependent /dɪˈpɛndənt/
dependent on /dɪˈpɛndənt ɑn/
distracting /dɪˈstræktɪŋ/
distraction /dɪˈstrækʃən/
economic /ˌɛkəˈnɑmɪk/
economical /ˌɛkəˈnɑmɪkəl/
eventually /ɪˈvɛntʃəli/
(face-to-face) socializing /(ˌfeɪs tə ˈfeɪs) ˌsoʊʃəlaɪzɪŋ/
focus on sth /ˈfoʊkəs ɑn sʌmθɪŋ/
focused /ˈfoʊkəst/
for hours on end /fər ˌaʊɚz ɑn ˈɛnd/
genial /ˈdʒiniəl/
have a (bad) effect on /ˌhæv ə (bæd) ɪˈfɛkt ɑn/
help with sth /ˈhɛlp wɪð sʌmθɪŋ/
historic /hɪˈstɑrɪk/
historical /hɪˈstɑrɪkəl/
in an instant /ˌɪn ən ˈɪnstənt/
inactivity /ˌɪnækˈtɪvət̬i/
include /ɪnˈklud/
instant /ˈɪnstənt/
keep/lose track of time /ˌkip/ˌluz ˌtræk əv ˈtaɪm/
lately /ˈleɪtli/
lay /leɪ/
lead to /ˈlid tə/
lie /laɪ/
lifespan /ˈlaɪfspæn/
line sb's pockets /ˌlaɪn ˌsʌmbɑdiz ˈpɑkɪts/
lone /loʊn/
lonely /ˈloʊnli/
loose /lus/
occasion /əˈkeɪʒən/
on a daily/hourly basis /ɑn ə ˌdeɪli/ˌaʊɚli ˈbeɪsɪs/
on purpose /ˌɑn ˈpɚpəs/
on time /ˌɑn ˈtaɪm/
opportunity /ˌɑpɚˈtunət̬i/
play a crucial/vital role in /ˌpleɪ ə ˌkruʃəl/ˌvaɪtl ˈroʊl ɪn/
predict /prɪˈdɪkt/
raise /reɪz/
rediscover /ˌridɪˈskʌvɚ/
revolutionize /ˌrɛvəˈluʃənaɪz/
safe in the knowledge that /ˌseɪf ɪn ðə ˈnɑlɪdʒ ðæt/
security measures /sɪˈkyʊrət̬i ˌmɛʒɚz/
short/limited attention span /ˌʃɔrt/ˌlɪmɪt̬ɪd əˈtɛnʃən spæn/
stay on top of sth /ˌsteɪ ɑn ˈtɑp əv sʌmθɪŋ/
supplement /ˈsʌpləmənt/
the next frontier /ðə ˌnɛkst frʌnˈtɪr/
travel light /ˌtrævəl ˈlaɪt/
undeniable /ˌʌndɪˈnaɪəbəl/
undeniably /ˌʌndɪˈnaɪəbli/
use sth to your advantage /ˌyuz ˌsʌmθɪŋ tə yɚ ədˈvæntɪdʒ/
visible /ˈvɪzəbəl/

FOCUS REVIEW 7

VOCABULARY AND GRAMMAR

1 Complete the sentences with words from the unit. The first letter of each word is given.

1 Many doctors are concerned by the number of children who have a **s**edentary lifestyle.
2 I asked him to **c**ast an eye over my essay before I submitted it.
3 Whenever you **b**rowse the web, your Internet provider collects information about websites you visit.
4 It's easy to **l**ose track of time when you're online.
5 With all kinds of information at our **f**ingertips, doing homework should be a piece of cake.
6 We will have finished our experiments soon, and then the whole lab wil be at your **d**isposal.

2 Complete the sentences with the correct form of the words in capitals.

1 Well-balanced meals at school might help to solve the problem of obesity among pupils. **OBESE**
2 Has it been scientifically proven that bilingual children have better cognitive skills? **SCIENCE**
3 We need to find an economical yet effective way to protect the system against hackers. **ECONOMY**
4 Teens may suffer from various withdrawal symptoms when deprived of access to their cell phones. **WITHDRAW**

3 Complete the sentences with the correct passive form of the verbs in parentheses.

1 I'm sure you will be shown (show) the test results soon.
2 Your invention needs to be described (describe) in greater detail before you submit it to the Patent Office.
3 I don't mind not being paid (not pay) much for testing video games because I'd be playing them anyway.
4 The spare parts should have been delivered (deliver) a week ago. I'll call the company to see why they aren't here yet.
5 Mr. Jenkins was made to (make) undergo a stomach operation by his surgeon.

4 Rewrite the sentences in the passive.

1 One report argued that the archaeologists had damaged some artefacts during the excavations.
It ________ the archaeologists had damaged some artefacts during the excavations.
2 Some writers believe that the lost city of Atlantis existed until the ninth century BC.
The lost city of Atlantis ________ until the ninth century BC.
3 It's not clear why the lights went out. They say there was a short circuit.
It's not clear why the lights went out. There ________ a short circuit.
4 The police think that a dangerous hacker has been stealing sensitive data for over a year.
A dangerous hacker ________ sensitive data for over a year.

Exercise 4
1 was argued that
2 is believed to have existed
3 is said to have been
4 is thought to have been stealing

Exercise 6
1 is believed to have crashed
2 must have done the trick
3 doesn't enjoy being told
4 was offered to Imogen
5 are expected to do

LANGUAGE IN USE

5 Read the text and choose the correct answer, A, B, C, or D.

Planes and helicopters are a common sight in the sky nowadays. We can see them overhead almost everywhere. One kind that is thought [1]______ popularity recently is drones, i.e. unmanned aerial vehicles.

There has been an increase in the use of drones, mainly [2]______ the realization that, apart from military operations, there is a huge market for commercial use. Drones fitted with cameras can give farmers aerial views of their crops, survey flooded areas, or help ecologists monitor endangered animals. They [3]______ to deliver medical supplies in remote places and, in the near future, our shopping.

The possibilities of using drones commercially or recreationally are endless, and it's [4]______ that soon the Internet will be full of drone footage taken at all kinds of locations and times. Obviously, this causes some concerns – we will soon need to [5]______ the issue of lack of privacy when drones fly over somebody's property and take photos without their consent.

1 A to be gained　B to have been gaining (circled)　C to having been gained　D to gain
2 A because　B provided　C due to (circled)　D even though
3 A may be used (circled)　B may be using　C may have used　D may have been used
4 A questionable　B doubtful　C unmistakable　D undeniable (circled)
5 A answer　B address (circled)　C deal　D solve

6 Complete the sentences with the correct form of the words in parentheses. Add any necessary words.

1 Amelia Earhart ________ (believe/crash) somewhere near the Howland Island in the Pacific Ocean.
2 When I saw Julia last week, she looked much better, so I guess the treatment she received ________ (must/do/trick).
3 My younger brother ________ (not/enjoy/tell) to turn his computer off every evening at 8 p.m.
4 A place at the research station ________ (offer/Imogen) because she was the best candidate.
5 Even grade school students ________ (expect/do) many experiments nowadays.

REFERENCES
AUDIO SCRIPT ››› *pp. 212–213*

EXTRA ACTIVITIES
• Photocopiable resource 56B (multiple choice – 12 mins) MultiROM and ActiveTeach
• Photocopiable resource 63 (mini-test 2 – 15 mins) MultiROM and ActiveTeach
• Photocopiable resource 47 (Speaking – 12 mins) MultiROM and ActiveTeach
• Photocopiable resource 48 (Writing – 12 mins) MultiROM and ActiveTeach

WORKBOOK
Use of English 7.9, pp. 102–103; Self-assessment 7.10, p. 104

LISTENING

7 CD•3.28 MP3•113 **Listen to people in six different situations and choose the correct answer, A, B, or C.**

1 What will the new scheme do?
   - A It will stop Internet piracy.
   - (B) It will warn illegal downloaders.
   - C It will punish illegal downloaders more severely.

2 What does the woman believe?
   - (A) The man's moods are affected by playing the game.
   - B The man ought to play a different game.
   - C The man shouldn't play the game when their friends are there.

3 Which statement is true?
   - A There is a 'connect' option in the settings.
   - (B) The phone has got some pre-installed applications.
   - C The 'wi-fi' option isn't on.

4 What should students try to do for the contest?
   - A Invent something that shows their scientific abilities.
   - (B) Invent something that is original.
   - C Invent something related to a particular category.

5 What is the girl's attitude to the new Science teacher?
   - A The teacher is better than they had expected.
   - B The teacher is a very clever scientist.
   - (C) The teacher engaged the class well.

6 Why does the boy not want to stop texting?
   - (A) He likes to do two things at the same time.
   - B He thinks his thumb will improve with exercises.
   - C He enjoys texting with his finger.

SPEAKING

8 With a partner, complete the speaking task.

Here are some places where robots might make changes to our lives in the future. Talk to each other about the changes robots might make in these places.

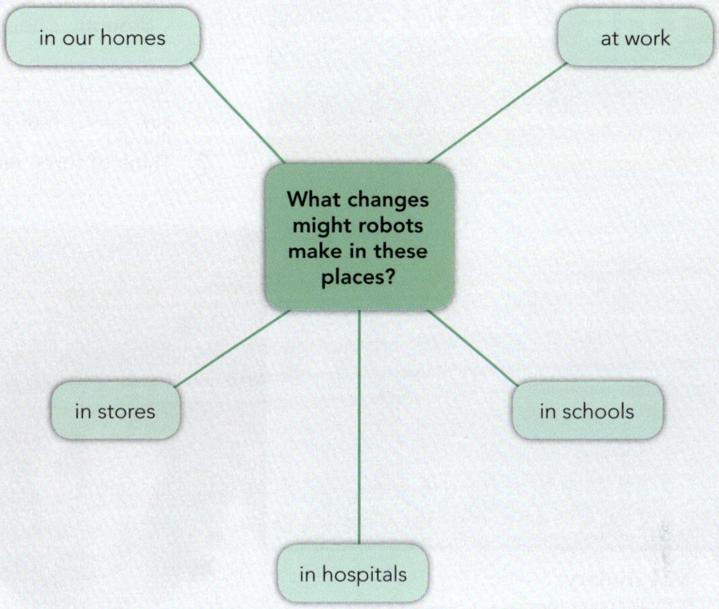

In which place would robots help us the most?

9 With a partner, discuss the questions.

1 Do you think robots will ever be able to think like human beings?
2 What other kinds of technological changes will change our lives in the future?
3 Do you think we rely on computers too much? Why?/Why not?
4 Some people think Science classes are boring. How can teachers make them more interesting?
5 Some people believe the computer is the most important invention ever. Do you agree?

WRITING

10 Complete the writing task.

In your English class you have been talking about social media. Now your English teacher has asked you to write an essay. Write an essay using all the notes and give reasons for your point of view.

More and more people are sharing information on social network sites. What are the advantages and disadvantages of this?

Notes

Write about:

- keeping in touch
- privacy
- ______ (your own idea)

Write your essay in 140–190 words.

137

NEXT CLASS

- Ask students to do Self-check 7.11, WB p. 105 as homework.
- Ask students to prepare for Unit test 7 (*Focus* Assessment Package).

8 AROUND THE GLOBE

We know that when we protect our oceans, we're protecting our future.

BILL CLINTON (B. 1946), A FORMER US PRESIDENT

UNIT LANGUAGE AND SKILLS

Vocabulary:
- *Show what you know* – land and water
- the natural world
- hazards and pollutants
- compound nouns
- collocations
- word families
- *Word in Focus – around*

Grammar:
- unreal past regrets
- emphasis – cleft sentences and inversion

Listening:
- an interview about intelligent animals
- multiple choice

Reading:
- four summaries of movies about journeys
- multiple matching

Speaking:
- a presentation about a natural wonder

Writing:
- a review of a travel destination

FOCUS EXTRA

- Grammar Focus pages 172–173
- WORD STORE booklet pages 16–17
- Workbook pages 106–119 or MyEnglishLab
- MP3s – www.english.com/focus

8.1 Vocabulary

The natural world • Pollution • Compound nouns

I can talk about pollution and the environment.

SHOW WHAT YOU KNOW

1 With a partner, put the words in the box under an appropriate heading. Explain your choices.

~~bay~~ cliff dam float foothills fossil fuel glacier drought flood melt pond stream

Suggestions	Land	Water
	bay cliff foothills fossil fuel drought dam glacier	bay float flood melt pond stream dam glacier

2 Think of three more words for each category.

CAN A TEENAGE ENVIRONMENTALIST CLEAN UP OUR OCEANS?

Boyan Slat is a young Dutchman with a mission to save the oceans from the consequences of our throwaway society.

THE FACTS

Oceans cover seventy-one percent of the earth's surface. From the fresh water of the polar ice caps to the seabed seven miles below the surface at the deepest point of the Pacific Ocean, the ocean is home to over half of all living **species**. Over the past 100 years, due to global warming, the sea level has risen four to ten inches.

THE PROBLEM

The oceans are being used as garbage dumps. Thirty-three percent of toxic contaminants in oceans come from air pollution such as acid rain and debris blown from landfills. Other pollutants are sewage, industrial waste, and pollution from oilfields and ships. The plastic debris concentrates in five rotating **currents** like giant **whirlpools** called gyres. The largest gyre, called the Pacific Garbage Patch, is twice the size of France and is located between Hawaii and California.

the five gyres

At least 1 million seabirds and 100,000 marine mammals die each year due to plastic pollution. When plastic breaks up into smaller particles, it becomes a hazard for marine wildlife. Seabirds, whales, turtles, and other sea creatures regularly consume waste products, which can be easily mistaken for jellyfish or other **prey** but cannot be degraded in the stomach. The animals die from starvation because they're not getting the **nutrients** they need. Plastics also slowly release toxins and other chemical substances that work their way up the marine food chain.

REFERENCES

CULTURE NOTES ››› *p. 198*

EXTRA ACTIVITIES

- Photocopiable resource 49 (the natural world – 12 mins) MultiROM and ActiveTeach
- Photocopiable resource 52 (Test yourself partner work activities) MultiROM and ActiveTeach
- MyEnglishLab – assignable *Show what you have learned* mini-test

WORKBOOK

pp. 106–107

NEXT CLASS

- Ask students to prepare for a 10–15 minute vocabulary quiz: *Focus* Assessment Package, Unit 8.1, Vocabulary.

3 **With a partner, guess the correct answers.**

1 Oceans cover *sixty-one percent* / *seventy-one percent* of the earth's surface. (circled: *seventy-one percent*)
2 The deepest point of the Pacific Ocean is *4 mi* / *7 mi* below the surface. (circled: *7 mi*)
3 Sea levels have risen *4–10 in* / *2–4 in* over the last 100 years. (circled: *4–10 in*)
4 Plastic waste *remains* / *disappears* in the oceans. (circled: *remains*)
5 Plastic pollution kills at least 1 million *seabirds* / *marine mammals* every year. (circled: *seabirds*)

4 **Read the article and check your answers. What solution to plastic pollution does Boyan Slat propose?**
An Ocean Clean-up device – a floating barrier 62 mi in length

5 **Answer the questions. Then check your answers in the article.**

1 Apart from plastic, what other things pollute the oceans?
2 What is a 'gyre', how many are there, and where is the biggest one?
3 Why is plastic pollution a problem for marine wildlife?
4 How is Slat's device different from other 'clean-up' devices?
5 What two claims does Slat make about the effectiveness of his device?

6 **SPEAKING With a partner, discuss the questions.**

1 How much plastic does your family throw away in a typical week?
2 Do you know what happens to your plastic waste? Where does it go?
3 What could you do to cut down on your use of plastic?

A SOLUTION

At the age of nineteen, Boyan Slat invented a device that he claims could clean up to 20 billion tons of plastic waste from the world's oceans. Unlike conventional methods of cleaning up plastic using ships and nets, Boyan Slat's 'Ocean Clean-up' concept is based on a simple idea: with its waves, **tides**, and currents, the ocean never stops moving, so instead of going after the plastics, as most traditional methods do, you could simply wait for the plastic to come to you. A floating barrier 62 miles in length would catch the debris, enabling a platform to extract it afterwards. The ocean current would pass underneath the barriers, taking all sea life with it. Boyan Slat believes that his innovation could clean up half of the Pacific Garbage Patch over a period of ten years, and would make up to 500 million dollars a year from recycling the waste collected.

Boyan Slat's floating barrier

Go to WORD STORE 8 page 17.

WORD STORE 8A

7 CD•3.29 MP3•114 **Complete WORD STORE 8A with the base form of the words in red in the article. Then listen, check, and repeat.**

8 **Complete the sentences with words from WORD STORE 8A.**

1 Most of all living *species* live in the ocean.
2 Coastal regions usually have a high *tide* twice a day.
3 Jellyfish are typical *prey* for seabirds.
4 Plastic doesn't contain any *nutrients* to help wildlife live.
5 The movement of garbage in the gyres is dependent on strong *currents*.
6 Gyres are like huge *whirlpools* of plastic garbage.

WORD STORE 8B

9 CD•3.30 MP3•115 **Complete WORD STORE 8B with words from the article. Use these definitions to help you. What is the mystery word? Listen, check, and repeat.**

1 rain that contains a high concentration of pollutants *acid rain*
2 a general word for human waste *sewage*
3 places where unwanted waste is thrown out *garbage dump*
4 material you get rid of when it has been through the factory process *industrial waste*
5 a general word for substances that pollute or poison *contaminants*
6 things that can be dangerous or cause damage *hazards*

10 **What do you think are the most worrying hazards and pollutants in the ocean? Why?**

WORD STORE 8C

11 CD•3.31 MP3•116 **Complete the compound nouns in WORD STORE 8C with the underlined words in the article. Then listen, check, and repeat. Add a translation.**

12 **With a partner, complete the list of environmental problems with compound nouns from WORD STORE 8C.**

1 melting *ice caps* ☐
2 rising *sea levels* ☐
3 chemicals and toxins in the *food chain* ☐
4 more non-biodegradable waste and so more *landfills* ☐
5 onshore and offshore *oilfields* ☐

13 **SPEAKING With a partner, discuss how dangerous (1 = not very dangerous, 5 = extremely dangerous) you think the problems in Exercise 12 are for our planet.**

WORD STORE 8D

14 CD•3.32 MP3•117 **Complete WORD STORE 8D with more compound nouns. Then listen, check, and repeat. Write example sentences.**

Exercise 5
1 Acid rain, debris, sewage, industrial waste, oil, ships.
2 A giant collection of plastic; there are five; the biggest one is in the Pacific.
3 It can't be digested; it contains no nutrients and kills wildlife.
4 It uses ocean currents to move the waste through the device.
5 It could clean up half of the Pacific Garbage Patch over ten years and make up to 500 million dollars a year.

8.2 Grammar

Unreal past and regrets – *wish, if only, it's time,* and *would rather*

I can express wishes and regrets using phrases like it's time *and* would rather.

1 **SPEAKING With a partner, discuss your idea of an ideal vacation and a nightmare vacation. Use the words in the box and your own ideas.**

adventure alone beach camping great nightlife historic monuments hot mountains museums no wi-fi peace and quiet sun water sports with the family with friends

Exercise 2
1 go back to the same campsite; something exciting/an adventure; something cultural; safari/trekking; sail across the ocean; white water rafting
2 white water rafting

2 CD•3.33 MP3•118 **Listen to the Moss family discussing what to do for their next vacation. Answer the questions.**

1 What suggestions do they make?
2 What do you think they will probably do?

3 CD•3.33 MP3•118 **Who said what? Write *B* for Ben, *E* for Ellie, *M* for Mom and *D* for Dad. Then listen again and check.**

1 '<u>If only</u> **we could go** somewhere exciting for a change.' E
2 'I think <u>it's time</u> **we did** something cultural.' D
3 'I <u>wish</u> **you all realized** how much I look forward to doing nothing for two weeks.' M
4 '<u>I'd rather</u> **we went** to the same campsite we went to last year.' B

4 **Read GRAMMAR FOCUS I and answer the questions about the sentences in Exercise 3.**

1 Which sentences refer to the present and which refer to the future? present = 3 / future = 1, 2, 4
2 Which tense is used after the underlined phrases? past simple

GRAMMAR FOCUS I

Unreal past

- You use ***wish/if only* + sb + a past tense** to say that somebody really wants a present or future situation to be different.
- You use ***it's (about) time* + sb + a past tense** to say that somebody should do something (now or in the future).
- You use ***would rather* + sb + a past tense** to say what somebody would prefer somebody else to do (now or in the future).

140

REFERENCES
AUDIO SCRIPT ››› *p. 213*

EXTRA ACTIVITIES
- Photocopiable resource 50 (unreal past – 15 mins) MultiROM and ActiveTeach
- MyEnglishLab – assignable *Show what you have learned* mini-test

WORKBOOK
p. 108

NEXT CLASS
- Ask students to prepare for a 10–15 minute grammar quiz: *Focus* Assessment Package, Unit 8.2, Grammar.

5 Complete the second sentence so that it has a similar meaning to the first. Then check the sentences that are true for you.

1 It isn't summer. I wish it was summer.
2 We always go to the mountains but I prefer the beach. I'd rather we … went to the beach.
3 I ought to learn how to ski. It's time I … learned how to ski.
4 I can't drive. I wish I … knew how to drive / could drive.
5 I really need to plan my next vacation. It's about time I … planned my next vacation.
6 It's raining. If only it … wasn't raining.

6 CD•3.34 MP3•119 **Listen to the Moss family talking after the vacation. Choose the correct verb form to explain the meaning of these extracts.**

1 'If only **I'd worn** more sunscreen.' =
Ellie *wore* / *didn't wear* enough sunscreen.
2 'I wish **I hadn't forgotten** my camera.' =
Ben *had* / *didn't have* his camera with him.
3 'I wish you'd fallen in, too.' =
Ben *fell out* / *didn't fall out* of the raft with Ellie.
4 'I just wish I'd known about the mosquitoes.' =
Mom *knew* / *didn't know* that there were mosquitoes.

7 Complete GRAMMAR FOCUS II with the phrases in blue in Exercise 6.

GRAMMAR FOCUS II

Past regrets

You use ***wish/if only* + sb + Past Perfect** to talk about past regrets.

If only [1] I'd worn *more sunscreen.*
I wish [2] I hadn't forgotten *my camera.*

Note: ***If only*** is stronger than ***wish***.

8 Complete the sentences with the correct form of the verbs in parentheses. Do you have any of these regrets?

1 I wish I 'd gone (go) on vacation with my friends last summer.
2 If only I 'd studied (study) more for my last English test.
3 I wish my parents had been (be) born in another country.
4 I wish I hadn't given up (not give up) piano lessons a few years ago.
5 I wish my brother/sister hadn't been (not be) so horrible to me when we were kids.
6 If only I 'd gone (go) to bed earlier last night.

9 Complete the sentences to make them true for you. Then compare with a partner.

1 I wish I could …
2 It's about time I …
3 I'd rather people didn't …
4 If only I hadn't …
5 I wish my parents …
6 If only my friends …

Grammar Focus page 172

8.3 Listening

Multiple choice

I can understand the main points of an interview.

1 **Which of the adjectives in the box would you use to describe the animals in the photos?**

> adorable aggressive agile friendly gentle independent intelligent
> loyal playful sociable stupid wise

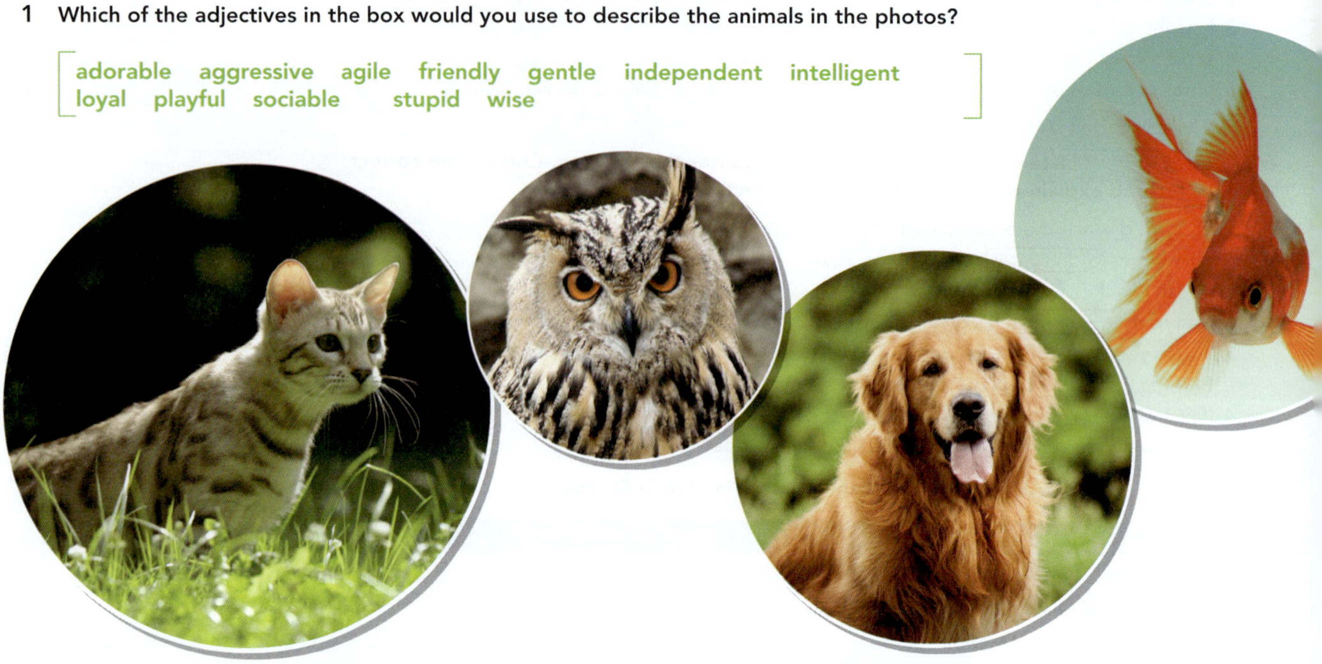

2 CD•3.35 MP3•120 **With a partner, decide if the statements are true (T) or false (F). Then listen to an interview with a wildlife expert and check your ideas.**

1 Chimpanzees share exactly half of the same genes as humans. F
2 Dolphins sometimes attack each other. T
3 Owls are intelligent birds. F
4 Cats have bigger brains than dogs. F

EXAM FOCUS Multiple choice

3 CD•3.35 MP3•120 **Listen again and choose the correct answer, A, B, or C.**

1 What is true about chimps?
  A They kill for pleasure.
  B They are affectionate towards humans.
  (C) They have strong family links.
2 Which characteristics do dolphins share with chimpanzees?
  A They are soon independent of their mothers.
  (B) Social relationships are important to them.
  C The males are aggressive towards the females.
3 Dr. Matthews believes that sheep
  A are as stupid as they look.
  B don't do very well in intelligence tests.
  (C) show signs that they can learn.
4 Why are dogs smarter than cats?
  A Cats have been domesticated for longer.
  (B) Dogs spend more time with humans.
  C Dogs learn through helping humans.
5 Which of the following statements best sums up the interview?
  A Appearances can be deceptive.
  B Animals form stable communities.
  (C) What we think about animals isn't always true.

142

REFERENCES
AUDIO SCRIPT ››› *pp. 213–214*
WORKBOOK
p. 109

4 **Complete the sentences with the correct form of the words in capitals.**

1 The radio series *Animal World* examines animals' behavior in the wild. **BEHAVE**
2 Chimpanzees experience adolescence in a similar way to humans. **ADOLESCENT**
3 Dolphins are undoubtedly intelligent. **DOUBT**
4 Dolphins can be competitive with one another. **COMPETE**
5 The intelligence of sheep is undervalued. **VALUE**
6 The idea that owls are intelligent is a common misconception **CONCEIVE**
7 Cats' brains have not evolved since they were first domesticated by the Egyptians. **DOMESTIC**
8 Cats don't need the approval of humans to do things. **APPROVE**

5 **SPEAKING With a partner, add at least four more animals to each column. Then discuss the questions.**

Domestic animals	Farm animals	Wild animals
dogs, cats,	cows, sheep,	lions, dolphins

Which animal is:
a the wildest/tamest?
b the most/least lovable?
c the most/least useful to society?

PRONUNCIATION FOCUS

6 CD•3.36 MP3•121 **Listen and repeat.**

1 sheep /ʃip/ ship /ʃɪp/
2 cats /kæts/ cuts /kʌts/
3 prove /pruv/ proof /pruf/
4 bag /bæg/ back /bæk/

7 CD•3.37 MP3•122 **Listen and write down the five words from Exercise 6 you hear.**

8 **Choose five words from Exercise 6. Then, with a partner, take turns to dictate them to your partner. Check: has he/she written down the correct word?**

Exercise 7
1 cuts
2 back
3 sheep
4 prove

WORD STORE 8E

9 CD•3.38 MP3•123 **Complete WORD STORE 8E. Add the adjectives in the box to complete the collocations. Then listen, check, and repeat.**

143

8.4 Reading

Multiple matching

I can find specific details in movie summaries.

1 SPEAKING With a partner, discuss the questions.

1 Would you rather visit Alaska, Australia, or the Pacific coast?
2 Who would you choose as your traveling companion? Or would you prefer to travel alone?
3 What are the pros and cons of traveling alone?

EXAM FOCUS Multiple matching

2 Read the texts about four movies based on true stories of journeys. For questions 1–10, choose from the texts (A–D). You can choose each text more than once.

In this movie, the main character(s):

1 wanted to cross the western part of this country and reach the West coast. C
2 became very sick because of his/her food. B
3 took too many things on a journey. D
4 rejected his/her family after a betrayal. B
5 wanted to be reunited with family members. A
6 had to do a lot of climbing on the journey. D
7 planned to test personal limits of endurance with no help. B
8 wanted to rediscover something lost. D
9 was/were affected by a political decision. A
10 appreciated the wide open spaces on the journey. C

3 Complete the questions with the prepositions in the box. Then answer the questions.

about	by	in	of	on	over	through	to	with

Text A

1 Who did the 1869 Protection Act give the Australian Government power _over_?
2 What kind of journey did Molly, Daisy, and Gracie set off _on_?
3 Who were Molly and Daisy pursued _by_?

Text B

4 What kind of family did Chris McCandless grow up _in_?
5 What secret did McCandless find out _about_?
6 What did McCandless take pride _in_?

Text C

7 What animals did Robyn Davidson start out _with_?
8 What kind of landscape did Davidson's route take her _through_
9 What did Davidson lose all sense _of_?

Text D

10 What was Cheryl devastated _by_?
11 What did she turn _to_?
12 What did she struggle _through_

Exercise 3
1 the lives of aboriginal people
2 an arduous one – nine-week journey
3 the authorities
4 an affluent one
5 his father's second family
6 living simply with few belongings
7 four camels and a dog
8 inhospitable/remote
9 self, space, and time
10 the loss of her mother
11 drugs
12 wilderness, and crossing nine mountain ranges

4 Complete the collocations with the adjectives in blue in the texts.

1 distant/inaccessible/_remote_ REGIONS
2 empty/bleak/_inhospitable_ PLACES
3 a tough/punishing/_arduous_ JOURNEY
4 baking/burning/_scorching_ TEMPERATURES
5 unexpected/deep _record_ SNOWFALL
6 a deserted/barren/_desolate_ WILDERNESS

5 With a partner, match collocations from Exercise 4 with the places in the box.

the Gobi Desert	Death Valley	the Sahara Desert
Mount Everest	the South Pole	Siberia
the Nile		

6 SPEAKING With a partner, discuss the questions.

1 Which of the four movies in this lesson would you most/least like to see? Why?
2 What other movies or books about extraordinary journeys do you know?
3 Which movies or books have inspired you to visit a place? Where and why?

WORD STORE 8F

7 CD•3.40 MP3•125 **Complete WORD STORE 8F with adjectives or nouns from the lesson. Then listen, check, and repeat.**

C TRACKS

In early 1977, Robyn Davidson started out with only four camels and her dog to walk 1,700 miles from the central Australian desert to the Indian Ocean off the western coast. Nine months later, ragged, blistered and burned black by the sun, she reached her destination. An Aboriginal man, Mr. Eddie, accompanied her for three weeks, while photographer Rich Smolan joined her three times during the journey. Davidson, now sixty-five, is back in the limelight. The book of her journey, *Tracks*, has been reissued and a movie adaptation came out in 2013.

Her route to the sea took her through **remote** regions and some of Australia's most **inhospitable** places. During nine long, hard months she battled **scorching** temperatures, rotten food, thirst, navigation errors, and injured camels. But far more challengi Davidson found herself being swallowed by the v space, and time.

Despite that, she says, 'I love the desert and its i Aborigines and learning from them. I like the free growth and learning processes that develop from

REFERENCES
CULTURE NOTES ››› *pp. 198–199*

EXTRA ACTIVITIES
• Photocopiable resource 51 (journeys – 10 mins) MultiROM and ActiveTeach

WORKBOOK
pp. 110–111

NEXT CLASS
• Ask students to write a short summary of a movie they have seen.

D•3.39 MP3•124

**his week, Movie Blog is bringing you four true stories about extraordinary people.
heir stories don't always end happily, but their journeys will move and inspire you.**

A THE RABBIT-PROOF FENCE

In Australia in 1931, three Aboriginal girls ran away from their white captors and walked 1,500 miles to get back home. Their story is told in a movie entitled *Rabbit-Proof Fence*. The Aboriginal Protection Act of 1869 gave the government powers over the lives of Aboriginal people, including the power to forcibly remove mixed race children – those born to a white parent and a black parent – from their families.

This story follows three little girls: Molly, fourteen, her sister, eight-year-old Daisy, and their ten-year-old cousin Gracie, as they are taken from their family to a camp. Upset at being so far from their mothers and their home, the young girls escape and set off on an **arduous** journey to find their way home, pursued by the authorities. Molly remembered her father once telling her about the Rabbit-Proof Fence that crosses western Australia from north to south. Her goal was simple: to find the fence and follow it home. After nine weeks of walking and hiding, they finally arrive home and are reunited with their family.

B INTO THE WILD

The lonely death of Chris McCandless inspired a book *Into the Wild*, and a movie by the same name. Chris McCandless was a young American graduate who grew up in an affluent family in Washington, DC. When he found out about his father's secret second family, he was so upset that he distanced himself from his family. He abandoned his real name and never contacted his parents or his sister again. After two years of hitchhiking around the Northwest, he decided to push himself to the extreme and hiked alone into the **desolate** wilderness of Alaska. He took pride in living simply and surviving with few belongings.

He spent the next sixteen weeks completely alone, hunting, reading, and 'camping' in a deserted bus. In late July it is thought that he ate some poisonous seeds that made him extremely sick and too weak to hunt for food. Realizing that he was going to die, Chris wrote a goodbye message, and a few weeks later some hunters found his body in the bus. This was his message: 'I have had a happy life and thank the Lord. Goodbye and may God bless all!'

chological aspects. At one point
esert and losing all sense of self,

ise of space. I enjoy being with
eing on my own, and I like the
'

D WILD

Cheryl Strayed's surname is not her original name. It's a name she invented for herself. After the death of her mother in 1991, Cheryl's grief caused her to lose her way in life; she felt she had 'strayed'. Devastated by the loss of her mother to cancer, Cheryl turned to drugs. Then her husband divorced her and, finally, she realized that she had lost her own sense of identity.

Cheryl decided to challenge herself by hiking along the Pacific Crest Trail in an attempt to find the person she used to be. This was not an easy task. The PCT runs for 1,100 miles through California from Mexico to Canada and is certainly not a journey for novices. But Cheryl filled a backpack to bursting and set off. Three months later, after struggling through wilderness and crossing nine mountain ranges, Cheryl made it to the end. The journey had been physically and mentally hard for the inexperienced hiker. She had endured 100-degree temperatures and **record** snowfalls, and she encountered bears and rattlesnakes. The giant backpack was so heavy that she called it 'Monster'! But the journey had done what she wanted. It had healed her.

Cheryl wrote a book about her journey and this, in turn, inspired an amazing movie called *Wild*, starring Reese Witherspoon as Cheryl. It shows the healing power of a journey in the wild.

8.5 Grammar

Emphasis – cleft sentences and inversion

I can use a range of sentence structures to express emphasis.

1 CD•3.41 MP3•126 **Read and listen to a conversation between two friends. Why does Will get angry?** *Because Emma doesn't think humans are responsible for climate change.*

Will: I've been watching a show about extreme weather events – interesting but very scary! **What they did was show** the effects of some recent floods where people had lost absolutely everything. **Rarely have I seen** such devastating scenes. **What I find shocking is that** some people still believe that humans have nothing to do with climate change.

Emma: I don't think you can blame humans.

Will: What? **It's those kind of comments that** really annoy me. How can you say that?

Emma: **All I'm saying is that** there's no link between carbon emissions and climate change. **What's happened is that** scientists have invented global warming so they can get more funding.

Will: Are you serious? **Not only are you** making ridiculous accusations, **but** you don't even know the basic facts. Of course it's carbon emissions that are to blame for global warming.

EXTRA ACTIVITIES
- Photocopiable resource 52 (Test yourself partner work activities) MultiROM and ActiveTeach
- MyEnglishLab – assignable *Show what you have learned* mini-test

WORKBOOK
p. 112

NEXT CLASS
- Ask students to prepare for a 10–15 minute grammar quiz: *Focus* Assessment Package, Unit 8.5, Grammar.

2 Read and complete the GRAMMAR FOCUS with the words in blue in the conversation.

GRAMMAR FOCUS

Emphasis

You can emphasize a piece of information in a sentence in a number of different ways:

- Cleft sentences: 'divide' a sentence by adding a clause to emphasize key information
  What's [1]*happened is* (*that*) *scientists have invented …* (= Scientists have invented …)
  What they [2] did *was* (*to*) *show the effects of …* (= They showed the effects of …)
  [3] What *I find shocking is* (*that*) … (= I find it shocking (that) …)
  [4] It's *those kind of comments that …* (= Those kind of comments …)
  [5] All *I'm saying is* (*that*) … (= I'm just saying (that) …)
- Inversion: negative expression (*never, rarely, not only*, etc.) + auxiliary verb + subject (formal)
  [6] Rarely *have I seen …* (= I have rarely seen …)
  [7] Not only *are you making ridiculous accusations, but you don't even know the basic facts.*
  (= You are making … and you don't even know …)

3 Rewrite the sentences using structures from the GRAMMAR FOCUS and the word in capitals.

1 Will and Emma had an argument. **HAPPENED**
What happened was (that) Will and Emma had an argument.
2 Will (not Emma) started talking about climate change. **IT**
3 Will told Emma how strongly he felt. **DID**
4 Emma only suggested that you couldn't blame humans. **ALL**
5 Will couldn't believe Emma's views on scientists. **WHAT**
6 Will hadn't ever heard such ridiculous accusations. **NEVER**

Exercise 3
2 It was Will that started talking about climate change.
3 What Will did was (to) tell Emma how strongly he felt.
4 All Emma suggested was that you couldn't blame humans.
5 What Will couldn't believe was/were Emma's views on scientists.
6 Never had Will heard such ridiculous accusations.

4 Complete the sentences with the words in the box. There are two extra words.

all	are	do	does	is	it's	has	what

1 It's the gases from industrialization that have caused the greenhouse effect.
2 What scientists do is analyze air that's 800,000 years old trapped under the ice in Antarctica.
3 Never has there been more carbon dioxide in the atmosphere than there is now.
4 What happened was that average temperatures rose by 2 degrees Fahrenheit last century.
5 Not only are we observing a rise in sea levels, but also many extreme weather events.
6 If we don't act now, all we're doing is creating problems for future generations.

5 Put the words in the correct order to make sentences. Begin with the underlined words.

1 worry about most / I / is / pollution / what
2 I / money / my birthday / all / for / want / is
3 it gets dark so early / what / winter / I / about / that / hate / is
4 most / the food / what / I / my country / about / love / is
5 who / in our house / the cooking / my father / does / it's
6 to do / what / buy a laptop / is / want / I
7 my clothes / to any of my friends / under no circumstances / lend / would / I

Exercise 5
1 What I worry about most is pollution.
2 All I want for my birthday is money.
3 What I hate about winter is that it gets dark so early.
4 What I love most about my country is the food.
5 It's my father who does the cooking in our house.
6 What I want to do is buy a laptop.
7 Under no circumstances would I lend my clothes to any of my friends.

6 With a partner, check the sentences in Exercise 5 that are true for you. Write more true sentences beginning with the underlined words.

What I worry about most is …

Grammar Focus page 172

8.6 Speaking

Giving a presentation

I can give a presentation on a natural wonder.

1 **SPEAKING With a partner, follow the instructions.**

- Make a list of well-known natural wonders.
- Compare your list with another pair.
- In groups of four, discuss which of the places you have visited or would like to visit.

2 **SPEAKING Look at the photo and describe it using the words in the box.**

cave/cavern crystal minerals geologists underground

Giant Crystal Cave

Exercise 3
1 when mineral miners from the town of Naica in Northern Mexico discovered the cave
2 the age of the enormous crystals of Cueva de los Cristales
3 the weight of the largest crystal in the cave
4 the temperature in the cave
5 it is impossible to remain underground in the cave for more than 10 minutes at a time

3 CD•3.42 MP3•127 **You are going to listen to a presentation about the Giant Crystal Cave. How will the information below relate to the topic? Listen and check.**

1 the year 2000
2 half a million years
3 55 tons
4 136 degrees Fahrenheit
5 10 minutes

REFERENCES
CULTURE NOTES ››› p. 199
AUDIO SCRIPT ››› p. 214

WORKBOOK
p. 113

4 CD•3.42 MP3•127 **Complete the SPEAKING FOCUS with the words in the box. Then listen again and check.**

[aware during free familiar realize wondered]

SPEAKING FOCUS

Introducing the topic

Have you ever thought about/considered/[1] _wondered_ how/why/what … ?

[2] _During_ my/this presentation, I plan to tell you about …

You may be wondering why I've chosen to talk about … today. Well, let me explain …

Introducing familiar information

We are (probably) all [3] _familiar_ with …

You may be [4] _aware_ that …

You may already know that …

Maybe you have heard of/about …

Introducing surprising information

Most people aren't aware/don't [5] _realize_ …

… , but did you know that … ?

You might not know that …

Finishing your presentation

OK, that's all from me.

Thank you for listening.

I hope you found the presentation interesting.

If anyone has any questions, please feel [6] _free_ to ask now.

5 **Complete the extracts with words and phrases from the SPEAKING FOCUS.**

1 You may be _wondering_ why I've chosen to talk about Ha Long Bay today. Well, let me explain.
2 You may already _know_ that Komodo, an island in Indonesia, is home to the famous Komodo Dragon, the biggest lizard alive on the planet today.
3 Maybe you have _heard_ of Table Mountain in South Africa. It rises high above Cape Town.
4 We are probably all familiar with the Amazon River, in South America, but most people aren't _aware_ that it was chosen as one of the new Seven Wonders of the World in 2011.
5 Thanks for listening. If _anyone_ has any questions, please feel free to ask now.

6 **Which of these are good tips on giving presentations? Check one sentence in each pair. Then compare with a partner.**

1 a Speak with a clear voice at a natural speed. ✓
  b Speak quickly and quietly.
2 a Don't look at the audience.
  b Make eye contact with the audience. ✓
3 a Ask the audience questions to keep them involved. ✓
  b Don't ask the audience questions.
4 a Write a script and read out every word when you present.
  b Have some notes with you but don't read them out. ✓
5 a If you forget something, keep going. No one will notice. ✓
  b If you forget something, say sorry and end the presentation.
6 a When you finish, sit down as quickly as possible.
  b When you finish, thank the audience and invite questions. ✓

7 SPEAKING **Prepare a presentation on a natural wonder. Follow these steps.**

1 Select a natural wonder that interests you.
2 Do some research and plan your presentation.
3 Find some interesting photos to illustrate the presentation if possible.
4 Select useful language from the SPEAKING FOCUS.
5 Study and practice your presentation.
6 Give your presentation to the class. Follow the advice in Exercise 6.

8.7 Writing

A review of a travel destination

I can write a review of a travel destination and make recommendations.

1 **SPEAKING With a partner, discuss the questions. Use the collocations in the box to help you.**

1 Why are some areas made into national parks?
2 Describe a well-known national park you know.

cultural heritage	**diverse landscapes**	**environmental impact**	**natural beauty**
sustainable tourism	**wildlife protection**		

2 **Read Alice's comments in *Young Traveler* magazine. Do you agree with her point of view?**

3 **Read Nick's review. Would you like to visit the place he describes? Why?/Why not?**

4 **With a partner, answer the questions.**

In which paragraph does Nick:

a describe the location of the place? [2]
b say which place he is writing about and why? [1]
c make a final recommendation? [4]
d give details of the protective measures taken in the place chosen? [3]

5 **Complete the WRITING FOCUS with the words in the box.**

because	cause and result	~~concession~~
contrast	reason	

6 **Read Nick's review again and find an example for each category in the WRITING FOCUS.** See ( ) in text.

WRITING FOCUS

Using introductory words and phrases

You can use introductory words and phrases to:

- express [1] *concession* .
  While/Though there are still problems, the situation has improved.
  Despite/In spite of the laws, some new hotels have still been built.
- express [2] *reason* formally using participle clauses.
  Having seen a turtle swim, I know how graceful they are in the water.
  Being a responsible tourist, I am happy to follow the rules.
- express [3] *cause and result* .
  The river was so polluted that something had to be done.
  Litter became such a problem that the area was closed to visitors.
- express [4] *contrast* .
  While/Whereas many parts of the forest are protected, others are not.
  Some tourists behave responsibly while/whereas others do not.
- express reason with alternatives to [5] *because* (*of*).
  Governments are often reluctant to limit tourism, as/since it generates huge income.
  Certain paths have been closed due to erosion caused by visitors.

Making recommendations

This destination would be ideal for …
If you're looking for … , then this is the place for you.
I can thoroughly recommend …
… is definitely worth visiting.
All in all, I would highly recommend …

Have your say …

Last month we asked you: Is enough being done to protect the natural environment in popular tourist destinations?

Alice, 17, wrote:

I'm a nature lover and it seems to me that governments and tour operators care mainly about the money that tourism generates and not about the negative impacts that visitors have on natural environments. Development of facilities for tourists often takes priority over protection of areas of natural beauty and local wildlife, and not enough is done to establish national parks or develop tourism responsibly.

YOUNG TRAVELER

Olly201: I get what you're saying, Alice, but there are places out there that offer eco-friendly vacations! Check out the links in my last post.

YOUNG TRAVELER

Have your say …

Nick, 17, wrote:

Zakynthos

1 If you're looking for a vacation destination where a great deal is being done to promote wildlife protection and preserve natural beauty, then the Greek island of Zakynthos is the place for you.

2 (Having just returned from a vacation to beautiful Zakynthos, I have personally seen sustainable tourism in action.) Zakynthos is a picturesque island **off** the west coast of mainland Greece. It is **surrounded** by turquoise waters, but only a small part of its **coastline** is sandy beach. In the southern part of the island **lies** the Bay of Laganas, a major nesting area for the loggerhead sea turtle. During my trip to the island, my friends and I learnt about the ways in which the turtles are being protected.

150

REFERENCES
CULTURE NOTES ››› *pp. 199–200*

EXTRA ACTIVITIES
• MyEnglishLab – assignable *Show what you have learned* writing task and *Show that you have checked* checklist

WORKBOOK
p. 114

7 **Complete the LANGUAGE FOCUS with the words in purple in Nick's review.**

LANGUAGE FOCUS

Describing the location of a place

Use the following structures to describe the location of a place:

- A reef/An island [1] ___off___ the (west) coast (of) …
  … is a town/resort/region on the (east) coast (of) …/inland from …/to the south of …/high in the mountains/deep in the forest, etc.
- It is [2] ___surrounded___ by turquoise waters/majestic mountains/lush forests/vast deserts.
- In the southern part of the island/country [3] ___lies___ the Bay of Laganas/the resort of …
- Part of its [4] ___coastline___ is sandy beach/the region is a national park/the beach is closed to tourists.

8 **SPEAKING With a partner, choose a famous tourist destination in your country and describe its location. Use the LANGUAGE FOCUS to help you. Can your partner guess the place you are describing?**

9 **Read the notice from the Young Traveler website. Then follow the instructions below.**

MORE ECO-VACATION REVIEWS WANTED!

We hope you enjoy the reviews on this page and find them useful. We would like to include more reviews from readers who have been to eco-friendly places on vacation. This might be a particular hotel, restaurant or a whole area. Send us a review describing the place and how it is attempting to be environmentally friendly.

1 Decide which place you are going to write about and do some research. Choose from these places or use your own idea:
- Masai Mara National Reserve, Kenya
- Fraser Island, Great Sandy National Park, Australia
- Punta Tombo Penguin Rookery, Argentina
- Yellowstone National Park, the US

(***Hint:*** *search for 'visitor rules' or 'visitors' guide'.*)

2 Follow the paragraph plan in Nick's review (see Exercise 4).

10 **Write your review in 140–190 words. Use the WRITING FOCUS and the LANGUAGE FOCUS to help you.**

3 YOUNG TRAVELER

Under pressure from environmental groups, the Greek government made parts of the coastline into a marine national park in 1999. As a result, building is not allowed, and vehicles and artificial lights 3
are banned near the beach. Similarly, speedboats are so disruptive that they are not permitted, and there are no night flights to Zakynthos because the noise scares the turtles. While tourists can 1, 4
visit some of the nesting beaches, this can only be done at certain
4 times and there are strict rules about contact.

So, for people who care about the environment and want to make an environmentally-friendly vacation choice, I can thoroughly recommend a visit to Zakynthos. If you're looking for somewhere beautiful and peaceful too, then this is the place for you.

151

8.8 Language in focus

Word families – prefixes and suffixes

I can recognize and form a wide range of words using prefixes and suffixes.

1 Read the information. Then check the example words you know. Try to guess the meaning of the other words.

Prefixes, as well as suffixes, can be added to the same root word to create word families. For example, from the root word *use* you can form ***re**use*, ***mis**use*, ***dis**used*, and ***re**usable*. The table lists some common prefixes and their meanings.

PREFIX	MEANING	EXAMPLES
un- in- dis- il- im- ir-	not (mainly adjectives)	uneven, illogical
un- dis-	opposite (mainly verbs)	undo, disallow
re-	do again	rebuild, redistribute
mis-	badly, wrongly	misbehave, mismanage
multi-	many, several	multicolored, multinational
over- under-	too much/not enough	overwork, underpay
pro-/anti-	in favor/against	pro-democracy, anti-communist
pre- post-	before/after	pre-owned, postwar

2 Translate the example words in Exercise 1. Are there similar prefixes in your language?

Exercise 3
il- = adjectives beginning with *l-*
im- = adjectives beginning with *m-* or *p-*
ir- = adjectives beginning with *r-*

3 Write the negative form of the words in the box next to the correct prefix. What spelling rules can you work out for *il-*, *im-* and *ir-*?

ability believe capable fair formal legible literate mature patient pleasant regular relevant

1 dis- *ability*, *believe*
2 il- *legible*, *literate*
3 im- *mature*, *patient*
4 in- *capable*, *formal*
5 ir- *regular*, *relevant*
6 un- *fair*, *pleasant*

4 Give these statements the opposite meaning by changing the underlined word. Which statements do you agree with?

1 It's <u>probable</u> that people will live on Mars one day. *improbable*
2 The money I get from my parents every week is <u>adequate</u>. *inadequate*
3 It ought to be <u>legal</u> to ride a bicycle without a helmet. *illegal*
4 Most people would describe me as <u>responsible</u>. *irresponsible*
5 The roads in my country are really <u>safe</u>. *unsafe*
6 Doctors are <u>underpaid</u> for the job they do. *overpaid*
7 People who are <u>pro-nuclear</u> don't understand the dangers. *anti-nuclear*
8 <u>Pre-match</u> interviews with footballers are usually boring. *Post-match*

Exercise 5
1 unemployment
2 renewable
3 misinformation
4 understaffed
5 pre-election
6 multicultural

5 Complete the sentences with the correct form of the word in capitals. Use a prefix and a suffix each time. Do you share any of these worries?

I worry about:
1 jobs. Youth ________ is a big problem in my country. **EMPLOY**
2 the environment. People should use more ________ energy. **NEW**
3 the media. There is too much ________ : you can't trust anybody. **INFORM**
4 health. There aren't enough doctors. Hospitals are ________ . **STAFF**
5 politics. Politicians should be made to keep their ________ promises. **ELECT**
6 our society. I think it should be more ________ . **CULTURE**

152

08 WORD LIST

Geographical features

bay /beɪ/
cave/cavern /keɪv/ˈkævɚn/
cliff /klɪf/
coast /koʊst/
coastal region /ˈkoʊstl ˌridʒən/
coastline /ˈkoʊstlaɪn/
current /ˈkʌrənt/
dam /dæm/
diverse landscape /dəˌvɚs ˈlændskeɪp/
foothills /ˈfʊtˌhɪlz/
glacier /ˈgleɪʃɚ/
gyre/whirlpool /ˈdʒaɪɚ/ˈwɚlpul/
ice cap /ˈaɪs kæp/
(lush) forest /(ˌlʌʃ) ˈfɑrəst/
(majestic) mountains /(məˌdʒɛstɪk) ˈmaʊnt̚nz/
natural wonder /ˌnætʃərəl ˈwʌndɚ/
pond /pɑnd/
(sandy) beach /(ˌsændi) ˈbitʃ/
seabed /ˈsibɛd/
seashore /ˈsiʃɔr/
stream /strim/
tide /taɪd/
(vast) desert /(ˌvæst) ˈdɛzɚt/
wave /weɪv/

Describing location

above/below the surface /əˌbʌv/bɪˌloʊ ðə ˈsɚfəs/
cover /ˈkʌvɚ/
deep in the forest /ˌdip ɪn ðə ˈfɑrəst/
high in the mountains /ˌhaɪ ɪn ðə ˈmaʊnt̚nz/
in the northern/southern/eastern/western part of an island/country /ɪn ðə ˌnɔrðɚn/ˌsʌðɚn/ˌistɚn/ˌwɛstɚn pɑrt əv ən ˈaɪlənd/ˈkʌntri/
inland from /ˈɪnlænd frəm/
lie /laɪ/
mainland /ˈmeɪnlænd/
off the coast /ɔf ðə ˈkoʊst/
on the (east/west) coast (of Australia) /ɑn ðə (ˌist/ˌwɛst) ˌkoʊst (əv ɔˈstreɪliə)/
surrounded by sth /səˈraʊndɪd baɪ/
to the north/south/east/west of /tə ðə ˈnɔrθ/ˈsaʊθ/ˈist/ˈwɛst əv/
underground /ˈʌndɚgraʊnd/

Animals

camel /ˈkæməl/
chimpanzee /ˌtʃɪmpænˈzi/
domestic/farm/wild animal /dəˌmɛstɪk/ˌfɑrm/ˌwaɪld ˈænɪməl/
jellyfish /ˈdʒɛlifɪʃ/
lizard /ˈlɪzɚd/
(marine) mammal /(məˌrin) ˈmæməl/
owl /aʊl/
rabbit /ˈræbɪt/
(sea) creature /(ˈsi) ˌkritʃɚ/
seabird /ˈsibɚd/
sea lion /ˈsi ˌlaɪən/
sheep /ʃip/
turtle /ˈtɚt̲l/
whale /weɪl/

Describing animals

adorable/loveable /əˈdɔrəbəl/ˈlʌvəbəl/
aggressive towards /əˈgrɛsɪv təˌwɔrdz/
agile /ˈædʒaɪl/
be competitive against /bi kəmˈpɛt̲ət̲ɪv əˌgɛnst/
behavior /bɪˈheɪvyɚ/
childhood/adolescence /ˈtʃaɪldhʊd/ˌædəˈlɛsəns/
develop powerful bonds /dɪˌvɛləp ˌpaʊɚfəl ˈbɑndz/
do well in intelligence tests /du ˌwɛl ɪn ɪnˈtɛlədʒəns tɛsts/
domesticate /dəˈmɛstɪkeɪt/
(extremely) violent /(ɪkˌstrimli) ˈvaɪələnt/
evolve /ɪˈvɑlv/
follow the crowd /ˌfɑloʊ ðə ˈkraʊd/
food chain /ˈfud tʃeɪn/
form (stable) communities /ˌfɔrm (ˌsteɪbəl) kəˈmyunət̲iz/
gentle /ˈdʒɛntəl/
graceful /ˈgreɪsfəl/
in the wild /ˌɪn ðə ˈwaɪld/
independent (of sb/sth) /ˌɪndəˈpɛndənt (əv sʌmbɑdi/sʌmθɪŋ)/

EXTRA ACTIVITIES
• Photocopiable resource 53 (word formation – 15 mins) MultiROM and ActiveTeach

WORKBOOK
p. 115

NEXT CLASS
• Ask students to study the Word list on pp. 152–153.
• Ask students to review for Focus review 8.

(living) species /(ˌlɪvɪŋ) ˈspiʃiz/
lay eggs /ˌleɪ ˈɛgz/
male/female /meɪl/ˈfimeɪl/
natural habitat /ˌnætʃərəl ˈhæbəˌtæt/
nesting area /ˈnɛstɪŋ ˌɛriə/
playful /ˈpleɪfəl/
prey /preɪ/
rival gang /ˌraɪvəl ˈgæŋ/
rookery /ˈrʊkəri/
sea life /ˈsi laɪf/
social/sociable /ˈsoʊʃəl/ˈsoʊʃəbəl/
social relationships /ˌsoʊʃəl riˈleɪʃənʃɪps/
stupid /ˈstupɪd/
tame /teɪm/
undervalued /ˌʌndɚˈvælyud/
useful to society /yusfəl tə səˈsaɪəṭi/
wise /waɪz/

Environmental problems and protection

acid rain /ˌæsɪd ˈreɪn/
(air) pollution /(ˈɛr) pəˌluʃən/
atmosphere /ˈætməsfɪr/
average temperature /ˌævrɪdʒ ˈtɛmprətʃɚ/
behave responsibly /bɪˌheɪv rɪˈspɑnsəbli/
carbon dioxide /ˌkɑrbən daɪˈɑksaɪd/
carbon emissions /ˈkɑrbən ɪˌmɪʃənz/
climate change /ˈklaɪmət tʃeɪndʒ/
consume /kənˈsum/
contaminant /kənˈtæmɪnənt/
drift /drɪft/
dump unwanted garbage /ˌdʌmp ʌnˌwɑntɪd ˈgɑrbɪdʒ/
environmental group /ɪnˌvaɪɚnˈmɛntl ˈgrup/
environmental impact /ɪnˌvaɪɚnˈmɛntl ˈɪmpækt/
environmentalist /ɪnˌvaɪɚnˈmɛntl-ɪst/
erosion /ɪˈroʊʒən/
establish national parks /ɪˌstæblɪʃ ˌnæʃənəl ˈpɑrks/
extract /ɪkˈstrækt/
floating barrier /ˌfloʊṭɪŋ ˈbæriɚ/
fossil fuel /ˈfɑsəl ˌfyuəl/
fresh water /ˌfrɛʃ ˈwɔṭɚ/
funding /ˈfʌndɪŋ/
garbage dump/landfill /ˈgɑrbɪdʒ dʌmp/ˈlændfɪl/
garbage/litter/waste/debris /ˈgɑrbɪdʒ/ˈlɪṭɚ/weɪst/dɪˈbri/
garbage patch /ˈgɑrbɪdʒ pætʃ/
gas /gæs/
global warming /ˌgloʊbəl ˈwɔrmɪŋ/
hazard /ˈhæzɚd/
industrial/non-biodegradable waste /ɪnˌdʌstriəl/nɑn ˌbaɪoʊdɪˌgreɪdəbəl ˈweɪst/
industrialization /ɪnˌdʌstriələˈzeɪʃən/
(local/marine) wildlife /(ˌloʊkəl/məˌrin) ˈwaɪldlaɪf/
make efforts /ˌmeɪk ˈɛfɚts/
melt /mɛlt/
(negative) impact /(ˌnɛgəṭɪv) ˈɪmpækt/
nutrient /ˈnutriənt/
oil well /ˈɔɪl wɛl/
onshore/offshore oilfield /ˌɑnʃɔr/ɔfˌʃɔr ˈɔɪlfild/
(plastic) pollution/pollution from /(ˈplæstɪk) pəˌluʃən/pəˈluʃən frəm/
plastic waste /ˌplæstɪk ˈweɪst/
pollutant /pəˈlutˀnt/
pollute /pəˈlut/
pro-nuclear /proʊ ˈnukliɚ/
recycle /ˌriˈsaɪkəl/
release toxins/chemical substances /rɪˌlis ˈtɑksɪnz/ˌkɛmɪkəl ˈsʌbstənsɪz/
renewable energy /rɪˌnuəbəl ˈɛnɚdʒi/
rise (by one degree Fahrenheit) /ˌraɪz (baɪ wʌn dɪˌgri ˈfærənhaɪt)/
rise in sea level/rising sea level /ˌraɪz ɪn ˈsi ˌlɛvəl/ˌraɪzɪŋ ˈsi ˌlɛvəl/
sewage /ˈsuɪdʒ/
solution /səˈluʃən/
toxic /ˈtɑksɪk/
toxin /ˈtɑksɪn/
(wildlife) protection /(ˈwaɪldlaɪf) prəˌtɛkʃən/

Extreme weather, natural disasters

baking/burning/scorching temperatures /ˌbeɪkɪŋ/ˌbɚnɪŋ/ˌskɔrtʃɪŋ ˈtɛmprətʃɚz/
drought /draʊt/
flood /flʌd/
landslide /ˈlændslaɪd/
starvation /stɑrˈveɪʃən/

Traveling and tourism

area of natural beauty /ˌɛriə əv ˌnætʃərəl ˈbyuṭi/
around the globe /əˌraʊnd ðə ˈgloʊb/
cross /krɔs/
cultural heritage /ˌkʌltʃərəl ˈhɛrəṭɪdʒ/
degrade /dɪˈgreɪd/
deserted/barren/desolate wilderness /dɪˌzɚṭɪd/ˌbærən/ˌdɛsəlɪt ˈwɪldɚnəs/
distant/remote/inaccessible region /ˌdɪstənt/rɪˌmoʊt/ɪnəkˌsɛsəbəl ˈridʒən/
empty/bleak/inhospitable place /ˌɛmpti/ˌblik/ɪnhɑˌspɪṭəbəl ˈpleɪs/
facilities for tourists /fəˌsɪləṭiz fɚ ˈtʊrɪsts/
goal (of the journey) /ˈgoʊl (əv ðə ˌdʒɚni)/
hunt (for sth) /hʌnt (fɔr)/
limit tourism /ˌlɪmət ˈtʊrɪzəm/
lose all sense of space/time /ˌluz ɔl sɛns əv ˈspeɪs/ˈtaɪm/
navigation error /ˌnævɪˈgeɪʃən ˌɛrɚ/
path /pæθ/
picturesque /ˌpɪktʃəˈrɛsk/
reach your destination /ˌritʃ yɚ ˌdɛstəˈneɪʃən/
resort /rɪˈzɔrt/
speedboat /ˈspidboʊt/
survive /sɚˈvaɪv/
sustainable tourism /səˌsteɪnəbəl ˈtʊrɪzəm/
tough/punishing/arduous journey /ˌtʌf/ˌpʌnɪʃɪŋ/ˌɑrdʒuəs ˈdʒɚni/
tour operator /ˈtʊr ˌɑpəreɪṭɚ/
tourist destination /ˈtʊrɪst ˌdɛstəˈneɪʃən/
traveling companion /ˈtrævəlɪŋ kəmˌpænyən/
visitor /ˈvɪzəṭɚ/

Phrasal verbs

break up into (smaller particles) /ˌbreɪk ˈʌp ˌɪntə (smɔlɚ pɑrṭɪkəls)/
follow around /ˌfɑloʊ əˈraʊnd/
go around /ˌgoʊ əˈraʊnd/
sit around /ˌsɪt əˈraʊnd/
start out /ˌstɑrt ˈaʊt/
turn around and around /ˌtɚn əˈraʊnd ənd əˈraʊnd/

Other

approval /əˈpruvəl/
around/approximately /əˈraʊnd/əˈprɑksɪmətli/
challenge /ˈtʃæləndʒ/
challenging /ˈtʃæləndʒɪŋ/
common misconception /ˌkɑmən ˌmɪskənˈsɛpʃən/
crystal /ˈkrɪstəl/
distance yourself from /ˈdɪstəns yɚˌsɛlf frəm/
food poisoning /ˈfud ˌpɔɪzənɪŋ/
geologist /dʒiˈɑlədʒɪst/
grown /groʊn/
growth /groʊθ/
incomparable /ɪnˈkɑmpərəbəl/
inherent /ɪnˈhɛrənt/
injured /ˈɪndʒɚd/
injury /ˈɪndʒəri/
mineral /ˈmɪnərəl/
poison /ˈpɔɪzən/
poisonous /ˈpɔɪzənəs/
pursue /pɚˈsu/
rag /ræg/
ragged /ˈrægɪd/
scientific research /ˌsaɪənˈtɪfɪk rɪˈsɚtʃ/
seed /sid/
take a chance /ˌteɪk ə ˈtʃæns/
thirst /θɚst/
thirsty /ˈθɚsti/
undoubtedly /ʌnˈdaʊṭɪdli/
unlike /ʌnˈlaɪk/
vastness /ˈvæstnəs/

FOCUS REVIEW 8

VOCABULARY AND GRAMMAR

1 Complete the sentences with the words in the box. There are two extra words.

species debris habitat inhospitable field prey wells

1 After the hurricane there was so much debris scattered around that it took weeks to clean it up.
2 Animals use a number of techniques to catch their prey , such as stalking or waiting camouflaged for the most appropriate moment.
3 The first oil wells in Europe were drilled 98–165 feet deep in Bóbrka, Poland.
4 Deforestation is a serious problem partly because it contributes to the loss of natural habitat of the animals living in the forest.
5 The middle of the Sahara is one of the most inhospitable places on the planet. There's hardly any life.

2 Complete the sentences with the correct form of the words in capitals.

1 The idea that space exploration is the main reason for the loss of the ozone layer is a common misconception. **CONCEIVE**
2 He stood on the shore admiring the ocean and feeling overwhelmed by its vastness . **VAST**
3 It is feared that the contract for a new power plant has been mismanaged, and this may cause a serious delay to its opening. **MANAGE**
4 Despite the scorching temperatures in Death Valley, we decided to go for a drive across it. **SCORCH**
5 The residents expressed their strong disapproval of the authorities' plan to extend the supermarket in place of a park. **APPROVE**
6 Environmentalists worry about the industrial waste in our area. **INDUSTRY**

3 Complete the sentences with the correct form of the verbs in parentheses.

1 I wish I had chosen (choose) to do a presentation about endangered species. I'm struggling with the topic of acid rain.
2 It's about time you started (start) cycling to school. It's not too far.
3 If only the highway hadn't been built (not build) near the nature reserve. It wouldn't have affected the local wildlife so much.
4 I'd rather you used (use) reusable bags while shopping instead of those plastic ones.
5 I wish my parents had asked (ask) me what breed of dog I wanted to get before buying me a poodle.

4 Complete the second sentence so that it has a similar meaning to the first.

1 You are not allowed to use the equipment without supervision under any circumstances.
Under ________ the equipment without supervision.
2 Tim not only saw a school of dolphins, but he also spotted a whale.
Not ________ a school of dolphins, but he also spotted a whale.
3 Claudia needs to mow the lawn before she goes on vacation.
What ________ the lawn before she goes on vacation.
4 We have never experienced such cold weather while skiing.
Never ________ such cold weather while skiing.
5 Josh only recommended you should buy more organic food.
All ________ should buy more organic food.

154

Exercise 4
1 no circumstances are you allowed to use
2 only did Tim see
3 Claudia needs to do is (to) mow
4 have we experienced
5 Josh recommended was that you

Exercise 6
1 you trained your dog/your dog was trained
2 have I seen so many robins in the garden
3 the rescue workers could have some hot food and a rest
4 I had listened to my brother when he told me about the weather
5 no circumstances should we go home now because there's a tornado approaching
6 the teacher didn't give us so many photocopies

LANGUAGE IN USE

5 Complete the text with one word in each blank.

A KANGAROO AT LARGE

A couple of weeks ago, the police received a strange phone call. It turned out that a kangaroo had escaped from an animal park situated in the suburbs. [1] Having arrived at the scene, the police discovered that the kangaroo had got out through a hole in the fence.

The public and all police patrols were notified about the missing kangaroo. Immediately, the police received a [2] lot/number of phone calls from members of the public with reported sightings of the escaped animal. Unfortunately, [3] despite the police getting to these places quickly, the kangaroo managed to stay one hop ahead of everyone. After a couple of days, the police finally realized that the kangaroo was grazing on the grass in the park near the police station. [4] What everybody found quite surprising was how calm the animal seemed to be and how easy it was to catch.

When it was safely returned to the animal park, one policeman said, 'I wish we [5] had more cases like that.'

6 Complete the second sentence so that it has a similar meaning to the first.

1 Your dog needs training.
It's about time ________________.
2 I have never seen so many robins in the garden before.
Never before ________________.
3 The rescue workers really want some hot food and a rest.
If only ________________.
4 It's too bad I didn't listen to my brother when he told me about the weather.
I wish ________________.
5 We mustn't go home now because there's a tornado approaching.
Under ________________.
6 I don't like the fact that the teacher gives us so many photocopies.
I'd rather ________________.

EXTRA ACTIVITIES
- Photocopiable resource 57B (fill in the blanks – 20 mins) MultiROM and ActiveTeach
- Photocopiable resource 64 (mini-test 3 – 15 mins) MultiROM and ActiveTeach
- Photocopiable resource 54 (Speaking – 15 mins) MultiROM and ActiveTeach
- Photocopiable resource 55 (Writing – 15 mins) MultiROM and ActiveTeach

WORKBOOK
Use of English 8.9, pp. 116–117; Self-assessment 8.10, p. 118

READING

7 Read the texts about travelers. For questions 1–5, choose from the texts (A–C). You can choose each text more than once.

Which text mentions a person who:

1 needed a number of accomplishments to achieve their ambition? C
2 achieved something that had first been done many years before? A
3 had to compete against another person trying to achieve the same goal? A
4 became famous for a discovery that many others had failed to make? B
5 was in danger? C

A **Krystyna Chojnowska-Liskiewicz** (born July 15 1936) was the first woman to sail solo around the globe, a journey initially completed by Joshua Slocum in 1900. Chojnowska-Liskiewicz set off from the Canary Islands on February 28 1976 in the 30-foot vessel *Mazurek*, whose construction team was headed by her husband. She circumnavigated 31,166 nautical miles before returning to the spot where she had started some 401 days later, on April 21 1978. In completing her voyage, she officially became the first woman to sail single-handedly around the world, beating New Zealander Naomi James, who completed her circumnavigation on June 8 the same year.

B **Jacek Pałkiewicz** (born June 2 1942) is a Polish journalist, traveler, and explorer who has written over thirty books and became an internationally recognized expert on survival skills. Notable trips include his first major expedition in which he crossed the Sahara Desert on foot in 1972, a journey to the coldest place in Siberia (-72°C) in 1989, and crossing the jungles of Vietnam on elephants in 1992. He is best known, however, for his 1996 trek to the Andes, where he led the scientific expedition that indisputably established the sought-after source of the Amazon River.

C **Junko Tabei** (born September 22 1939) is a Japanese mountain climber who became the first woman to climb Mount Everest. During the ascent, the camp Tabei was staying at was struck by an avalanche. She was buried under the snow and lost consciousness but her Sherpa guide dug her out. Twelve days after the avalanche, on May 16 1975, Tabei reached the summit of Mount Everest. Tabei had set herself the goal of becoming the first woman to scale the Seven Summits, the highest mountains on each of the seven continents. She achieved her goal in June 1992, when she climbed Puncak Jaya on the island of New Guinea. Tabei also climbed the highest peaks in different countries around the world, and by 2009 she had reached fifty-six of them. Apart from climbing, she is also working for an organization aiming to preserve mountain environments.

SPEAKING

8 With a partner, complete the speaking task.

Student A, your photos show people doing things to help the environment. Compare the photos and say how the people's actions are helping the environment.

A

B

Student B, have you ever taken part in a beach cleanup?

9 Now go to WORD STORE page 24 and complete another speaking task.

10 With a partner, discuss the questions.

1 What could be done to persuade people to recycle more?
2 How can you use social media to promote an environmentally friendly lifestyle?
3 Is the work of environmental organizations effective? What makes you think it is or is not?
4 What are the advantages of living next to large green areas?

WRITING

11 Complete the writing task.

You have seen this announcement on an English-language website.

Movie reviews wanted
Have you seen a movie that was made in a particularly beautiful part of the world? Write a review for our website, describing the location and how it was important for the movie. Say whether you would recommend the movie to others and why.

Write your review in 140–190 words.

NEXT CLASS
- Ask students to do Self-check 8.11, WB p. 119 as homework.
- Ask students to prepare for Unit test 8 and Review test 4 (*Focus* Assessment Package).

GRAMMAR FOCUS

0.1 Present tenses – review

Present Simple

We use the Present Simple to talk about:

- actions that are repeated regularly:
  I always ***drive*** *to work.*
- states and permanent situations:
  The chef ***doesn't come*** *from Italy.*
- with verbs expressing emotions (*hate*, *like*, *love*, etc.), states of mind (*believe*, *know*, *need*, *prefer*, *remember*, *seem*, *think*, *understand*, *want*, etc.) or senses (*feel*, *hear*, *see*, etc.):
  Do *you* ***prefer*** *Indian food or Chinese food?*

Present Continuous

We use the Present Continuous to talk about:

- actions happening at the time of speaking:
  Most of the guests ***are sitting*** *on the outdoor patio at the moment.*
- temporary situations:
  I'm working *at Tuco's bar during the summer break.*

Present Perfect Simple

We use the Present Perfect Simple to talk about actions and situations that:

- finished in the past and have a result in the present (and we don't know or it's not important when exactly they happened):
  I've made *coffee. Would you like some?*
- started in the past and continue into the present:
  How long ***have*** *you* ***owned*** *this restaurant?*

Present Perfect Continuous

We use the Present Perfect Continuous to talk about:

- actions that started in the past and continue into the present:
  Zoe ***has been sleeping*** *since two o'clock.*
- actions that lasted for some time (and possibly still continue) and whose results we can see now:
  I'm tired because ***I've been cleaning*** *the house all day.*

Present Perfect Simple vs Present Perfect Continuous

We use the Present Perfect Continuous to focus on the action or process (which may or may not be complete):
I've been baking *cookies all morning.*
We use the Present Perfect Simple to focus on the result of a finished action:
I've baked *200 cookies.*

Choose the correct options.

1 I'm really tired. I *have cooked* / *have been cooking* all day.
2 I *haven't seen* / *haven't been seeing* Margaret recently. How is she?
3 She *thinks* / *is thinking* she'll have the steak, but she can't decide.
4 *Do you hear* / *Are you hearing* that noise? I wonder what it is.
5 I'm watching my weight, so I *prefer* / *am preferring* not to have any sugar in my coffee.
6 The meeting *is taking place* / *takes place* upstairs today because of the flood damage on the ground floor.
7 Margaret *has been writing* / *has written* the reports. Can you take them up to Mr. Jones?

0.2 Past tenses – review

Past Simple

We use the Past Simple to talk about:

- actions and situations that started and finished in the past. We often say when they happened:
  We ***bought*** *this house in 2013.*
- a series of actions that happened one after the other:
  Messi ***kicked*** *the ball and it* ***flew*** *into the net.*

Past Continuous

We use the Past Continuous:

- to talk about actions that were in progress at a particular time in the past:
  'What ***were*** *you* ***doing*** *at eight yesterday evening?'*
  *'****I was watching*** *a football game on TV.'*
- to talk about an action that was in progress when another action took place (for the shorter action, which happened while the longer action was in progress, we use the Past Simple):
  When she ***was skiing*** *down the slope, another skier* ***crashed*** *into her.*
- to describe background states for other events:
  On the day of the match, the sun ***was shining*** *and a light breeze* ***was blowing***.

Past Perfect Simple

We use the Past Perfect Simple to talk about an action that happened before a particular time in the past or before another past action (for the action that happened first, we use the Past Simple):
The party ***had finished*** *by midnight.*
Beasley ***had scored*** *two goals before the coach* ***decided*** *to substitute him.*

Choose the correct answer, A, B, or C.

1 I went ice-skating last weekend – it was the first time I ____ it.
A tried B had tried C was trying

2 No, I ____ that you were moving overseas. That's news to me!
A wasn't hearing B don't hear C hadn't heard

3 I ____ first prize in a chess contest once.
A had won B won C was winning

4 I'm sorry. I ____ about something else. What did you say?
A thought B was thinking C had thought

5 I broke a bone once. I ____ my bike and I crashed into a tree.
A rode B had ridden C was riding

6 Had he ever ____ a basketball team before he took on the school team?
A coached B coaching C been coaching

Complete the sentences with the correct form of the verbs in parentheses.

1 I wish I hadn't eaten (not eat) so much. I feel a little sick now.

2 If I hadn't helped (not help) my mother around the house this afternoon, she wouldn't have let (not let) me use the Internet in the evening.

3 If I could (can) meet anyone, dead or alive, I would choose (choose) to meet John Lennon.

4 You wouldn't have been able (not be able) to buy a new laptop last year if I hadn't lent (not lend) you the money.

5 I'd love to visit Rio de Janeiro one day. If only I could (can) afford to go.

6 Jane's little brother is so spoiled. If you don't give (not give) him what he wants, he gets (get) really angry.

0.3 Conditionals • *wish* and *if only*

Conditionals

- We use Zero Conditional sentences (*if/when* + Present Simple, Present Simple) to talk about things that are always true:
  If the temperature ***drops*** *below 32°F, water* ***freezes****.*
  When babies ***are*** *hungry, they* ***cry****.*
- We use First Conditional sentences (*if* + Present Simple, *will/could/might* + infinitive) to talk about things that will happen in the future under certain conditions:
  If you ***leave*** *a message, they****'ll call*** *you back.*
- We use Second Conditional sentences (*if* + Past Simple, *would/could/might* + infinitive) to talk about present or future situations or states that are impossible or unlikely:
  Would *you* ***tell*** *him the truth if he* ***asked*** *you?*
- We use Third Conditional sentences (*if* + Past Perfect, *would have/might have/could have* + Past Participle) to talk about events in the past that did not happen:
  If you ***had accepted*** *my help, you* ***would have avoided*** *a lot of trouble.*

wish and *if only*

- We use *wish/if only* + Past Simple to express regret and dissatisfaction with a present situation:
  John ***wishes*** *he* ***didn't have to*** *sell the house.*
  If only *I* ***could*** *help you.*
- We use *wish/if only* + *would* + infinitive to express annoyance about a present situation that we would like to be different. It usually refers to things we can't change or control:
  I ***wish*** *they****'d stop*** *playing loud music in the evenings.*
  If only *you****'d come back*** *to me.*
- *Wish* and *if only* have a similar meaning, but *if only* is more emphatic. It expresses a greater degree of regret.
- We use *wish/if only* + Past Perfect to express regret about a past situation:
  I ***wish*** *I* ***hadn't bought*** *this dress – it's awful!*
  It's too late now. ***If only*** *I****'d followed*** *my dad's advice!*

0.4 Modal verbs for speculation

- When speculating about present or future situations, we use *must/might/may/could/might not/may not/can't* + infinitive.
- When speculating about past situations or events, we use *must/might/may/could/might not/may not/couldn't* + *have* + past participle.
- *Must* expresses a strong belief (bordering on certainty) that something is or was true:
  There ***must be*** *something wrong with the engine.*
  She ***must have made*** *a mistake in her calculations.*
- *Might, may* and *could* express a possibility that something is, will be or was possible or probable:
  This ***might/may/could*** *be the article I'm looking for.*
  Scientists disagree on what ***might/may/could happen*** *to the Earth in the future.*
  Life on Earth ***might/may/could have originated*** *from another planet.*
- *Might not* and *may not* express a weak possibility that something is not, will not be, or was not true:
  Black holes ***might not/may not exist*** *at all.*
  Here are some facts you ***may not/might not have heard*** *about.*
- *Can't* and *couldn't* express a strong belief (bordering on certainty) that something is not or was not true:
  He ***can't be*** *American; his accent is too strong.*
  This book ***couldn't have been written*** *by a real expert.*

Complete the second sentence so that it has a similar meaning to the first, using the word in capitals. Do not change the word in capitals.

1 I'm certain that he didn't see me. **COULDN'T**
He _couldn't have seen_ me.

2 I'm not sure she believes me. **MIGHT**
She _might not believe_ me.

3 I'm positive that John broke it. No one else was here. **MUST**
John _must have broken_ it. No one else was here.

4 Maybe the instructions fell behind the dresser. **MAY**
The _instructions may have fallen_ behind the dresser.

5 I'm convinced there's no life on other planets. **CAN'T**
There _can't be life_ on other planets.

6 I'm sure he is satisfied with the results of his research. **MUST**
He _must be satisfied_ with the results of his research.

0.5 Reported Speech

Statements

In Reported Speech we often report the speaker's words using verbs such as **say** or **tell** and the pronoun **that** (which can be omitted). The verb **tell** takes an object:
*'I bought a bunch of flowers for my wife.' → He **told me/said** (**that**) he had bought a bunch of flowers for his wife.*

We make the following changes in Reported Speech:

- tenses:

Direct Speech	Reported Speech
Present Simple Rose: 'I go shopping on weekends.'	**Past Simple** Rose said (that) she went shopping on weekends.
Present Continuous Rose: 'I am going shopping.'	**Past Continuous** Rose said (that) she was going shopping.
Present Perfect Rose: 'I have already been shopping.'	**Past Perfect** Rose said (that) she had already been shopping.
Past Simple Rose: 'I didn't go shopping this morning.'	**Past Perfect** Rose said (that) she hadn't been shopping that morning.
Past Perfect Rose: 'I hadn't been shopping before the party.'	**Past Perfect** Rose said (that) she hadn't been shopping before the party.
can/can't Rose: 'I can't go shopping.'	***could/couldn't*** Rose said (that) she couldn't go shopping.
will/won't Rose: 'I won't go shopping alone.'	***would/wouldn't*** Rose said (that) she wouldn't go shopping alone.
be going to Rose: 'I'm going shopping on Saturday.'	***was/were going to*** Rose said (that) she was going to go shopping on Saturday.

- time expressions and words referring to places (depending on the context):

Direct Speech	Reported Speech
now	at that time/then
today	that day
yesterday	the day before/the previous day
two hours ago	two hours earlier/before
tomorrow	the next day/the following day
here	there

- demonstrative pronouns, personal pronouns, object pronouns, and possessive adjectives (depending on the context):

Direct Speech	Reported Speech
this/these	that/those
I/we	he/she/they
me/us	him/her/them
my	his/her
our	their

Questions

To report questions, we use verbs and phrases such as **ask**, **enquire**, or **want to know** and make the same changes as in reported statements (tenses, pronouns, time expressions, words referring to places, etc.). The word order in reported questions is the same as in affirmative sentences (the subject comes before the verb).

- To report *yes/no* questions, we use *if* or *whether*:
  *'**Can** I speak to the manager?' → The customer asked **if/whether** he **could** speak to the manager.*
  *'**Do** you often **watch** movies on TV?' → I asked her **if/whether** she often **watched** movies on TV.*
- To report *wh-* questions, we keep the question word (e.g. *what, who, how, where, when*):
  *'**How many** bottles of cola **did** you **buy**?' → I asked my son **how many** bottles of cola he **had bought**.*
  *'**When are** you **coming** back?' → Dorothy wanted to know **when** I **was coming** back.*

Imperatives

To report imperatives (orders or requests) we use verbs such as **ask** or **tell** or other reporting verbs, an object, and **(not) + to-infinitive:**
*'Please refund my money.' → The customer **asked** the manager **to refund** his money.*
*'**Don't apply** the cream more than twice a day.' → The store assistant **advised** the customer **not to apply** the cream more than twice a day.*

Report the statements, questions, and imperatives.

1 'Our bus left two hours ago,' they told us.
They told us ______________________ .
2 'Are you from this part of town?' the stranger asked Greg.
The stranger asked Greg ______________________ .
3 'Do you like going to the movies?' asked Pauline.
Pauline asked me ______________________ .
4 'Please don't play in the kitchen,' Barbara told the children.
Barbara told the children ______________________ .
5 'You need to get the assignment back to me by 4 p.m. tomorrow,' said Mr. Roberts.
Mr. Roberts said ______________________ .
6 'Please get some of my special toothpaste from the pharmacy,' Sylvia told me.
Sylvia asked me ______________________ .
7 'I have never bought anything because of an advertisement,' said Ricardo.
Ricardo said ______________________ .

0.6 Articles

Indefinite article (*a/an*)

We use ***a/an*** with singular countable nouns:

- when we mention something for the first time:
  *There is **a** piano in the school auditorium.*
- when we refer to one of many things:
  *I need **a** new laptop.*
- when we talk about someone's job:
  Brad is **an** actor.
- in expressions with the verb *have* and *take* (e.g. *have a chat/ take a walk/have a talk/take a look*):
  *Let's take **a** look around.*
- in expressions about time, frequency, speed, and price per amount:
  *twice **a** year*
  *100 miles **an** hour*
  *$1.50 **a** pound*

Definite article (*the*)

We use **the** with singular and plural nouns and uncountable nouns:

- to refer to something that we have mentioned before:
  *There is **a** piano in the school auditorium. **The** piano is very old.*
- to refer to something that both the speaker and the listener know:
  *Let's go to **the** restaurant we went to last week.*
- to refer to something unique or one of a kind:
  ***The** sun sets at 7 p.m.*
  *Who is **the** music director of La Scala?*
- with *theater, movies,* and *radio*:
  *I love going to **the** theater.*
  *I heard it on **the** radio today.*
- with *morning, afternoon, evening* (but not *noon*):
  *Let's watch a movie in **the** evening.*
- with musical instruments, when referring to someone playing them:
  *Julia plays **the** flute and **the** trumpet.*
- with the superlative form of adjectives:
  ***the** most famous*
- with ordinal numbers:
  ***the** third*
- with certain names of countries (if the name is in plural form or includes a common noun):
  ***the** Netherlands*
  ***the** United States*
  ***the** United Kingdom*
  ***the** Czech Republic*
- with geographical regions, mountain ranges, rivers, seas, oceans, archipelagos, and deserts:
  ***the** Himalayas*
  ***the** Mississippi*
  ***the** Caribbean Sea*
  ***the** Bahamas*

Zero article

We do not use an article:

- with uncountable nouns or plural countable nouns when we are talking about something in general:
  ***Music** is very important in my life.*
  *Pete loves **ice cream**.*
  ***Pop stars** are often demanding and self-centered.*
- with meals:
  *Let's have **dinner**.*
- with the names of continents, most countries, cities (exception: *the Hague*), lakes, islands, and mountains:
  South America
  Brazil
  Manchester
  Lake Nicaragua
  Easter Island
  Mount Aconcagua

Complete the sentences with *a/an, the,* or Ø (no article).

1 I'm going to __the__ movies tomorrow. Would you like to come?
2 Did you know that __the__ place with __the__ longest name is in __ø__ New Zealand? It's a hill called Taumatawhakatangihangakoauauotamatea-turipukakapiki-maungahoronukupokaiwhenuakitanatahu.
3 I just saw __a__ cat with really short, silvery fur. Is that what they call a Russian Blue?
4 What time do you want to have __ø__ lunch?
5 I've decided I'm going to have __a__ haircut. I'm tired of having long hair.
6 Isn't he __the__ actor who's in that new soap opera?
7 Did you know that __the__ capital of __ø__ Syria is Damascus?

0.5
1 (that) our bus had left two hours before
2 if he was from that part of town
3 if I liked going to the movies
4 not to play in the kitchen
5 (that) I needed to get the assignment back to him by 4 p.m. the following/next day
6 to get some of her special toothpaste from the pharmacy
7 (that) he had never bought anything because of an advertisement

0.7 Comparative structures

Adjectives

We form the comparative and superlative forms of adjectives as follows:

Adjectives		Comparative	Superlative
one-syllable adjectives	young nice hot	younger nicer hotter	the youngest the nicest the hottest
one- or two-syllable adjectives ending in -y	pretty dry	prettier drier	the prettiest the driest
two-syllable or longer adjectives	dangerous	more dangerous	the most dangerous
irregular adjectives	good bad far	better worse further	the best the worst the furthest

- *less* + adjective:
  Marie is ***less ambitious*** *than Tess.*
- *the least* + adjective:
  His last book was ***the least interesting****.*

Adverbs

We form the comparative and superlative forms of adverbs as follows:

Adverbs		Comparative	Superlative
most adverbs	quietly carefully	more quietly more carefully	the most quietly the most carefully
adverbs same as adjectives	hard near early late fast	harder nearer earlier later faster	the hardest the nearest the earliest the latest the fastest
irregular adverbs	well badly far little a lot/ much	better worse further less more	the best the worst the furthest the least the most

- *less* + adverb:
  From now on this page will be updated ***less regularly****.*
- *the least* + adverb:
  This country is one of ***the least effectively*** *governed countries in the world.*

Other forms of comparison

- To compare two people, things, or activities, we can use *than*:
  The inside of the hospital is more modern ***than*** *the outside.*
  Does brown hair grow more quickly ***than*** *blond hair?*
- We can also use (*not*) *as* + adjective/adverb + *as*:
  Your essay is ***not as good as*** *mine.*
- To talk about a small difference between two people, things, or activities, we can use ***a little/a bit/slightly*** + adjective/ adverb in the comparative form:
  Boys are a ***little more likely*** *than girls to be born early.*
  The event was received ***slightly more positively*** *than the previous one.*
- To talk about a big difference, we can use *quite a bit/far/ much/a lot* + adjective/adverb in the comparative form:
  We're going to need a ***much more powerful*** *telescope.*
  The new system works ***far better*** *than everyone expected.*
- We use *not* + adjective/adverb + ***enough*** to say we have less than we need or want and ***too*** + adjective/adverb to say we have more than we need or want:
  The new version of this video game is still ***not realistic enough****.*
  I didn't play ***well enough*** *to win.*
  The survivors were ***too exhausted*** *to answer any questions.*
  We left the hotel ***too early*** *to have breakfast there.*
- To say that with one change (to a certain degree) comes another change (to the same degree), we use *the* + comparative, *the* + comparative:
  The sooner *you get here,* ***the better****.*
  The harder *I try,* ***the worse*** *the situation becomes.*

Complete the sentences with the correct form of the words in parentheses.

1 He really is ________ (talented) singer I've ever heard.
2 Cozumel isn't ________ (expensive) as I thought it would be.
3 Is it possible for you to come over a little ________ (early)?
4 He's far ________ (intelligent) you might think.
5 It's much ________ (far) I expected.
6 Driving is the ________ (safe) way of traveling. All other ways are safer.
7 'When do you want to leave?' 'The ________ (soon, good), to be honest.'

0.7
1 the most talented
2 as expensive
3 earlier
4 more intelligent than
5 farther/further than
6 least safe
7 sooner, the better

0.8 The passive; *have something done*

The passive

- We use the passive when we are more interested in the action itself than the person (the agent) performing it:
  The presidential election ***will be held*** *in July.*
- If we want to say who performed the action, we use the word **by**:
  The telephone ***was invented*** *in 1876* ***by*** *Alexander Graham Bell.*
- We form the passive with an appropriate form of the verb *to be* and the past participle of the main verb.

Present Simple	*Coffee* ***is grown*** *and* ***exported*** *by over fifty developing countries.*
Present Continuous	*The report* ***is*** *still* ***being examined.***
Past Simple	*When* ***was*** *the Willis Tower* ***built?***
Past Continuous	*At 11 p.m. the suspect* ***was*** *still* ***being questioned.***
Present Perfect	*A new community center* ***has*** *just* ***been opened*** *in my town.*
Past Perfect	*I found out that my application* ***had been accepted.***
will	*Over 1,000 companies* ***will be affected*** *by the new regulations.*

have something done

We use *have* + object + past participle to talk about actions that someone else (typically an expert or a contractor) does at our request. Compare the two sentences:
After the burglary, the Jacksons ***changed*** *their locks.* (They did it themselves.)
After the burglary, the Jacksons ***had their locks changed.*** (They hired a locksmith to do it.)

Present Simple	*We* ***have*** *the office* ***cleaned*** *twice a week.*
Present Continuous	*Why* ***are*** *you* ***having*** *your windows* ***replaced?***
Past Simple	*We* ***had*** *all the installations* ***checked.***
Past Continuous	*Last year in June my neighbors* ***were having*** *their house* ***painted.***
Present Perfect	***Have*** *you ever* ***had*** *your nails* ***done?***
will	*When* ***will*** *you* ***have*** *your tires* ***changed?***
be going to	***I'm going to have*** *a burglar alarm* ***installed.***

We can usually replace the verb *have* with the verb *get*:
We ***had*** *the documents translated.* =
We ***got*** *the documents translated.*

Complete the sentences with the correct form of the words in parentheses. Use the passive or *have something done*.

1 He ________ (stop) by the police and ________ (ask) for his ID.
2 I think everybody – both road-users and pedestrians – ________ (affect) by the introduction of self-driving cars in the near future.
3 Where ________ (you/your laptop/repair) last month? I think mine's broken now.
4 Smoking in public places ________ (ban) for several years now.
5 Actually, I ________ (never/my photo/take) by a professional photographer.
6 More drivers ________ (fine) for speeding than for drink-driving.
7 An increasing number of teenagers ________ (teach) how to cook by their parents nowadays.

0.8
1 was stopped, asked
2 will be affected
3 did you have your laptop repaired
4 has been banned
5 have never had my photo taken
6 are fined
7 are being taught

GRAMMAR FOCUS

1.2 Present and past habits

To talk about someone's habits and typical behavior, we can use:

- the Present Simple or the Past Simple, to talk about repeated present or past actions or states:
  When I ***get*** *home, I* ***do*** *my homework and then* ***practice*** *the violin.*
  My grandfather ***picked*** *me* ***up*** *from school every day.*
- *used to* + infinitive to talk about states (e.g. with the verbs *be, have, believe, like*) or actions that happened regularly in the past but are no longer happening in the present. We do not use this structure to talk about single past actions:
  When I your age, I ***used to be*** *very eager to learn.*
  I ***didn't use to fall behind*** *with my homework.*
  Did *you* ***use to like*** *Chemistry?*
- *would* + infinitive to talk about past actions or behavior typical for someone (but not states):
  Our Math teacher ***would give*** *us loads of homework.*
- *will* + infinitive to talk about present actions or typical behavior (but not states):
  *She****'ll watch*** *TV or play games all day instead of studying for her exams.*
  Note: We do not use the verbs *will/would* in this meaning in questions.
- the Present Continuous or Past Continuous with the adverb *always* to complain about someone's behavior:
  *She****'s always putting*** *things off and she's never on time.*
  My neighbors ***were always complaining*** *about the noise.*

Choose the correct options.

1 When Mario and I shared a dorm room, he was always borrowing / *will always borrow* my things without asking.
2 When I was a kid, I *would believe* / used to believe that my dad was a spy.
3 Did you use to like / *Would you like* your elementary school?
4 It's so annoying! She *will always lose* / is always losing her notebook.
5 Martha would ask / *was asking* the teacher a lot of questions after every lesson. She was very curious.
6 I always forget / *will forget* to bring a pen. Can I borrow one of yours?

1.5 Verb patterns

- verb + *to*-infinitive, e.g. *agree, arrange, can't afford, decide, intend, learn, manage, offer, prefer, refuse, remember, seem, tend*:
  I ***decided to leave*** *school and find a job.*
  My sister ***agreed to help*** *me with my homework.*
- verb + object + *to*-infinitive, e.g. *advise, allow, cause, enable, encourage, expect, force, remind, urge, warn*:
  Robert's mother ***encouraged him to study*** *Law.*
  The teacher ***reminded us not to use*** *our cell phones during class.*
- verb + object + infinitive without *to*, e.g. *make, let*:
  Do his parents ***let him hang out*** *with his friends?*
  My parents used to ***make me do*** *a lot of house chores.*
- verb + *-ing* form, e.g. *admit, avoid, can't help, can't stand, enjoy, fancy, imagine, keep, miss, practice, spend/waste time, stop*:
  I ***can't stand wearing*** *a school uniform.*
  She recently ***stopped eating*** *fast food and she feels better already.*
- verb + *-ing* form/*to*-infinitive:
  After the verbs *begin, continue, hate, intend, like, love, prefer*, and *start*, we can use both the *-ing* form and the *to*-infinitive. The meaning stays the same or changes very slightly:
  I ***started playing*** *chess. I* ***started to play*** *chess.*
  He ***intends using*** *the school website. He* ***intends to use*** *the school website.*

Change in meaning

- After the verbs *remember, forget, stop*, and *try*, we can use both the *-ing* form and the *to*-infinitive. However, the meaning of the sentence changes:

  Jenny ***remembers locking*** *the door.* (She remembers that she locked the door.)
  Jenny ***remembers to lock*** *the door.* (She always remembers to lock the door.)

  Dad'll ***forget giving*** *me the money.* (He will forget that he gave me the money.)
  Dad'll ***forget to give*** *me the money.* (He hasn't given me the money and he'll forget to do it.)

  Liz ***stopped drinking*** *coffee.* (Liz doesn't drink coffee anymore.)
  Liz ***stopped to drink*** *some coffee.* (Liz stopped doing something in order to drink coffee.)

  I ***tried turning*** *the computer* ***off*** *and* ***on*** *again, but it didn't help.* (I tried this as an experiment to see if it would work).
  I ***tried to turn*** *the computer off, but the shutdown command didn't work.* (I made an effort to turn the computer off).

- We use *feel, hear, see, watch* + infinitive without *to* when we want to say that we saw the whole action from beginning to end:
  *I **watched** Mary **paint** a picture.* (I saw Mary start on the painting, paint it, and finish painting).
- We use *feel, hear, see, watch* + *-ing* form when we witness only a part of the action:
  *I **watched Mary painting** a picture.* (Mary was painting a picture when I saw her).

Complete the second sentence so that it has a similar meaning to the first, using the word in capitals. Do not change the word in capitals.

1 You're looking for volunteers? You could put a poster up in the school. **TRIED**
Have you __________ a poster in the school?
2 It's really important that you hand in your assignment on Friday. **REMEMBER**
You must __________ your assignment on Friday.
3 Would Juan like to come to the concert on Sunday? **FEEL**
Does Juan __________ the concert on Sunday?
4 I told him that dropping Spanish was a bad idea. **ENCOURAGED**
I __________ Spanish.
5 Those boots are much too expensive for me to buy. **AFFORD**
I __________ those boots.
6 Jake has been forbidden from using his dad's computer. **ALLOWED**
Jake __________ his dad's computer.
7 Janice doesn't go to dance class any more. She quit two weeks ago. **STOPPED**
Janice __________ two weeks ago.

1.5
1 tried putting up
2 remember to hand in
3 feel like coming to
4 encouraged him not to drop
5 can't afford to buy
6 is not allowed to use
7 stopped going to dance class

2.2 Past Perfect Simple and Continuous

Past Perfect Simple

We use the Past Perfect Simple:

- to talk about actions that happened before a particular time or event in the past (for which we usually use the Past Simple):
  *When I arrived at the wedding reception, the bride's father **had** already **made** his speech.*
  *By the age of sixteen, he **had learnt** to speak three foreign languages.*
- to talk about states that were true or happening before a particular time in the past:
  *When my parents got married, they **had known** each other for fifteen years.*

Past Perfect Continuous

We use the Past Perfect Continuous to talk about actions that were in progress up to a particular time in the past (or finished shortly before it):
*The guests **had been waiting** in front of the church for forty minutes before the bus picked them up.*
*We **hadn't been thinking** about selling the house, but then we got this great offer.*
*How long **had** you **been watching** me before I woke up?*

Affirmative	Negative
I/You/He/She/It/We/They had been sleeping.	I/You/He/She/It/We/They hadn't been (had not been) sleeping.

Yes/No questions	Short answers
Had I/you/he/she/it/we/they been sleeping?	Yes, I/you/he/she/it/we/they had. No, I/you/he/she/it/we/they hadn't.

Wh- questions	Subject questions
How long had I/you/he/she/it/we/they been sleeping?	Who had been sleeping?

Past Perfect Simple vs Past Perfect Continuous

- We use the Past Perfect Simple:
  - to talk about finished actions:
    *My father **had visited** his American relatives twice before he finally went to live with them.*
  - to talk about states using stative verbs, e.g. *be, have, know, see, believe*:
    *I **had** never **seen** such a magnificent church before I visited St. Paul's Cathedral.*
- We use the Past Perfect Continuous to talk about actions but not states. We stress the duration of the action rather than the result:
  *We **had been waiting** for three hours when they finally arrived.*

GRAMMAR FOCUS

Complete the sentences with the Past Perfect Simple or Continuous form of the verbs in parentheses.

1 Roberto watches a lot of French movies but fortunately, he _hadn't seen_ (not see) that movie before. He loved it!

2 I didn't speak to Janet at the reception. By the time I arrived, she _had already left_ (already/leave).

3 It was such a shame. She _had been decorating_ (decorate) the Christmas tree for an hour and then it fell over!

4 I was really tired when I arrived. I _had driven_ (drive) all the way there without stopping.

5 Mike locked the cat in the closet by mistake. The poor thing _had been crying_ (cry) for hours before he finally let it out.

6 Barbara _knew_ (know) that Alex was going to be at the concert.

2.5 Relative clauses

Defining relative clauses

- Defining relative clauses provides information integral to the sentence (without which the sentence makes no sense):
  A stepfather is a man ***who is married to your mother but isn't your father.***
- We do not use commas to separate a defining relative clause from the rest of the sentence:
  The girl ***who is sitting next to the bride*** *is her sister Kerry.*
- Defining relative clauses can start with:
  - *who* or *that*, when talking about people:
    Mrs. Wilkes is the person ***who/that*** *moved in last week.*
  - *that*, when talking about things:
    Would you like to see the house ***that*** *is for sale?*
  - ***whose***, when talking about possession or ownership:
    I know a girl ***whose*** *parents own a yacht.*
    You shouldn't drive a car ***whose*** *bumper is about to fall off.*
  - *where*, when talking about places:
    This is the place ***where*** *my parents first met.*
- We can leave out the relative pronouns *who* and *that* when they are followed by a noun or a pronoun:
  He is the man (***who/that***) *I want to marry.*
  BUT: *This is the man* ***who/that*** *wants to marry me.*

Non-defining relative clauses

- Non-defining relative clauses always include a relative pronoun:
  Hector, ***who*** *is a brilliant actor, took the main role.*
- They give additional information, without which the sentence still makes sense:
  Jill, ***who used to be my neighbor****, is going to marry my nephew.*
- They are separated by commas from the rest of the sentence:
  *The new movie****,*** *which stars Leonardo DiCaprio****,*** *will be a huge success.*
- They start with the same relative pronouns as defining relative clauses, except that *which* replaces *that*:
  Ed, ***who*** *lives in Montreal, couldn't come to the funeral.*
  Joyce's new Lexus, ***which*** *she bought last month, cost a fortune.*
  St. Mary's Church, ***where*** *the wedding is going to be held, was built in 1645.*
  Yesterday I bumped into Angus White, ***whose*** *brother is studying Medicine.*
- Non-defining relative clauses can also comment on the rest of the sentence, beginning with the pronoun *which*:
  Tom was late for Thanksgiving dinner again, ***which*** *made his mother furious.*
  The bartender continued to stare at me, ***which*** *I found extremely annoying.*

Reduced relative clauses

- We use the present participle (in the active voice) or the past participle (in the passive voice) instead of the relative pronoun and the verb:
  Elderly people ***living*** *alone* (= who live alone) *should have friends or family to care for them.*
  Children ***raised*** (= who were raised) *in a bilingual environment may begin to speak a little later.*
- They can be both defining and non-defining:
  Do you know the man ***talking*** (= who is talking) *to Mr. Schwartz?* (defining)
  Rich people, ***accustomed*** (= who are accustomed) *to luxurious living, will never understand poor people.* (non-defining)

Choose the correct answer, A, B, or C.

1 Kim's the one ____ likes to be the center of attention the whole time.
(A) who B whom C which

2 There's a new magazine on the market ____ you how to play guitar.
(A) that teaches B taught C teaching

3 Barbara is an only child, ____ a lot about her behavior.
A explaining (B) which explains C that explains

4 Isn't this the same place ____ we saw on the way here?
A what (B) – C where

5 The wedding I went to, ____ was in Albuquerque, was very nice.
A where B that (C) which

6 According to some parents, children ____ to break rules become more independent.
(A) taught B teaching C that taught

7 That's the priest ____ conducted the wedding ceremony. Doesn't he look different in casual clothes?
A – (B) that C which

3.2 Future forms

Future Continuous

We use the Future Continuous:

- to talk about actions that will be in progress at a particular time in the future:
  *This time tomorrow we**'ll be flying** to the Bahamas.*
- to talk about planned or routine future events, actions or situations:
  ***I'll be going** to the supermarket after work.*
- to form polite questions or requests:
  ***Will** you be **taking** the first aid course this month?*
  ***Will** you be **using** your car tomorrow?* (because I'd like to borrow it)

Affirmative	Negative
I/You/He/She/It/We/They 'll (will) be sleeping.	I/You/He/She/It/We/They won't (will not) be sleeping.

Yes/No questions	Short answers
Will I/you/he/she/it/we/they be sleeping?	Yes, I/you/he/she/it/we/they **will**. No, I/you/he/she/it/we/they **won't**.

Wh- questions	Subject questions
How long will I/you/he/she/it/we/they be sleeping?	Who will be sleeping?

Future Perfect Simple

We use the Future Perfect Simple to talk about actions or situations that will be completed before a certain time in the future:

*They **will have crossed** the border by five o'clock.*

Affirmative	Negative
I/You/He/She/It/We/They will have finished by ten o'clock.	I/You/He/She/It/We/They won't (will not) have finished by ten o'clock.

Yes/No questions	Short answers
Will I/you/he/she/it/we/they have finished by ten o'clock?	Yes, I/you/he/she/it/we/they **will**. No, I/you/he/she/it/we/they **won't**.

Wh- questions	Subject questions
When will I/you/he/she/it/we/they have finished?	Who will have finished by ten o'clock?

Future Perfect Continuous

We use the Future Perfect Continuous to talk about actions or states that will have been in progress for some time by a certain time in the future:

*By the end of the year we **will have been living** in Toronto for eight years.*

Affirmative	Negative
I/You/He/She/It/We/They will have been working for ten hours.	I/You/He/She/It/We/They won't (will not) have been working for ten hours.

Yes/No questions	Short answers
Will I/you/he/she/it/we/they have been working for ten hours?	Yes, I/you/he/she/it/we/they **will**. No, I/you/he/she/it/we/they **won't**.

Wh- questions	Subject questions
How long will I/you/he/she/it/we/they have been working?	Who will have been working for ten hours?

Typical time expressions used with the Future Perfect Simple and Future Perfect Continuous are:

- *by 2030/next month/next year*
- *by then*
- *by the time*
- *in two days/three weeks/one month's time/ten years' time*

Complete the sentences with the correct future form of the verbs in parentheses.

1 This time next week I _________ (work) here for three years. Doesn't time fly?
2 Robert can't meet us at 6 p.m. He _________ (not finish) his homework by then.
3 _________ (you/read) that book by Friday? I promised to lend it to George.
4 Tomorrow Magda _________ (visit) her grandfather, so we can't meet for coffee as we usually do.
5 I _________ (be) couch surfing three years in a row after this summer.
6 This article says we _________ (not live) in space for at least another 200 years.
7 _________ (you/collect) Marge from the train station tomorrow or do I need to go?

3.2
1 will have been working
2 won't have finished
3 Will you have read
4 will be visiting
5 will have been
6 won't be living
7 Will you collect/Will you be collecting

3.5 Quantifiers

Quantifiers	Countable nouns	Uncountable nouns
every, each, all	each/every **Each/Every** *book cost $10.* all **All the** *books were quite cheap.*	 **All the** *furniture was quite cheap.*
most	most **Most** *books were quite cheap.*	**Most of the** *furniture was quite cheap.*
whole	whole *I've read the* **whole** *book.*	
many, much, a great deal of, a lot of, lots of, loads of, plenty of	many *Do you have* **many** *books?* *I don't have* **many** *books.* a lot of/ lots of/loads of/plenty of *I have* **a lot of/lots of/loads of/plenty of** *books.*	much/a great deal of *Do you have* **much/a great deal of** *furniture?* *I don't have* **much/a great deal of** *furniture.* *I have* **a lot of/lots of/loads of/plenty of** *furniture.*
a number of, several, a few, a couple of, a little, some	a number of/several/a few/a couple of *I have* **a number of/several/a few/a couple of** *books.* some *I have* **some** *books.*	a little *I have* **a little** *furniture.* *I have* **some** *furniture.*
few, little	few *I have very* **few** *books.*	little *I have* **little** *furniture.*
both	both **Both** *of these books are mine.*	
either	either *You can buy* **either** *book.*	
neither	neither **Neither** *book was expensive.*	
no, none of	no *I have* **no** *books.* none of **None of** *the books belongs to me.*	 *I have* **no** *furniture.* **None of** *the furniture belongs to me.*

- *A few* and *a little* have a similar meaning to *some*, whereas *few* and *little* mean 'not as many or as much as we'd like'.
  We're staying in London for **a few** *days.*
  He has **few** *interests outside his work.*
  Don't worry, we still have **a little** *time left.*
  Unfortunately, there is **little** *hope of success.*
- The following quantifiers are always used with the preposition *of*: *a number of, a couple of, a great deal of, a lot of, lots of, loads of, plenty of, none of.*
- All other quantifiers (except *no* and *every*) can be used with the preposition *of*, if it is followed by a personal pronoun, a pronoun (possessive or demonstrative) + noun, or the article *the*.
  Most *shops/***Most of the** *shops were open.*
  Julio spent **most of** *his life on a farm.*
  Most *research/***Most of the** *research was carried out in the US.*
  A few of us *took a taxi home.*

another/other/others

another	+ singular countable noun or the pronoun *one*

*Can I have **another** cup of tea?*
*We're visiting one museum today and **another** one tomorrow.*

other	+ plural noun or the pronoun *ones*

*I've got **other** doubts, too.*
*These rolls are stale. Do you have any **other** ones?*

the others	-

*Are you alone? Where are **the others**?*

- Use *another* when you mean one more person of the same thing, additional.
- Use *other* when you mean *different* people or things to the ones you've already mentioned.
- Use *the other* when you refer to the second of two people or things, the one you haven't already mentioned.
- Use *the others* to refer to all the people or things in a group apart from the one you have already mentioned.

Choose the correct answer, A, B, C, or D.

1 I'm afraid only ________ people decided to come, so we won't be putting on the show.
(A) a few B little C few
2 I hear that ________ people are unaware of the plans to build a parking lot in the center of town.
A most of (B) most C none of
3 The principal said that ________ of the students that caused the fire will be allowed to go on the trip.
(A) none B no C very little
4 This apartment has a slightly bigger living room than the other one we saw, but I'm afraid ________ of them have cable TV.
A either B both (C) neither
5 Why is there only ________ water left? Barbara bought three bottles for the trip.
A any B a few (C) a little
6 We have decided that ________ students that contribute to the school website will receive a small prize.
A each (B) all C every
7 There is very ________ nightlife in Richmond, so you'll have to provide your own entertainment.
(A) little B a little C few
8 A ________ of people think New York City is the best place to live.
(A) lot B lots C loads
9 We have ________ bread left. We need to buy some more.
(A) little B few C loads of
10 ________ dogs are very friendly.
A Neither B Either (C) Both
11 This cake is delicious! Can I have ________ piece?
A other B others (C) another
12 I'm sorry, we are completely booked. You can try ________ hostels in town.
(A) other B another C others

4.2 Question tags and reply questions

Question tags

- Question tags are short questions added at the end of the sentence to ask for confirmation (falling intonation) or ask a question (rising intonation).
- We form question tags using an auxiliary (e.g. *be, do, have*) or modal verb (e.g. *can, should*) and the pronoun corresponding to the subject (e.g. *I, you, she, they*).
- Question tags for affirmative sentences are usually negative:
*You've already been to this coffee shop, **haven't you?***
*They **made** a formal complaint, **didn't they?***
- Question tags for negative sentences are usually affirmative:
*She **can't** swim, **can she?***
*You **aren't** going to reduce the price, **are you?***
- The question tag for *I am* is **aren't I?**:
I'm** late, **aren't I?
- In imperative sentences we use the question tag **will you?**:
Wait** for me here, **will you?
Don't spend** too much, **will you?
- The question tag for *let's* is **shall we?**:
Let's** meet for a coffee later, **shall we?
- In sentences where the pronoun *something* or *nothing* is the subject, we use a question tag with the pronoun *it*. If the subject is *nothing*, we always use an affirmative question tag:
Something** is wrong, **isn't it?
Nothing** can be done, **can it?
- In sentences with adverbs such as *never, rarely, seldom, hardly,* or *barely*, we use an affirmative question tag:
*I **hardly** know you, **do I?***
*They **never** listen to you, **do they?***
- In sentences with *everybody, everyone, no one,* or *nobody* as the subject, we use a question tag with the pronoun *they* and the plural form of the verb. If the subject is *no one* or *nobody*, we always use an affirmative question tag:
Everybody/Everyone** will ask questions, **won't they?
Nobody/No one** signed up for the dressmaking class, **did they?
- In sentences with the pronoun *that* as the subject, we use a question tag with the pronoun *it*.
That's** your new car over there, **isn't it?
- In sentences with *there is/there are* (in all tenses), we repeat the pronoun *there* in the question tag:
***There** was a security alarm in the store, **wasn't there**?*
***There** won't be any problems with the complaint, **will there**?*

Reply questions

We use reply questions to show interest in what somebody is saying and to signal that we want more details.

- With affirmative sentences, we use affirmative reply questions:
*'I **went** to the gym yesterday.' '**Did you**?'*
*'Your dad **lent** me some money.' '**Did he**?'*
- With negative sentences, we use negative reply questions:
*'Chris and Lisa **aren't flying** to Japan after all.' '**Aren't they?**'*
*'I **never buy** shoes online.' '**Don't you?**'*

GRAMMAR FOCUS

Complete the sentences with question tags or reply questions.

1 You've forgotten to mail my letters, haven't you ?
2 Frank can lend you some money, can't he ?
3 No matter what we do, nothing will change, will it ?
4 Don't get lost, will you ?
5 A: I'm not going to the movies tomorrow.
B: Aren't you ?
6 A: My brother never buys anything online.
B: Doesn't he ?
7 Everybody decided not to visit the museum, didn't they ?

4.5 Present and past modal structures

The present

To give advice or express necessity/lack of necessity, we use:

- *should/shouldn't* and *ought to/oughtn't to*:
  You ***should/ought to eat*** *more fruit and vegetables.*
  You ***shouldn't/oughtn't to spend*** *so much on clothes.*
- *must/mustn't*:
  You ***must try*** *fish spa – it's really wonderful!*
  You ***mustn't spoil*** *me like this – you're too generous!*
- *need to/don't need to*:
  You ***need to study*** *harder to pass this exam.*
  I can hear you, you ***don't need to shout****.*
- *had better/had better not*:
  *You****'d better check*** *the price online before you buy a phone here.*
  *You****'d better not be*** *late this time.*

The past

- To say that something was or wasn't necessary, we use *had to/didn't have to*:
  Ella's car broke down, so she ***had to*** *take a taxi.*
  Luckily, I ***didn't have to*** *wait long.*
- To express regret or criticism about something that happened or didn't happen, or to give advice, we use *ought (not) to/should (not)* + *have* + past participle:
  We ***should have booked/ought to have booked*** *a different hotel. This one is terrible.*
  My parents ***shouldn't have sold/oughtn't to have sold*** *their camper van.*
- To say that an action was not necessary, we can also use *didn't need to* + infinitive:
  I ***didn't need to cook*** *dinner for the children yesterday because they were away.*
- *Must* and *had better* are not used in the past.

Complete the sentences with the correct form of the verbs in parentheses and a modal structure. Sometimes more than one answer is possible.

1 You really shouldn't have told (tell) her that I was leaving. I thought I could trust you not to say anything.
2 My train was canceled but fortunately, I didn't have to wait (wait) long for another.
3 It wasn't until they got to the auction that they realized they didn't have to buy (buy) tickets in advance. There were still plenty on sale on the door.
4 Apparently, Patricia had to return (return) the shoes the next day because the sole came off.
5 You must/should apologize (apologize) for the mistake. Simon was very upset.
6 I didn't realize we had to dress (dress) up. No wonder they wouldn't let me in wearing these baggy jeans!
7 You really shouldn't/don't need to worry (worry) about the driving test. I'm sure you'll be fine.

5.2 Reported speech

- In Reported Speech we change the following:
  - time expressions and words referring to places (depending on the context).
  - demonstrative pronouns, personal pronouns, object pronouns, and possessive adjectives (depending on the context).
  - most tenses in affirmative sentences and in questions, but only when the reporting verb is in the past tense (e.g. *he said, she told me, he asked*).
- If the reporting verb is in the present tense (e.g. Present Simple or Present Perfect), we do not change the tense in Reported Speech:
  *'I****'m not*** *satisfied with your performance.'* →
  The teacher ***has said*** *she* ***is not*** *satisfied with my performance.*
  'How ***do*** *you* ***handle*** *stress?'* →
  She ***wants to know*** *how I* ***handle*** *stress.*
- Even when the reporting verb is in the past tense, we do not change the following in Reported Speech:
  - verbs in the Past Perfect Simple and Past Perfect Continuous:
    'Before my resignation I ***had been working*** *on an environmental project.'* →
    The candidate said that before his resignation he ***had been working*** *on an environmental project.*
    *'****Had*** *you ever* ***been*** *to a job interview before that last one?'* →
    I asked my neighbor if she ***had*** *ever* ***been*** *to a job interview before that last one.*
  - modal verbs *would, should, could, might* and *must*.
    'During the interview you ***should*** *try to make eye contact.'* → *The advisor told me that during the interview I* ***should*** *try to make eye contact.*
    'We ***must*** *all try harder.'* → *The manager said that we* ***must*** *all try harder.*

Report the statements and questions.

1 'You need to fill out an application form.'
She says *(that) you need to fill out an application form* .

2 'Can you wait here for a few minutes?'
She wants to know *if you/we can wait here for a few minutes* .

3 'I really love my new job.'
Ben told me *(that) he really loves his new job* .

4 'I'd like to express my interest in this vacant post.'
He said *(that) he would like to express his interest in that vacant post* .

5 'Could you give me the report by noon today?'
John asked *(me) if I could give him the report by noon that day* .

6 'I had never had a job interview before.'
Paula said *(that) she had never had a job interview before* .

7 'Did you get the job?'
She wants to know *if I got the job* .

5.5 Reporting verbs

say and *tell*

We usually use the verbs *say* or *tell* to report what someone said:

- *say*
  He ***said*** *(that) he was getting married.*
- *say* + *to* + object
  He ***said to me*** *(that) he was getting married.*
- *tell* + object
  He ***told me*** *(that) he was getting married.*

Verbs without a direct object

- verb + (*that*) (e.g. *add, admit, agree, claim, complain, deny, explain, insist, promise, propose, recommend, regret, suggest*):
  'I wasted a lot of money.' →
  Sue ***complained (that)*** *she had wasted a lot of money.*
- verb + to-infinitive (e.g. *agree, claim, decide, offer, promise, refuse, threaten*):
  'I'll hire two new employees.' →
  The manager ***decided to hire*** *two new employees.*
- verb + *-ing* form (e.g. *admit, deny, propose, recommend, regret, suggest*):
  'I didn't take the money.' →
  The cashier ***denied taking*** *the money.*
- verb + preposition + *-ing* form (e.g. *apologize for, insist on, object to*):
  'I'm sorry I was rude.' →
  I ***apologized for being*** *rude.*

Verbs with a direct object

- verb + object + (*that*) (e.g. *advise, assure, convince, inform, persuade, promise, remind, tell, warn*):
  'The meeting will start in an hour.' →
  The secretary ***reminded them (that)*** *the meeting would start in an hour.*
- verb + object + to-infinitive (e.g. *advise, ask, beg, convince, encourage, invite, order, persuade, recommend, remind, tell, warn, urge*):
  'You really should apply for this job.' →
  Everybody ***encouraged me to apply*** *for that job.*
- verb + object + preposition + *-ing* form (e.g. *accuse sb of, blame sb for, criticize sb for, congratulate sb on, praise sb for, suspect sb of, thank sb for*):
  'It's your fault that the car was damaged.' →
  Joe's boss ***blames him for damaging*** *the car.*

Complete the sentences with the correct form of the verbs in parentheses.

1 She reminded me *to fulfill* (fulfil) my duties.
2 Jonathan suggested *hiring* (hire) an interior designer.
3 She persuaded me *not to step down* (not step down).
4 I was blamed *for causing* (cause) unnecessary problems.
5 He threatened *to tell* (tell) the boss about my lack of experience.
6 She congratulated me *on winning* (win) first prize.
7 Would you advise me *to take* (take) a course in accountancy?

6.2 Conditional clauses – alternatives to *if*

To form Zero, First, Second and Third Conditional sentences, we can use the following words and structures:

- *if*
  If *we had retouched the photo, you would have looked younger.*
- *unless*
  I won't tell you what happened ***if*** *you* ***don't*** *promise to keep it secret.* →
  I won't tell you what happened ***unless*** *you promise to keep it secret.*
- *provided* (*that*)/*providing* (*that*)
  You can go with us ***if*** *you pay for your own meals.* →
  You can go with us, ***provided that*** *you pay for your own meals.*
- *Imagine … or Suppose/Supposing …* (in questions):
  If someone published a private email from you on Facebook, would you be angry? →
  Imagine/Suppose/Supposing *someone published a private email from you on Facebook, would you be angry?*

GRAMMAR FOCUS

Inversion

- We use inversion in formal language, mostly in writing, to emphasize the rhetorical effect of the sentence.
- We can use inversion in sentences with the auxiliary verbs *were* and *had*. The verb *were* is also used with the first and third person singular:
  If it ***were*** *my photograph, I wouldn't let anyone publish it.* →
  Were *it my photograph, I would not let anyone publish it.*
  If I ***had considered*** *all the aspects more carefully, I would probably have made the right decision.* →
  Had *I* ***considered*** *all the aspects more carefully, I would probably have made the right decision.*
- We can also use inversion with *should* if we want to say that the condition is rather improbable. Note that *should* in these types of sentences doesn't imply obligation:
  If *you* ***are dissatisfied*** *with the product, you are entitled to a refund.* (the least formal) →
  If *you* ***should be*** *dissatisfied with the product, you are entitled to a refund.* (more formal) →
  Should *you* ***be*** *dissatisfied with the product, you are entitled to a refund.* (the most formal)
- When using inversion, we do not use contractions with negatives in the dependent clauses:
  If I ***hadn't told*** *the police the truth, an innocent person would have been arrested.* →
  Had *I* ***not told*** *the police the truth, an innocent person would have been arrested.*

Choose the correct options.

1 I won't help you *if* / *unless* you stop misleading me.
2 I'll lend you the book *providing* / *supposing* you give it back to me on Friday.
3 You would never have met her *unless* / *if* you hadn't come with us that night.
4 *Providing* / *Supposing* I refuse to doctor the picture, what would you do?
5 *Imagine* / *Provided* you won the lottery, what would you buy?
6 *Had I not* / *Hadn't I distorted* the truth, there would have been even more trouble.
7 *Should* / *If* you be unhappy with the portrait, you can always get a photo taken.

6.5 Mixed conditionals

We can mix Second and Third Conditional forms, creating mixed conditional sentences Type I or Type II.

Mixed conditionals Type I: *if* + Past Simple, *would/wouldn't have* + past participle

We use Type I mixed conditionals to speculate about permanent states or situations that had a result in the past:
If Sergio ***didn't speak*** *English with an accent, he* ***wouldn't have been recognized*** *and arrested last month.*
(But because he speaks with an accent, he was arrested.)
If I ***was taller,*** *I* ***would have gotten*** *the main role in the school play.* (But I didn't get the role because I'm not taller.)

Mixed conditionals Type II: *if* + Past Perfect, *would/wouldn't* + infinitive

We use Type II mixed conditionals to speculate about past events that didn't happen, and this has certain effects or consequences in the present:
If she ***hadn't split up*** *with Harold two years ago, Gina* ***wouldn't be*** *so unhappy now.* (But she did, and now she is unhappy.)
He ***would be*** *a free man now if the police* ***had stopped*** *looking for him then.* (But the police didn't stop looking, and he isn't free.)
As with all types of conditionals, we can use *could*, *might*, or *should* instead of *would* in mixed conditional sentences.

Complete the sentences with the correct form of the verbs in parentheses.

1 If she __hadn't had__ (not have) plastic surgery, she __wouldn't look__ (not look) so good now.
2 Jared __would be__ (be) a much better actor today if he __had taken__ (take) lessons when he was younger.
3 I hope she appreciated your help. I __wouldn't have helped__ (not help) her if I __were__ (be) you.
4 If you __hadn't eaten__ (not eat) so much, you __wouldn't feel__ (feel) sick now.
5 She __wouldn't be__ (be) angry with you now if you __had told__ (tell) the truth this morning.
6 If Gina __was/were__ (be) a better liar, they __might have believed__ (might/believe) the story she told them.

7.2 Advanced passive forms

Passive forms with modal structures

We can use the passive:

- with modal verbs in the present (modal verb + *be* + past participle):
  The project ***must be completed*** *by tomorrow.*
  Cell phones ***may be used*** *as directed by the staff.*
- with modal verbs in the past (modal verb + *have been* + past participle):
  The contest ***should have been canceled*** *after the accident.*
  The server ***couldn't have been repaired*** *properly yesterday.*
  Her Facebook profile ***must have been removed*** *because I can't find it.*

Passive forms with verbs that take two objects

- Some verbs, e.g. *ask, bring, buy, give, hand, offer, pay, promise, sell, send, show, teach, tell*, etc., can take a direct and an indirect object:
  The general manager promised ***John*** (direct object) ***a raise***. (indirect object)
  The students gave ***the teacher*** (direct object) ***a bunch of flowers***. (indirect object)

- Depending on what we want to emphasize, we can begin with either the direct or the indirect object:
  ***A raise** was promised to John by the general manager.* (indirect object becomes the subject, with emphasis on *a raise*)
  ***John** was promised a raise by the general manager.* (direct object becomes the subject, with emphasis on *John*)
  ***A bunch of flowers** was given to the teacher by the students.* (indirect object becomes the subject, with emphasis on *a bunch of flowers*)
  ***The teacher** was given a bunch of flowers by the students.* (direct object becomes the subject, with emphasis on *the teacher*)

Passive infinitive and *-ing* forms

- After verbs and phrases followed by an *-ing* form (e.g. *be interested in, can't stand, don't mind, enjoy, get tired of, hate, like/dislike, love, miss*) we form the passive *-ing* form with *being* + past participle:
  *My teacher **doesn't mind being asked** millions of questions.*
  *I **got tired of being criticized** for my ideas.*
- After verbs and phrases followed by a *to*-infinitive (e.g. *can't afford, choose, decide, hope, need, prefer, pretend, refuse, want, would like*) we form the passive infinitive with *to be* + past participle:
  *Millions of people **hope to be cured** of the disease.*
  *At some point your son will **need to be told** the truth.*

The passive of *make somebody do something*

- In the passive we use the *to*-infinitive after *made*:
  *My mom **made me clean** my room.* (Active)
  *I **was made to clean** my room (by my mom).* (Passive)

Complete the second sentence so that it has a similar meaning to the first, using the word in capitals. Do not change the word in capitals.

1 It's a bad idea not to address all the issues. **OUGHT**
All the issues ___ought to be___ addressed.
2 Everybody could hear the music despite closing the windows. **COULD**
The music ___could be heard___ despite closing the windows.
3 She had shown me the password the previous day. **HAD**
I ___had been shown the password___ the previous day.
4 They said that I mustn't go online. **TOLD**
I ___was told not to___ go online.
5 I don't like it when someone orders me around. **BEING**
I ___don't like being ordered___ around.
6 The babysitter made the children go to bed early. **MADE**
The children ___were made to go to___ bed early by the babysitter.
7 I'm sure somebody stole my sunglasses. **MUST**
My glasses ___must have been stolen___ .

7.5 Passive reporting structures

Impersonal passive structures

To talk about general opinions and views, we use verbs such as *agree, believe, claim, consider, expect, feel, hope, know, report, say, think, understand,* etc., and the following structures:

- *it* + passive verb (present or past) + *that*:
  People generally claim that optimists live longer. →
  ***It is** generally **claimed that** optimists live longer.*
  People believed that Mathematics was the link between God and the world. →
  *It **was believed that** Mathematics was the link between God and the world.*
- subject + passive verb (present or past) + *to*-infinitive:
  People consider wearable technology to be the future of computing. →
  ***Wearable technology is considered to be** the future of computing.*
  People know that almonds protect against diabetes and high blood pressure. →
  ***Almonds are known to protect** against diabetes and high blood pressure.*
- subject + passive verb (present or past) + *to have* + past participle:
  People believe that the earthquake has killed more than 1,000 people. →
  ***The earthquake is believed to have killed** more than 1,000 people.*
  The press previously reported that the company's profit had reached $100 million. →
  ***The company's profit was** previously **reported to have** reached $100 million.*
- *there* + passive verb (present or past) + *to be*:
  People expect that there will be a rise in the number of jobs offered across the US. →
  ***There is expected to be** a rise in the number of jobs offered across the US.*
- *there* + passive verb (present or past) + *to have been*
  People think that there were over twenty inventors who invented various light sources before Edison. →
  ***There are thought to have been** over twenty inventors who invented various light sources before Edison.*

GRAMMAR FOCUS

Rewrite the sentences using impersonal passive structures.

1 Many people consider Bob Dylan to be the most influential musician of the twentieth century.
Bob Dylan *is considered to be the most influential musician of the twentieth century*.

2 In February, newspapers reported that crime levels were falling faster.
It *was reported in February that crime levels were falling faster*.

3 Linguists expect that by 2050, 7,000 languages will disappear.
7,000 languages *will disappear/will have disappeared by 2050*.

4 Nutritionists say that kale is the most nutrient-dense food there is.
Kale *is said to be the most nutrient-dense food there is*.

5 Palaeontologists think there were over 500 different species of dinosaur.
There *are thought to have been over 500 different species of dinosaur*.

6 Experts believe that 1.24 million people were killed in road traffic accidents in 2010.
Road traffic accidents *are believed to have killed 1.24 million people in 2010*.

7 We now know that cats are able to produce about ninety different sounds more than dogs.
Cats *are known to be able to produce about ninety different sounds* more than dogs.

8.2 Unreal past and regrets – *wish, if only, it's time,* and *would rather*

Present and future

- To express regret about a present situation that seems to be impossible to change, we use *wish/if only* + subject + Past Simple:
- *Wish* and *if only* have a similar meaning, but *if only* is more emphatic than *wish*. It expresses greater regret:
  I ***wish I knew*** *more about ecology.*
  I ***wish oceans*** *weren't used as garbage dumps.*
  If only we could *save sea animals from starvation.*
  If only I didn't have *to work so much.*
- To say that we believe somebody should do something in the present or in the near future, we use *it's (about) time* + subject + Past Simple:
  It's about time people stopped *driving cars in cities.*
  It's about time you started *recycling your garbage.*
- To say what we would prefer somebody to do in the present or future, we use *would rather* + subject + Past Simple:
  I'd rather we switched *to organic fruit and vegetables.*
  My mom ***would rather I didn't eat*** *in my room.*

Past

To express regret about a past situation, we use *wish/if only* + subject + Past Perfect:
I ***wish we had done*** *more to prevent this tragedy.*
My ex-boyfriend ***wishes we hadn't broken up***.
If only the city council hadn't reduced *the funds for environmental protection.*
If only I had listened *to you when you advised me not to go on that expedition!*

Choose the correct options.

1 If only I *lost* / *hadn't lost* / *didn't lose* my camera on the beach that day. (*hadn't lost*)

2 It's about time we *stop* / *stopped* / *had stopped* dumping waste in the seas. (*stopped*)

3 My back's all red. I wish I *had* / *did* / *would* put on more sun block. (*had*)

4 I'd rather she *couldn't* / *didn't* / *won't* go swimming alone. (*didn't*)

5 If only I *hadn't to* / *had to* / *didn't have to* go camping. I hate sleeping in tents. (*didn't have to*)

6 I wish you *knew* / *had known* / *know* just how much effort I put into this trip. (*knew*)

7 If only I had *seen* / *saw* / *did see* her earlier. I'd have asked her to join us. (*seen*)

8.5 Emphasis – cleft sentences and inversion

Cleft sentences

- Cleft sentences are used to give emphasis to the person performing an action or to the place, time, or reason of the action:
  I love helping other people. →
  What I really love *is helping other people.*
- They start with *what, it* or *all*:
  The company covered up the scandal. →
  What the company did was (to) cover up *the scandal.*
  I raised the subject of sewage being dumped into the river. →
  It was me who raised *the subject of sewage being dumped into the river.*
  We helped the flood victims clean up the debris. →
  All we did was (to) help *the flood victims clean up the debris.*
  You need love. → ***All you need is*** *love.*

Inversion

- We use inversion in sentences that start with negative adverbs, e.g. *never, rarely, seldom, hardly, barely, scarcely, no sooner*, or phrases with *no* or *not*, e.g. *under no circumstances, on no condition, on no account, at no time, in no way, not until, not only*. In these sentences an affirmative sentence takes on the order and verb form of a question: negative adverb/phrase with *no* or *not* + auxiliary verb + subject + main verb:
  He had never been so devastated. →
  Never had he been *so devastated.*
  We rarely hear about such powerful mother and child bonds in animals. →
  Rarely do we hear *about such powerful mother and child bonds in animals.*
  She had not only survived the disaster, but she had saved two other people as well. →
  Not only had she survived *the disaster, but she had saved two other people as well.*
  You are not permitted to leave the building under any circumstances. →
  Under no circumstances are you permitted *to leave the building.*

Rewrite the sentences to add emphasis.

1 Tess promised to help clean up the yard.
It was *Tess who promised to help clean up the yard* .
2 We are only handing out leaflets in protest.
All *we are doing is handing out leaflets in protest* .
3 She has never been so disappointed by the results.
Never *has she been so disappointed by the results* .
4 You are not going out in that raging storm under any circumstances.
Under *no circumstances are you going out in that raging storm* .
5 I want to know who started the violence.
What *I want to know is who started the violence* .
6 We rarely see such high temperatures at this time of year.
Rarely *do we see such high temperatures at this time of year* .
7 They had just gotten back to the apartment when they heard the news.
Hardly *had they gotten back to the apartment when they heard the news*
8 I don't believe in telling lies.
What *I don't believe in is telling lies* .

IRREGULAR VERBS

Infinitive	Past Simple	Past participle
be [bi]	was/were [wɑz/wɚ]	been [bin]
beat [bit]	beat [bit]	beaten [bitn]
become [bɪ'kʌm]	became [bɪ'keɪm]	become [bɪ'kʌm]
begin [bɪ'gɪn]	began [bɪ'gæn]	begun [bɪ'gʌn]
bite [baɪt]	bit [bɪt]	bitten ['bɪtn]
break [breɪk]	broke [broʊk]	broken ['broʊkən]
bring [brɪŋ]	brought [brɔt]	brought [brɔt]
broadcast ['brɔdkæst]	broadcast ['brɔdkæst]	broadcast ['brɔdkæst]
build [bɪld]	built [bɪlt]	built [bɪlt]
burn [bɚn]	burned [bɚnd]	burned [bɚnd]
burst [bɚst]	burst [bɚst]	burst [bɚst]
buy [baɪ]	bought [bɔt]	bought [bɔt]
can [kæn]	could [kʊd]	been able to [bin 'eɪbl tə]
catch [kætʃ]	caught [kɔt]	caught [kɔt]
choose [tʃuz]	chose [tʃoʊz]	chosen ['tʃoʊzn]
come [kʌm]	came [keɪm]	come [kʌm]
cost [kɑst]	cost [kɑst]	cost [kɑst]
cut [kʌt]	cut [kʌt]	cut [kʌt]
deal [dil]	dealt [dɛlt]	dealt [dɛlt]
dig [dɪg]	dug [dʌg]	dug [dʌg]
do [du]	did [dɪd]	done [dʌn]
draw [drɔ]	drew [dru]	drawn [drɔn]
dream [drim]	dreamed [drimd]	dreamed [drimd]
drink [drɪnk]	drank [dræŋk]	drunk [drʌnk]
drive [draɪv]	drove [droʊv]	driven ['drɪvn]
eat [it]	ate [eɪt]	eaten ['itn]
fall [fɔl]	fell [fɛl]	fallen ['fɔln]
feed [fid]	fed [fɛd]	fed [fɛd]
feel [fil]	felt [fɛlt]	felt [fɛlt]
fight [faɪt]	fought [fɔt]	fought [fɔt]
find [faɪnd]	found [faʊnd]	found [faʊnd]
fit [fɪt]	fit [fɪt]	fit [fɪt]
fly [flaɪ]	flew [flʊ]	flown [floʊn]
forget [fɚ'gɛt]	forgot [fɚ'gɑt]	forgotten [fɚ'gɑtn]
forgive [fɚ'gɪv]	forgave [fɚ'geɪv]	forgiven [fɚ'gɪvn]
freeze [friz]	froze [froʊz]	frozen ['froʊzən]
get [gɛt]	got [gɑt]	got [gɑt]
give [gɪv]	gave [geɪv]	given ['gɪvn]
go [goʊ]	went [wɛnt]	gone [gɑn]/
grow [groʊ]	grew [gru]	grown [groʊn]
hang [hæŋ]	hung [hʌŋ]	hung [hʌŋ]
have [hæv]	had [hæd]	had [hæd]
hear [hɪr]	heard [hɚd]	heard [hɚd]
hide [haɪd]	hid [hɪd]	hidden ['hɪdn]
hit [hɪt]	hit [hɪt]	hit [hɪt]
hold [hoʊld]	held [hɛld]	held [hɛld]
hurt [hɚt]	hurt [hɚt]	hurt [hɚt]
keep [kip]	kept [kɛpt]	kept [kɛpt]
know [noʊ]	knew [nyʊ]	known [noʊn]
lead [lid]	led [lɛd]	led [lɛd]
leap [lip]	leapt [lɛpt]	leapt [lɛpt]
learn [lɚn]	learned [lɚnd]	learned [lɚnd]
leave [liv]	left [lɛft]	left [lɛft]
lend [lɛnd]	lent [lɛnt]	lent [lɛnt]
let [lɛt]	let [lɛt]	let [lɛt]
lie [laɪ]	lay [leɪ]	lain [leɪn]
light [laɪt]	lit [lɪt]	lit [lɪt]
lose [luz]	lost [lɑst]	lost [lɑst]
make [meɪk]	made [meɪd]	made [meɪd]
mean [min]	meant [mɛnt]	meant [mɛnt]
meet [mit]	met [mɛt]	met [mɛt]
pay [peɪ]	paid [peɪd]	paid [peɪd]
put [pʊt]	put [pʊt]	put [pʊt]
read [rid]	read [rɛd]	read [rɛd]
ride [raɪd]	rode [roʊd]	ridden ['rɪdn]
ring [rɪŋ]	rang [ræŋ]	rung [rʌŋ]
run [rʌn]	ran [ræn]	run [rʌn]
say [seɪ]	said [sɛd]	said [sɛd]
see [si]	saw [sɔ]	seen [sin]
sell [sɛl]	sold [soʊld]	sold [soʊld]
send [sɛnd]	sent [sɛnt]	sent [sɛnt]
set [sɛt]	set [sɛt]	set [sɛt]
shine [ʃaɪn]	shone [ʃɑn]	shone [ʃɑn]
show [ʃoʊ]	showed [ʃoʊd]	shown [ʃoʊn]
shut [ʃʌt]	shut [ʃʌt]	shut [ʃʌt]
sing [sɪŋ]	sang [sæŋ]	sung [sʌŋ]
sit [sɪt]	sat [sæt]	sat [sæt]
sleep [slip]	slept [slɛpt]	slept [slɛpt]
slide [slaɪd]	slid [slɪd]	slid [slɪd]
smell [smɛl]	smelled [smɛld]	smelled [smɛld]
speak [spik]	spoke [spoʊk]	spoken ['spoʊkən]
speed [spid]	sped [spɛd]	sped [spɛd]
spend [spɛnd]	spent [spɛnt]	spent [spɛnt]
spill [spɪl]	spilled [spɪld]	spilled [spɪld]
split [splɪt]	split [splɪt]	split [splɪt]
stand [stæŋd]	stood [stʊd]	stood [stʊd]
steal [stil]	stole [stoʊl]	stolen ['stoʊlən]
stick [stɪk]	stuck [stʌk]	stuck [stʌk]
sting [stɪŋ]	stung [stʌŋ]	stung [stʌŋ]
strike [straɪk]	struck [strʌk]	struck [strʌk]
swear [swɛr]	swore [swɔr]	sworn [swɔrn]
swell [swɛl]	swelled [swɛld]	swollen ['swoʊln]
swim [swɪm]	swam [swæm]	swum [swʌm]
take [teɪk]	took [tʊk]	taken ['teɪkən]
teach [titʃ]	taught [tɔt]	taught [tɔt]
tear [tɛr]	tore [tɔr]	torn [tɔrn]
tell [tɛl]	told [toʊld]	told [toʊld]
think [θɪnk]	thought [θɔt]	thought [θɔt]
throw [θroʊ]	threw [θru]	thrown [θroʊn]
understand [ˌʌndɚ'stænd]	understood [ˌʌndɚ'stʊd]	understood [ˌʌndɚ'stʊd]
upset [ʌp'sɛt]	upset [ʌp'sɛt]	upset [ʌp'sɛt]
wake [weɪk]	woke [woʊk]	woken ['woʊkən]
wear [wɛr]	wore [wɔr]	worn [wɔrn]
win [wɪn]	won [wʌn]	won [wʌn]
write [raɪt]	wrote [roʊt]	written ['rɪtn]

Culture notes

0.1

The Paleo diet is a fad diet based on the notion that we should only eat foods presumably available to our Paleolithic hunter-gatherer ancestors. Its advocates assume that our nutritional needs have not been able to adapt to the foods produced by modern agriculture and that these foods are the foundation of today's obesity and diabetes epidemics. Consequently, the followers of the Paleo diet should avoid grains, legumes (like peas, beans, or soybeans), dairy products, refined sugar and oils, as well as any other processed foods. The staples of the Paleo diet include meat and seafood, non-starchy vegetables, fruit, and nuts. The diet grew in popularity thanks to the 2002 book by Loren Cordain *The Paleo Diet*.

Thai food is the traditional cuisine of Thailand. It is characterized as being aromatic and spicy. One of its fundamental principles is the combination of at least three out of the five basic tastes in a dish or a whole meal, namely sweet, sour, bitter, salty, and spicy. It is also crucially important that Thai food is beautifully presented. The most popular Thai dishes include coconut curries and rice or noodle stir-fries. The typical fragrance and taste of the dishes are attributed to lemon grass, kaffir lime (a type of citrus tree) leaves, chilies, and fish sauce. Most dishes are served with rice, which is the staple ingredient.

0.2

The **FA Cup**, or Football Association Challenge Cup, is the oldest annual soccer competition in the world. It has been held in England since the 1871–1872 season and is organized by the Football Association. Clubs of all standards can participate, providing they qualify, and the tournament has become famous for the fact that teams from the lower divisions get the chance to beat and eliminate top clubs from the tournament and could then theoretically go on to win the Cup. For example, in 2012–2013, 758 clubs took part in the FA Cup tournament and Luton Town beat Norwich City, but were unfortunately knocked out before reaching the final.

A **triathlon** is a three-sport athletic competition. The event is a test of ability, strength, and endurance since the sports are done one after the other. The most common ones include swimming, cycling, and running over various distances. It is believed that the triathlon originated in France in the twentieth century. It was introduced into the Olympics in 2000, in Sydney, Australia. One of the most famous triathlons is the Ironman Triathlon, which takes place in Hawaii.

0.6

Tinie Tempah (b. 1988) is the stage name of Patrick Chukwuemeka Okogwu, an English rapper. He won fame after releasing his 2010 debut album *Disc-Overy*, which brought him two Brit Awards for Best British Breakthrough Act and Best British Single.

Stephen Mangan (b. 1968) is an English actor. He is known for his critically-acclaimed theatrical roles, as well as comedy roles in the British sitcoms *Green Wing* and *I'm Alan Partridge*.

Sara Pascoe (b. 1981) is an English stand-up comedian and actress. She has been performing stand-up since 2007. Her highly-acclaimed show *Sara Pascoe vs History* earned her a nomination for the Foster's Edinburgh Comedy Award 2014 for Best Comedy Show.

0.7

Andy Roddick (b. 1982) is an American tennis player. In 2003 he became the world number one player, according to the ATP (Association of Tennis Professionals) rating. He is well-known for his swift serve and powerful forehand. In 2000 Roddick established the Andy Roddick Foundation with the mission of expanding opportunities for children to learn and succeed. He retired from professional tennis in 2012.

Andy Murray (b. 1987) is a Scottish tennis player. He was ranked world number two on the ATP list in 2009. Murray won the gold medal in the men's singles final at the 2012 London Olympic Games, defeating Roger Federer.

One World Trade Center (1 WTC), initially named the Freedom Tower, is a skyscraper in lower Manhattan, New York City, USA. Standing at a height of 541 meters, this 104-story building is the tallest skyscraper in the USA, and the fourth tallest in the world. It was built on the site of New York's World Trade Center, destroyed in the terrorist attacks of September 11 2001. 1 WTC was designed by the world-famous architect Daniel Libeskind, whose project won the 2002 competition for the building to replace the World Trade Center. The project underwent numerous changes before actual construction began in 2006. 1 WTC opened in November 2014.

The Shard is a skyscraper located in central London. Rising to 309 meters, this 95-story building dominates the skyline of the City of London. It is also the tallest building in the whole European Union. The name of the Shard, or the Shard of Glass as it is sometimes called, reflects the acutely pyramidal shape of the building. The Shard was opened in 2012 and it houses offices, restaurants, a hotel, and a viewing gallery with an open-air observation deck.

Boston is the capital city of the state of Massachusetts on the north-eastern coast of the USA. It was founded by Puritan colonists in 1630, which makes it one of the oldest cities in the USA. It was the scene of some major events of the American Revolution, and as a result of its rich history, it is very popular with tourists. Boston is also famous for being host to the oldest and one of the most prestigious annual marathons in the world. Additionally, the Boston area is where some of the most renowned American universities such as Harvard University and the Massachusetts Institute of Technology are located.

Big Ben is the common name for the main bell of the clock located at the Palace of Westminster (the Houses of Parliament) in London, UK. It is located in the Elizabeth Tower, previously known as the Clock Tower. The tower was renamed to mark the Diamond Jubilee of Queen Elizabeth II in 2012. Big Ben weighs almost 14 tons and it first rang in 1859, one year after the completion of the tower. With some interruptions, it has struck the hours ever since. The sound of Big Ben and the image of its tower are probably the most recognizable icons of London and the UK. The name Big Ben is also informally used to refer to the Elizabeth Tower and the clock, officially known as the Great Westminster Clock.

The Statue of Liberty is a landmark sculpture located on Liberty Island in New York Harbor, New York City, USA. The 93-meter monument depicts a female figure raising a torch in her right hand and holding a tablet in her left hand. The inscription on the tablet is the date of the American Declaration of Independence. The Statue of Liberty was designed by the French sculptor Frédéric Auguste Bartholdi. It was presented to the USA as a gift of friendship from the people of France in 1886. The statue symbolizes freedom and has become one of the most recognizable symbols of the USA. It used to welcome millions of immigrants arriving at the immigrant inspection station on nearby Ellis Island. Since 1984, the Statue of Liberty has been a UNESCO World Heritage Site.

0.8

The United States **Congress** is the legislative branch of the American government, located in the Capitol, Washington, DC. It consists of the Senate (100 Senators elected for six-year terms) and the House of Representatives (435 Representatives elected for two-year terms). Each state is represented by two senators. The number of representatives, however, depends on the size of the state's population.

The **Houses of Parliament** is the common name for the Palace of Westminster, the seat of the British Parliament, which consists of the House of Commons and the House of Lords. It is situated on the River Thames in central London, next to Westminster Bridge. The Palace of Westminster has three main towers, the most famous of which is Elizabeth Tower, commonly referred to as Big Ben. The Palace has been on the UNESCO World Heritage Site list since 1987.

A **constitutional monarchy** is a form of government. The king or queen is the head of the country but they do not have absolute power – their power is limited and defined by the country's laws. Britain has been a constitutional monarchy since the late 1860s.

A **county** is a territorial unit used in some English-speaking countries, mainly for administrative purposes. County boundaries are often based on historical divisions. The word *county* is abbreviated to *Co.* in the UK and Ireland and *Cnty.* in the USA.

Conservatives refers to the Conservative and Unionist Party in the UK. It is a big center-right political party, founded in 1834 from the Tory Party. The Conservatives are still called Tories. The party strongly supports a free-market economy and is often associated with conservative values and Euroskepticism. Some well-known Conservative Prime Ministers are: Winston Churchill, Margaret Thatcher, John Major, and David Cameron.

Labour refers to the Labour Party in the UK, the main rival of the Conservatives. It is a left-of-center political party, formed in 1900. Its main goal is to represent the interests of ordinary working people and support social equality. Some well-known Labour Prime Ministers were: Clement Attlee and Tony Blair.

Democrats is the popular name for the Democratic Party, one of the two major political parties in the USA. Formed in 1828, it is the world's oldest political party. Over the years it has changed its political profile and become a center-left party that supports organized labor and the civil rights of minorities and advocates government intervention and regulation in the economy. Among the fifteen Democrats who have held the office of US president are: Franklin D. Roosevelt (1933–1945), Harry S. Truman (1945–1953), John F. Kennedy (1961–1963), Jimmy Carter (1977–1981), Bill Clinton (1993–2001), and Barack Obama, the first African American president.

Republicans is the common name for the Republican Party, one of the two major political parties in the USA. It was founded in 1854 by anti-slavery advocates. The contemporary Republican Party, or the GOP (Grand Old Party), as it is often called, represents American conservatism as opposed to American liberalism, which is associated with the Democrats. It supports free market capitalism and objects to strong government intervention in the economy and the labor market. The first Republican US president was Abraham Lincoln (1861–1865). Other well-known republicans who have served as president are: Ronald Reagan (1981–1989), George Bush (1989–1993), and George W. Bush (2001–2009).

King Harold II (b. circa 1022–d. 1066), or Harold Godwinson, was the last Anglo-Saxon King of England. He was chosen by Witan (the King's Council) to be the successor of King Edward the Confessor, who died without an heir. He ascended the throne on January 6 1066 and only reigned for ten months. He was killed in battle near Hastings on October 14 1066, trying to defend England against the Normans led by William the Conqueror.

William the Conqueror (circa 1028–1087) was the first Norman King of England. As Duke William of Normandy, he challenged King Harold's right to the English throne and, in 1066, he began the Norman conquest of England. Having defeated Harold at the Battle of Hastings on October 14 1066, he marched to London. He was crowned King of England in Westminster Abbey on Christmas Day 1066, which marked the beginning of Norman rule over England. The conquest, however, continued for another five years, bringing death and destruction. William's reign changed England drastically. Almost all Saxon landlords lost their land, which was given to Norman nobles. The organization of the kingdom was based on the feudal system, in which Saxons became an unpaid workforce for the new Norman landlords.

Abraham Lincoln (1809–1865) was the sixteenth president of the USA. He is considered one of the most influential US presidents and he made history by abolishing slavery and preserving the unity of the USA. He had only been in office for one month when the American Civil War broke out in 1861. He took command of the Union in the war, leading it to victory. In 1863 Lincoln issued the Emancipation Proclamation, which announced the freedom of slaves. On April 14 1865, John Wilkes Booth, an actor and Confederate spy, shot Lincoln in Ford's Theatre in Washington, DC. Lincoln died the following day, a month before the Civil War formally ended.

Henry VIII (1491–1547) was King of England, the second monarch of the Tudor dynasty. He reigned from 1509 until his death. Henry VIII is mainly remembered as the founder of the Church of England and as being 'the king with six wives.' The separation from Rome began with Henry's wish to get the Pope's permission to divorce his first wife Catherine of Aragon. The Pope's refusal caused Henry to break away from the Roman Catholic Church and make himself the head of the Church of England. This political decision allowed Henry to centralize his authority and, on a personal level, to marry again. Having divorced Catherine, Henry married five more times, mainly in search of a male heir. His second wife, Anne Boleyn, gave birth to Elizabeth, the future Queen of England. Anne Boleyn and Henry's fifth wife, Kathryn Howard, were executed for being unfaithful.

Christopher Columbus (1450 or 1451–1506) was an Italian explorer and sailor from Genoa. He is widely believed to have reached America in 1492, when he accidentally landed in the modern-day Bahamas, Cuba, and Haiti in his attempt to find a new sea route to Asia. After completing his first voyage, he set out on another three voyages, organized with the help and support of the Spanish crown. During the third and fourth voyages, Columbus eventually reached the American mainland. Although the Icelander Leif Ericson is now thought to be the first European to reach America, it was Columbus's discoveries that clearly made history and marked the beginning of the European colonization and exploration of the American continents.

Unit 1 Do your best

1.2

Gillian Lynne (b. 1926) is a legendary British ballet dancer, choreographer, and director. She is renowned for the choreography of such successful Broadway shows as *Cats* and *The Phantom of the Opera*. At the age of 88, in recognition of her lifetime artistic achievements, she received the honor of Dame Commander of the Order of the British Empire.

Ken Robinson (b. 1950) is a British author and speaker, whose main area of interest is education in the arts and through the arts. His best-known books are *Out of Our Minds: Learning to be Creative* and *The Element: How Finding Your Passion Changes Everything*, in which he analyzes the success of popular artists such as Paul McCartney, Meg Ryan, or Gillian Lynne. Sir Ken Robinson advises different organizations and governments on using art in education. He is a charismatic speaker and often gives talks at conferences.

1.4

Sugata Mitra (b. 1951) is an Indian scientist and Professor of Educational Technology at the University of Newcastle, UK. Mitra has a PhD in Physics and is responsible for more than twenty-five inventions in the field of educational technology and cognitive science. His most famous achievement, however, is The Hole in the Wall experiment, in which New Delhi slum children had access to a free computer placed in a wall. The experiment proved that children were able to teach themselves how to use a computer without any external instructions. In 2013 his inspiring work brought him the one-million-dollar TED award, which helped him finance another educational project, called The School in the Cloud.

Skype is a software application, first launched in 2003, which enables phone calls and video calls to be made across the Internet. Its enormous popularity results from the fact that Skype-to-Skype calls are free of charge. Skype can also be used to call landlines and cell phones worldwide at competitive prices.

New Delhi is the capital of India and the seat of the Indian Government. Although administratively separate, it is one of the eleven districts that constitute the National Capital Territory of Delhi (usually referred to as Delhi). The population of the whole megalopolis of Delhi, including the suburban areas, is estimated at twenty-five million people.

Vikas Swarup (b. 1963) is an Indian diplomat and writer. What brought him international fame was his highly-acclaimed debut book from 2005, *Q & A*. It is a story about a young waiter who scoops record winnings in a TV quiz show only to be later accused of cheating. The book was loosely inspired by professor Mitra's Hole in the Wall experiment. *Q & A* was later made into a movie, entitled ***Slumdog Millionaire***. It was directed by Danny Boyle and filmed in India, where the plot is set. It is a story about Jamal Malik, a young man from Mumbai's slums who, despite groundless suspicions about his honesty, manages to win the grand prize in the Indian version of *Who Wants To Be a Millionaire?* The movie hit theaters in 2009, becoming a worldwide blockbuster. It won eight Oscars in the same year.

TED is a non-profit organization whose main aim and mission is to spread innovative ideas ('Ideas worth spreading') in all fields – from science to global problems to art. The formula of TED is based on inspirational short talks given by influential people, available in more than 100 languages to everyone on the Internet since 2006. TED started in 1984 as a one-off conference. Its name stands for *Technology, Entertainment and Design*.

1.5

Rafael 'Rafa' Nadal (b. 1986) is a prize-winning Spanish tennis player. He is considered one of the best tennis players in history and is often called the King of Clay because of his exceptional skills on clay courts. Among many other records he holds, Rafael Nadal is the only tennis player who has won a singles Grand Slam tournament nine times. He is also the 2008 Olympic gold medalist in singles.

Leonardo da Vinci (1452–1519) was a versatile Italian artist, scientist, and inventor, regarded as one of the most gifted and influential Renaissance men. He is mostly known for his paintings such as *The Last Supper* and the *Mona Lisa*, to name but a few. Leonardo da Vinci is famous for his engineering projects and visionary inventions, including flying machines.

Mahatma Gandhi (1869–1948) was the leader of the Indian independence movement and one of the founders of the modern Indian state, often referred to as the 'father of the nation.' He is known for using non-violent methods to achieve his political goals. Gandhi was born in India, into a well-off family. He studied law in London and worked as a lawyer in South Africa, where he first involved himself in civil rights movements. He continued his work as an activist after returning to India in 1915. He was assassinated by a Hindu nationalist, only half a year after India gained independence from Britain.

Albert Einstein (1879–1955) was a theoretical physicist and philosopher of science. He is most famous for developing the Theory of Relativity. He was born in Germany and studied Physics and Mathematics in Zurich. He became a lecturer at Bern University first and then a full professor at the Charles Ferdinand University in Prague in 1911. He moved to America in 1933 and became an American citizen in 1940. He won the Nobel Prize in Physics in 1921. He wrote over 300 scientific papers and 150 non-scientific ones. He also had a love of music and played the piano and violin.

Winston Churchill (1874–1965) was a British politician and artist. He was the UK Prime Minister during the last five years of World War II, playing a crucial role in wartime world politics. He became prime minister again in 1951 and retired in April 1955 because of ill health. As well as being an influential politician, Winston Churchill was also a painter and a writer. In 1953 he was awarded the Nobel Prize in Literature.

Marie Skłodowska-Curie (1867–1934) was a Polish-French chemist and physicist, known for her research on radioactivity and the discovery of two radioactive elements, polonium and radium. In 1891 Maria Skłodowska left Poland for Paris to study at the Sorbonne, where she continued her scientific work throughout her life and became the first woman professor in the history of the university. She was also the first woman to win a Nobel Prize and the first person with two Nobel Prizes in different disciplines, the first in Physics (in 1903) and the other in Chemistry (in 1911). She was awarded the 1903 Nobel Prize together with her husband, Pierre Curie, and Henri Becquerel.

Barack Obama (b. 1961) became the forty-fourth US President and the first black president in 2008. He was re-elected for a second term as president in 2012. In 2009 he won the Nobel Peace Prize. He is known for reforming health care laws and for working to end US military involvement abroad.

Unit 2 It takes all sorts

2.4

Michael Grant (b. 1954) is an American novelist, the author and co-author of more than 150 books for young adults, most of which were written as series. He is known for the *Animorphs, Everworld,* and *Making Out* book series, which he wrote with his wife. Grant's best-selling series, however, is ***Gone***. It tells a story about Perdido Beach, an imaginary town in America where everyone aged fifteen or older mysteriously disappears. There are six books in the series: *Gone, Hunger, Lies, Plague, Fear,* and *Light*.

The Civil War in American history refers to the war between eleven rebellious southern states where slavery was legal (often referred to as the 'South' or the 'Confederacy') and the remaining states loyal to the federal government (called the 'North' or the 'Union'). The war broke out in 1861, when seven slave states rebelled against the US government and formed the Confederate States of America, which were soon joined by four other states. The war lasted four years and cost the lives of 600,000 soldiers. It ended in 1865 with the victory of the Union. As a result of the war, slavery was abolished and the integrity of the USA was preserved.

The Royal Navy (RN) is the oldest part of the British armed forces, dating from the sixteenth century. For over 200 years, until the twentieth century, it was the world's most powerful navy. The RN played a crucial role in the foundation of the British Empire. Currently its main role is to protect the UK's interests and contribute to NATO operations. The Royal Navy maintains a fleet of highly specialized ships and submarines as well as aircraft.

The Bermuda Triangle is a popular term referring to the area in the west of the Northern Atlantic whose vertices are roughly marked by the tip of the Florida peninsula, Puerto Rico, and Bermuda. In popular culture the area has become infamous for mysterious disappearances of planes and ships. However, neither the US Navy nor the WWF (World Wide Fund for Nature) considers the Bermuda Triangle as dangerous waters for shipping.

USS Cyclops was an American cargo ship meant for carrying coal, built for the US Navy before World War I. *USS Cyclops* disappeared during its voyage from Bahia, Brazil, to Baltimore, USA. It probably sank somewhere within the Bermuda Triangle after March 4 1918, with over 300 crew members on board. The shipwreck has never been found, making the loss of *USS Cyclops* one of the greatest maritime mysteries ever.

Flight 19 refers to the flight of five US Navy bombers which disappeared without a trace with all fourteen crew members over the Bermuda Triangle on December 5 1945. They had taken off from Florida for routine navigation training. To make matters worse, the plane sent to search for Flight 19 vanished too. What caused the loss of the planes has never been clearly determined.

2.7

John Gray (b. 1951) is an American author and personal relationship counselor. He made his name as the author of the famous self-help book ***Men Are from Mars, Women Are from Venus***, published in 1992. With millions of copies sold, the book is one of the best-selling non-fiction books in history. It aims to explain problems in relationships between men and women through characteristic tendencies in each gender. Despite huge commercial success, *Men Are from Mars, Women Are from Venus* did not receive much recognition among academics, who often maintain that it is rather simplistic and largely stereotypical. All Gray's later books grew out of his bestseller and pivot around the same theme of relationships and personal growth.

Unit 3 A place to live

3.1

Toronto is the biggest city in Canada, with a population of over 5.5 million, including the residents of the Greater Toronto Area. Toronto lies on Lake Ontario and it is the capital of the province of Ontario. The city, originally called York, was founded in the eighteenth century and in 1834 was renamed Toronto. The city is considered Canada's financial and commercial center. Being a gateway to Canada for generations of immigrants, Toronto has preserved a strong multicultural character.

The CN Tower is the landmark of Toronto. The tower is 553.33 meters high and it is the tallest free-standing structure in the whole Western Hemisphere. It is also the third tallest tower in the world. It was the tallest man-made structure for thirty-four years following its construction in 1976. The CN Tower features a revolving restaurant, an observation deck (LookOut), located at 346 meters above street level and a spectacular glass floor, one level below the LookOut. The CN Tower is visited by more than two million people every year.

Berlin is the capital of Germany and the largest German city, with a population of 3.5 million people. As a result of World War II, the city was divided into East Berlin, which became the capital of East Germany, and West Berlin, which was a West German enclave within East Germany. Between 1961 and 1989 West Berlin and East Berlin were separated by the Berlin Wall. The fall of the Wall marked the reunification of the city and the whole country. The reunified city became the capital of all Germany in 1990.

New York, located on America's east coast, is the biggest city in the USA, with almost 8.5 million inhabitants. To distinguish it from the state of New York, where the city lies, it is usually called New York City. The city consists of five main parts, called boroughs: Brooklyn, Queens, Manhattan, the Bronx, and Staten Island. The city was founded in 1624 by Dutch settlers, who named it New Amsterdam. It was changed to New York when the city came under English control in 1664. These days New York is sometimes nicknamed The Big Apple. For years, New York City was the first stop for many immigrants to America.

3.3

The Freedom Ship is the name of a floating city project, put forward in the late 1990s. It would be a series of huge barges, connected to each other into a 1,317-meter-long ship-like complex. It would consist of apartments for 50,000 residents and any facilities a modern city can offer, such as schools, stores, hotels, a hospital, and a rooftop airport. Although the Freedom Ship would be continuously traveling around the world, it would not be a cruise liner. Its main aim is to create a unique place to live for the world's first mobile community.

3.4

The International Space Station (ISS) is the largest satellite in the Earth's orbit and a huge science laboratory, where the resident astronauts conduct unique experiments in all kinds of fields, from biology to meteorology. The ISS is an international project brought to life by the collaboration of five space agencies. The station is made of modules, the first of which was launched in 1998. It consists of two main sections: the Russian Orbital Segment and the US Orbital Segment. They are both shared by an international crew of up to six people. The ISS weighs more than 400 tons and is the size of a soccer field. It orbits the Earth every ninety minutes at an altitude of 354 kilometers. It is visible to the naked eye.

3.5

Wi-Fi is a set of standards for radio-based wireless networks which allow compatible devices to connect to network access points without cables or wires. The Wi-Fi logo is issued by the Wi-Fi Alliance, a non-profit organization that promotes Wi-Fi technology and certifies that devices and products are compliant with Wi-Fi standards. Wi-Fi is thought to be an abbreviation for *Wireless Fidelity*.

Unit 4 The cost of living

4.3

The Rose Bowl Flea Market is a huge flea market in Pasadena, California. It features about 2,500 vendors selling furniture, jewelry, vintage clothing, and much more. Each month, about 20,000 buyers visit in search of the perfect item. Even celebrities shop at the Rose Bowl Flea Market. Actors, models, and rock stars like Rod Stewart, Flea, Madonna, and Cher have been spotted shopping there.

eBay refers to the commercial website, eBay.com, owned by an American multinational corporation. It is an online auction and shopping site, allowing its users to buy and sell a wide range of products and services. eBay operates in more than thirty countries worldwide.

An auction is a sale in which goods or property are sold to the highest bidder. All sorts of items are sold at auctions, from artwork and jewelry to cattle and land. An auctioneer leads the auction by telling about the items for sale and keeping track of the bidding. Bidders compete with each other to pay a certain amount for items for sale at the auction.

4.4

Nimes is a city in southern France with a population of about 150,000 people. It was founded by the Romans and played an important role in Roman Gaul. Due to its history and numerous ancient monuments in the city and in its vicinity, Nimes is sometimes nicknamed 'the French Rome.'

Genoa is an Italian city situated on the northern Mediterranean coast. It has about 600,000 inhabitants, making it the sixth largest city in Italy. Genoa prides itself on its rich history, which has always been closely connected with the sea. For centuries it was an independent city-state and one of the Maritime Republics. It is still the largest seaport in Italy, also known for its shipbuilding industry. Genoa is the birthplace of Christopher Columbus and Niccolo Paganini.

The Californian Gold Rush started on January 24 1848, when James W. Marshall found gold at a sawmill located in the Sierra Nevada mountains in California. The news spread quickly, enticing 300,000 people from all over the world to come to California in the hope of making a quick fortune. In the early days gold was easy to find and a few gold-seekers, called 'forty-niners,' struck it rich. The Gold Rush, which lasted until 1855, contributed to the development of the region. As a result, new roads were built, San Francisco became a boom town, and California was admitted to the USA.

Levi Strauss (1829–1902) was a German-American businessman of Jewish origin and the founder of Levi Strauss & Co, the firm he set up in 1853 in San Francisco. It was the first company that produced blue jeans.

Jacob W. Davis (1831–1908) was a Latvian-American tailor who revolutionized the world of clothing by reinforcing work pants with copper rivets. He came up with the idea in 1870 and three years later, with the financial support of Levi Strauss, he patented his new fastening. At that point he started working for Strauss, who had launched the production of Davis's reinforced jeans in a new tailor store. He went on working for Strauss until his death.

James Dean (1931–1955) was an American actor. He is especially known for his role as a troubled teenager in the movie *Rebel Without a Cause*. Dean's great passion was racing and sports cars. He died in a car crash at the age of twenty-four, having acted in only three movies. His early death, exceptional acting talent, and the rebellious characters he played made him a legend and an icon of American pop culture.

Unit 5 The world at your feet

5.1

The Great Barrier Reef is the largest coral reef system in the world. It is off the coast of Queensland, Australia, and has been called one of the seven natural wonders of the world. A large part of the reef is a protected marine park. It is a popular tourist destination.

Hamilton Island is an island in Australia, located off the central coast of Queensland in the Great Barrier Reef. Covering five square kilometers, it is the biggest of the Whitsunday Islands. The island is inhabited by over 1,200 people and it is a popular vacation destination. It gained a lot of international attention through the promotion project Best Job In The World.

Queensland is the second largest state in Australia, located in the northeast of the continent. It is popular with tourists thanks to its long coastline with pristine beaches and warm weather. Queensland is often nicknamed the 'Sunshine State.' The capital of Queensland is Brisbane.

The Outback refers to the remote dry areas of the Australian interior, far away from any cities. It is often contrasted with the term *Bush*, which refers to the immediate countryside outside the main urban areas. However, there is no clear division line between the Outback and the Bush. The Outback is mostly uninhabited. The most famous outback town is Alice Springs, located in the geographic center of Australia. Despite its inhospitable character, the Outback has a few popular tourist destinations such as Uluru (also known as Ayers Rock) and the Alice Springs Desert Park.

Sydney is the biggest city in Australia and, as such, it is often mistaken for the country's capital. (The national capital of Australia is Canberra.) It is located on the east coast in one of the world's largest natural harbors. Sydney was established in 1788 as a British penal settlement, but the area had been inhabited by Aboriginal peoples for thousands of years. Nowadays it has over 4.7 million inhabitants, almost a third of whom were born abroad. This ethnic diversity makes Sydney the most multicultural city in Australia.

Melbourne is the second largest city in Australia, with over 4.4 million residents, and the capital of the state of Victoria. Melbourne was founded by European settlers in 1835, but indigenous semi-nomadic tribes had lived in the area for thousands of years before. Located on the south-eastern coast, it is the busiest container and cargo port in Australia. It is also an important financial and cultural center.

5.4

Harper's Magazine is an American monthly magazine with an average circulation of 220,000 copies. It focuses on social, political, and cultural issues. It has been continuously published since 1850 and is the second oldest monthly magazine in the USA.

Bill Bryson (b. 1951) is an American writer, renowned for his best-selling humorous books. He mostly writes about travel, the English language and science. Bryson's most widely-acclaimed books are *Notes from a Small Island* and *A Really Short History of Nearly Everything*. In 2006 he published his memoir *The Life and Times of the Thunderbolt Kid*.

Pearl Harbor is a lagoon harbor and an American naval base on the Hawaiian island of Oahu. Many people associate it with the attack on December 7 1941. The attack was a Japanese surprise air raid on the American base which destroyed most of the American fleet and aircraft. The attack on Pearl Harbor caused the USA to enter World War II.

Des Moines is the capital city of the state of Iowa, in the Midwestern USA. It is also the largest city in Iowa, with a population of over 203,000. The city is named after the Des Moines River. Des Moines is known as a major center of the American insurance industry.

Unit 6 True or false?

6.1

Nelson Mandela (1918–2013) was a South-African human rights activist and politician, who became known for his relentless struggle against apartheid and racism. Mandela was imprisoned for his political involvement for twenty-seven years, serving most of his sentence on Robben Island, near Cape Town. Eventually, his fight brought about revolutionary changes in South Africa. When he was set free in 1990, he took part in negotiations with President F.W. de Klerk to end apartheid. These led to the first fully democratic elections in 1994, in which Mandela was chosen as the first black president of South Africa. Together, Mandela and de Klerk were awarded the Nobel Peace Prize in 1993. He is highly respected among South Africans and is often called the 'Father of the Nation' or just 'Tata' (Father).

Brad Pitt (b. 1963) is an American actor and producer and one of the most recognizable Hollywood names. He rose to fame after his role as a young hitchhiker in *Thelma and Louise*. He starred in such blockbusters as *Interview with the Vampire, Legends of the Fall, Seven, Fight Club, Troy,* and *Mr. and Mrs. Smith*. He is married to the American actress Angelina Jolie and the couple are constantly in the public eye. Pitt is known for his humanitarian work. Together with his wife, he runs the Maddox Jolie-Pitt Foundation, which assists with humanitarian crises.

Lorde (b. 1996) is the stage pseudonym of Ella Marija Lani Yelich-O'Connor, a New Zealand singer. In 2013 Lorde released her debut single *Royals*, which reached number one on the US Billboard Hot 100, bringing her international popularity. The single was followed by her debut studio album *Pure Heroine*, which has sold more than one million copies worldwide.

Keira Knightley (b. 1985) is a popular British actress. She appeared in her first movie at the age of ten. Her role in the British comedy-drama *Bend It like Beckham* in 2002 was a springboard for her international career. She shot to stardom after appearing in the *Pirates of the Caribbean* movie series. Knightley is known for her period drama movies, such as *Pride and Prejudice*, which brought her an Oscar nomination.

6.3

Banksy is an elusive British artist, movie director, and political activist. He is known for his provocative, satirical graffiti and other kinds of street art. He has placed his works in visible places in different cities all over the world. Through his art Banksy comments on important political and social issues. He works anonymously and has never revealed his true identity. Most people believe that his secrecy may result from the illegal character of graffiti.

6.5

Daniel Radcliffe (b. 1989) is a British actor, mainly known for playing the title character in the *Harry Potter* movie series. The director of *Harry Potter and the Sorcerer's Stone* cast Radcliffe when he was eleven. He continued to play Harry Potter throughout the series for over ten years.

Harry Potter is the main character in a fantasy series written by the British author J.K. Rowling. He is a young wizard and a student of Hogwarts School of Witchcraft and Wizardry, who tries to conquer the villain Lord Voldemort. Harry Potter's adventures constitute the focus of the whole series, which consists of seven books: *Harry Potter and the Sorcerer's Stone, Harry Potter and the Chamber of Secrets, Harry Potter and the Prisoner of Azkaban, Harry Potter and the Goblet of Fire, Harry Potter and the Order of the Phoenix, Harry Potter and the Half-Blood Prince,* and *Harry Potter and the Deathly Hallows.* The series was an enormous commercial success, with over 400 million copies sold worldwide. All the books in the series have been made into movies and Harry Potter has become a valuable brand name.

Robert Pattinson (b. 1986) is an English actor who was born in London. He is most famous for his role as Edward Cullen in *The Twilight Saga*. He was also in *Harry Potter and the Goblet of Fire*. When he was younger, he used to be a model. He is also a musician and song writer; he plays both the piano and guitar. He sang one of his own songs, Never Think, on the *Twilight* soundtrack.

The Twilight Saga is a series of fantasy romance movies for young adults based on the novels by Stephenie Meyer. The movies are about a teenage girl named Bella Swan (played by Kristen Stewart) who falls in love with a vampire named **Edward Cullen** (played by Robert Pattinson). There are five movies in the Saga: *Twilight, New Moon, Eclipse, Breaking Dawn Part I,* and *Breaking Dawn Part II.*

Unit 7 Log on

7.1

Google is an Internet search engine. It allows you to search all the websites on the Internet to find information using key words and phrases. It was started in 1998 by Larry Page and Sergey Brin, two American students who wanted to organize the world's information and make it easy to use. By 2000, Google was the world's largest search engine. Now Google also offers other software applications such as Gmail (email), a blogging site, and a social networking site called Google+. Google has approximately one billion search requests every day and we now often use the verb *to google* when we mean 'to look something up on the Internet.'

Global Positioning System (GPS) is a space-based satellite navigation system. It provides location and time information anywhere in the world with sufficient GPS satellites. It is maintained by the United States government and is freely available to anyone with a GPS receiver. It is commonly used in car navigation systems but also has many commercial and military uses. It has been in operation since 1993 and uses more than twenty-four satellites in various orbits around the globe. Other countries such as Japan, Russia, India, and China are now developing their own GPS systems. The European Union is also developing the Galileo positioning system.

7.2

Bill Gates (b. 1955) is a successful American entrepreneur, philanthropist, and inventor. He is best known for being the co-founder of Microsoft. According to the Forbes list, he has been ranked as one of the richest people in the world since 1995. In 2015 his fortune was estimated at almost eighty billion dollars. In 2000 Gates established the Bill & Melinda Gates Foundation, through which he has donated substantial funds to charitable organizations and various research programs. Gates is also the author of two books: *The Road Ahead* and *Business @ the Speed of Thought*.

The American company **Apple** designs and sells consumer electronics, computer software, and computers. It is most famous for Mac computers, the iPod music player, the iPhone, and the iPad tablet computer. It was founded in 1976 by Steve Jobs, Steve Wozniak, and Ronald Wayne.

YouTube is a popular video-sharing website started in 2005 by Steve Chen, Chad Hurley, and Jawed Karim. People upload video clips to share with others. Some TV companies also upload clips. In 2006 the website was bought by Google.

The Nobel Prize refers to a set of the most prestigious international awards for great achievements in various categories. The prizes were established by the Swedish inventor Alfred Nobel in his will in 1895. Since 1901 the prizes have been awarded in the following categories: Physics, Chemistry, Medicine, Literature, and Peace. In 1968 the Central Bank of Sweden established a related award in Economics, called the Nobel Memorial Prize in Economic Sciences. All the prizes are presented in Stockholm, Sweden, with the exception of the Nobel Peace Prize, which is awarded in Oslo, Norway.

7.4

Denver is the capital city of the US state of Colorado, with a population of 600,000 inhabitants. It is sometimes called the Mile-High City due to its elevation at exactly one mile above sea level. Denver is only twenty kilometers east of the mineral-rich Rocky Mountains, which made it a convenient location for mining and energy companies. The city developed rapidly in the 1970s and early 1980s as a result of the energy crisis and soaring oil prices. This period of the city's economic boom was depicted in the soap opera *Dynasty*.

LinkedIn is a social networking website which allows its users to create profiles with information about their professional lives. It is mostly used to form relationships of a business nature. The website was launched in 2003 and it is available in a number of different languages, with users in over 200 countries.

7.5

Pythagoras (circa 570–circa 495BC) was a Greek mathematician and philosopher. He is famous for developing the Pythagorean Theorem, which states that in every right-angled triangle the square built on the longest side has the same area as the two squares built on the other sides put together.

Archimedes (circa 287–circa 212BC) was a Greek mathematician and inventor. Despite sparse information about his life, he is often considered the greatest mathematician in antiquity, whose work contributed a lot to the development of geometry. However, Archimedes is mostly known for discovering Archimedes' Principle, one of the basic rules of hydrostatics. It states that a body immersed in a fluid loses as much of its weight as the weight of the fluid displaced. Archimedes was a great engineer too. He built defensive war machines to protect Syracuse, the Greek city in Sicily, where he lived.

The Maya people are diverse ethnic groups from Central America who speak the Mayan languages. They are native inhabitants of southern Mexico, Guatemala, Belize, and Honduras. The ancestors of the Maya people created the Maya civilization, one of the finest pre-Columbian cultures of city-states, which flourished in the Yucatan Peninsula in the first millennium of the modern era. There were eight million Maya people living in the region before the arrival of Europeans in the fifteenth century. These days the Maya population is estimated at seven million.

7.6

Mario is a Nintendo video game character, created by Shigeru Miyamoto. Mario is an Italian plumber living in the Mushroom Kingdom. His main goal is to rescue Princess Peach from the hands of a villain named Bowser. Mario first appeared in the early 1980s and has been in over 200 games since then, as well as numerous TV shows, movies, and comics.

Minecraft is a video game released in 2009. In its core version, the game consists of moving around in a world made of 3D cubes and breaking them up to build new constructions. The cubes represent various materials which the player gathers and uses to create new structures. The world consists of different types of terrain such as deserts, mountains, forests, or seas. There are several game modes, in which the player has different options and goals.

Unit 8 Around the globe

8.1

Hawaii is a group of islands in the Pacific Ocean. It is the newest of the fifty states of the USA. It has hundreds of islands, although there are only eight main ones. Its original culture is mainly Polynesian. Until around 1820 there was no written Hawaiian language; history and culture were passed on by oral tradition until American missionaries wrote a language based on the sounds they heard. Hawaii is a popular tourist destination because of its warm climate, beautiful beaches, and volcanoes. It is the only state which is not in the Americas. The highest mountain in Hawaii is Mauna Kea and is 4,205 meters high. However, if you measure the mountain from its base on the seabed of the Pacific Ocean to the top, it is higher than Mount Everest, at 10,200 meters!

California is an American state, located in the southwest of the USA, on the Pacific coast. It is the most populated US state, with thirty-eight million people residing on 424,345 square kilometers. The capital of California is Sacramento, but the state's biggest cities are Los Angeles, San Diego, San Jose, and San Francisco. California officially joined the USA under the Compromise of 1850. At the same time California began to boom as a consequence of the Gold Rush. California is home to the Hollywood movie industry and innovative high-tech companies in Silicon Valley. It is also known for the production of fruit and wine.

8.4

Rabbit-Proof Fence is an Australian movie from 2002, directed by Phillip Noyce. It is a screen adaptation of the book *Follow the Rabbit-Proof Fence,* by Doris Pilkington Garimara. It is based on a true story of three Aboriginal girls, including the author's mother, who ran away from the Moore River Native Settlement in Western Australia and walked for nine weeks along a rabbit-proof fence to go back to their families. The rabbit-proof fence, currently called the State Barrier Fence of Western Australia, was constructed to prevent rabbits and other pest animals spreading to Western Australia from the east. The girls belonged to the so-called Stolen Generation of mixed-race children who were taken away from their Aboriginal parents by force in the early twentieth century. The movie opened to excellent reviews and has received numerous international awards and nominations. The movie's musical soundtrack was composed by Peter Gabriel.

The Aboriginal Protection Act of 1869 empowered the government of the then colony of Victoria in Australia to make decisions about the lives of Aboriginal people. It controlled such aspects as their residence, employment, and marriage. The Act was soon expanded by the Half-Caste Act, which permitted authorities to remove Aboriginal people of mixed origin from their families and homeland to make them adapt to white society.

Chris McCandless (1968–1992) was a young American hiker. In 1992 he went into the Alaskan wilderness in pursuit of a simple solitary lifestyle. His frail body was found four months later. He is thought to have starved to death, probably as a result of plant poisoning, which prevented him from hunting or gathering food. His travels and adventures inspired Jon Krakauer to write the non-fiction book ***Into the Wild***, published in 1996. The book elaborates on an extensive article about McCandless that Krakauer had published in the American magazine *Outside* three years earlier. *Into the Wild* is also the title of the 2007 movie adaptation directed by Sean Penn.

Robyn Davidson (b. 1950) is an Australian writer and traveler. She is mostly known for her book ***Tracks***, in which she writes about her 2,700-kilometer journey on foot across the deserts of west Australia. In 1977, accompanied by a dog and four camels, she set out on a nine-month trek from

Alice Springs to the west coast. A year later she described the experience in an article for *National Geographic Magazine*. The article generated so much interest that Davidson went on to write a book. *Tracks* came out in 1980 and was highly acclaimed by critics and readers. In 2013 *Tracks* was made into a movie, directed by John Curran and starring Mia Wasikowska as Robyn Davidson.

Cheryl Strayed is an American writer. Her work has been published in various magazines and newspapers and she has also written three books. Her second book, *Wild: From Lost to Found on the Pacific Crest Trail*, was published in 2012 and describes her journey on foot along a 1,100-mile trail. After a series of tragedies and disasters in her personal life, including the death of her mother and the breakdown of her marriage, she set out on the three-month hike. The long, physically-demanding journey helped her to overcome her problems and find innerpeace. Her book was made into an acclaimed movie starring Reese Witherspoon in 2014.

The Pacific Crest Trail (PCT) is a long-distance hiking trail which goes through the Sierra Nevada and Cascade mountains. It begins at the American border with Mexico and ends at the US-Canadian border and is 4,286 kilometers long.

The Gobi is a large desert in Asia, which covers an area of almost 1.3 million square kilometers in northern China and southern Mongolia. The dry climate of the Gobi results from the Himalayas preventing rain-carrying clouds from reaching the area. The Gobi is known for numerous discoveries of dinosaur fossils.

Death Valley is a desert valley in the US state of California, near the border with Nevada. It is part of the Mojave Desert. It is also the deepest depression in North America, lying at eighty-six meters below sea level at its lowest point, called Badwater Basin. It is the depth of Death Valley and its surroundings that make it one of the hottest places on Earth, with the highest temperature ever recorded being 56.7°C.

The Sahara Desert is the largest hot desert in the world. It covers most of North Africa, stretching across the whole continent from the Atlantic to the Red Sea. It covers an area of 9.4 million square kilometers. The name Sahara comes from the Arabic word for desert. In places, Saharan sand dunes are as high as 180 meters above sea level.

The South Pole is the southernmost point on the surface of the Earth, located in Antarctica. It is determined by the point where the Earth's axis and the Earth's surface intersect. It is one of the coldest places on Earth, with an average yearly temperature of -49.3°C. On December 14 1911 the Norwegian Roald Amundsen and his companions became the first people to reach the South Pole. In 1956 the USA built a scientific research station there called the Amundsen-Scott South Pole Station. Since then the South Pole has been continuously inhabited.

Siberia refers to the vast region of northern Asia that extends from the Ural Mountains to the Pacific. It has been part of Russia since the seventeenth century. Siberia is characterized by a severe climate with extremely low winter temperatures, an abundance of natural resources, and low population density. It is also infamous for having been used as a place of imprisonment and exile in the former Soviet Union.

8.6

The Giant Crystal Cave is a cave in Naica, a mining town in the north of Mexico. It is part of a working lead, zinc, and silver mine. The cave is famous for enormous gypsum crystals, some of the world's largest crystals ever discovered. The biggest specimen weighs fifty-five tons and it is twelve meters long. The cave lies 300 meters below the surface and is difficult to explore due to the inside temperature reaching up to 58°C and extremely high humidity.

Ha Long Bay is located in north-eastern Vietnam, near the mouth of the Bach Dang river, covering an area of 1,553 square kilometers. It is famous for its spectacular scenery and, as such, is one of the biggest tourist attractions in East Asia. There are over 1,600 limestone islands and islets, which make a unique seascape, created in a process of erosion over millions of years. Ha Long Bay was designated a UNESCO World Heritage site in 1994.

Cape Town is the second largest city in South Africa, with 3.7 million people living in the metropolitan area. Its population constitutes one of the world's most multicultural cities. Cape Town is located on the shore of Table Bay, on the Atlantic Coast, near the southernmost tip of the African continent. It is a famous tourist destination thanks to its beautiful harbor and two scenic landmarks: Table Mountain and Cape Point. Cape Town was founded by the Dutch in 1652 as a supply station for Dutch merchant ships and soon became the economic hub of the region. It is now the second biggest economic center in South Africa. As its legislative capital, it is the seat of the National Parliament.

Table Mountain is the 1,084-meter landmark mountain which overlooks the South African city of Cape Town. As its name suggests, the flat top of the mountain resembles a table top. The top is almost three kilometers long and has steep vertical cliffs at the edges. Table Mountain is part of the Table Mountain National Park and is a famous tourist destination. It can be easily reached by cableway, but it also attracts hikers thanks to a network of over 550 trails.

8.7

Zakynthos is a Greek island located in the Ionian Sea. It is a popular vacation destination, famous for its picturesque 123-kilometer-long coastline. Since 1999 it has been the site of the National Marine Park of Zakynthos, located in the southern part of the island. The Park is famous for the Bay of Laganas and its beaches, which are used by the loggerhead sea turtle as nesting grounds.

The loggerhead sea turtle is the biggest hard-shell turtle in the world. The average adult measures about ninety centimeters and weighs 135 kilograms, but specimens twice as long as this, weighing almost half a ton, have also been found. The loggerhead inhabits all the world's oceans and the Mediterranean Sea. It is considered an endangered species. Its population, estimated at 200,000, has decreased due to industrial fishing nets, its slow reproduction rate, and the loss of nesting sites.

The Masai Mara National Reserve is a wildlife reserve, located in south-west Kenya, on the border with Tanzania. It adjoins the Serengeti National Park in Tanzania, and is one of Africa's most diverse and fascinating eco-systems. The whole area is famous for the Great Migration, the world's largest mammal migration, in which countless herds of gnus (also called wildebeest), zebras, and Thomson's gazelles move to and fro between the Masai Mara and the Serengeti on a yearly cycle. Africa's big cats – the lion, the cheetah, and the leopard – can be found in the Masai Mara in relatively large numbers. There are also elephants, buffaloes, black rhinoceroses, hippopotamuses, and Nile crocodiles. The unique and rich wildlife attracts many tourists, making the reserve the most popular safari destination in Africa.

Fraser Island is an island located off the eastern coast of Australia. It spans 1,840 square kilometers and is the largest sand island in the world. It is made up of sand it has been accumulating for over 750,000 years. Almost the whole island is now part of the Great Sandy National Park. In 1992 the island was declared a UNESCO World Heritage Site. Fraser Island has about 200 permanent residents but it is extremely popular with tourists because of its unique landscape and varied wildlife. It is home to the last remaining pure dingoes in Eastern Australia. To protect the species, dogs are not allowed on the island.

Punta Tombo is a peninsula located on the Atlantic coast of Argentina. It is three kilometers long and 600 meters wide and it is famous for being the nesting site of Magellanic penguins. They arrive in Punta Tombo between September and April, to lay their eggs and look after their offspring. It is one of the world's largest penguin colonies and also one of the most accessible and as such it attracts about 100,000 visitors every year.

Yellowstone National Park is a nature reserve in the USA, with an area of more than 8,900 square kilometers. It is famous for its active volcano and hot water springs and is home to hundreds of different bird and mammal species. Approximately four million people visit the park every year.

Students' Book audio script

Starter unit

0.7 The UK vs The US

CD•1.7 MP3•7 Exercise 2, page 10

Jo = John, Je = Jess

Jo: How are you finding life in the UK?
Je: Oh, it's great, but everything's so expensive here.
Jo: Really? More expensive than in the States?
Je: Oh yes, the cost of living is a lot higher in the UK and salaries are quite a bit lower.
Jo: Oh, I didn't know that. I thought that things were pretty similar in the UK and the US. Apart from the fact that everything is much bigger in the States.
Je: Hahaha, yes, that's so true. When you go into a restaurant in the States, food portions are enormous. A lot bigger than here in the UK. I never finish a meal in the States.
Jo: Oh dear, what a waste!
Je: Not really. You can take the leftovers back home.
Jo: Oh, that's good. So what else is different?
Je: The most noticeable thing is the size of houses. They're much much smaller here. Most houses in the States have basements and far more space. For instance, in the States I have a walk-in closet for my clothes.
Jo: Closet?
Je: Oh, that's a wardrobe. Here in the UK I have a small wardrobe for all my clothes – it's horrible! The other thing that's hard is housework – it's a lot harder here because there are fewer appliances than in the States. I need my American washer-dryer set!
Jo: Is there anything that's better here?
Je: Oh sure. Here I can go to the doctor for free. Health care isn't as expensive as in the States. The other really good thing here is that employees get a lot more time off than they do in the States. And I love all the museums and historical buildings. British people visit museums far more frequently than Americans.
Jo: Do you think you'll ever get used to living in the UK?
Je: Oh yes, the longer I live here, the more I like it.

0.8 The US vs The UK

CD•1.8 MP3•8 Exercise 4, page 11

1 The UK hasn't been invaded since 1066, when King Harold was defeated by William the Conqueror.

2 Until 1913, it was legal to have children sent to other parts of the US by the postal service.

3 One in eight workers in the US has been employed by McDonalds at one time or another.

4 80 percent of everything on sale in the UK is bought by women.

5 When Abraham Lincoln became President of the US in 1861, slaves were still being imported from Africa. During his presidency, Lincoln had slavery abolished.

6 In 1918 women over thirty were allowed to vote in elections in the UK. Women over twenty-one weren't allowed to vote until 1928.

7 Eight billion chickens are consumed in the US each year.

8 The English king, Henry VIII, had been married six times and had two of his wives executed by the time he died in 1547.

Unit 1 Do your best

1.2 Grammar

CD•1.13 MP3•13 Exercise 2, page 14

A: What are you reading?
B: Oh, this? It's a book about people who become successful because they do what they love doing.
A: Oh, that sounds good. What kind of thing?
B: Well, I'm just reading about a famous ballet dancer called Gillian Lynne. When she was a little girl, her teachers at school complained that she didn't pay attention and was always fidgeting and disturbing her classmates. So her mother arranged for her to see a psychologist to find out what her problem was.
A: Oh OK.
B: Anyway, the psychologist talked to the girl's mother, and then he put some music on the radio and left Gillian on her own in his office. He told the mother to watch Gillian through a window and as soon as they left the room, the little girl got up and started dancing.
A: Ah – that's so clever!
B: I know – the psychologist realized that Gillian didn't have a problem, she just had a gift for dancing.
A: So what did the mother do?
B: She sent her daughter to a dance school and Gillian ended up being a famous ballet dancer and choreographer.
A: Wow, that's a great story.

1.3 Listening

CD•1.15 MP3•15 Exercises 4 and 5, page 17

1 My earliest memory? I have very clear memories from the Christmas before my third birthday, I also remember my third birthday party vividly, and I remember other events very clearly from when I was three years old. Some people say I must have confused a memory with photos I've seen of the same events. But I've asked my mom about it and she agrees that my memories are accurate. For some of them, there's no photographic evidence or anything that I could have used to 'create' the memories in my head, so I believe they're real.

2 Most people in my family have terrible memories, but my grandfather's amazing. He's not like other old people who are losing their memory and get confused – he's really sharp. He remembers dates and names and places. He can even recall in detail events that happened fifty years ago – and he's seventy-seven! I'm sixteen and I can't remember what I did yesterday! I wish I had his memory – it would help me a lot in my exams. I asked him how he manages to remember things so well, and he says it's because he drinks green tea! I think it's because he reads a lot and stays active. He walks every day – he's in much better shape than I am.

3 I've read that a lot of innocent people get convicted of crimes they didn't commit because a witness has identified them wrongly. That's terrible. Apparently, it's hard for most people to remember someone's face correctly, especially if you only see them for a few brief moments. I think I'd be really good at recognizing criminals and I'm sure I wouldn't choose the wrong person in an identity parade because I never forget a face. I only have to see someone once, and I can remember them in detail. I just wish I had an equally good memory for names.

4 I saw a documentary last night about a boy who can't forget anything about his past life. He can tell you exactly what he was doing on a date and at a time in the past – and he can tell you details like what he was wearing, what he ate, what the weather was like. So you can say 'What did you do for your fifteenth birthday?' and he can remember everything about it. He's the only one in his family with a memory like that. In fact, they said he has a very rare condition – it has a name but I can't remember it. It's slipped my mind!

1.5 Grammar

CD•1.21 MP3•21 Exercises 1 and 2, page 20

Part one

What do Barack Obama, Prince William, Paul McCartney, Diego Maradona, and Bart Simpson have in common? They're all left-handed. In fact 10 percent of the world population is left-handed, and I'm one of them.

I have no idea why I use my left hand or what causes someone to be left-handed, but according to studies, it's a combination of genes and the environment that make someone use one hand rather than the other.

In left-handed people, the right hemisphere of the brain is dominant. This means left-handers tend to be creative and visual thinkers. You would therefore expect to find more left-handers working in music, the arts, and media in general. Dominance of the right hemisphere also enables left-handers to be better at 3D perception, so it's no surprise that a high proportion of left-handers decide to become architects.

Left-handers have good coordination too, which may explain why a greater number manage to pass their driving test first time. There is also a high percentage of lefties in the world of sport. Tennis champion Rafael Nadal is naturally right-handed but he has chosen to play tennis with his left hand. He keeps winning, so it's a decision that seems to have worked out well for him.

1.6 Speaking

CD•1.24 MP3•24 Exercises 6 and 7, page 23

Personally, I think it's absolutely vital. Actually, I'm having lessons right now and I intend to take my test next year. My family and I live on the outskirts of the city and it takes me ages to get to the center on the bus for school, or to meet my friends. Driving into the city would be so much more convenient, so for this reason I feel it's really important that I learn.

Focus review 1

CD•1.25 MP3•25 Exercise 8, page 29

1 I was beginning to fall behind in Biology class, so I decided to go along to the local Science center where they were advertising some free workshops. I'm really interested in Science but the classes in school are pretty dull and the teacher doesn't seem very motivated, but dropping out's not an option. At the center, though, things are very different, much more hands-on, and the instructor is really supportive. He actually voted my last project as the best in the group. That makes me want to work even harder. And, the funny thing is, my grades at school have actually started to improve as a result.

2 I'm really into science fiction and was curious about what a course on creative writing would involve. One thing I didn't expect was that the course would be so demanding, and I've already fallen behind a little. I'm not sure what the tutor will say if I don't catch up on the work that's due. I mean, it's free and we're all there voluntarily – even the tutor, I believe – so I doubt I'll be asked to quit the course. I've never been the most hard-working person and the other students in class strike me as being rather studious, so I know I can't put off doing the work indefinitely.

3 I've always wanted to do a drama class, so when the opportunity came up to do one nearby, I jumped at the chance. The tutor's great and the other students on the course all seem very self-motivated, which I guess is important on a free course such as this otherwise you just wouldn't go, right? I plan to go on and study drama at college and I dream of one day making a living out of being on stage. Naturally, I'm keen to soak up as much knowledge as I can in the hope that this will help me improve my acting skills.

4 My high school grades in Art are fine but I just wanted to try some new approaches and was looking for inspiration. I was a little worried initially as I've never been a very sociable person but everybody at the art club struck me as being really open. The tutor came across as being very hard-working and focused – which I wasn't expecting as you hear about these volunteer teachers being a bit lazy and unmotivated. The next assignment, painting or sketching something about our earliest memory, is rather challenging but I have lots of ideas and I'm feeling really creative again!

Unit 2 It takes all kinds

2.3 Listening

CD•1.30 MP3•30 **Exercises 2 and 3, page 34**

Good morning everyone. Thanks for coming to this talk about the science of love. My name is Ruby Niverton and I'm a neurologist – that means I study what goes on in people's brains. It wasn't my original career plan – that was to be a biologist – but I later discovered that for me the brain is a lot more interesting than the body. And the fact is that there is so much that we still don't understand about the workings of the mind. Something that neuroscientists have been taking an interest in recently is the nature of 'love.' Experts from all over the world have been doing research into this fascinating aspect of human behavior; here in the UK, but also in China, where the most important recent research has been done. Those studies show that the feeling we call 'love' is actually a chemical reaction in the brain and they have done tests to show this. It appears that the powerful feeling of 'loving' someone has similar roots in the brain to the reasons we become hungry or thirsty. It's a very strong chemical need! In other words, it's like a drug.

And as with a drug, this need builds up, or rather – it develops. First you're attracted to another person. Then you start going out with them and you really fall for them. You start to think about them all the time and then you realize that you are madly in love. What has really happened is that you've developed an addiction. You can't live without the reaction you get from being with or thinking about this person.

The evidence for this has come from different types of tests. One was filming the reactions of people when they were put in different situations, asked questions or shown photos of people they loved. What the Chinese scientists also did was to put people in brain scanners to look at their brain activity when they looked at the photos. They then compared the results with the brain activity when the people were shown photos of people they had NO feelings for. The results were pretty dramatic!

It seems that deep in the center of the brain there is a very primitive part that developed a long time ago – about sixty-five million years in fact! Long, long before the time – about four million years ago – when man is thought to have stood on two legs for the first time. Scientists believe that this is linked to very basic needs related to survival. It makes us want the things we need to live – like food, water and ... love – because love leads to a continuation of our species!

Not just having babies, but bringing them up in secure family units until they are grown. Strangely, scientists have also found that this area of the brain related to addiction is also active when we eat chocolate! And, as with other things that we can be obsessed with, it's hard to cut off that obsession when we want to. Just as it's hard to stop eating chocolate, it's also very hard to stop loving someone – even if you split up with that person. However, scientists are working on a cure for love – who knows, maybe in a few years a pill will be on sale that can stop us hurting so much when the love of our life leaves us! Now would that be a good or a bad thing? Let's have some questions first ...

CD•1.33 MP3•33 **Exercise 10, page 35**

1 Ruby Niverton specializes in neurology.

2 She is passionate about her latest project.

3 She focused on observing brain activity.

4 Some broken-hearted people were involved in the experiment.

5 She concluded that love is associated with two different areas in the brain.

2.6 Speaking

CD•1.37 MP3•37 **Exercises 4 and 5, pages 40–41**

OK, a memorable day trip. Hmm, let's see. Right, so I'm going to tell you about a great day trip that I had at the local lake. This took place about a month ago, on a Saturday, and I had been working really hard studying after school in the evenings and on weekends. I hadn't been out for weeks and I felt like I really needed a break. So I called my friend, Lisa, and we decided we would take a picnic and go to the lake not far from our village. The weather wasn't great, but we went anyway and as soon as we got there, the sun came out. Initially, we were the only people there, but it's a popular spot and, as expected, other people soon started arriving. As we were sitting there on our blanket, another group of teenagers came and sat down right next to us. They were really friendly and we chatted for a bit then someone got a flying disc out. All of a sudden, the weather changed and, out of the blue, it started pouring with rain. We were going to go and then someone said we might as well go for a swim as we were wet anyway. Swimming in the rain was fantastic and fortunately, after it stopped raining, the sun came out again and we ended up staying all afternoon. Eventually, the evening came and it started to get cold, so we headed home. Without a doubt, it was one of the best days I've had in ages and a welcome break from studying. We're planning to meet our new friends again as soon as we've finished our exams. Funnily enough, the best days are often the ones you don't really plan.

Focus review 2

CD•1.39 MP3•39 **Exercise 8, page 47**

I'm here today to talk about a very special family relationship – twins. It's an interesting topic for me for two reasons. Firstly, I'm a psychologist, and the relationship between twins has always fascinated people of my profession. Secondly, and maybe more importantly because it has given me a special interest – I'm a twin myself! As you all know, I'm sure, there are different types of twins, identical and fraternal. Fraternal twins are more common – these are twins that are born from different eggs in the mother. That's what me and my brother are. The other type of twin is 'identical.' These are babies born from the same egg and this is rarer. In fact only one third of all the twins in the world are identical. There's another interesting point. The percentage of identical twins around the world is more or less the same in every country – but it seems that geography has an effect on the number of fraternal twins. For example, in Japan, for every thousand births there are about six sets of twins. However, in some parts of Africa there are twenty sets! There's actually a school in England that at one point had twenty sets of twins attending classes. That beat the world record by twelve sets! A year ago six sets of identical twins started the school at the same time. All students at the school wear uniforms, so it was very hard to know who was who.

Although the similar appearance of twins is very interesting, psychologists are particularly interested in another connection. A lot of people believe that twins have a psychic relationship – that they know what their brother or sister is thinking. But how true is this? Can twins communicate without words? Do they know when their twin is in danger? It's interesting and here my reactions are different! As a scientist I say no, psychic ability doesn't exist – but as a twin I have to say that I'm not sure!

There are many stories about twins around the world that have had big coincidences in their lives. Twin mothers in the US had baby sons within two hours of each other although they were supposed to have been born four weeks apart. And there's the famous case of 'twin Jims' who were separated at birth and brought up by different families. They went on to first marry wives with the same name 'Linda,' then got married a second time to wives with the same name 'Betty'! They gave their sons the same name and both of them called their dogs 'Toy'!

Many people would love to have a twin but not all twins are happy about it! As a twin myself, I know that twins can have a lot of problems. One of these is that there is often a lot of competition between them, particularly when they are young. Both children want the parents' attention.

Also twins don't like looking the same and when they are older they try to dress differently and have different careers in order to be seen as individuals. The problem is that our appearance, abilities, interests, and so on develop because of our DNA and therefore twins can't escape their similarity!

Unit 3 A place to live

3.1 Vocabulary

CD•2.1 MP3•40 **Exercise 3, page 48**

We went into the student cafeteria at London University and asked the question: What makes a city a good place for young people?

1 Lisa
My number one priority is open spaces for running. I like a city with plenty of parks and cheap sports facilities. I can't stand places where everything closes at six o'clock in the evening! I love cities that are hectic and never sleep and where you have great nightlife with a wide choice of things to do – movies, theater, music, restaurants … but young people don't have much money to spend, so it's important that all those things are affordable.

2 Gudrun
I'm into art and fashion, so I love places like London, where you can see some really crazy fashions, and some good graffiti and other street art. I can't afford to go into expensive designer stores, so I like flea markets and second-hand clothes stores. Buses and underground are really expensive in London. Where I come from, I can go everywhere by bicycle, but it's too dangerous here. The cycle lanes are too narrow and I'm afraid to use my bike. So I walk, but London's enormous, so I walk a lot. I guess it helps me stay in shape, but my ideal city has cheap public transportation and safe cycle lanes.

3 Liang
I'm studying here now, but when I've finished my degree I'll go back to China. I live in Shanghai and it's an exciting modern city full of gleaming skyscrapers, but that's not important for me. It's a very expensive place to live, and often the smog is so thick that you can't see to the other side of the road. I'd rather live somewhere less polluted. But the best thing about Shanghai is that there are plenty of job opportunities – I just hope I get a good job when I go back.

4 Josh
Well, one of the most important things for me is to be in a place with lots of other young people. I come from a picturesque town on the coast. Tourists love it – it's got quaint little backstreets, leafy neighborhoods, and breathtaking views over the sea. But I don't care about those things. My hometown is full of retired people, so there's nothing for young people to do. I'd prefer to live in a run-down, inner-city area in a big city where there's a lot going on. I think a city is more interesting if it's multicultural too. Where I'm from, most of the people who live there were born there.

3.3 Listening

CD•2.7 MP3•46 **Exercises 3 and 4, page 53**

1
Welcome to the *Lifestyle Show*. Let's start with the shocking results of a recent survey: Thirty-five percent of American people do not know any of their neighbors. Well, it's not a problem for residents of Springhill co-housing project in the southwest of England. Springhill is a new housing development of thirty-five homes in a typical residential area. Residents have their own self-contained apartments or houses and gardens but share a common house for communal meals. The co-housing idea comes from Denmark, where it is well-established, and according to the latest government housing figures, eight percent of Danish people live in this way. There is growing interest around the world in the model as a provider of affordable, sustainable social housing. Building materials are natural or recycled.
Springhill is not only sustainable in building terms, but in human terms too, encouraging the daily social contact that we know is a key to health and happiness. We're sure there'll be a hundred percent improvement in neighborly relations at Springhill. And now for a look at a different kind of ...

2
R = Rick, T = Tom
R: Come on, we're going to be late for school. What are you reading?
T: Oh, it's one of Dad's business magazines. Have you seen the plans for this Freedom Ship?
R: No, what is it?
T: Well, it's just a concept right now, but they're planning to build a huge ship that looks like a floating high-rise building with an airport on top.
R: That sounds a bit unstable if you ask me. Let's have a look. Oh, that's amazing. It looks like a multi-story parking lot! I wouldn't like to be on it in bad weather. Are they really going to build it?
T: Only if it can be profitable, so if you ask me, I'd be surprised. They need billions of dollars to even start, so it may never happen. It says here that there are people with disposable income who want to invest in the project and use it as their second home, but I shouldn't think many people would want to live on it. They want to make it nearly a mile and a half long – nearly a mile and a half long! That doesn't sound possible!
R: Where will it dock?
T: According to this article, no ports will be big enough for it to enter, so it'll just be sailing around the world non-stop with 50,000 people on board.
R: Well, I won't be one of them! Come on, it's time to go.

3
Today I'm reporting from *The House and Home Show* and I'm going to start with a question – where will you be living twenty years from now? Well, I think I've found the answer to that question. You'll probably be living in the kind of house on show here. I'm looking around a fully connected smart home and it's like walking into the future! But what is a smart home and how will smart technology benefit our lives?
OK, a smart home can be rewired so household appliances such as fridges, light fixtures, security systems, and thermostats can be controlled by the homeowner using a mobile device.

One benefit is that the smart home can save energy costs – even when you're not at home, with the tap of a finger on your cell phone, you can turn off lights, close windows, and control the heating. With the smart home you gain more hours in the day – when you're running low on milk, your fridge can order more and it can be programmed to manage all your shopping. The fridge will even advise on recipes based on what you've got in stock. Domestic chores just got a lot easier! This is my dream home!

Unit 4 The cost of living

4.2 Grammar

CD•2.19 MP3•58 **Exercises 1 and 2, page 68**

L = Laura, M = Mom
L: Mom! Guess what – Jamie got tickets for us to see Beyoncé tonight. It was sold out but he got them online.
M: You know it's risky buying tickets online, don't you?
L: Is it? The guy's meeting us outside the concert with the tickets.
M: OK, but just be careful, won't you? Don't give him any money until you see the tickets.
L: Don't worry! It'll be fine. Right, Jamie's picking me up in five minutes.
M: Jamie? But he hasn't passed his driving test, has he?
L: Yes, Mom, he passed it weeks ago.
M: Oh OK ... Wait a minute. You're not wearing my earrings, are you?
L: Oh, erm yes, I am. I forgot to ask you. Sorry.
M: You know they're worth a lot of money, don't you?
L: Are they? But you never wear them, do you?
M: Look, it's fine but just don't lose them, will you? It's so easy to lose things at concerts.
L: Stop worrying about everything, Mom. I'm always careful when I borrow your things, aren't I?

4.3 Listening

CD•2.22 MP3•61 Exercises 3 and 4, pages 70–71

I = Interviewer, M = Martin

I: Welcome to *The Shopping Show*. In this episode we're looking at the growing market in the US for second-hand goods and the different places where you can buy and sell these pre-owned items. To get us started, we have a guest in the studio. Hello and welcome, Martin Richards. Martin, you sell second-hand goods on the market, don't you? Can you tell us where you get them from?

M: Yes. Hello. Basically, I buy and sell the contents of luggage that is lost at airports and unclaimed by their owners.

I: There are thousands of bags and suitcases that get lost at airports, aren't there?

M: Yes, absolutely. Twenty-six million checked bags get lost from international flights around the world every year. Heathrow is one of the busiest airports in the world with nearly 200,000 people passing through the airport each day. Unsurprisingly, 45,000 bags get lost every month.

I: Amazing! So how do you get hold of this unclaimed lost luggage and what do you do with it?

M: Well, I certainly don't get them from the owners! I go to an auction house in London – they buy the lost property from Heathrow Airport, and sell it weekly to individuals like me. Then I have a stall on a market where I sell the clothes that come out of the lost suitcases.

I: So how much do you pay, and what kind of things do you get?

M: Well, there's an element of chance when you buy a suitcase because you can't look inside before you bid for it. The better the suitcase, the more likely you are to find designer clothes. But you could be very unlucky with a high-quality bag and just find dirty socks – that's the chance you take. Luckily, the auctioneers open the bags and throw away anything horrible like food that's gone bad or wet stuff that's gone moldy. When you buy suitcases, you just get clothes. Then they take out electrical goods and shoes and they sell those in separate lots.

I: If we could just go back to what you were saying before, it's really surprising how many bags get lost! Have you any idea how this happens?

M: Apparently, the most common cause of lost luggage is when people check in their bags either too far in advance, or at the very last minute. Things can also get lost if passengers transfer to other flights. But you wouldn't believe what the most commonly lost thing is – children's buggies! That's what I find most shocking – I just don't understand how people can leave the airport carrying the child and not remember the buggy!

I: One last question, Martin. Do you feel a bit strange handling people's personal belongings?

M: Um. That's a good question. The easy answer is no – I try to think about it as a job. But if I'm honest, I do often wonder who these people are, where they're from, and where they were going. Once I found a wedding dress in one of the suitcases – I just hope they lost it on the way home.

I: Absolutely. I'm sure those suitcases could tell a few stories. Thank you, Martin. Now …

4.5 Grammar

CD•2.29 MP3•68 Exercises 1 and 2, page 74

J = James, E = Ellie

J: It's Bella's birthday tomorrow and I haven't got a present yet. Can you give me some ideas? Clothes?

E: You definitely shouldn't buy clothes unless you know the correct size. If you get too small, she'll think she's fat, and if you get too big, she'll think you think she's fat.

J: Oh, right, not clothes. How about jewelry? A nice ring?

E: A ring? You need to be careful not to give the wrong message – a ring has a special meaning.

J: Hm. A bracelet?

E: Yes, with a bracelet you don't need to worry about giving the wrong message. But it must be something really nice. Something she'll be proud to wear. How much do you want to spend?

J: I don't know – no more than twenty-five dollars.

E: Right – you ought to forget jewelry. What's she into?

J: Music. I could get concert tickets.

E: That's good – but you ought to avoid buying them for too far ahead. You may split up and then it would be a waste of money.

J: Oh yeah. I know – perfume!

E: Do you know what she likes?

J: No.

E: Well you ought to!

J: I could get her the same as Mom wears.

E: No! You mustn't do that! That's a really bad idea! Moms and teenagers don't wear the same perfume.

J: Why? Mom's perfume's nice. Oh dear, this is more difficult than I thought. I wish I had more time. Should I get a gift certificate or is that boring?

E: It's boring. You'd better ask her friends for some ideas before the stores shut. They'll know exactly what she likes. Hurry, though, because you're running out of time …

CD•2.31 MP3•70 Exercise 8, page 75

A

A: You look tired today.

B: I am. I didn't have a very good evening yesterday.

A: What happened?

B: I went to the movies with my brother. The ticket cost a lot and the movie was terrible and very long. So it was an expensive evening and we went to bed late.

B
A: Have you seen Katy's new haircut?
B: No, what's it like?
A: I don't think it suits her. I told her it made her nose look big. She was upset.

C
A: That new girl came to my brother's birthday party last week.
B: Oh, what's she like?
A: I'm not sure if she's shy or rude, but she didn't speak to anyone and she left really early.

4.6 Speaking

CD•2.32 MP3•71 Exercises 2 and 3, page 76

O = Oscar, E = Emma
O: What a week! I'm exhausted. I'm glad it's Saturday.
E: Well, don't relax too much; we need to do some food shopping. We don't even have coffee.
O: Don't we? Well, you could've said something earlier. How am I supposed to function without coffee?
E: Er ... well, you should've noticed yourself if it's so important to you. Anyway, there's a food market on West Street today. I say we get there early.
O: What, you mean leave the apartment?
E: Well, how else do you suggest we do the shopping, Oscar?
O: Er ... online? I really can't be bothered to go out, Emma. Going to the market is time consuming and takes effort, but shopping online is quick and convenient. Click, click, click and it's done. Miraculous! It's the only way of shopping that allows you to stay on the sofa ... and therefore, it's clearly the best choice. Another reason is that, instead of carrying heavy bags half-way across town, someone will deliver everything to the door. What could be easier?
E: You are so lazy, Oscar! OK, when you compare the two, shopping online might require less effort, but I wouldn't choose it because you can't actually pick the fresh food yourself, can you? If you order online, they can send you all the old stuff. That's why I'd opt for the market. On top of that, it is actually good to leave the house and interact with other real people sometimes, you know?
O: Hmmm?
E: I mean, I prefer going to the market simply because it's a colorful and lively place to spend some time. Also, shopping online isn't the best choice if you consider the environment – all those delivery trucks speeding around the city. Plus, don't forget it's much more likely that the food at the market is locally grown and it's definitely the cheaper option.
O: OK, OK! I get the message. How about you go to the market and I stay here?
E: That's fine, Oscar. You can clean the kitchen and the bathroom while I do the shopping.
O: On second thoughts, I'll come with you and help carry the bags.
E: Oh, my hero!

Focus Review 4

CD•2.33 MP3•72 Exercise 7, page 83

P = Presenter, A = Anne
P: I'm here in the studio with Anne Knight – a mystery shopper. It's very much a niche job and one that's full of secrecy. Can you tell me a little about your job and what it actually entails?
A: Sure. Basically I'm assigned a number of different stores, in different locations and cities, and asked to buy a certain something from a specific department or from a new product range. It could be in a chain of supermarkets, for example, a fast food restaurant, or a large department store. I take extensive notes on the appearance and cleanliness of the store, the progression of the queue, and the quality of customer service. I then have to write up detailed reports on the overall shopping experience. It's not as glamorous as most people think.
P: Companies are spending millions each year, there's an increasing need for mystery shoppers, and salaries can be impressive, I hear. Do your clients get good value for money?
A: I believe so. Retailers are becoming increasingly aware of the competition from online stores and profits are being threatened. They are responding to the fact that shoppers who are actually prepared to set foot inside a store need to be offered a higher quality of service – a more unique and enjoyable shopping experience than they get online. Attracting new customers is desirable through improved customer service but central to the idea keeping regular visitors coming back.
P: Does it work?
A: Oh, definitely. Once the report has been produced clients might respond, for example, by employing more cashiers to work the tills, which results in queues moving faster. Or maybe store floors are cleaner or reorganized to make them more shopper-friendly. In particular, though, a few of the places I've visited have been awarded for the good quality of service to their customers. I'm totally convinced that it's a result of my efforts and that what I'm doing benefits everyone who goes shopping – and that's most satisfying.
P: What else do you like about being a mystery shopper?
A: Occasionally, we get an exclusive assignment such as checking out a five-star restaurant, or doing a report on a store that's on a cruise ship. Companies really have to spend vast sums for such a service and the pay is very good, so understandably such jobs are quite rare – but it does add to the whole unpredictability of the work, which is nice.
P: In many ways the perfect job.

A: Believe it or not, it's actually quite hard to enjoy a meal that costs a fortune in a plush restaurant because you can't sit there and take notes like you can in a store. Remembering lots of tiny details about the meal, the overall quality of the service, and the food being served, as well as the much more personal interaction with the waiting staff – all of that can actually distract from the whole experience. And then having to go home or back to the hotel late at night to write reports on everything while it's still fresh. You really do need to remain focused and detail oriented. Hardly the perfect way to spend an evening.
P: So, it's not all just about free meals, is it? Thank you, Anne. Stay tuned because next up Michael Bridges will be talking to …

Unit 5 The world at your feet

5.2 Grammar

CD•2.38 MP3•77 **Exercises 1 and 2, page 86**

1
A: Tell us about your weaknesses.
B: I'm not a morning person. In fact, I struggled to get up this morning. I'd like to be able to start work after lunch.

2
A: It's a pity you haven't had any experience of restaurant work.
B: Don't worry!
C: We are very good at eating …
B: … and that's why we think we should get the job.

3
A: Do you like the job you have now?
B: No, I don't because I have to answer the phone a lot and I hate that.

5.3 Listening

CD•2.39 MP3•78 **Exercises 2 and 3, page 88**

P = Presenter, DA = Dr. Atkins
P: In today's show we're taking a look into the future of work. With us in the studio we have a specialist in future trends in the workplace – Dr. Atkins. Dr. Atkins, what do you think the world of work will look like ten years from now?
DA: Well, it certainly won't look the same as now. Technology now enables us to work anywhere and so there's been a steady rise in people working from home and a sharp drop in the number of people commuting to work.
P: As technology takes over tasks that people used to do, what kind of skills will be useful for people in the future?
DA: People will have to focus on the kind of skills that can't be done by a machine or a robot such as leadership and management jobs or caring for other humans.
P: So you don't think that dentists and teachers should worry about their jobs just yet?
DA: No, definitely not. Jobs in the medical and teaching professions will be unchanged. Many of the traditional jobs will still be necessary ten or twenty years from now – we'll always need lawyers, politicians, fire fighters, and so on. And we mustn't forget the creative industries: we'll always need artists, writers, and actors. I also think there will be a marked increase in jobs connected with alternative energy.
P: What kind of jobs would they be?
DA: Well things like solar panel engineers or wind turbine technicians.
P: Right, I see. So which jobs do you think are at risk in the future?
DA: Um, I think there will be a gradual decline in jobs in retail – store assistants aren't required in the days of online shopping. Any office jobs and factory jobs that can be done by computers and robots will disappear.
P: Finally, can you name any job titles that don't exist now and will in the future?
DA: I think we'll see jobs like body-part maker, robot mechanics, and space tourist guide. But I could be completely wrong!

CD•2.40 MP3•79 **Exercises 6 and 7, page 89**

P = Presenter, J = Julie, G = Geoffrey, A = Angie, M = Mark
P: Welcome back to our show exploring the future of work. We asked four people their thoughts on their careers and where they saw them in the future. Our first speaker is Julie Robinson, a LAWYER.
J: A career in law is stable because laws don't tend to change fast. It's challenging and potentially well-paid if you get a high-powered job in a top law firm. However, I believe there's been a sharp drop in law graduates recently because it's so expensive to study law at university for six years. Some law firms are offering apprenticeships so that trainees can start work and earn a salary while they're training. Technology has had an effect on our profession – some of the jobs that lawyers used to do can now be done online. Fortunately, these tend to be tedious tasks that nobody liked doing. On the whole, being a lawyer can be an extremely rewarding and lucrative career.
P: Our second speaker is Geoffrey Smith, a DENTIST.
G: My dental practice is always busy, and I can't see that changing in the future. As far as clients are concerned, I've noticed a marked increase in elderly patients who want to keep their teeth in good condition. Technology has changed the way I work and will probably continue to make my job easier. There have been great advances in the medication we use to manage pain, so my patients can relax a bit more. I know people hate coming to see me! I don't blame them, but I don't think they'd be any happier if I was replaced by a robot.

P: Our third speaker is Angie Walters, a STORE ASSISTANT.
A: The supermarket where I work is always busy, so it's hard to believe my job is going to disappear. If you ask me, people want to see what they're buying – I do! But the experts say that there will be a gradual decline in supermarket sales, and so my job isn't secure. I'd hate to lose my job because I think I've got great interpersonal skills and I'm quite good at handling difficult customers. Some people think my job's monotonous, but I find this human contact with the customers very fulfilling. If we close down, I worry that some of my elderly customers will never go out and see anyone. That's not progress, is it?
P: Finally, our fourth speaker is Mark Pomroy, a WIND TURBINE TECHNICIAN.
M: I'm working in the alternative energy industry. To work with wind turbines, you need to do a two-year course in Applied Sciences and this will teach you the basic technology. The skills you need are to be good with your hands, and it helps to have some experience in mechanics. In my free time I enjoy taking car engines apart and putting them back together, so that helps. After studying the basics, I did an internship with a company and learned on the job. My job's demanding, but I think it will be an important career in the near future.
P: Well thank you to our four speakers. It's interesting to hear …

5.6 Speaking

CD•2.45 MP3•84 **Exercises 2 and 3, page 94**

D = Daniel, H = Hannah
Friends Hannah and Daniel are working in Daniel's dad's bike store during the summer vacations. Today they are responsible for opening the store.
D: Right, here we are. Have you got the keys?
H: Yep.
D: Thanks … OK … er …
H: What's the matter?
D: I've no idea. I can't seem to open it.
H: What do you mean? Just put the key in and turn it.
D: Yes, thank you, Einstein. Every time I try to turn it, it gets stuck.
H: Well, what's up with it?
D: How should I know? Maybe there's something wrong with the lock.
H: Well, have you tried turning it the other way?
D: The other way? I doubt that'll work, but let's see.
H: And?
D: No, that doesn't make any difference. Now what?
H: Let me try.
D: OK … Careful. Not too hard, it'll …
H: Whoops! It's broken off in the lock.
D: Hannah! Why in the world did you do that?
H: I didn't do it on purpose.
D: What are we supposed to do now?
H: Calm down. I think I might have left the restroom window open around the back. Maybe if I climb through, I'll be able to open the door from the inside. At least then we can open the store on time. We'll work out what to do about the lock later.

At the back of the store
H: Yes! It's open. Problem solved. Help me up.
D: OK, be careful. I'm not sure this is a good idea. It looks a bit small. Are you sure you'll fit?
H: Are you saying I'm fat?
D: What?
H: I'm joking, Daniel. OK, 1 … 2 … 3 … oooof … ah … ouch! Oh, I can't get my leg through.
D: Are you OK?
H: No! I can't move.
D: OK, this isn't going to work. Come back out.
H: Oh, OK … ah … ooof … ouch! Daniel, I can't …
D: What are you doing?
H: I'm stuck! What am I going to do now?
D: Well, you should have thought about that earlier.
D: Oh no! That's it. My dad is going to kill us.

Unit 6 True or false?

6.3 Listening

CD•3.5 MP3•90 **Exercise 2, page 106**

Reports are coming in from London of a new mural by enigmatic street artist, Banksy. Banksy's real identity is unknown. Some people believe his real name is Robert Banks while others say that he's Robin Gunningham, who was born in Bristol in 1973. Banksy has never confirmed or denied any of these reports and his identity remains a mystery even though his art is recognized worldwide. There is an unconfirmed rumor that he trained to be a butcher before becoming a street artist. His graffiti art became famous in the 1990s in Bristol and London, but he chose to remain anonymous at first to avoid being arrested for acts of vandalism. So far he has managed to protect his true identity and has remained out of reach of the authorities. When a new 'Banksy' appears in the street, he posts it on his website. This is how he authenticates his street art and confirms to the public that it is genuine and not a fake. His artworks can fetch hundreds of thousands of dollars in auction. It is unclear how much of this money goes to Banksy himself, though people say he is worth twenty million dollars.

CD•3.6 MP3•91 **Exercises 4 and 5, page 107**

A = Alice, R = Robert
A: What are you doing?
R: I'm trying to find some information on the Internet for my Art project. I have to do an essay about artists who raise ethical issues through their work.

A: Ooh, that sounds interesting. I worked on a similar project for my degree. You should write about street artists like Banksy who make statements about society through graffiti.
R: I don't know much about him. Do you?
A: Quite a bit, yes. I used to think he was American because he's done a lot of work in New York, but it turns out that he's actually British. He's been doing street art for twenty-five years but I've no idea how old he was when he started. Actually it's amazing how he's managed to stay so enigmatic but apparently his friends are really loyal and committed to helping him remain anonymous. I don't know much about his background – nobody does – but I can tell you about his murals and his painting techniques if you like.
R: Yes, that would be good.
A: OK, he started off painting onto walls and then later he started using stencils and spray cans to speed up the painting process. When you want your identity to remain a secret you don't want to hang around the streets too long doing something illegal! I mean, he is breaking the law.
R: Yeah, I suppose he is. Right, let me just finish writing that down. OK, so what's he trying to achieve with all this – what does he believe in?
A: Well, he's quite political – he calls himself an activist and he's against authority in general. He has strong beliefs about people and the way we live our lives.
R: So which issues is he most interested in?
A: He's anti-war, so some of his murals show soldiers holding flowers instead of guns to make people aware of the stupidity of war. Look, I'll show you on this website about him.
R: Ah, right. I like the one of the protestor who's about to throw a bouquet of flowers.
A: Yes, that's a good one and it's quite obvious what it's about – it stands for peaceful protest. Banksy also does a lot of paintings of children. His most popular image is a girl with a red heart-shaped balloon. Here it is.
R: Oh yes, I love that one. But it's a bit sad – the balloon is floating away from the little girl. I'm not sure what the underlying message is, but his art really makes you think, doesn't it?
A: Yes, that's right. The meaning isn't always obvious but I know he's a strong believer in fairness and equality – that's why he's a good subject for your essay.

6.6 Speaking

CD•3.12 MP3•97 **Exercises 3 and 4, pages 112–113**

1 I firmly believe they do. During the 1980s, due to pressure from anti-fur campaigners, the number of fashion designers using fur fell sharply. Sadly, fur seems to be fashionable again these days, so I would say that campaigns and protests are more important than ever. Obviously, protesting is a good way to promote awareness, but I think it is important to make your point peacefully. The anti-fur movement has received criticism in the past for using violent or illegal protests and I also believe these do more harm than good. It could be argued that some of the more shocking images used in protests actually prevent some people from engaging with the movement. Frankly, I find some of the pictures extremely difficult to look at.

2 Well, one obvious advantage is their ability to deliver a message to huge groups of people. Clearly, a lot of the general public are interested in the lives and opinions of public figures and celebrities. When a celebrity supports the anti-fur movement, lots of people take notice. Regrettably, the opposite is also true. When celebrities are seen wearing fur products, it sends the message that fur is glamorous and desirable. If you ask me, there is nothing glamorous or desirable about killing animals for the sake of fashion.

3 I think I'd emphasize just how many animals have died to make their coat, or hat, or whatever it is they are wearing. Often, people don't realize that to make a single coat from fox fur, for example, fifteen to twenty animals have to be killed. I'd like them to think about these poor creatures every time they put on their 'beautiful' coat. Can they really justify that much killing, just so they can wear fur? In my opinion, fur is beautiful, but only when it's on the animals to which it belongs. For those who really can't do without the 'fur look,' there are synthetic products that look exactly the same as the real thing. Some protesters feel that even synthetic fur is wrong as it encourages the fashion to continue, but I don't feel particularly strongly about that.

Unit 7 Log on

7.1 Vocabulary

CD•3.15 MP3•100 **Exercise 9, page 121**

1
D = Doctor, P = Patient
D: Good morning. What seems to be the problem?
P: Hello, doctor. I'm not feeling very well. I keep getting headaches.
D: OK, I think we need to take your blood pressure. Hmm, it's a bit high.
P: Oh dear. What should I do?
D: You need to do more exercise and try not to put too much salt on your food.
P: Oh no, I love salt!

2
B = Boy, G = Girl
B: I think I need to change my glasses.
G: Why? They look OK.
B: Because my eyes hurt all the time.
G: Maybe you're spending too much time looking at your computer screen.
B: Hm, that's what my mom says.

3
G = Girl, B = Boy
B: Did you go to bed late last night?
G: No, but I couldn't sleep – I was still awake at four o'clock this morning.
B: Oh dear, that's horrible. I used to have problems sleeping, but since I started running I sleep like a baby!

4
M = Man, W = Woman
M: I think I need to get a better office chair.
W: Really?
M: Yes, my knees hurt when I stand up.
W: Well, I suppose you do spend most of your time sitting at your desk. But good office chairs can be very expensive.

5
G = Girl, B = Boy
G: I'm worried about my mom. She has to take medication every day.
B: Why's that? She looks OK.
G: She has too much sugar in her blood and it can be dangerous. But the medication helps.

6
M = Mother, B = Boy
M: Jo, stop playing that game now and come and have dinner.
B: OK, I'll be there in a minute.
M: Jo! Stop that now. You've been playing that game for five hours! Time to stop.

7.3 Listening

CD•3.18 MP3•103 **Exercises 2 and 3, page 124**

1
SA: Store Assistant, J = Julie
SA: Good afternoon. Can I help you?
J: Oh yes, I'm looking for a new laptop. I have a budget of $500.
SA: Right. You won't be looking at a top-of-the-line model for that amount, but I'm happy to show you what you can get for $500. Let's start here. This one's a basic laptop with a capacity of 500 gigabytes.
J: That sounds good.
SA: Well, compared with how computers used to be, it's not bad. If you just want to do word processing and social networking, it's a waste of money to buy a more powerful computer. But if you want to do gaming and store movies and music, you can get the same computer with a one-terabyte hard drive for just $550, that's just $50 more.
J: I do want to store movies and music, but do I need one terabyte?
SA: Well, you may be able to do without the extra storage now, but you need to think about the future. If you want to store music and movies, it's well worth spending a bit more. For just $50 you get a hard drive twice the size.
J: Hm, I'm not sure. I need to think it over.
SA: Of course. If it helps you to make a decision, I'll throw in an external drive with the one-terabyte model.

2
S = Sat-nav, K = Kate, L = Luke
S: *At the junction take the third exit. Take the exit.*
L: Are you sure this is right?
K: Well, the sat-nav seems to think it is. Why?
L: I thought we should be on the highway by now. I'm going to go towards the highway.
S: *Make a legal U-turn where possible.*
K: The sat-nav didn't like that! I don't know why you're going on the highway when the sat-nav was taking us another route?
S: *Exit ahead.*
K: Now it's trying to make us leave the highway. I really don't think we should be on the highway at all.
L: Do we have a map anywhere?
K: Why would we need a map? I think we should do what the sat-nav tells us to do.
S: *In 500 feet take the exit.*
L: But I think it's wrong. Why don't we stop at the next service station and have a look at a map. Then we can figure out where to go.
K: OK, but I don't know why you bother to have a sat-nav if you don't think it works.
L: It was you who talked me into getting it! I hate sat-navs – they just get on my nerves.
K: You just don't like being told what to do.
L: Sorry?
K: Nothing.
S: *Turn around where possible.*

3
A report into street crime in the UK has revealed that 700,000 handsets were stolen last year. Children under fifteen were the most common targets, with up to half a million young people aged between eleven and fifteen falling victim to phone theft last year. The report said that cell phone robbery was mainly carried out by male teenagers. Overall, cell phone theft has risen 190 percent since 1995 and police have warned that if present trends continue, thefts are likely to reach one million by the end of this year. Since these figures came out, the government have urged cell phone companies to bring in new security measures. This would allow accounts to be cut off when customers reported the number of their stolen handset.

7.5 Grammar

CD•3.24 MP3•109 **Exercise 1, page 128**

Nobody knows exactly how numbers originated but, maybe unsurprisingly, it is thought that numbers and counting began with the number one. The first evidence of this is the Ishango bone that was found in the Congo region of Africa. The bone is believed to be more than 20,000 years old. It is thought that lines cut into the bone at regular intervals were used for counting.

Arithmetic is considered to have originated around 6,000 years ago in Sumeria, an ancient civilization in modern-day Iraq. There was a system of tokens in use; if you had ten chickens you were given ten tokens. Then when you sold or killed one of your chickens, a token was removed. It is thought that this is how subtraction, and therefore arithmetic, was invented.

Around the time when they were building the pyramids, the Egyptians are known to have invented the numbers one thousand and one million.

It might surprise you to know that before 1500, the term 'mathematics' was understood to mean 'astrology.' It only changed to its present meaning between 1500 to 1800. In a world dominated by technology, there are said to be unlimited opportunities for mathematicians and an increasing number of students are expected to be doing Math in college in the future.

7.6 Speaking

CD•3.26 MP3•111 **Exercises 3 and 4, pages 130–131**

M = Mia, L = Lucas, S = Sam

M: Whoa! What's this? It looks a bit scary.
L: I'm not sure, to be honest.
S: Hi and welcome to 'Mind-blowing Machines.' I'm Sam and I'm an 'Explainer' here at the exhibition. Would you like to know a little bit more about this incredible machine?
M: Er ... sure. What is it?
S: It's actually a fully-automated remote surgical unit.
L: Er ... I'm afraid you've lost me there. It's a what?
S: Well, basically, it's a kind of robotic surgeon that can be controlled from anywhere in the world.
L: A robotic surgeon? Sounds like something from a nightmare! You'd never get me anywhere near that thing.
S: Ha, yes. Quite a few people say that, but it's perfectly safe. It's operated by a real human surgeon, of course. The two robotic arms here are actually steadier and provide a greater range of movement than the human hand. The machine makes it possible to provide expert surgical services to patients all around the world without the need to travel.
M: Are you saying that the surgeon doesn't actually have to be in the place where the operation takes place?
S: Yes, precisely. Using an ultra-fast telecommunications system, the machine would allow a surgeon here in London, for example, to perform an operation on a patient in Australia or Africa, or anywhere in the world, in fact.
M: That's amazing.
S: Mind-blowing, huh?

Focus review 7

CD•3.28 MP3•113 **Exercise 7, page 137**

1

The entertainment industry is set to launch a new scheme in an effort to combat the high levels of Internet piracy. The project, backed by UK Internet service providers, will see people suspected of downloading illegal content alerted via 'educational' letters informing them of where they can download the same content through more official channels. Reports suggest that one in five American people engage in some form of copyright infringement, but many believe that the new measures are not severe enough to curb the growing number of Internet users downloading illegally.

2

W = Woman, M = Man

W: What are you doing? I thought you were doing the washing up.
M: Later. I just thought I'd get half an hour in before we go out?
W: Seriously? So I have to do the washing up again? You play that silly video game for hours every day. You'd be better off studying for your exam next month. Don't come crying to me if you fail.
M: Oh, it's just a little harmless fun and it helps me to relax.
W: Relax!? That's a joke. You get so wound up that you're miserable for ages afterwards. And with your high blood pressure ...
M: Oh, come on. Don't exaggerate.
W: Look at last Wednesday when Anne and Bob came over. You could hardly be bothered to talk to them because you'd lost on that game.

3

B = Boy, G = Girl

B: I don't know why I let myself get talked into buying this smartphone.
G: What's the problem? It's supposed to be a good phone. It has some pre-installed applications – you can see a complete list here. Just keep playing around with it.
B: But nothing seems to work. To connect to the Internet, you should go to settings and press connect. At least that's what you'd expect. But look, there's no connect option.
G: That's weird. It should be simple enough. Is the wi-fi option on?
B: It's hard to tell. When I try to check, the thing just reboots. Nothing does what it's supposed to do. I'll have to take it back to the store.

4

Do you and your classmates enjoy science? Do you have ideas for new inventions? Then enter the Young Inventors Contest. The contest is open to groups of eleven- to sixteen-year-old students and entries will be accepted up to July thirty-first. Although the judges will be looking at good basic scientific knowledge, what is most likely to get their attention is an idea that is new and different. In the past, the contest has targeted specific types of inventions. For example, last year's students were asked to design something to help the environment. This year the topic is completely open, so let your imaginations roam free! More details can be found on our website at ...

5

B = Boy, G = Girl

B: So, how was the dreaded Science class today?
G: Actually, not as bad as I'd thought! We've got a new teacher and I think she's going to make Science classes a lot more interesting.
B: That's good! But I can't imagine how she's going to do that. Science is Science is Science!
G: I know, and I'm really not very good at it. But she started today by showing us part of a science fiction movie in class. Then we had a great discussion about how likely it is that the inventions they showed will actually happen.
B: Now, that's MY kind of science class.

6

G = Girl, B = Boy

G: Are you OK? Why are you moving your hand and fingers around in that weird way?
B: I'm just doing some exercises. I've got a really sore thumb. I think it's because I've been doing so much writing recently.
G: I don't think so! It's all the texting you do. You never stop!
B: You know, I hadn't thought of that. You might have a point there. Since this started hurting I've had to try texting with my fingers and that's really hard. It takes ages too.
G: The easy answer is to cut down on the texting and phone people for a while. You'll be surprised how quickly it clears up.
B: Don't be silly. If I keep phoning people, I won't be able to chat to the people I'm with as well, will I?

Unit 8 Around the globe

8.2 Grammar

CD•3.33 MP3•118 **Exercises 2 and 3, page 140**

B = Ben, E = Ellie, D = Dad, M = Mom

B: Mom, where are we going on vacation this year? I wish we could go back to that campsite we went to last year.
E: And the year before, and the year before that, and the yea —
D: OK Ellie we get the message!
E: Well, it's boring to go to the same place every year. If only we could go somewhere exciting for a change.
M: Like where?
E: I don't know – I just wish we could do something different, have an adventure.
D: Yes, I agree. I think it's time we did something cultural. I've had enough of lounging on sunbeds – let's go somewhere where we can learn something about the culture.
M: Well, I don't see what's wrong with sunbeds myself. I wish you all realized how much I look forward to doing nothing for two weeks! I've got a stressful job and I look after you lot too.
D: Look, we can do both – we can go somewhere where you can lie in the sun and we can go and explore the museums and churches ...
E: Dad, that wasn't what I meant. I want to have an experience. If only we could go on safari or go trekking in the Himalayas or sail across the ocean.
M: Ha, sail across the ocean? Can I remind you that we HAVEN'T won the lottery recently!
B: Hmm, I'd rather we went to the campsite we went to last year.
E: But Ben, we don't do anything there – we just go to the beach every day.
M: Fine by me.
D: No, Ellie's right. It's time we went outside our comfort zone. We should have a family adventure. I've always wanted to do white water rafting. Let's go to France. It'll be hot – Mom can sunbathe and we can have an adventure.
E: I'd rather go to the Himalayas.
D: We can go there when you become a millionaire! Here, let's google *white water rafting in France*.

CD•3.34 MP3•119 **Exercise 6, page 141**

D = Dad, E = Ellie, B = Ben, M = Mom

D: So what was the best part of the vacation for you?
E: Definitely not the sunburn. If only I'd worn more sunscreen.
D: Hm yes, you really suffered, didn't you, Ellie?
B: Hahaha you were so red. But the best part for me was when you fell out of the raft. I wish I hadn't forgotten my camera. It would have been a great photo!
E: I wish you'd fallen in too, Ben! Then you wouldn't think it was so funny. The water was freezing!
M: Ugh, it sounds awful. I'm so glad I stayed at the campsite – I just wish I'd known about the mosquitoes. I was bitten to death. But it's better than being frightened to death in the raft.
D: Yes, I must admit it was frightening, but we wanted to go outside our comfort zone, and we certainly did.

8.3 Listening

CD•3.35 MP3•120 **Exercises 2 and 3, page 142**

P = Presenter, D = Dr. Matthews

P: Welcome to *Animal World*, the series in which we examine animals' behavior in their natural habitats. This week, we're turning our attention to some of the smartest animals on the planet. Here to help us is wildlife expert and animal rights campaigner Dr. Roger Matthews. Thank you for joining us, Dr. Matthews.
D: Thank you for inviting me.
P: Dr. Matthews, if humans are intelligent, then chimpanzees must be intelligent too because they share ninety-eight percent of the same genes as humans. Is that right?
D: Yes, it is. And when you spend time with chimpanzees, you can see how close they are

to humans in so many ways: they embrace and kiss and hug each other, and they laugh when they're playing. They experience adolescence and develop powerful mother and child bonds. They are also similar to humans in that they attack and kill rival gangs of chimpanzees when they want to extend their territory.

P: Oh, that really is quite shocking. I thought chimps were like humans, but nicer.

D: It's the same with dolphins. When you think of dolphins, words like 'friendly,' 'gentle,' 'playful,' 'intelligent' come to mind. Well, they are undoubtedly intelligent – dolphins have large brains and they have a number of things in common with humans and chimpanzees. They form stable communities and live in social groups. And they're totally dependent on their parents during childhood. But they're also good at defending themselves and can be quite competitive against one another. When they want to show who's boss, or keep other males away from a female, they can be quite aggressive.

P: If we could come nearer to home, Dr. Matthews, what about the animals we see every day around us?

D: Right, let's think about farm animals – which do you think are the least intelligent?

P: Hmm, least intelligent. Cows, maybe, or no – sheep?

D: Right, sheep have the reputation for being stupid because they follow the crowd and frankly, they don't look very bright. However, scientific research shows that they've been seriously undervalued for their intelligence. Sheep are capable of learning. In intelligence tests, they perform at a level very similar to monkeys, and they can recognize people and respond when you call their name. So sheep are in fact quite intelligent animals.

P: Extraordinary!

D: It proves that it isn't the animals that look intelligent that are intelligent. Look at owls – we call them 'wise,' but it's a common misconception. Owls are not very clever at all.

P: Yes, things are not always as they appear! Now, before we go any further, there's a question I'd like to ask. Which are smarter, dogs or cats?

D: Well, cats seem to have strong personalities while dogs can be rather silly. But in fact, dogs have bigger brains. Their brains have been developing for centuries, while cats' brains have remained unchanged since they were first domesticated by the ancient Egyptians.

P: Why is that?

D: It's down to one simple fact – dogs are more social than cats, and the more social the animal, the bigger the brain and therefore the smarter the animal. If you think about it, dogs come when you call and spend a lot of time trying to please their owner. They're used as rescue dogs, police dogs, guide dogs. Cats, on the other hand, are loners.

P: Ah, I'm going to defend cats here – dogs do tricks because they've been trained to come when you call their name, or to fetch the ball and things like that. I'm sure my cat could do that if she wanted to, but she's too independent to do tricks and she doesn't need the approval of humans like dogs do.

D: Well, everybody thinks their own pet is the smartest. I've got a goldfish and I'm sure he can tell the time.

P: Hahaha, thank you very much, Dr. Matthews. In future, I won't judge an animal on what it looks like. Next week we're talking about elephants. But until then, goodbye.

8.6 Speaking

CD•3.42 MP3•127 **Exercises 3 and 4, pages 148–149**

Have you ever wondered what mysteries lie directly beneath your feet? Of course, there are your socks and shoes, and the floor, then possibly a cellar, then probably earth and rocks and then, maybe an underground lake, or maybe, something altogether more unexpected; something ancient and astonishingly beautiful.

In 2000, mineral miners from the town of Naica, in Northern Mexico, made an astounding discovery beneath the ground. What they found took the idea of 'buried treasure' to a whole new level. During this presentation, I plan to tell you more about Cueva De Los Cristales, a truly incredible natural wonder.

We are all familiar with underground caves from films and documentaries, even if we have never actually been in one ourselves. You may be aware that caves can be very dangerous places but also fascinating places. Most people don't realize, however, just how stunning they can actually be.

When those Mexican miners drained the water from a system of underground caverns at the beginning of the new millennium, their discovery proved that caves can be among the most awe-inspiring environments on the planet.

Hiding and growing in the darkness for half a million years, the enormous crystals of Cueva De Los Cristales or Giant Crystal Cave – now on the screen – are some of the biggest ever discovered. The largest is forty feet long, thirteen feet in diameter and weighs fifty-five tons. Unfortunately, you won't be able to visit them any time soon as the caves are extremely hot. Temperatures of up to 136 degrees Fahrenheit mean that, without proper protection, it is impossible to remain underground there for more than ten minutes at a time. As you can see in this picture, scientists exploring the caves in 2006 had to wear breathing equipment and specially designed suits to keep them cool.

It is believed that there are more undiscovered caverns at Naica, but exploring them would mean demolishing many of the crystals already uncovered. Instead, the plan is to finish doing research then re-flood the caves with water and seal them up again

OK, that's all from me. Thank you for listening. I hope you found the presentation interesting. If anyone has any questions, please feel free to ask now.

Workbook answer key

0.1 Diet

1
1 dried
2 bitter
3 ripe
4 fresh
5 greasy
6 raw
7 sour
8 stale
9 fattening

2
1 doesn't cook
2 've become
3 aren't working
4 've been waiting
5 have you been cooking?

3
1 've never heard
2 see
3 eat
4 are you doing
5 'm making
6 Do you think
7 have you been boiling
8 think

0.2 Fun and games

1
1 broke
2 scored
3 beat
4 win
5 staying
6 going
7 throwing

2
1 completed
2 were watching
3 reached
4 had climbed
5 was shining
6 pulled

3
1 had already scored
2 Did you remember
3 Were you watching
4 threw
5 forgot
6 wasn't concentrating

0.3 Teenage types

1
1 assertive
2 fussy
3 spoiled
4 selfish
5 rude
6 immature

2
1 wouldn't make
2 I had
3 would call
4 there was
5 I wasn't
6 wouldn't tap

3
1 'll never remember
2 would've bought
3 saw
4 'd known
5 sit
6 wouldn't behave

0.4 Visitors from space

1
1 explore
2 observations
3 analyzed
4 concluded
5 research
6 evolved
7 preserved
8 destruction

2
1 B
2 A
3 B
4 B
5 A

3
1 must've missed
2 might've gotten/ may have gotten/ could've gotten
3 can't be
4 might arrive/may arrive/could arrive
5 might not even have mailed/may not even have mailed
6 must not have left

0.5 Advertising

1
1 box
2 bunch
3 can
4 jar
5 bag
6 pair
7 tube

2
1 to taste the drink and describe the flavor
2 I would like to try their new service for free for a month
3 to contact them and let them know what I thought
4 I had ever thought of trying a different brand of lipstick
5 not to forget to take one pill before breakfast and the other one before bed
6 who was going to pay for the damage to her computer

3
1 would be there the following/next day if I could come back then
2 the advertising executives were arriving that night
3 he had seen the new ad on TV for the first time that day
4 they were going to open the new branch of their coffee shop the following/next week
5 she was sorry, but my doctor's appointment for that day had been canceled
6 she couldn't promise anything right then

0.6 Performers

1
1 novel
2 watercolor
3 ballet
4 screen
5 action
6 costume drama

2
1 a
2 Ø
3 The
4 Ø
5 the
6 a
7 the
8 the

3
1 the festival
2 the
3 a
4 lunch
5 a
6 The swimming pool
7 the only music

0.7 UK vs US

1
1 holiday
2 underground
3 lift
4 pavement
5 wardrobe

2
1 the best-paid
2 than
3 much
4 healthy
5 The
6 best-dressed

3
1 the ugliest
2 not as good as
3 not as far from us as
4 more you practice
5 healthier than

0.8 US vs UK

1
1 d
2 e
3 f
4 b
5 a
6 c

2
1 am never asked for my opinion
2 was told (by my teacher) that I spoke with an American accent (by my teacher)
3 was given to me to add to my cup of tea
4 was sent to America (by my parents) for the summer to learn English (by my parents)
5 am being met (by my American friend) at the airport in New York (by my American friend)
6 will always be remembered as the only American in my school

3
1 had your phone fixed yet
2 doesn't get his hair cut
3 didn't have her teeth whitened
4 has her toenails painted
5 is having the tattoo removed
6 got her hair cut

1 Do your best

1.1 Vocabulary

1
1 catch
2 put
3 fallen
4 turned
5 went

2
1 deep – P
2 attention – P
3 eager – A
4 gift – A
5 soak – P
6 reached – A

3
1 bright
2 single-minded
3 analytic
4 curious
5 studious

4
1 single-minded
2 studious
3 curious
4 analytic
5 bright

5
1 diligent
2 fun-loving
3 inquisitive
4 rational
5 persistent

1.2 Grammar

1
1 is always talking
2 were always playing
3 're always putting
4 are you always hanging

2
1 are
2 performed
3 used
4 didn't use to
5 would

3
1 is always/ constantly biting
2 used to be
3 will leave
4 was always/ constantly stealing
5 would pick and eat

1.3 Listening language practice

1
1 vividly
2 accurate
3 have
4 losing
5 recall
6 remember
7 manages

2
1 personal
2 recognition
3 visualize
4 familiarize
5 memorable

1.4 Reading

1
3

2
A 4
B 2
C –
D 5
E 1
F 3

3
1 F
2 T
3 F
4 T
5 T
6 F
7 F

4
1 put e
2 make c
3 have a
4 read d
5 see b

5
1 form
2 high
3 setting up
4 innate

1.5 Grammar

1
1 to laugh
2 to meet
3 to recycle
4 working
5 talking

2
1 a ii
b i
2 a i
b ii
3 a i
b ii
4 a ii
b i

3
1 hearing Mom and Dad talking
2 trying to get
3 stop thinking
4 forgotten to do
5 tried counting

1.6 Speaking language practice

1
1 c
2 a
3 b
4 f
5 d
6 e

2
1 frustrated
2 thrilled
3 relieved
4 terrified
5 enthusiastic
6 confused

3
1 e
2 d
3 a
4 b
5 c
6 f

4
1 tell
2 by
3 Clearly
4 chances
5 looks
6 definitely
7 might

5
1 I think, For this reason (I) feel
2 To be honest
3 In my opinion, That's why (I) think
4 intend, Actually
a = 3
b = 2
c = 1
d = 4

1.7 Writing
1
A Introduction
B Refreshments
C Events
D Charity fundraising
E Conclusion

2
1 C
2 E
3 D
4 A
5 B

3
1 It is hoped that
2 A lot of points were discussed
3 The purpose of this report is
4 It would assist the organizers if
5 there are still a number of decisions to be made

4
1 to wear
2 that we would invite
3 are
4 having
5 give
6 to announce

5
1 F
2 T
3 T
4 F
5 F
6 T

1.8 Language in focus
1
1 is always complaining
2 Not answering the phone
3 Keep practicing
4 stopped watching
5 is tired of dieting
6 has been barking
7 waste time worrying

2
1 looking
2 eating
3 turning
4 Being
5 terrifying
6 taking

3
1 There
2 It
3 There
4 there
5 It
6 it

1.9 Use of English
1
1 C
2 B
3 A
4 B
5 D
6 D
7 C
8 D

2
1 knowledge
2 priority
3 sporty
4 visitor
5 competitions
6 representative
7 enthusiastically
8 motivated

1.11 Self-check
1
1 gregarious
2 pursue
3 catch
4 recognizable
5 thinker

2
1 personalized
2 memorable
3 studious
4 visual
5 familiarize

3
1 will draw
2 is always playing
3 use
4 would ask
5 used to

4
1 spends too much money buying
2 do not (don't) feel like staying up
3 urged us to pay
4 remember to bring
5 heard him talking

5
1 was always speaking
2 reminded me to set a date
3 there any point in starting
4 take free education for granted
5 caught up on each other's

6
1 thirst
2 let
3 no
4 being
5 go

2 It takes all kinds

2.1 Vocabulary
1
1 ceremony
2 immediate/extended
3 extended/immediate
4 reception
5 gathering
6 shrines

2
1 a blessing
b Bless
2 a massive
b masses
3 a children
b childish
4 a receptionist
b receptions
5 a distant
b distance

3
1 showered
2 made
3 throats
4 proposed
5 lose

4
1 a frog
1 b lump
2 a toast
b motion
3 a fool
b fuss
4 a praise
b gifts
5 a sight
b count

5
1 worth (the) effort
2 centre (of) attention, highlight
3 once (in a) lifetime experience, time (of my) life

2.2 Grammar
1
1 b had been feeling
c had done
d had failed
e hadn't worked
2 a had been biking
b had he started out
c had been
d had been looking forward to
e had done

2
1 a had been living
b had known
2 a had been sneaking
b had sneaked
3 a had received
b had been receiving
4 a had been sleeping
b had slept

3
1 had loved
2 had always started
3 had done
4 had put up
5 had been receiving
6 had correctly predicted
7 had heard
8 had been looking forward
9 had snowed
10 had gone off

2.3 Listening language practice
1
1 a lot
2 the most
3 similar
4 like
5 compared

2
1 A
2 B
3 C
4 A
5 B

3
1 a passionate
b about
2 a focus
b on
3 a take part
b in
4 a associated
b with

2.4 Reading
1
1 F
2
1 C
2 B
3 C
4 A
5 D

3
1 concept
2 disappearance
3 explosion
4 illustrate
5 abduction
6 suppressed

2.5 Grammar
1
1 b
2 c
3 d
4 a

2
1 Ø
2 who/that
3 , whose
4 Ø
5 , which

3
1 Prince William Bridge, built in 2012, is the newest in the city.
2 There's a Japanese death metal band playing at the club on Saturday.
3 Most of the buildings destroyed in the war have been rebuilt.
4 Pupils living in the hills have to walk several hours to get to school.
5 Cannot be rewritten

2.6 Speaking language practice
1
1 expected, the mass was lengthy and tedious
2 I look back on that day now, I always smile to myself
3 of a sudden, we turned a corner and there she was
4 of the blue, a car appeared on the horizon
5 turned out to be worth all the effort in the end
6 soon as we left, it started snowing heavily

2
b 3, 6
c 1,4
d 2,5

3
1 Suddenly, d
2 Unexpectedly, b
3 Out of the blue, d
4 While, b
5 All of a sudden, c

4
1 place
2 Just
3 predictably
4 Fortunately
5 When
6 unexpectedly
7 enough
8 Without

5
A 4
B 2
C 1
D 5
E 3

2.7 Writing
1
1 attention
2 Define, introduction
3 develop, question
4 personal, think
5 concerned, opinion, shouldn't

2
1 d, ii
2 a, iii
3 e, iii
4 c, i
5 b, iv

3
in any order …
1 b followed by f
2 h followed by d
3 g followed by e

4
b followed by f

5
a 1
b 2
c 3
d 7
e 6
f –
g 5
h 4
i 0
j –

6
1 Having never had a female friend before,
2 Spending so much of their time together,
3 Having gained each other's trust,

2.8 Language in focus
1
1 middle
2 good
3 true
4 softly
5 ate
6 stayed
7 sandwiches

2
1 a personal
b person
2 a proud
b pride
3 a faith
b faithfully
4 a loss
b loser

3
1 vivid
2 disappointed
3 acquaintance
4 secrets
5 expecting

2.9 Use of English
1
1 was
2 it
3 who
4 gotten
5 had
6 which
7 worth
8 out

2
1 didn't use to
2 should avoid eating
3 let us leave early
4 after we had made
5 yelled at me
6 had been planning the wedding

2.11 Self-check
1
1 distant
2 propose
3 fool
4 about
5 take

2
1 disappearance
2 illustrations
3 suppression
4 concept
5 spoiled

3
1 had been seeing
2 were just leaving
3 had never been
4 had been painting
5 had learned

4
1 whose
2 which
3 who / that
4 which
5 which

5
1 got in trouble with
2 had known each other for
3 fell for her
4 the author whose book
5 had been preparing the party

6
1 A
2 C
3 D
4 B
5 D

3 A place to live

3.1 Vocabulary
1
1 b for
2 a offset
b by
3 a benefiting
b from
4 a steeped
b in
5 a packed
b with
6 a prides itself
b on

2
1 A
2 B
3 C
4 B
5 A
6 C
7 B

3
1 I
2 j
3 c

4 g
5 h
6 b
7 d
8 k
9 e
10 a
11 i

4
1 the historical heart of
2 main sight and most famous landmark
3 a reliable network of buses and trains
4 easy to get around
5 within walking distance
6 youth-friendly place
7 best kept secrets

3.2 Grammar

1
1 'll have finished
2 won't have gone
3 will have started
4 will have been waiting
5 will have been living
6 'll be eating

2
1 b In July people will be shopping there.
1 c By Christmas the center will have been in business for six months.
2 a At 11 p.m. the first horror movie will have finished.
2 b By midnight the audience will be watching the second movie.
2 c By 4 a.m. the audience will have been sitting in the movie theater for eight hours.

3
1 will be living
2 will have constructed
3 will be designing
4 will have been using
5 will have become
6 will be recycling

3.3 Listening language practice

1
Welcome to *The Lifestyle Show.* Let's start with the shocking results **of** a recent survey: thirty-five percent **of** American people do not know any **of** their neighbors. Well, it's not a problem for residents **of** Springhill co-housing project in the southwest **of** England. Springhill is a new housing development **of** thirty-five homes in a typical residential area.

2
1 affordable
2 latest
3 daily
4 well-established
5 neighborly
6 communal

3
1 well-established
2 latest
3 affordable
4 sustainable
5 daily
6 neighborly

5
1 extravagant, overpriced
2 infrequent, occasional, irregular
3 hostile, unsociable, cold
4 temporary, damaging, wasteful

6
1 disposable
2 profiting
3 reliable
4 respect
5 suitable
6 sustain

3.4 Reading

1
3

2
1 F
2 F
3 T
4 T
5 T
6 F

3
a 7
b 4
c 1
d 3
e 6
f 2
g 5

4
1 highly flammable
2 Three-story dwellings
3 common practice
4 cramped conditions
5 sewerage system
6 Striking architecture
7 Thatched roofs

5
1 striking architecture
2 cramped conditions
3 thatched roofs
4 financial hub
5 sewerage system
6 Three-story houses

6
1 in
2 on
3 on
4 in
5 on
6 in

3.5 Grammar

1
1 A couple **of** my friends are deep thinkers, which makes them interesting to talk to about life's ups and downs.
2 Though normally confident, many **of** the people on the stage that night were actually very nervous.
3 –
4 –
5 Elsa's pen broke, but luckily none **of** the ink spilled out into her purse.
6 –

2
1 there are several only children
2 so you can borrow either of
3 All (of) the people who attended
4 Every student
5 No animals

3
1 B
2 A
3 C
4 B
5 B
6 A
7 C
8 B

3.6 Speaking language practice

1
1 joking
2 half
3 settled
4 choice
5 convinced
6 agree
7 compromise
8 saying

2
1 O
2 C
3 A
4 S
5 O
6 A
7 C
8 O

3
1 not convinced
2 Given the choice
3 completely
4 what you're saying
5 why don't we meet halfway
6 must be joking

4
1 No way!
2 I know what (you) mean
3 could split/share
4 (I) guess (so)
5 What would (you) say if
6 (You're) absolutely right
7 If you agree (to do the kitchen,) I'll (do the bathroom.)
8 why don't (we) compromise

9 that's settled
10 totally

3.7 Writing

1
1 ✗
2 ✓
3 ✗
4 ✓
5 ✓
6 ✗
7 ✓
8 ✗

2
1 urbanites
2 urban
3 rural
4 shrunk
5 disposable income
6 enrich

3
1 Equally
2 further
3 persuasive
4 minuses
5 considered
6 Personally

4
a 4
b 6
c 3
d 2
e 5
f 1

5
1 e
2 b
3 c
4 f
5 a
6 d

6
Although this suggests that life in the city may be superior in some ways, there are definitely pros and cons to metropolitan living.
… despite the fact that cities can be lonely and dangerous places to live, I feel the benefits outweigh the drawbacks.

7
1 Although
2 Even though
3 in spite of
4 Although
5 despite

3.8 Language in focus

1
1 both
2 whole
3 each
4 every
5 others
6 another

2
1 all the
2 both of them
3 The whole, every one of
4 the others, one of them, another one
5 all of them
6 each of the

3.9 Use of English

1
1 C
2 B
3 D
4 A
5 D
6 B
7 C
8 C

2
1 tested each other
2 look up to
3 stopped us (from) flying
4 will have received
5 will have been working
6 my whole apartment

3.11 Self-check

1
1 within
2 in
3 on
4 in
5 from

2
1 run-down
2 mouth-watering
3 disposable
4 hectic
5 quaint

3
1 will be enjoying
2 will have painted
3 will be installing
4 will have been resurfacing
5 will have owned

4
1 neither
2 no
3 deal
4 either
5 some

5
1 will have married
2 within walking distance
3 will have been building
4 great deal of
5 at an altitude of

6
1 B
2 A
3 D
4 C
5 D

4 The cost of living

4.1 Vocabulary

1
1 around
2 out
3 out
4 off
5 up
6 off

2
1 bring out
2 forking out
3 knock (a considerable amount) off
4 shop around
5 snap up
6 ripped off

3
1 paid through the nose
2 you're broke
3 make ends meet
4 money to burn

4
1 f
2 d
3 a
4 e
5 g
6 b
7 c

5
1 attract
2 niche
3 fortune
4 chain
5 discounted
6 deals
7 range

6
1 launch
2 make
3 attract
4 fill
5 spend
6 serve

7
1 make
2 cutting
3 launch
4 deal
5 supplying

4.2 Grammar

1
1 d
2 a
3 b
4 f
5 c
6 e

2
1 is, Will you
2 weren't, Were they
3 will, Are they
4 did, Aren't you
5 won't, Can't you

3
b shall 3
c did 6
d isn't 5
e don't 1
f didn't 4
g isn't 2

4.3 Listening language practice

1
1 A
2 C
3 B
4 C
5 A
6 B
7 B

2
1 have missed
2 flights
3 property
4 dresses
5 goods

4.4 Reading

1
1 B
2 C
3 A

2
1 Text C
2 Text A
3 Text C
4 Text B

3
1 B
2 B
3 C
4 A
5 B
6 C
7 C
8 A

4
1 Australia
2 they are carefully locked away
3 their durability
4 six months
5 agricultural compost
6 58 billion pounds

5
1 shred
2 conceal
3 switch
4 issue
5 compact
6 manufacture
7 sidestep

6
1 shred
2 issuing
3 compact
4 manufactures
5 switch
6 sidestep
7 concealed

7
1 production, traditional
2 enthusiasm, expertise, environment
3 producer, perfect
4 enthusiasts, tradition
5 perfection, experts
6 perfectionist, traditionalist

4.5 Grammar

1
1 –
2 You'd better ~~to~~ avoid the dark backstreets late at night unless you want to get into trouble.
3 –
4 Visitors simply must ~~to~~ experience the vibrant nightlife of Rio during the week of the carnival.
5 –
6 –

2
2 ought not to have worked
3 ought to have had
4 should not have lost touch
5 should have let

3
1 had to go
2 shouldn't have splashed out
3 didn't need to cancel
4 didn't need to bother
5 shouldn't have spent
6 didn't need to bother

4.6 Speaking language practice

1
1 is definitely the more suitable choice because
2 main reason that X would be my choice
3 is much more likely that
4 is clearly the least suitable option because
5 might be cheaper but I wouldn't choose it because
6 isn't the best choice if you consider

2
1 a choice
b opt
2 a compare
b likely
c go for
3 a but
b simply

3
1 the best choice
2 why (I'd) opt for
3 might (be cheap,) but (I) wouldn't
4 main reason (is) that
5 Another reason (I) wouldn't pick
6 the (only) option that

4.7 Writing

1
1 begin
2 summarizing
3 narrative tenses
4 reaction
5 happen
6 reply

2
1 c
2 f
3 a
4 b
5 d
6 e

3
1 took place
2 approached
3 accused
4 reason with
5 make matters worse
6 humiliated
7 decided (to) contact (you and complain)
8 ask (that you) investigate (the) matter
9 simply unfair (to) treat
10 look forward (to your) reply

4
1 such
2 so
3 such a
4 such an
5 so

5
1 accused us of
2 such a disappointment
3 The fact
4 urge you to
5 We were so humiliated
6 on behalf of

4.8 Language in focus

1
1 forbidden
2 certain
3 obliged
4 sure
5 unable
6 succeeded in

2
1 wearing
2 to use
3 hitting
4 to report
5 to visit
6 entering

3
1 obliged
2 permitted
3 sure
4 unlikely
5 aren't able
6 supposed

4.9 Use of English

1
1 B
2 D
3 A
4 C
5 B
6 D
7 B
8 D

2
1 Personally
2 fashionable
3 designer
4 affordable
5 stylish
6 quirky
7 salesperson
8 enables

4.11 Self-check

1
1 cost
2 bad
3 pick
4 arm
5 chain

2
1 niche
2 broke
3 launch
4 shop
5 burn

3
1 Is he
2 Is she
3 doesn't she
4 will you
5 didn't he

4
1 supposed
2 have brought
3 banned
4 unlikely
5 should

5
1 have
2 help
3 priced
4 knock
5 had

6
1 ought not to have wasted
2 was supposed to have
3 are not allowed to withdraw
4 snap up
5 am not forking out

5 The world at your feet

5.1 Vocabulary

1
1 qualifications
2 training
3 experience
4 terms
5 salary
6 working
7 place

2
1 stepped
2 taking
3 drawn
4 taking
5 picked

3
1 expressing
2 filled
3 expenses
4 responsibilities
5 process
6 youth
7 sense

4
1 the terms and conditions
2 salary
3 positions
4 train
5 a date
6 qualifications in something
7 accommodation
8 employment

5
1 sense of achievement
2 passport expired
3 express concern about
4 living standards
5 application process
6 collective responsibility
7 created a vacancy
8 target the pre-school market

6
1 a campaign
b campaigners
2 a employees
b employers
3 a interviewee
b Interviewers
4 a recruits
b Recruitment
5 a review
b reviewers

5.2 Grammar

1
1 is
2 you are
3 he was
4 look
5 not to
6 you
7 loves
8 to wait

2
1 him whether the company had filled
2 me if I had
3 us whether we had both applied

3
1 the company had been attempting to target the youth market since the year before.
2 whether/if he could interview me there and then.
3 she gets a real sense of achievement from her job.
4 he might miss the meeting the following day.
5 to wait there.
6 not to forget to renew my passport the following month.
7 how long I had been campaigning for a change in the law.

5.3 Listening language practice

1
1 a drop
2 sharp
3 constant
4 rapid
5 growing

2
1 gradual decline
2 marked increase
3 unchanged
4 sharp drop
5 steady rise

3
1 A
2 B
3 C
4 B
5 C
6 A

4
2 rewarding
3 lucrative
4 monotonous
5 important
6 no synonym
7 stable

5.4 Reading

1
2 Technology news

3
1 B
2 C
3 C
4 A
5 C

4
1 F
2 F
3 T
4 F
5 F
6 T

5
1 in, e
2 at, d
3 on, a
4 in, b
5 to, c

6
1 to the highest bidder
2 at a mark-up
3 his eye on
4 is back in the news

7
1 contrary
2 rule
3 fact
4 top
5 circumstances

5.5 Grammar

1
1 being
2 to pay
3 them to give
4 that he would increase
5 of
6 wearing

2
1 The judge refused to continue the case until the lawyer returned.
2 I begged her not to contact my parents, but she ignored me and called my mom there and then.
3 They haven't invited us to the mass, so we will just go straight to the reception.
4 Taylor apologized for being so grumpy and explained that she was very tired.
5 I only had a couple of dollars, but fortunately the manager insisted on paying for my taxi home.
6 Jasmine didn't object to spicy food as long as it wasn't ridiculously hot.

3
1 advised us not to work for free/that we shouldn't work for free.
2 congratulated me on getting the job.
3 urged her to visit us again the following/next month.
4 reminded them to count the money that night/that they should count the money that night.
5 admitted forgetting to place the order the day before/that he had forgotten to place the order the day before.

5.6 Speaking language practice

1
1 I have no idea
2 there's (a) problem with
3 Have you tried
4 make any difference
5 doubt (that'll) work, (but) let's see

6 Why (in the) world
7 are (we) supposed (to do) now

2
1 f
2 a
3 g
4 e
5 c
6 b
7 d

3
1 the matter with it
2 should I know
3 should've thought
4 time
5 you tried
6 make any difference
7 solved

5.7 Writing

1
A 3
B 2
C 1
D 4

2
1 Broadly speaking
2 Most people agree that
3 In almost all cases
4 tend not to

3
1 In
2 tends
3 general
4 agree
5 Some
6 cases

4
1 choice
2 all options possible
3 results
4 cause
5 outcome

5
1 stimulating
2 greater
3 fortunate
4 dull
5 miserable
6 fascinating

5.8 Language in focus

1
1 come, I
2 give, I
3 looks, L
4 hold, I

2
1 across, back
2 of, put, by

3
1 look up to him
2 makes up bedtime stories
3 taken on
4 broken up
5 was laid off
6 picked it up

5.9 Use of English

1
1 monotonous
2 rewarding
3 accountant
4 entertainment
5 celebrations
6 totally
7 secrecy
8 unemployed

2
1 suggested that we
2 takes on
3 should have read
4 warned me not to spend/against spending
5 is likely to reply
6 put too much pressure on

5.11 Self-check

1
1 expires
2 take
3 contrary
4 step down
5 vacancy

2
1 applicants
2 recruitment
3 monotonous
4 achievement
5 campaigners

3
1 denied taking
2 objected to working
3 reminded me to lock
4 blamed me for not finishing
5 advised me to rest

4
1 came
2 look
3 get
4 broke
5 laid

5
1 insisted on preparing the draft
2 suggested wearing/suggested we wear/suggested that we should wear our new sweatshirts
3 Bob had handed in his
4 had broken/was broken
5 made up for

6
1 D
2 B
3 C
4 D
5 A

6 True or false?

6.1 Vocabulary

1
1 authentic
2 misleading
3 distort
4 sensationalize
5 fake
6 doctored
7 deceive
8 manipulate
9 illusion

2
1 at
2 with, pinch
3 responsibility, for
4 for, granted
5 of, context
6 pride, in

3
1 B
2 B
3 A
4 B
5 C
6 A

4
1 reaching
2 faced
3 timed
4 tax
5 streetwise
6 Kind

6.2 Grammar

1
1 provided/providing
2 unless
3 Unless
4 Provided/Providing
5 provided/providing
6 unless

2
1 Suppose the Apollo moon landings had been fake, b
2 Supposing I said I didn't want to go to college, e
3 Imagine we didn't have to go to school today, d
4 Imagine you had been born fifty years ago, a
5 Supposing we could live anywhere, c
6 Imagine you could have any job, f

3
1 Should I not return
2 Were Helen not so two-faced
3 Had the announcement not been so ill-timed
4 Should you see Meredith
5 Were it not summer

6.3 Listening language practice

1
1 for
2 about
3 through
4 for
5 about
6 about
7 through
8 about

2
1 to stay
2 remain
3 painting
4 using
5 to remain
6 writing
7 to achieve
8 holding

4
1 a belief
b believable
2 a fairness
b fair
3 a equal
b equality
4 a anonymous
b anonymity
5 a loyal
b loyalty
6 a enigma
b enigmatic
7 a mystery
b mysterious

6.4 Reading

1
2

2
A 3
B 1
C 5
D –
E 4
F 2

3
1 –
2 E
3 A
4 –
5 D
6 C
7 B

4
1 ran away
2 go through
3 take in
4 settle in
5 look into
6 showed up

6.5 Grammar

1
1 had, is
2 don't enjoy, didn't
3 didn't fork out, can
4 am, didn't ask
5 like, invited

2
1 liked
2 'd kept
3 'd have
4 would've left

3
1 wouldn't look, hadn't been airbrushed
2 was/were, would've let her
3 would be, hadn't forgotten
4 wouldn't have driven, wasn't/weren't
5 wouldn't have, hadn't had

6.6 Speaking language practice

1
1 Frankly
2 Sadly
3 Clearly
4 honest
5 Regrettably

2
1 R
2 W
3 U
4 R
5 W

3
1 one obvious disadvantage is that
2 quite important, I think, because
3 well as reducing their energy consumption, other things include
4 I don't have a strong opinion about
b 1
c 4
d 2
e 3

4
1 explain
2 argued
3 Regrettably
4 firmly
5 Obviously
6 significant
7 advantage
8 suppose

6.7 Writing

1
6 Restate your main opinion.
2 Say which two points of view or aspects will be discussed.
4 Expand the discussion by giving examples.
7 Include a final comment.
5 Use a linking phrase to introduce a conclusion.
3 Discuss different aspects of the issue and support the main opinion you stated in the introduction.

2
1 intention
2 perspective
3 terms
4 consider
5 issue
6 considered

3
A 3
B 1
C 4
D 2

4
While these attitudes are very different, they both seem unsatisfactory in one way or another.

5
1 a Adults understand that not everything is affordable, whereas/while children find this more difficult to appreciate.
b While adults understand that not everything is affordable, children find this more difficult to appreciate.
2 a Older viewers are aware that ads are designed to manipulate emotions, while/whereas many children are not mature enough to realize this.
b Whereas older viewers are aware that ads are designed to manipulate emotions, many children are not mature enough to realize this.
3 a Certain experts say such marketing techniques should be banned, while/whereas others admit that banning ads will not stop children wanting things.
b While certain experts say such marketing techniques should be banned, others admit that banning ads will not stop children wanting things.
4 a Some people believe advertisers are to blame, while/whereas other people argue that it is parents' responsibility to control what their children watch.
b Whereas some people believe advertisers are to blame, other people argue that it is parents' responsibility to control what their children watch.

6.8 Language in focus

1
1 A
2 C
3 C
4 B
5 C
6 B

2
1 <u>pur</u>ity
2 be<u>liev</u>able
3 <u>pac</u>ifists
4 cre<u>a</u>tion
5 de<u>pend</u>ent
6 em<u>ploy</u>ment

3
1 succeed
2 relationships
3 importance
4 trust
5 communication
6 innovative

6.9 Use of English

1
1 D
2 D
3 A
4 D
5 B
6 C
7 D
8 C

2
1 about
2 such
3 If
4 had
5 can
6 told

7 many
8 Unless

6.11 Self-check

1
1 showed
2 genuine
3 fake
4 distorted
5 stupidity

2
1 wouldn't be angry with her if she hadn't gotten involved
2 had a wrinkle-free face, she would have gotten
3 I weren't/wasn't very/so busy, I would have sent you
4 wouldn't have talked to him about his mortgage if he hadn't lied
5 hadn't started taking photos of us at home, we would feel

3
1 doubt
2 made
3 in
4 were
5 unless

4
1 C
2 A
3 C
4 B
5 A

5
1 pinch
2 doctored
3 look into
4 stony-faced
5 face

6
1 unless they break
2 Supposing you find
3 you hadn't forgotten
4 wouldn't have employed
5 out of context

7 Log on

7.1 Vocabulary

1
1 A
2 B
3 C
4 B
5 A
6 A

2
1 diabetes
2 high blood pressure
3 repetitive strain injury
4 addiction
5 joint pain
6 eye strain
7 obesity

3
1 eye strain
2 insomnia
3 diabetes
4 repetitive strain injury
5 joint pain
6 high blood pressure
7 addiction

4
1 at his fingertips
2 long attention span
3 At the expense of
4 sedentary lifestyles
5 played a crucial role
6 withdrawal symptoms
7 address the issue

5
1 a
2 f
3 g
4 d
5 e
6 c
7 b

7.2 Grammar

1
1 approached
2 have been
3 had been
4 have been
5 being
6 be
7 had
8 have been

2
1 being told
2 to be sent
3 to be treated
4 being taken over
5 being asked
6 to be beaten

3
1 is being bought
2 is going to be given
3 has been promised
4 was offered to Brian
5 had been/was taught

7.3 Listening language practice

1
1 B
2 C
3 C
4 A
5 B
6 C
7 A
8 B

2
1 mid-range
2 premium
3 custom-made
4 branded
5 generic
6 cutting-edge
7 user-friendly

3
1 user-friendly
2 premium
3 mid-range
4 cutting-edge
5 generic
6 branded
7 custom-made

4
1 external drive
2 handset
3 sat-nav
4 remote control
5 landline

7.4 Reading

1
A Safety
B Parking
C Free time
D Congestion
E Environment
F Freedom

2
1 B
2 C
3 B
4 A
5 B
6 C

3
1 break
2 behind
3 parallel
4 circles
5 winding
6 eight-lane
7 dealership
8 license
9 run

4
1 driving in circles
2 behind the wheel
3 driver's license
4 the school run
5 car dealership
6 winding country roads
7 breaking the speed limit
8 Eight-lane highways
9 parallel parking

5
1 casting (an) eye
2 browsed
3 beamed
4 dashing around
5 wandering around
6 stare
7 frowning

7.5 Grammar

1
1 There
2 It
3 It
4 There
5 It

2
1 It is thought that
2 There are understood to be
3 It was agreed by
4 am expected not to be

3
1 are known to have woken
2 are not believed to have been
3 there are understood to be
4 is considered to be
5 it is thought that
6 are caused by
7 It is also said that

7.6 Speaking language practice

1
1 words
2 with
3 What
4 follow
5 meant
6 lost
7 understand
8 mean
9 precisely
10 pretty
11 saying

2
2 S
3 C
4 S
5 C
6 S
7 U
8 S
9 C
10 C
11 U

3
Conversation 1
b I'm not sure I follow you
c Yes, that's exactly it
1 Yes, that's exactly it
2 I'm not sure I follow you
Conversation 2
a What I meant was
b Are you saying
c that's not quite what I meant
d I'm not with you
3 I'm not with you
4 Are you saying
5 That's not quite what I meant
6 What I meant was
Conversation 3
a that's pretty much it
b I'm afraid you've lost me there
c If I understand you correctly, you mean
d in other words
7 in other words
8 that's pretty much it
9 I'm afraid you've lost me there
10 If I understand you correctly, you mean

4
1 What
2 do
3 Shall
4 to
5 been
6 ask

7.7 Writing

1
1 Undoubtedly, there are certain benefits to this idea.
2 The evidence may be strong, but nevertheless some people refuse to accept it.
3 It may actually be very easy to make this happen.
4 That said, there are also reasons to object to this.
5 As long as the rules are followed, this approach seems acceptable.
6 Provided that everyone agrees, this appears to be an effective solution.

2
A 3
B 1
C 4
D 2

3
1 undoubtedly
2 yet
3 Even
4 Without
5 actually
6 Providing
7 doubt

4
1 because
2 Since
3 because
4 since
5 Due to
6 Due to

7.8 Language in focus

1
1 C
2 B
3 B
4 A
5 C
6 C

2
1 practicing
2 practice
3 breathe
4 affecting
5 advise
6 breath
7 effect

3
1 economic
2 historic
3 conscious
4 occasion
5 continual

4
1 Currently
2 complements
3 Eventually
4 compliment
5 possibly

7.9 Use of English

1
1 C
2 C
3 D
4 B
5 A
6 C
7 D
8 B

2
1 recently
2 engineering
3 reality
4 movements
5 unlike
6 repetitive
7 revolutionize
8 undeniably

7.11 Self-check

1
1 eye strain
2 withdrawal
3 updated
4 hectic
5 frowned

2
1 bookmark
2 landline
3 insomnia
4 wander
5 sedentary

3
1 being forced
2 have been charged
3 had been sent
4 to be installed
5 being criticized

4
1 was thought that
2 is said to have had
3 were estimated to be
4 is claimed to often cause
5 is known to have revolutionized

5
1 be
2 who
3 because
4 were
5 fingertips

6
1 undoubtedly
2 unlimited
3 beneficial
4 privacy
5 advances

8 Around the globe

8.1 Vocabulary

1
1 melts
2 drought
3 float
4 foothills
5 fossil fuels

2
1 species
2 tides
3 currents
4 whirlpools
5 nutrients
6 prey

3
1 sewage
2 garbage dumps
3 industrial
4 contaminants
5 hazard

4
1 A
2 C
3 B
4 C
5 B

5
1 poisoning
2 oil
3 slide
4 shore(s)

8.2 Grammar

1
1 didn't
2 are
3 didn't perform
4 is
5 has

2
1 drove (instead of me)
2 I had set
3 you bought your girlfriend some
4 had learned to swim
5 not sit

3
1 could have gone
2 had lived
3 didn't live
4 wasn't/weren't

4
1 invested
2 could
3 made
4 had spent
5 had begun

8.3 Listening language practice

1
1 natural
2 campaigner
3 adolescence
4 powerful
5 shocking
6 undoubtedly
7 dependent
8 childhood
9 competitive
10 aggressive

2
1 d
2 a
3 c
4 e
5 b

8.4 Reading

1
2 extinction

2
1 C
2 A
3 B
4 A
5 D
6 C
7 D
8 A
9 B
10 C

3
1 T
2 F
3 T
4 F
5 F
6 T
7 F
8 T

4
1 widespread
2 partial
3 enormous
4 severe
5 immigration
6 herbivore
7 shrink
8 ancient

5
1 severe
2 eventual
3 widespread
4 ancient
5 shrink
6 minuscule
7 carnivore
8 grow
9 partial
10 enormous

6
1 a vastness
b vast
2 a injured
b injury
3 a rag
b ragged
4 a thirst
b thirsty
5 a growth
b grown
6 a poisonous
b poison

8.5 Grammar

1
1 what scientists managed to do was
2 Never before has there been
3 Not only did
4 What is most amazing is that
5 It's these kinds of achievements that

2
1 happened was
2 have I
3 It's
4 is that
5 we are
6 he did was
7 have the temperatures
8 do you

3
1 It was a documentary about a man snowboarding on an iceberg that distracted him.
2 What the film crew did was fly out to the North Atlantic by helicopter.
3 What happened was they dropped the man onto the top of the huge iceberg.
4 All the man did was ride down it for about half a minute, but the shots were amazing.
5 Never had Ryan seen anyone snowboarding in such an unusual place.
6 What he found most impressive was the effort that the whole team went to.

8.6 Speaking language practice

1
1 contact
2 involved
3 notes
4 forget
5 invite

2
1 You may be wondering why I've chosen to talk about, e
2 We are probably all familiar with, a
3 You may already know that, c
4 You might not know that, f
5 That's all from me, b
6 If anyone has any questions, please feel free to ask now, d

3
1 plan
2 aware
3 heard
4 realize
5 listening
6 found

4
Beginning
1 a Have you ever tried holding your breath for more than a minute? It's not easy, is it? Well, today
2 d I plan to explain how we can all train ourselves to easily hold our breath for longer. So, let's
3 c get going. Now, maybe some of you have heard of an extreme sport called free diving.
4 e You may be aware that free divers are able to stay under water for several minutes at a time,
5 b but did you know that the world record holder is able to hold his breath for almost ten minutes?

End
1 a OK, everybody, that's
2 e all from me. I'd like to thank you
3 c for listening, and I hope
4 f that you found the presentation interesting.
5 d If you would like to ask any questions,
6 b please feel free to do so now.

8.7 Writing

1
1 c
2 e
3 a
4 d
5 f
6 b

2
1 cultural heritage
2 diverse landscapes
3 environmental impact
4 natural beauty
5 sustainable tourism
6 wildlife protection

3
1 in
2 from
3 banks
4 by
5 so
6 Whereas
7 Even though
8 as
9 Since
10 Although

4
1 such
2 whereas
3 Having
4 despite
5 Being
6 so
7 Since

5
1 Being
2 Even though
3 Despite
4 while
5 Due to
6 Because

8.8 Language in focus

1
1 disallow
2 postwar
3 misbehave
4 illogical
5 rebuild
6 underpaid
7 pro-democracy
8 uneven
9 unfair
10 overwork
11 anti-corruption
12 pre-existing
13 insensitive
14 imperfect

2
1 disobedient
2 rewritten
3 misunderstood
4 pre-installed
5 imperfection
6 multilingual
7 anti-acne
8 underfeeding
9 irrelevant

3
1 irresponsibly
2 unmarried
3 undercook
4 disabled

8.9 Use of English

1
1 that
2 a
3 had
4 each
5 the
6 What
7 as
8 in

2
1 would/'d rather you didn't
2 if I hadn't worked
3 they did was to study
4 shouldn't have complained
5 is thought to have been
6 only did we stay

8.11 Self-check

1
1 contaminant
2 acid
3 sewage
4 species
5 current

2
1 thirst
2 whirlpools
3 poisoning
4 dumps
5 hazard

3
1 stopped
2 hadn't allowed
3 planted
4 hadn't given
5 had installed

4
1 Under no circumstances
2 Never before
3 All that happened
4 It was James
5 Not only

5
1 drought
2 incomparably
3 environmentalists
4 starvation
5 inaccessible

6
1 What Mark needs to do
2 wish we had preserved
3 would rather you thought
4 only we could join you
5 have we dumped

VOCABULARY BANK – PRACTICE EXERCISES

People

1
1 self-confident
2 immature
3 sporty
4 rebellious
5 persistent
6 fussy
7 strict
8 reliable
9 sensible
10 protective

2
1 dyed
2 hazel
3 outfit
4 tight
5 baggy
6 high heels
7 twenties
8 wrinkle-free
9 acne
10 slouch

3
1 lose
2 take
3 look
4 have
5 be

4
1 was passionate about
2 lost (her) temper
3 took pride in
4 had her priorities straight
5 look back on

House

1
1 building
2 residential
3 distance
4 appliances
5 rental price
6 convenient
7 unfurnished
8 run-down
9 noisy
10 safe

2
1 b
2 f
3 a
4 d
5 c
6 e

3
1 household / domestic chores
2 doormat
3 bill
4 campus
5 resident

School

1
1 complained
2 paid attention
3 fell behind
4 passed
5 signed up
6 Drama
7 active learning
8 degree

2
1 A
2 C
3 A
4 C
5 B

3
1 attended (a photography) course
2 doing research
3 skip (two) classes
4 take exams
5 dropped (a) course

Work

1
1 steady
2 tedious
3 commute
4 underpaid
5 left
6 applications
7 gain (new) skills
8 work from home
9 rewarding
10 well-paid

2

	Similar meaning	Opposite meaning
commute	travel to work	work from home
hire	take on	lay off
steady job	secure profession	working freelance
monotonous	tedious	interesting
find employment	accept a post	resign
fulfilling	rewarding	unsatisfying

Family and social life

1
1 h
2 g
3 e
4 i
5 d
6 a
7 b
8 c
9 f

2
1 ex-husband
2 fell in love
3 drifted apart
4 long-distance relationship
5 single mother
6 bring up my son
7 circle of friends
8 immediate family

9 worth the effort

Food

1
1 f
2 d
3 a
4 c
5 g
6 h
7 b
8 e

2
1 B
2 C
3 C
4 A
5 C

Shopping and services

1
1 bargain
2 cash
3 staff
4 launch
5 counter
6 reduced
7 sales

2
1 e
2 c
3 h
4 b
5 d
6 f
7 a
8 g

3
1 discounted price
2 niche market
3 shopping centers
4 earns a living
5 auction house
6 cost of living

Travelling and tourism

1
1 forest
2 sports facilities
3 dull
4 cruise ship
5 cycle lane
6 river bank
7 mainland
8 take off

2
1 world-class restaurants
2 vibrant nightlife
3 breathtaking views
4 tour operator
5 tourist destinations
6 picturesque
7 charted the route
8 started out
9 cruise ship
10 landmarks
11 market squares
12 cobbled

Culture

1
1 B
2 B
3 A
4 C
5 B
6 C

2
Mass media: review, editor, TV crew, piece of news
Photography: photo exhibition, selfie, zoom in, airbrushed
Art: paintbrush, stencil, watercolors, graffiti

Sports

1
1 e
2 f
3 a
4 d
5 c
6 b

2
1 stay in shape
2 go biking
3 score (any) goals
4 beat (their) opponents
5 broke (world) records
6 ride (my) bike

Health

1
1 B
2 C
3 A
4 B
5 D
6 D
7 A

2
1 poisoning
2 injured
3 circulation
4 breathe
5 weight
6 illness
7 digestive
8 obsessed

Science and technology

1

<table>
<tr><td></td><td></td><td>W</td><td>E</td><td>I</td><td>G</td><td>H</td><td>T</td><td>L</td><td>E</td><td>S</td><td>S</td><td>N</td><td>E</td><td>S</td><td>S</td><td>S</td></tr>
<tr><td></td><td></td><td></td><td>P</td><td>R</td><td>E</td><td>S</td><td>E</td><td>R</td><td>V</td><td>A</td><td>T</td><td>I</td><td>O</td><td>N</td><td></td><td></td></tr>
<tr><td></td><td></td><td>A</td><td>D</td><td>V</td><td>A</td><td>N</td><td>C</td><td>E</td><td>M</td><td>E</td><td>N</td><td>T</td><td></td><td></td><td></td><td></td></tr>
<tr><td></td><td></td><td>A</td><td>T</td><td>T</td><td>A</td><td>C</td><td>H</td><td>M</td><td>E</td><td>N</td><td>T</td><td></td><td></td><td></td><td></td><td></td></tr>
<tr><td></td><td></td><td></td><td></td><td></td><td>C</td><td>O</td><td>N</td><td>C</td><td>L</td><td>U</td><td>S</td><td>I</td><td>O</td><td>N</td><td></td><td></td></tr>
<tr><td></td><td></td><td></td><td>D</td><td>I</td><td>S</td><td>C</td><td>O</td><td>V</td><td>E</td><td>R</td><td>Y</td><td></td><td></td><td></td><td></td><td></td></tr>
<tr><td></td><td></td><td></td><td></td><td>E</td><td>V</td><td>O</td><td>L</td><td>U</td><td>T</td><td>I</td><td>O</td><td>N</td><td></td><td></td><td></td><td></td></tr>
<tr><td></td><td></td><td></td><td>E</td><td>X</td><td>P</td><td>L</td><td>O</td><td>S</td><td>I</td><td>O</td><td>N</td><td></td><td></td><td></td><td></td><td></td></tr>
<tr><td>I</td><td>N</td><td>V</td><td>E</td><td>S</td><td>T</td><td>I</td><td>G</td><td>A</td><td>T</td><td>I</td><td>O</td><td>N</td><td></td><td></td><td></td><td></td></tr>
<tr><td></td><td></td><td></td><td>A</td><td>N</td><td>A</td><td>L</td><td>Y</td><td>S</td><td>I</td><td>S</td><td></td><td></td><td></td><td></td><td></td><td></td></tr>
</table>

2
1 preservation
2 attachment
3 advancement
4 conclusion
5 Evolution

3
1 to
2 out
3 on
4 on
5 to
6 up
7 in
8 on / off

4
1 carry out
2 contribute to
3 access to
4 click on
5 rise in
6 on the horizon
7 set up
8 turn off

The natural world

1
1 h
2 i
3 e
4 b
5 g
6 a
7 c
8 d
9 f

2
1 climate change
2 average temperatures
3 global warming
4 fossil fuels
5 renewable energy
6 carbon dioxide
7 industrial waste
8 acid rain
9 national parks

3
1 fertilizers
2 wildlife
3 reptiles
4 pollutants
5 environment
6 earthquake
7 prey

4
1 Camels
2 Sheep, farm
3 glaciers
4 graceful
5 stream
6 nesting
7 waves
8 glaciers

5

Geographical features	Wild animals	Environmental problems
vast desert coastal region dense forest glacier peninsula	chimpanzee jellyfish marine mammal reptile seabird	acid rain carbon dioxide landfill oil well pollutant

The three extra words: sheep, food chain, earthquake

State and society

1
1 under
2 away
3 in
4 from
5 of
6 to
7 out
8 in
9 of

2
1 h
2 e
3 d
4 a
5 g
6 c
7 f
8 b

3
1 peaceful protests
2 indigenous cultures
3 fair treatment
4 security alarm
5 cyber crime (and) identity theft

Photocopiable resources

Contents on MultiROM and Active Teach

Resource	Language point	When to use	Time (minutes)
20 Doing up an apartment	Words related to home, suggesting, objecting, compromising, and agreeing	Before Focus review 3, Speaking, Ex. 8, p. 65	15
21 Advantages and disadvantages of …	Words related to renting accommodations and writing a 'for and against' essay	Before Focus review 3, Writing, Ex. 10, p. 65	15
Unit 4	The cost of living		
22 Good value for money	Money and shopping	After 4.1 Vocabulary, pp. 66–67	12
23 Question tag dominoes	Question tags	After 4.2 Grammar, pp. 68–69	10
24 I bet my best pair of jeans that it's correct!	Word formation	After 4.4 Reading, pp. 72–73	8
25 Test yourself partner work activities	Vocabulary: shopping and money	After 4.1 Vocabulary, pp. 66–67	10
	Grammar: present and past modal structures	After 4.5 Grammar, pp. 74–75	10
26 The focus of our debate today is …	Modality	After 4.8 Language in focus, p. 80	15
27 I am writing to complain about …	Expressing complaints and writing a letter of complaint	Before Focus review 4, Writing, Ex. 8, p. 83	10
28 What would you do if you won a lot of money?	Money	Before Focus review 4, Speaking, Ex. 9, p. 83	10
Unit 5	The world at your feet		
29 A short stint in a zoo	Employment	After 5.1 Vocabulary, pp. 84–85	8
30 Who said it?	Reported Speech	After 5.2 Grammar, pp. 86–87	12
31 These two are taboo	Words from the text on gender roles	After 5.4 Reading, pp. 90–91	10
32 Test yourself partner work activities	Vocabulary: employment	After 5.1 Vocabulary, pp. 84–85	10
	Grammar: reporting verbs	After 5.5 Grammar, pp. 92–93	10
33 Let's focus on phrasal verbs	Phrasal verbs	After 5.8 Language in focus, p. 98	10
34 Work and study	Words related to work, generalizing and describing consequences	Before Focus review 5, Writing, Ex. 9, p. 101	10
Unit 6	True or false?		
35 On the contrary	Appearance and the media	After 6.1 Vocabulary, pp. 102–103	10
36 Test yourself partner work activities	Vocabulary: truth and lies	After 6.1 Vocabulary, pp. 102–103	10
	Grammar: Conditionals	After 6.2 Grammar, pp. 104–105	10
37 Tic-tac-toe	Words from the text *The imposter*	After 6.4 Reading, pp. 108–109	10
38 Mix them well together	Mixed conditionals	After 6.5 Grammar, pp. 110–111	10
39 Society in focus	Word formation	After 6.8 Language in focus, p. 116	15
40 Choosing and rejecting	Choosing, rejecting, comparing and contrasting options, expressing opinions tentatively, and justifying a choice	Before Focus review 6, Speaking, Ex. 8, p. 119	12
41 Personally, I think …	Expressing a point of view and writing about different aspects of an issue	Before Focus review 6, Writing, Ex. 11, p. 119	15

Resource	Language point	When to use	Time (minutes)
Unit 7 Log on			
42 One down. Two across.	Technology and the effect it has on people	After 7.1 Vocabulary, pp. 120–121	10
43 Quick teen survey	Advanced passive forms	After 7.2 Grammar, pp. 122–123	15
44 At-signs, hashtags and asterisks	Word formation	After 7.4 Reading, pp. 126–127	12
45 Test yourself partner work activities	Vocabulary: health	After 7.1 Vocabulary, pp. 120–121	10
	Grammar: passive reporting structures	After 7.5 Grammar, pp. 128–129	10
46 On the confusion scale	Easily confused words	After 7.8 Language in focus, p. 134	20
47 How has technology developed?	Words related to technology, explaining points of view, and justifying opinions	Before Focus review 7, Speaking, Ex. 8, p. 137	12
48 Pros and cons of e-books	Words related to e-books, expressing certainty, contrast, and a condition	Before Focus review 7, Writing, Ex. 10, p. 137	12
Unit 8 Around the globe			
49 Save the polar bear cubs	The natural world	After 8.1 Vocabulary, pp. 138–139	12
50 Vote for us	Unreal past	After 8.2 Grammar, pp. 140–141	15
51 Do you have itchy feet?	Journeys	After 8.4 Reading, pp. 144–145	10
52 Test yourself partner work activities	Vocabulary: the natural world	After 8.1 Vocabulary, pp. 138–139	10
	Grammar: emphasis – cleft sentences and inversion	After 8.5 Grammar, pp. 146–147	10
53 We're word builders! We're bricklayers!	Word formation	After 8.8 Language in focus, p. 152	15
54 Different shades of green	Words related to the environment and presenting one's opinion	Before Focus review 8, Speaking, Ex. 8, p. 155	15
55 Eco-tours	Expressing an opinion, concession, contrast, reason, cause and result	Before Focus review 8, Writing, Ex. 11, p. 155	15
Language in use			
56 Multiple choice	Review	A: after Focus review 4, Ex. 5, p. 82 B: after Focus review 7, Ex. 5, p. 136	12 12
57 Fill in the blank		A: after Focus review 3, Ex. 5, p. 64 B: after Focus review 8, Ex. 5, p. 154	20 20
58 Word building		After Focus review 1, Ex. 5, p. 28	20
59 Word building cloze		A: after Focus review 2, Ex. 5, p. 46 B: after Focus review 5, Ex. 5, p. 100	20 20
60 Transformations		A: after Focus review 1, Ex. 6, p. 28 B: after Focus review 2, Ex. 7, p. 47 C: after Focus review 4, Ex. 6, p. 82 D: after Focus review 5, Ex. 6, p. 100	20 20 20 20
61 Sentence formation		A: after Focus review 3, Ex. 6, p. 64 B: after Focus review 6, Ex. 6, p. 118	12 12
62 Mini-test 1		After Focus review 6, Ex. 6, p. 118	15
63 Mini-test 2		After Focus review 7, Ex. 6, p. 136	15
64 Mini-test 3		After Focus review 8, Ex. 6, p. 154	15

Notes

Notes

Notes

Notes

Notes

Notes

Pearson Education Limited
Edinburgh Gate, Harlow
Essex, CM20 2JE, England
and Associated Companies throughout the world

www.english.com/focus/american

First published 2016

ISBN 978-1-292-12995-2 (Teacher's Book + MultiROM)
ISBN 978-1-292-12447-6 (MultiROM)
ISBN 978-1-292-12442-1 (Teacher's Book)

Set in Avenir
Printed and bound in Slovakia by Neografia.

The right of Arek Tkacz and Beata Trapnell to be identified as authors of this Work has been asserted by them in accordance with the Copyright, Designs and Patents Act 1988.

Acknowledgements
The publishers and authors would like to thank the following people for their feedback and comments during the development of the material: Humberto Santos Duran, Anna Maria Grochowska, Inga Lande, Magdalena Loska, Rosa Maria Maldonado, Juliana Queiroz Pereira, Tomasz Siuta, Renata Tomaka-Pasternak.

We are grateful to the following for permission to reproduce copyright material:

Students' Book figures: Book cover on page 30 from Gone by Michael Grant. Copyright © 2008 Michael Grant. Published by Egmont UK Ltd London and used with permission. and HarperCollins Children's Books US

Students' Book Text: Extract on page 14 adapted from 'The Element: how finding your passionchanges everything' (Ken Robinson and Lou Aronica Penguin 2010), Copyright © Ken Robinson and Lou Aronica, 2009, Penguin Books Ltd; Article on page 19 adapted from 'Our fantastic readers: how 200 of you volunteered', The Guardian, 16/03/2010 (Tobin L), Guardian News and Media Limited 2010; Extract on page 29 from 'Mao's Last Dancer', Fusion Press (Cunxin L 2003), Penguin Group (Australia) and Penguin Books Ltd, Copyright © 2003, 2009 Li Cunxin; Article on page 33 adapted from 'How long-lost love letter led to couple marrying after 16 years apart' Daily Mail, 20/07/2009 (Daily Mail reporter), MailOnline.com; Article on page adapted from 'Experience: I found my friend after 40 years, and married her' The Guardian, 26/10/2013 (Crisostomo J), Guardian News and Media Limited 2013; Extract on page 36 from 'Gone' by Michael Grant. Text copyright © 2008 Michael Grant. Published by Egmont UK Ltd, London and and HarperCollins Children's Books US used with permission; Article on page 55 adapted from 'Life aboard the International Space Station', The Guardian, 24/10/2010 (Sample I), Guardian News and Media Limited 2010; Article on page 65 adapted from 'The charms of Spain's cave houses', The Telegraph, 22/04/2014 (Gillilan L), © Telegraph Media Group Limited; Extract on page 90,91 adapted from 'The Life And Times Of The Thunderbolt Kid' New Ed edition, Black Swan; (Bryson,B) Published by Doubleday. Reprinted by permission of The Random House Group Limited. and Bill Bryson with permission; Article on page 102,103 from 'Michelle Obama was not unhappy during Nelson Mandela 'selfie', photographer insists', Telegraph (Clark N) The Telegraph 2013, copyright © Telegraph Media Group Limited; Article on page 119 adapted from 'Catch me if you can? Frank Abagnale is now the one busting fraudsters', The Telegraph, 16/08/2014 (Armitstead L), copyright © Telegraph Media Group Limited; 126,127

In some instances we have been unable to trace the owners of copyright material, and we would appreciate any information that would enable us to do so.

Illustration Acknowledgements
(Key: b-bottom; c-centre; l-left; r-right; t-top)
Students' Book pages: Joanna Balicka p. 4l, 8l, 100, Ewa Olejnik p. 58, 70, Kate Walker p. 99, Virus Group p. 411

Photo Acknowledgements
The publisher would like to thank the following for their kind permission to reproduce their photographs:
(Key: b-bottom; c-centre; l-left; r-right; t-top)

Students' Book pages: **123RF.com:** WS15bl, Ruud Morijn 70b, Edyta Pawlowska 74r, Cathy Yeulet WS23bl; **Alamy Images:** Agencja Free 94, Alamy Live News / Keith Mayhew 9cr, Blend Images 42b, 155b, WS24br, Michael Bracey 9b, Cultura RM 109, David R. Frazier Photolibrary, Inc. 49, Kathy deWitt 106r, Glowimages RM 133, Alistair Heap 52bl, Image Source Plus 31, Juice Images WS23tl, MBI 96b, 104, NASA Archive 55t, NASA Photo 55br, NG Images 55bl, OJO Images Ltd 41, Pixelbully 106bl, Martin Shields WS24bl, Tetra Images 69, TNT Magazine 67t, White House Photo 20; **Corbis:** Art in All of Us / Anthony Asael 19bl, Blend Images / Hill Street Studios WS24tl, Monalyn Gracia 114, Matthias Kulka 54, Robert Michael 140r, Reuters / Carlo Allegri 92, 93, Reuters / Daniel Munoz 85c; **Chris Dancy:** 127; **Fotolia.com:** 3dmavr 145 (background), Achimdiver 151, Agusyonok 19cr, Auremar 22b, Marilyn Barbone 60b, Mario Beauregard 119b, Elena Brodetskaya 142cr, Christofmuller 142cl, Contrastwerkstatt 88bl, Dreibirnen 72, ekostsov 122t, EpicStockMedia 138-139, Klaus Eppele 33r, Goce Fisteski 136, Vladimir Floyd 6, Fmarsicano 155t, Fotofeel 88tr, Stefano Garau 73 (background), Goodluz 12tl, 12tr, 12br, Gstockstudio 132, Nadine Haase 142l, Hidejaja 142r, luneWind 128, JiSign 64, Michael Jung 24c, Karelnoppe 40, Kartoxjm 37r, Kzenon 88tl, Xuejun li 76r, Magcom 11l, 11r, 60tl, 70t, 90tl, 126t, Maridav 66b, Michal812 84-85, Monkey Business 12bl, 22t, 100, 119t, Natureimmortal 112l, 113, Nickylarson974 82, Nitr 4t, Claudia Paulussen 29r, Photographee.eu 78-79, Qingwa 10bl, Dan Race 42t, 96t, Rzoog 126b, Samott 150-151, Giuseppe Savo 9t, Elena Schweitzer 7, Skampixelle 143c, Starbourne 65, Patrik Stedrak 143l, Stormy 38, Taesmileland 28, tashatuvango 84r, Theartofphoto 74l, vasosh 148bl, White 138b, Vladimir Wrangel 143r, Yarkovoy 140l, Ysbrandcosijn 37l; **Getty Images:** AFP / Stringer 108, Barcroft India / Niklas Halle'n 19t, Baron / Stringer 14, Keith Brofsky 51r, Berndt Fischer 101, Jim Franco 51l, Gamma-Rapho / David Lefranc 52tl, KidStock 47t, WS23tr, Mike Watson Images 24l, Tim Mosenfelder 102b, National Geographic / Speleoresearch & Films / Carsten Peter 148t, Yawar Nazir 146, omgimages 32, Dimitri Otis 102r, Marc Piasecki 110l, Rubberball 112r, Chris Ryan 47b, Stringer / Buddhika Weerasinghe 30, Stringer / Sascha Baumann 18cl, Mario Tama 67b, Michael Tran 110r; **Rex Shutterstock:** Imaginechina 66t, Newspix / Richard Hatherly 122b; **Shutterstock.com:** 3d brained WS15tl, Aletia 34, Andresr 10tl, Peter Bernik 29l, BestPhotoStudio 56, Bikeriderlondon 88br, Brisbane 103, Ron Ellis 10br, Featureflash 9cl, Ilya Genkin WS15tc, Julia Ivantsova WS15br, Deborah Kolb 103c, ktsdesign 16, Alina Ku-Ku 4b, Milles Studio 58, Monkey Business Images 79b, Ociacia 130br, oliveromg WS23cl, Tyler Olson WS23cr, Pakhnyushcha WS15tr, PGMart 52r, Picsfive 73, Pressmaster 42c, Rawpixel WS23br, RetroClipArt 90tr, ronstik WS15bc, She 48r, Spasiblo 130l, Boris Stroujko 48l, Syda Productions 121l, withGod WS24tr, Zeljkodan 121r, Zurijeta 76l; **SuperStock:** Blend Images 60c, Corbis 90bl; **The Kobal Collection:** Miramax / Dimension Films 145tl, River Road / Paramount 145tr, See-Saw Films 144-145; **TheOceanCleanup.com:** 138t, 139; **Tourism Australia:** Maxime Coquard 85t, Allan Dixon / 84l, Infinity Squared 85bl

All other images © Pearson Education

Illustrations
(Key: b-bottom; c-centre; l-left; r-right; t-top)
Joanna Balicka p. 4l, 8l, 126; Ewa Olejnik p. 72, 87; Kate Walker p. 124; Virus Group p. 4–11

All other images © Pearson Education

Every effort has been made to trace the copyright holders and we apologise in advance for any unintentional omissions. We would be pleased to insert the appropriate acknowledgement in any subsequent edition of this publication.